Global Integrated Supply Chain Systems

Yi-chen Lan
University of Western Sydney, Australia

Bhuvan Unhelkar
University of Western Sydney, Australia

 **IDEA GROUP PUBLISHING**

Singapore

Acquisitions Editor:	Renée Davies
Development Editor:	Kristin Roth
Senior Managing Editor:	Amanda Appicello
Managing Editor:	Jennifer Neidig
Copy Editor:	Sue VanderHook
Typesetter:	Sara Reed
Cover Design:	Lisa Tosheff
Printed at:	Integrated Book Technology

Published in the United States of America by
    Idea Group Publishing (an imprint of Idea Group Inc.)
    701 E. Chocolate Avenue
    Hershey PA 17033
    Tel: 717-533-8845
    Fax: 717-533-8661
    E-mail: cust@idea-group.com
    Web site: http://www.idea-group.com

and in the United Kingdom by
    Idea Group Publishing (an imprint of Idea Group Inc.)
    3 Henrietta Street
    Covent Garden
    London WC2E 8LU
    Tel: 44 20 7240 0856
    Fax: 44 20 7379 3313
    Web site: http://www.eurospan.co.uk

Product or company names used in this book are for identification purposes only. Inclusion of the names of the products or companies does not indicate a claim of ownership by IGI of the trademark or registered trademark.

Library of Congress Cataloging-in-Publication Data

Global integrated supply chain systems / Yi-chen Lan and Bhuvan Unhelkar, editors.
    p. cm.
  Summary: "This book discusses the business and technical reasons for integrating supply chain systems"--Provided by publisher.
  Includes bibliographical references and index.
  ISBN 1-59140-611-0 (hc) -- ISBN 1-59140-612-9 (sc) -- ISBN 1-59140-613-7 (ebook)
  1. Business logistics--Technological innovations. 2. Business logistics--Management. 3. Industrial procurement--Technological innovations. 4. International business enterprises--Technological innovations. I. Lan, Yi-chen, 1969- II. Unhelkar, Bhuvan.
  HD38.5.G575 2006
  658.7'2--dc22
               2005013551

British Cataloguing in Publication Data
A Cataloguing in Publication record for this book is available from the British Library.

All work contributed to this book is new, previously-unpublished material. Each chapter is assigned to at least 2-3 expert reviewers and is subject to a blind, peer review by these reviewers. The views expressed in this book are those of the authors, but not necessarily of the publisher.

Dedication

Bruce & Emily (YL)

Sudhanshu & Surbhi (BU)

Global Integrated Supply Chain Systems

Table of Contents

Preface

The evolution of Internet and Communication Technologies (ICT), most notably Web Services, has played a significant role in enabling enterprises to carry out their intra- and inter-organizational activities with dramatic efficiency and effectiveness. Global firms, in particular, have taken this opportunity to reengineer their business processes, enabling them to sustain their global competitive challenge. While a large part of the reengineering literature appears to be focusing on the customer side of the business processes, it is vital to consider in greater detail the supply side of the processes, as well. ICTs provide excellent opportunities for integration of processes, and supply chains are the ones that stand to benefit from this integration. A more comprehensive Enterprise Application Integration (EAI) than was previously achieved with technologies such as CORBA and DCOM can be envisaged. This edited book in your hand draws on the best of thoughts and practices in this vital supply chain aspect of business processes.

The focus in this book is the analysis and design aspect of development and implementation of global integrated supply chain systems. This is in contrast with most of the current literature that focuses on traditional operations and development of supply chain management systems. The book, however, discusses and documents the technical and managerial aspects of global integrated supply chain systems and provides insights into how the latest information technologies, such as Web services and mobile technology, could be incorporated within the supply chain systems. Furthermore, the chapters in this book also address the need for process improvement required to implement global integrated supply chain systems and how organizations handle the challenges of changes to their processes during the implementation of supply chain systems. Of particular interest should be the chapters that exchange concepts, new ideas, research results, experience, and other related issues that contribute not only to the academic domain but also benefit the corporate business community.

This edited work is addressed to a range of audiences, including senior managers, IT planners, consultants, and academic researchers. Specifically, this book provides valuable information to executives and operational managers in the industry in order to play a proactive role in global supply chain processes. Furthermore, higher degree students as well as academics will find the research base of this book quite attractive.

This book contributes to the literature on global integrated supply chain systems by addressing the need to understand, analyze, configure, develop, and manage the integrated supply chain systems to a global organization. We believe it fulfills a lacunae in the domain of integrated supply chain systems.

Organization of the Book

The systematic presentation of the 19 contributory chapters in this book provides an organized approach to the material. The chapters, embodying global research and experience reports, are summarized as follows:

Chapter I exposes some myths proposed by vendors with regard to the implementation of Integrated Supply Chain Environments (ISCE). It is followed by a proposed analysis methodology for Integrated Supply Chain Management systems. The chapter also examines some of the available literature regarding ISCE and proposes an analysis methodology, which intends to address some of the issues identified previously and construct a theoretical model for enterprises to adopt in the analysis phase of developing ISCM systems.

Chapter II highlights the current challenge of developing a process to deliver products in a timely fashion and of ensuring availability of items. It starts with exploring the impact of telecommunications, customer relationship management (CRM), and supply chain management (SCM) and their impact on meeting customers' expectations, regardless of location. The challenges, advantages, and future trends in each of these areas are also addressed and investigated. The chapter concludes with suggestions to help companies implement strategies that will effectively overcome the challenges of globalization.

Chapter III explores the role played by demand forecasting for the Internet age—an age where customers can be anywhere and want to have their needs addressed the moment they think about them. The organization that can fulfill the needs of the customers/consumers in the easiest, fastest, and most cost-effective way will win their business. The chapter helps the reader understand the challenges faced by organizations in forecasting demand in the net age, gives real life examples of these challenges, provides solutions for addressing them, and takes a look into the future.

Chapter IV initiates the concept of the customer-centric model in supply chain systems. It discusses various constraints of the present-day supply chain systems resulting from their roots being in logistics management and suggests an alternative next-level paradigm of a customer-centric matrix model. The chapter further demonstrates how this model would add value to the customer by taking the example of a healthcare information management system. It also delves into the limitations of and anticipated issues and challenges in implementing the suggested model.

Chapter V considers the importance of information sharing techniques and strategies employed by industry sectors. Well-developed supply chain management often brings with it improved buyer-supplier communication processes, and we consider the impact of these not only from an inter-sector point of view, but also from a cross-sector viewpoint. The chapter examines the particular perspectives of the small business within a supply chain structure and of the supply chain customer. The authors conclude that information sharing is a critical component of business success both inside and outside the supply chain structure. However, while globally and at the large business level, both development and implementation of such technologies have mushroomed, smaller enterprises have tended to be left behind to cope as best they can with multiple pressures to conform.

Chapter VI discusses the integrated operations of supply chain functions and high-lights the procurement function as a crucial link between the sources of supply and the organization. The chapter identifies four main challenges in e-procurement implementation coming from business process integration, technological issues, value creation, and change management.

Chapter VII discusses the concept of Supply Chain Management. It provides broad definitions of supply chain, the drivers for integrated supply chains design, and current challenges in global supply chains. More importantly, this chapter provides the reader an insight into aligning corporate strategy, people mindset, process design, and technology in designing integrated supply chain. A real-life example in health care industry is provided. The case example aims to give readers the identification of supply chain bottlenecks, the right methodology to map the as-is processes, and the redesign of simplified supply chain processes. Finally, the guidelines for Supply Chain Management implementation issues such as vendor selections and team building are further addressed.

Chapter VIII discusses the technologies that enable corporations to share information externally and to improve material flow within the supply chain. It identifies many benefits that can be realized from an integrated supply chain environment. On the other hand, many factors also are identified that lead to failed integrated supply chain implementations. The focus of this chapter is to introduce the Interaction Approach methodology as a framework for analyzing supply chains in the hope of improving the design, development, and implementation of integrated supply chain environments.

Chapter IX explores and evaluates the performance of supply chain management in using global logistics information technologies in Hong Kong firms. It reviews the role of functional information systems for supply chain management and identifies the characteristics of information systems utilized for supply chain management through survey data collected from 71 Hong Kong firms. A conceptual model and hypothesis relating to utilization of information systems, information technology, and SCM performance is developed. The chapter concludes with discussion and recommendations based on the research results.

Chapter X discusses the current status of supply chain management, challenges and solutions to supply chain management, critical issues, and the role of technology used in supply chain operations in China.

Chapter XI proposes a multi-objective model of global distribution for the Taiwan notebook computer. The proposed two-stage approach involves a mixed integer linear programming model and the fuzzy analytic hierarchy process (AHP) approach. The analytic method provides quantitative assessment of the relationships between manufacturers and customer services. To show the effectiveness of the proposed approach, a Taiwan notebook computer model is solved. The results of this multi-objective model show some dynamic characteristics among various performance criteria of the outbound logistics.

Chapter XII focuses on the development of an object-oriented enterprise business blueprint for e-supply chain inter-enterprise process integration. The approach described in this chapter will illustrate how the enterprise applications can be developed and woven into the very fabric of business practices by using object-oriented techniques. In contrast to an isolated IT system, this approach allows business processes to permeate different organizations, and communication in this system becomes process-to-process oriented.

Chapter XIII presents a software simulator, called LOSIMOPU. LOSIMOPU allows users to build a supply chain model and analyze the sensitivity of logistics on assigned policy and capacity under uncertainty. LOSIMOPU consists of five kinds of participants (end-customer, intermediate supplier, end-supplier, transportation server, and electronic payment server) and an e-marketplace for the supply chain. Each participant is implemented as a distributed object such that it runs concurrently and has capacity and policy for playing its role. The e-marketplace defines the trade protocol for the workflow management and transaction analysis. LOSIMOPU visualizes expected indices of assigned parameters for decision support. This chapter discusses the background of proposal, goal of simulator, milestone, technical issues for development, and the prototype system.

Chapter XIV deals with a time-dependent supply chain network equilibrium (TD-SCNE) problem, which allows product flows to be distributed over a network not only between two successive sectors in the same time period (a transaction) but also between two successive periods for the same agency (an inventory). This chapter proposes a three-loop nested diagonalization method, along with a specially designed super network representation, and the framework is demonstrated with a numerical example.

Chapter XV applies the multi-agent system paradigm to collaborative negotiation in a global manufacturing supply chain network. Multi-agent computational environments are suitable for dealing with a broad class of coordination and negotiation issues involving multiple autonomous or semi-autonomous problem-solving agents. An agent-based multi-contract negotiation system is proposed for global manufacturing supply chain coordination. This chapter includes a case study of mobile phone global manufacturing supply chain management.

Chapter XVI identifies the critical success factors in supply chain implementation through the empirical research. The authors studied the infrastructures enhancing the success of supply chain implementation, which influence the supply chain performance and adopt three categories of infrastructure as the critical success factors of supply chain implementation.

Chapter XVII discusses the applications of mobile technologies in various areas of supply chain management, the potential benefits of those technologies along the dimensions of reduced replenishment time, and transactions and billing cycles. Among other discussions, the role of mobile procurement, inventory management, product identification, package tracking, sales force, and field service automation technologies is highlighted. To substantiate the basis for adopting mobile technologies for supply chain management, different market drivers for mobile applications are exemplified and applied to the three macro level processes of supplier relationship management, internal supply chain management, and customer relationship management, and a resulting typology of mobile supply chain management applications is presented.

Chapter XVIII determines the critical success factors for the e-ISCS and examines their performance in supply chain. It adopts a factor analysis to determine four success factors: work performance quality, system quality, information quality, and service quality. A critical analysis of areas that require improvement also is conducted.

Chapter XIX discusses the significance of business continuity, a crucial ingredient of supply chain management, and the impact of business continuity on supply chain systems. The discussion is based on the author's experience of working in an environment that is dependent on supply chains, as well as helping many of his clients achieve uninterrupted business continuity.

Acknowledgments

First and foremost, the editors would like to acknowledge the individual authors who decided to share their thoughts and experiences in this book. The insight and acumen shown by the contributory authors is one of the best that we could find internationally. The effort in putting together the chapters is a phenomenal exercise that is deeply appreciated by the editors. Furthermore, a number of friends and colleagues helped review the chapters and pass on invaluable comments and constructive criticisms. Their help is specifically acknowledged.

Special thanks also go to the publishing team at Idea Group Inc. In particular, thanks to Michele Rossi, who continuously prodded via e-mail to keep the project on schedule, and to Mehdi Khosrow-Pour, whose enthusiasm motivated us initially to accept his invitation for taking on this project.

Finally, we would like to give special thanks to our families for their love and support to enable us to complete this project. YL: Thanks to my wife Anna, my children Bruce and Emily, and also my father Wen-hsiung and mother Su-chen for their moral support. BU: Thanks to my wife Asha, daughter Sonki Priyadarshini, and son Keshav Raja, as well as my extended family Girish and Chinar Mamdapur for all their support.

Yi-chen Lan, PhD, MACS
Bhuvan Unhelkar, PhD, FACS
Sydney, Australia
January 2005

Chapter I

A Methodology for Developing an Integrated Supply Chain Management System

Yi-chen Lan
University of Western Sydney, Australia

Bhuvan Unhelkar
University of Western Sydney, Australia

Abstract

Integrated Supply Chain Management (ISCM) involves the linking of suppliers and customers with the internal business processes of an organization. ISCM solutions allow organizations to automate workflows concerning the execution and analysis of planning, sourcing, making, delivering, returns handling, and maintenance, to name but a few. Many of today's ISCM systems use primarily Web technology as the supporting infrastructure. Undoubtedly, the electronic (Internet-based) ISCM systems deliver the enterprises with a competitive advantage by opening up opportunities to streamline processes, reduce costs, increase customer patronage, and enable thorough planning abilities. However, there has been significant customer backlash concerning the inability of software vendors to deliver easy integration and promised functionality. Although various researchers have suggested strategies to overcome some of the failures in operating ISCM systems, there appears to be a lacunae in terms of architectural investigations in the analysis stage. The methodology proposed in this chapter seeks to resolve these gaps and provides a fundamental framework for analyzing ISCM systems.

Introduction

This is the age of communication based on Internet technologies. As a result, enterprises are able to conduct inter- and intra-organizational activities efficiently and effectively. This efficiency of communication has percolated in all arenas of organizational activities, including customer relationships, resource planning, and, in the context of this discussion, supply chains. Given the cost of logistics and their importance in order fulfillment process, organizations may want to capitalize on this opportunity to communicate in order to reengineer their supply chain operations that would sustain them in the globally competitive and challenging world of electronic business. With this invigorated growth of e-business, software vendors and consultants have been promising businesses the utopian Internet-based supply chain systems that would provide them with the capability to respond in real-time to changing product demand and supply and offer an easy integration functionality with backend information systems (PeopleSoft, 2002; Turner, 1993).

Although a number of Internet-based supply chain systems (or integrated supply chain management systems—ISCM systems) are available for adoption, enterprises do not guarantee to implement the systems in conjunction with their existing information systems. Furthermore, the ISCM systems may not fulfill the connection and implementation requirements among participants in the supply chain.

After the e-commerce hype had dissipated, surveys undertaken in 2001 tend to paint a different picture as to the success of these implementations. Smith (2002) concludes that at least 15% of supply chain system implementations during 2001 and 2002 were abandoned in the US alone. Although several reasons can be identified as the cause of implementation failure, the main problem rests with the fundamental analysis of ISCM operations and requirements.

The purpose of this chapter is to debunk some myths proposed by vendors with regard to the implementation of Integrated Supply Chain Environments (ISCE) and propose an analysis methodology for Integrated Supply Chain Management systems.

First, the chapter will examine some of the available literature regarding ISCE. The fundamentals of ISCE—technologies and processes—will be investigated in some detail. Vendors were quick to promote the benefits of ISCE yet were not so forthcoming as to possible barriers and other issues to watch for. Both of these also will be discussed in this chapter.

Second, an analysis methodology is proposed, which intends to address some of the issues identified previously and construct a theoretical model for enterprises to adopt in the analysis phase of developing ISCM systems. This chapter concludes with a future research direction in investigating technological issues of ISCM systems operation.

Integrated Supply Chain Management Overview

ISCM involves the linking of suppliers and customers with the internal supply processes of an organization. Internal processes would include both vertically integrated functional areas, such as materials, sales and marketing, manufacturing, inventory and warehousing, distribution, and, perhaps, other independent companies involved in the supply chain (i.e., channel integration). Customers at one end of the process can potentially be a supplier downstream in the next process, ultimately supplying to the end user (Handfield et al., 1999; Turner, 1993).

ISCM Solutions

While, in many cases, ISCM systems are still in their infancy, the concept of establishing information flows between points in the supply chain has been around since the 1980s. Through Electronic Data Interchange (EDI), customers and suppliers have communicated supply data through direct dial-up interfaces and other mediums (Zieger, 2001). However, the ability for the Internet to create a common communication infrastructure has made integration much more cost-effective. ISCM has promised to deliver the right product to the right place at the right time and at the right price (Comptroller, 2002).

From the supply chain software development perspective, there are generally four large vendors identified; namely, Oracle, SAP, PeopleSoft, and Ariba, and a multitude of medium-sized vendors in the ISCM solution space (Armstrong, 2002). All claim that ISCM will enable the enterprise to respond in real time to changes in demand and supply.

For instance, current ISCM solutions allow organizations to automate workflows concerning the execution and analysis of the following business activities (Comptroller, 2002; Gledhill, 2002; Peoplesoft, 2002):

1. **Planning:** Demand and supply planning, manage planning infrastructure.
2. **Sourcing (buy-side):** Strategic sourcing, eprocurement, services procurement, catalog management, collaborative contract/supply management, e-settlements/vendor payments.
3. **Making (in-side):** Product life cycle management, demand planning, production management, production planning, flow production, event management.
4. **Delivering (sell-side):** Inventory, order management, promotions management, warehouse management, transportation management, delivery infrastructure management, e-bill payment, scm portal.
5. **Returns handling (from customers)**
6. **Maintenance**

ISCM Systems Architecture

Turner (1993) stated that information systems would be the enabler of integrated logistics. Armstrong (2002) affirms that Turner's view has come to fruition. Many of today's ISCM systems primarily use Web technology as the supporting infrastructure (Dalton et al., 1998). It is not uncommon in these instances to develop a three-tier or n-tier network architecture in order to provide robust support for ISCM systems.

For example, Advanced Software Design Inc. (2002) illustrated the three-tier ISCM integration architecture (Figure 1) in use by the US Department of Defense (DoD). Suppliers and customers access the DoD ISCM through the use of Web portals (the first tier of the ISCM). Web portals provide the necessary Web services to establish a common graphical interface for the DoD's stakeholders in accessing supply chain data. Customers, suppliers, distributors, and delivery agents can access custom information and services supplied by the ISCM. Supplier services could include access to business-to-business (B2B) marketplaces, support, and other push/pull supplier functionality. Alternately, customers can customize the site in order to access catalogs from the organization and external suppliers; customer transaction details; and other product, customer, and technical support.

The portals are supported by a messaging infrastructure (second tier), which provides the link to the underlying applications layer (third tier). The applications layer is independent of any particular interface (e.g., portals) and contains the necessary business logic and data access in order to perform operations. This includes access to SCM functionality, ERP systems, and decision support systems. Data and business logic also are stored independently.

The software architecture is constructed mostly in a Web-based environment that involves HTTP, server-side Java, and XML. ISCM systems are generally no different than other business applications but still require some interfacing with old technologies, such as aging ERPs and legacy systems (Zieger, 2001).

Figure 1. ISCM integration architecture

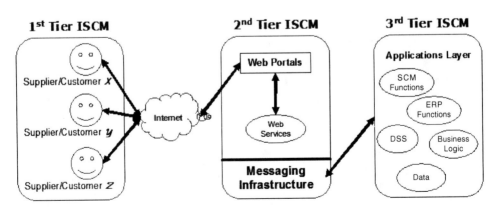

Benefits of ISCM Systems

ISCM delivers the enterprise with a competitive advantage by opening up opportunities to streamline processes, reduce costs, increase customer patronage, and utilize more thorough planning abilities (Turner, 1993). The benefits of ISCM systems are categorized into a number groups, including financial, customer, planning, production, and implementation. Each of these groups is further discussed in the following subsections.

1.   Financial

Cost Reduction: In some manufacturing organizations, the cost of the supply chain can represent 60-80% of their total cost base (Cottrill, 1997). One of the core benefits of driving efficiency through the supply chain is cost reduction. ISCM allows the organization to maximize profitability through reduced customer service, administration, and inventory costs. Less staff is required to maintain the supply chain, and order/inventory details can be made available to customers directly without human intervention (Comptroller, 2002; Cottrill, 1997; Gledhill, 2002). Some organizations have quoted 25% cost reductions per transaction, despite a 20% increase in orders (Turner, 1993).

Quality Financial Information: Another benefit is the improvement and reliability of financial information. ISCM systems maintain centralized databases that are linked to other enterprise systems (e.g., ERP, CRM) providing integrity, consistency, and real-time data access to managers so that they can manage the supply chain with an organizational perspective (Comptroller, 2002; Turner, 1993).

2.   Customer

Retention: Supply chain systems, through customer portals, provide customers with an instantaneous and holistic view of the progress of their transactions within the organization. This level of service (coupled with benefits derived from production) result in higher customer satisfaction levels and, in turn, improve the firm's ability to attract new customers and, more importantly, retain them. Organizations have achieved customer service levels of 97% following the introduction of ISCM systems. This retention translates into greater revenue (Bergert, 2001; Comptroller, 2002; Cottrill, 1997; Gledhill, 2002; Turner, 1993).

Behavior: The ability to capture customer transactions and preferences online provides the organization with the facility to track their behavior and, in turn, customize products and services to cater to them (Bragg, 2002).

Promise: Because of the level of workflow automation and inventory statistics, organizations are able to provide accurate estimates of when orders will be filled at the time of ordering. This is known as capable-to-promise (CTP) capability. This capability allows the organization's customers to plan more effectively (Gledhill, 2002).

3.   Planning

Companies with ISCM systems have the ability to mathematically and graphically observe the performance of the supply chain, giving the manager the power to plan and make things happen (Turner, 1993). ISCM systems provide the organization with the capabilities to derive more accurate demand planning with improved precision, create shorter planning and production cycles, establish one central data repository for the entire organization, and facilitate enhanced communications through rapid information dissemination (Bragg, 2002; Comptroller, 2002; Gledhill, 2002).

4.   Production

ISCM provides the ability to holistically manage the supply chain, allowing managers to respond dynamically to any situation that may arise so as to minimize its impact on production.

Inventory Management: By measuring the level of inventory and analyzing turnover, supply chain systems can improve turnover by reducing the need for safety stocks and the risk of retailer out-of-stocks. Inventory items need to be numbered consistently in order to facilitate measurement and tracking. These benefits reduce the overhead required to store high inventory levels (Cottrill, 1997; Gledhill, 2002). Turner's (1993) research claimed a 37% reduction in inventory levels as a result of ISCM implementation.

Efficiency: ISCM systems measure the performance of the supply chain through the generation of supply chain metrics. This allows process quality issues to be tracked and rectified, isolates bottlenecks in the process, and measures lead times so they can be aligned with available capacity in order to maximize plant utilization. All of this ensures quicker time-to-market for the firm's products (Bragg, 2002; Comptroller, 2002; Gledhill, 2002).

Other efficiency benefits include no data rekeying through simplified automated order placement, order status inquiries, delivery shipment, and invoicing (Bragg, 2002; Gledhill, 2002). ISCM implementations have resulted in a 50% overtime reduction for some organizations (Turner, 1993).

5.   Implementation

Consultants promise responsiveness and Plug & Play integrations. However, documented examples of supply chain failures by organizations such as Siemens AG, Nike, OPP Quimica, and Shell are evidence that the implementation of ISCM systems is not as easy as vendors claim. Claims of rapid integration and seamless linking seem to significantly underestimate the effort required to integrate ISCM with the rest of the enterprise (Oakton, 2003).

For Nike, i2 ISCM software required a significant degree of customization in order to integrate the software to the rest of the organization. Customization to enterprise software comes with great risk and significant cost for ongoing maintenance. Nike's summation of the software was that it just didn't work. OPP Quimica (a Brazilian chemicals company) required the use of third-party integration software in order to assimilate i2 to the rest of the enterprise architecture. Shell's implementation proved problematic with the need to tie 85 ERP sites to a single SCM platform (Smith, 2002).

Issues and Barriers in ISCM Analysis

Similar to the hype attached to Enterprise Resource Planning (ERP) applications, there has been significant customer backlash concerning the inability of software vendors to deliver easy integration and promised functionality (Smith, 2002). Turner (1993) believes that "few companies claim to have fully implemented SCM and have sustained the benefits proposed ISCM would create" (p. 52). In fact, Fontanella (2001) indicates that only 25% of ISCM users are utilizing the full suite of supply chain applications and that only 12% of users are receiving data from inbound suppliers and customers—far from an integrated supply chain.

Many of these issues stem from a failure to undertake thorough analysis in the following key areas.

- **Focus on transaction systems over strategic systems to manage supply chains:** Organizations are not taking a strategic view of ISCM systems. More so, they tend only to focus on transactions systems (e.g., inventory control, order processing, etc.), which provide little visibility of the enterprise (Fontanella, 2001; Turner, 1993).

- **Failure to preempt change to business processes:** In a majority of implementations, analysis has focused on the technical aspects of integrating ISCM systems with the remaining architecture. One area that has been neglected is the effect on business processes. Organizations expect staff either to just accept change or to customize the software. Both of these options are generally flawed. In order to reap the cost savings from ISCM systems, significant analysis must be conducted regarding process reengineering in order to ensure collaboration and to continue to sustain benefits (Fontanella, 2001; Mol et al., 1997; Turner, 1993).

- **Failure to appreciate geographical, relational, and environmental considerations between buyer and supplier:** The nature of ISCM (especially with multinational corporations) involves transacting across the world—24 hours a day, seven days a week, 360°. Analysts fail to appreciate the geographical, relational, and environmental inhibitors for ISCM implementations of this scope (Mol et al., 1997).

  Cross-borders logistics, culture, language and economics, and regulatory climate are just some considerations that can affect the integration of business processes between regional offices and external organizations, creating communication issues throughout the supply chain. One ill-performing participant in the supply chain will affect the performance of the entire supply chain (Strausl, 2001).

- **Failure to accurately identify the costs and benefits of ISCM implementation:** Many implementations have been classified as failures because of ISCM system's perceived inability to reap benefits and produce cost savings, as expected.

However, in many cases, it is the initial analysis of cost and benefits that has been flawed. Because of the nature and scope of ISCM implementations, it is difficult to accurately quantify attributable cost reductions from ISCM, because they could be derived throughout the supply chain and be complicated to calculate. In the same light, determining benefits share similar traits, with some having the additional complication of being intangible (e.g., benefits of a central database) and, therefore, difficult to quantify (New, 1994).

- **Insufficient capability:** The implementation and support of ISCM systems can be rather complex and, therefore, demands sophisticated resources and incremental implementations. Unfortunately, during the planning and analysis phases of implementation projects, organizations have failed to properly appreciate the level of complexity involved, resulting in significant under-resourcing. As a result, many organizations have suffered material cost overruns and delayed go-live times (Fontanella, 2001).

Proposed Methodology for ISCM Systems Analysis

Due to the extent of failed ISCM system implementations, it is imperative to construct an appropriate analysis and development methodology that can be adopted as the roadmap for enterprises flourishing in ISCM systems development and operations. The proposed methodology demonstrates an overall picture for constructing an ISCM system from recognizing problems and analyzing requirements to the implementation and operation. It embraces eight phases:

1. Identifying information management structure
2. Identifying connecting components
3. Ensuring appropriate business processes
4. Establishing and developing interfaces
5. Developing new business processes
6. Confirming strategic alignment
7. Implementing ISCM systems
8. Testing efficacy of implementation

Following is a discussion and culmination of those eight phases within the proposed iterative framework.

Identifying Information Management Structure

Given the global nature of supply chain systems and their level of required integration, a common ICT (information and communication technology) infrastructure must be able to extend around the globe, to support open and rapid communication, and to integrate easily with the architecture of not just the organization but also the architecture of customers and suppliers. This will be conducive to information sharing (Comptroller, 2002).

The enterprise's information systems architecture must be properly analyzed to ensure that it satisfies the needs of ISCM systems and can support security boundaries, largely distributed database operations, and event-driven applications. The architecture needs to be durable, flexible, and embedded with the appropriate middleware in order to integrate as easily as possible (Zieger, 2001). It also must be sufficiently robust in order to cater to firewalls and other security measures and have 24/7 global access and redundant systems and processes in order to handle events when ISCM systems need to be off-line for maintenance, emergency, and recovery purposes.

In accordance with these criteria, the Internet-based structure can be considered the most appropriate platform to satisfy these requirements. Nevertheless, participants in the supply chain have various capability and maturity levels in information management structure. Hence, prior to adopting the Internet technology for integration, the existing information management structure of each participant must be determined.

Identifying Connecting Components

One of the most critical functions of supply chain management is to ensure the effective integration of information and material flows through the system. This includes understanding the value added to products and its related information flows (inputs and outputs) as it progresses through the supply chain (Michael-Donovan, 2002). This embraces analysis of the supply chain's real costs and cost and performance drivers (Seirlis, 2001).

Turner (1993) identifies some of the key components that need to be functionally integrated. These components also are considered the connecting components (or connecting business functions) among participants in the supply chain. These components include order management, customer service, invoicing, forecasting, distribution requirements planning (DRP), warehouse and inventory management, manufacturing planning, production control (MRPII), and integrated logistics.

Ensuring Appropriate Business Processes

In order to enhance the supply chain processes, it is important to understand what happens currently. Generally, supply chain processes may include the procurement, production, ordering, delivery, and inventory paths, both within the company and external parties.

First, analysts should analyze the supply chain processes and be able to appreciate the company's mix of products, end configurations, volumes, life cycles, channels, customer segments, and delivery outlets (Tyndall et al., 2002).

Each process then should be prioritized and broken down into its subprocesses, identifying each of its sources, outputs, transformations, timings, resources utilized, and requirements. This also would be an opportune time to gather metrics concerning each of the processes in order to establish a baseline for identifying problems and to measure future process improvement.

Additionally, any opportunities to benefit from quick-wins should be taken advantage of at this point (Michael-Donovan, 2002).

Establishing and Developing Interfaces

Once architectural issues have been resolved and data requirements have been determined, a structure needs to be established to enable common linkages between data providers and data recipients of the ISCM (i.e., customers and suppliers) and linkages within ISCM processes. This will require the need to ascertain whether there are any missing links and to determine how the data required will be sourced or provided and in which format.

The emerging technology for interface communications is XML (eXtensible Markup Language). XML uses HTML tags to enable the definition, transmission, validation, and interpretation of data. However, effort for this task should not be underestimated (Zieger, 2001). Significant resources may be required in analyzing sources from ERP and anti-quated EDI systems. It has been suggested that third-party interface tools (e.g., Informatica & Brio) can be used to ease the transition for these types of systems (Zieger, 2001).

Developing New Business Processes

After conducting a detailed analysis of existing supply chain processes and identifying any inefficiencies and/or gaps in the process, a proposal should be created for the design of new processes. Not only should new processes cater to anticipated ISCM processing, but they also should be sufficiently visionary in order to accommodate other strategic initiatives (i.e., CRM, Supplier Management, Knowledge Management).

The new supply chain should be modeled in a manner so that supply chain blueprints can be generated (Comptroller, 2002; Zieger, 2001). Tyndall et al. (2002) suggest an iterative approach to process design, whereby a process is broken down into stages and then defined, analyzed, executed, assessed, and then redefined. This cycle continues until the appropriate performance expectations have been achieved. This process can become quite complex and convoluted, once organizations begin to incorporate backend systems and the processes of other organizations.

Based on metrics determined during the initial business process review, goals should be set for process improvement.

Confirm Strategic Alignment

At the completion of most of the analytical work, it is important to revisit some of the groundwork that would have been completed during the planning phase activity in the traditional SDLC.

It has been included in this framework to highlight the importance of ensuring an alignment between business strategy and expectations with the outcomes of the ISCM implementation—supply chain strategy is interdependent on the business strategic direction.

Analysts need to confirm that value is being delivered through ISCM by conducting a critical analysis on proposed benefits and costs in order to ensure that they are still realistic (Tyndall et al., 2002). In order to prevent misalignment of resources and skillsets, analysts also need to confirm that the business problem still can be solved with its current complement of staff.

Implementing ISCM Systems

This phase involves determining what activities will need to be undertaken to facilitate implementation of ISCM system—creating an action plan.

There are a number of factors that should be considered in this final phase of the methodology, such as setting up communication standards, developing business operation procedures, and establishing training programs.

Furthermore, this phase should be expanded to incorporate activities that can assist in the detailed analysis of implementation risks of the system. Conducting analyses in areas such as change management is one example. Inability to manage the implementation of change has been a key factor in project failure. Any enterprise system places great strain on the organization to adapt in order to reap the benefits. Change management involves more than simply conducting user-training programs but involves a continuing consultative relationship with end users to secure buy-in.

Conclusion and Future Challenge

This chapter endeavors to propose an analysis and development methodology for ISCM systems. The discussion started with review and investigation of the current ISCM solutions and architectures, and identified a number of benefits, issues, and problems regarding the implementation of ISCM systems. Based on the examination of existing ISCM status, the proposed methodology for ISCM systems analysis is constructed by an eight-phase development framework. The methodology tends to illustrate a systematic roadmap for enterprises in developing ISCM systems.

The future challenge for enterprises in operating and maintaining ISCM systems stressed the overall maturity of technological availability and the flexibility of business processes aligning with the ISCM architecture.

References

Advanced Software Design Inc. (2002). ASD supply chain solution. ASD Global. Retrieved July 21, 2003, from *http://www.asdglobal.com/products/dod.html*

Armstrong, E. (2002). The evolution of supply chain management software. *Logistics Management, 41*(9), 66-70.

Bergert, S, & Kazimer-Shockley, K. (2001). The customer rules. *Intelligent Enterprise, 4*(11), 31.

Bragg, S. (2002). 10 symptoms of poor supply chain performance. ARC Advisory Group. Retrieved July 21, 2003, from *http://www.idii.com/wp/arc_sc_perf.pdf*

Cottrill, K. (1997). Reforging the supply chain. *Journal of Business Strategy, 18*(6), 35-39.

Dalton, G., & Wilder, C. (1998). eBusiness—Global links—Companies are turning to the Internet for tighter integration with suppliers overseas. *Information Week, 674,* 18-20.

Fontanella, J. (2001). The overselling of supply chain suites. AMR Research. Retrieved July 21, 2003, from *http://www.amrresearch.com/Content/view.asp?pmillid=662&docid=8027*

Gledhill, J. (2002). Create values with IT investment: How to generate a healthy ROI across the enterprise. *Food Processing, 63*(9), 76-80.

Handfield, R., & Nichols Jr., E. (1999). *An introduction to supply chain management.* Prentice Hall.

Lan, Y., & Unhelkar, B. (2005). *Global enterprise transitions: Managing the process.* Hershey, PA: IRM Press.

Michael-Donovan, R. (2002). e-Supply chain management: Pre-requisites to success. Performance Improvement. Retrieved July 21, 2003, from *http://www.idii.com/wp/donovan_sc_part1.pdf*

Mol, M., & Koppius, O. (2002). Information technology and the internationalisation of the firm. *Journal of Global Information Management, 10*(4), 44-60.

New, S. (1994). A framework for analysing supply chain improvement. Manchester School of Management. Retrieved July 21, 2003, from *http://www.unf.edu/~ybolumol/tra_4202_011/Artiicles/sc_improvement.pdf*

Oakton. (2003). Manufacturing and supply chain solutions. Oakton Consulting. Retrieved July 21, 2003, from *http://www.infact.com.au/clients/manufacturing.htm*

OSD Comptroller iCenter. (2002). Integrated supply chain management: Optimising logistics support. Office of the Under Secretary of Defence. Retrieved July 21, 2003, from *http://www.dod.mil/comptroller/icenter/learn/iscmconcept.pdf*

Parkes, C. (2002). Supply chain management. Peoplesoft Inc. Retrieved July 21, 2003, from *http://peoplesoft.ittoolbox.com/documents/document.asp?i=836*

Seirlis, A. (2001). Integrated supply chain analysis. TLB Consulting. Retrieved July 21, 2003, from *http://www.tlb.co.za/library/comentary/intergrated.html*

Smith, T. (2002). Sharing the risk: How to avoid a supply-chain nightmare. Internet Week.com. Retrieved July 21, 2003, from *http://www.internetweek.com/supplyChain/INW20020725S0007*

Strausl, D. (2001). Four stages to building an effective supply chain network. *EBN,* (1251), 43.

Turner, R. (1993). Integrated supply chain management: What's wrong with this picture? *Industrial Engineering, 25*(12), 52-55.

Tyndall, G., et al. (2002). Making it happen: The value producing supply chain. Centre for Business Innovation—Ernst & Young. RetrievedJuly 21, 2003, from *http://www.cbi.cgey.com/journal/issue3/features/makin/makin.pdf*

Zieger, A. (2001). Preparing for supply chain architectures. PeerToPeerCentral.com. Retrieved July 21, 2003, from *http://www-106.ibm.com/developerworks/web/library/wa-supch.html?dwzone=web*

Chapter II

Going Global:
A Technology Review

Mahesh S. Raisinghani
Texas Woman's University, USA

Denise Taylor
University of Dallas, USA

Abstract

The World Wide Web opened the door for many organizations with international ambitions to go global. Organizations that did not have a global presence or access to international markets could create Web sites to offer products/services to a new customer base, and companies that were already internationally entrenched could make their products easily accessible. However, developing a process to deliver products in a timely fashion and ensuring availability of items is still a challenge. This chapter explores the impact of telecommunications, customer relationship management (CRM), and supply chain management (SCM) and its impact on meeting customers' expectations, regardless of location. We also address the challenges, advantages, and future trends in each of these areas. Finally, this chapter provides suggestions to help companies implement strategies that will effectively overcome the challenges of globalization.

Introduction

With the rapidly evolving telecommunications industry, especially in the US, it is becoming all the more challenging for companies to innovate and integrate. This is more so with businesses that choose to globalize, since even with the right telecommunications solution technologically, companies still need to ensure that they are communicating effectively with customers and providing them with detailed product information. This is where the supply chain systems become extremely important in modern globalization scenarios. An effective customer relationship management (CRM) solution will allow companies to provide timely and accurate data on customer orders and/or demand that can be used by the supply chain management (SCM) system to plan and schedule the manufacture of goods with minimal overruns. However, there is concern about whether domestic and/or global sourcing can effectively manage CRM, SCM, and telecommunications. These concerns arise from the fact that, although technology has evolved, the question of whether it is possible to improve the process of globalization by merely improving functionality of the technology in the areas of CRM, SCM, and telecommunications still remains. Before reviewing the technology components needed for globalization, it is imperative that a discussion occur on the means of communication. Implementation of a correct telecommunications solution is a key element in successfully managing and meeting customer demand. Therefore, a review of telecom technology and strategies will follow in order to understand the role it plays in the supply chain management process as well as the effect it has on meeting customer expectations. Later in this chapter, we provide an overview of the steps that companies can follow to review the customer needs and processes and develop a strategy that will help them achieve globalization.

Background

The introduction of the World Wide Web opened the door for many companies seeking to go global and made it easy for companies to create a way to view their products online. However, developing a process to deliver products in a timely fashion and ensure availability of items is the challenge. As companies strive to reduce expenditures by outsourcing jobs to locations beyond the US, they also want to grow revenues by attracting international business. This chapter explores the impact of telecommunications, customer relationship management (CRM), and supply chain management (SCM) and its impact on effectively meeting customers' expectations, regardless of the customers' locales. It addresses the challenges, advantages, and future trends in each of these areas. Finally, this chapter will provide suggestions to help companies implement strategies that will effectively help them overcome the challenges of globalization. Taking a closer look at all of these components will enable a review of the full cycle of customer processes, which will aid in developing a comprehensive global software strategy.

Role of Telecommunications in the Globalization Process

Telecommunications plays a significant role in globalization. Even with the implementation of good CRM and SCM systems, it is not likely that a company will realize the full potential of its business endeavors if the correct telecommunications strategy is not developed. The following section discusses the challenges and opportunities organizations face when embarking on global markets.

Telecommunications Challenges and Opportunities

When discussing global telecommunications' challenges, it is important to note that they differ from one country to another. While organizations in developed countries have stable infrastructures that are continuously enhanced by innovative technologies to manage electronic processing, in developing countries they do not have this luxury; rather, they tend to focus on how to exploit their in-house existing resources. Furthermore, unlike organizations in developed countries that can pick among giant telecommunications providers, in developing countries, organizations have been known to rely on a single source (usually owned by the government) for its telecommunications needs and support.

One of the ways developing countries have countered the telecomm obstacles is by using international host services to enter the market. Lake (2000) points out that an international hosting service raises the credibility of the enterprise and reduces fears that some consumers may have about purchasing from distant lands. In the research conducted by Wresch (2003), the US hosted about half of the Web sites of nine developing countries. Another way organizations in developing countries are overcoming the reliability issues in telecomm is by developing the talent within the organization and by exchanging the knowledge and expertise with fellow organizations in the country.

In a study conducted by Kaarst-Brown and Wang (2003), respondents in the Turks and Caicos Islands (TCI) in the British West Indies of the Caribbean indicated that customer service is negatively impacted by sporadic outages. In addition, the cost of maintaining adequate telecomm service was expensive, as Kaarst-Brown and Wang (2003) explained:

The major complaints over the quality of phone service reflect the impact of the telecommunications systems on customer service. How to find inexpensive vehicles to communicate with the customers has been an important issue in CRM in TCI. (Kaarst-Brown & Wang, 2003)

The weather was also a challenge for this set of respondents. Since TCI is an island nation, it had to find ways to maintain the infrastructure in spite of hurricanes and the salt in the air. TCI Cable & Wireless indicated:

Fiber optics, heavy duty towers, bite the bullet and maintain, maintain, maintain. Remote sites will help because we will put fiber between the remote sites and the exchange and the fiber is impervious to water. It reduces the propensity for error and faults. (Kaarst-Brown & Wang, 2003)

On the other hand, developed countries face a different set of challenges. While the infrastructure is developed, companies seeking to do business globally must find ways to reach austere regions of the world. Companies must enhance their telecommunications strategy to ensure swift and secure communications, regardless of where the transaction is delivered.

As companies move their operations to less-developed countries in search of cheap labor, they quickly discover that in these (often rural) locations, few carriers offer service. (Passmore, 2003)

Some solutions that companies can use to enhance their service are listed in Table 1. These solutions assist organizations in creating good telecommunications strategies. Since each option has its strengths and weaknesses, an organization must choose the

Table 1. Telecomm solutions (Passmore, 2003)

Service	Telecomm Solution
Single Service Provider	Find someone who can do everything, which is difficult. They assume end-to-end responsibility for meeting service level agreements. The Multiprotocol Label Switching-based backbone can deliver IP virtual private network services at Layer 3, ATM/frame relay services are provided at Layer 2, and circuit emulation or clear-channel bandwidth also may be available. But communications to some places is still restricted to lower-speed frame relay or X.25, and availability of specific services cannot be assumed.
Roll your own	Some large enterprises build their own private network to link global sites together. Because a private network potentially can be extended to wherever connectivity is needed, this approach usually solves the problem of reaching remote sites.
	The largest enterprises can leverage the same economies of scale that would apply to a carrier network. Because of the current worldwide glut of fiber on certain long-haul routes (especially in North America), companies may be able to obtain a great deal of bandwidth economically. However, such savings may be offset by the relatively high cost in many countries associated with leasing private network access circuits.
Stitch together multiple service provider clouds	Since a single service provider may not be able to deliver the desired network services to all of an enterprise's sites, an enterprise could try to combine different provider networks, either to extend geographic coverage or to create multiple carrier paths in the backbone for redundancy and higher availability. The enterprise would obtain IP-VPN, frame relay, ATM, or other services from each carrier and maintain a few peering points, where traffic would be handed off (routed) from one cloud to another.
Use a Virtual Network Organization (VNO)	VNOs offer more sophisticated services than traditional resellers, and there are currently two different models. (1) One type of VNO provides peering points between other carrier clouds, concatenating carrier services to provide end-to-end service across geographies. The peering points include performance-monitoring tools to enable the VNO to determine which carriers are meeting SLAs (or not). The result should be end-to-end service that meets SLAs on a global scale. (2) The other type uses IP-VPN services across provider networks. This cannot guarantee end-to-end performance, but they provide truly global reach. They leverage Internet connectivity and use the same access facilities for both site-to-site and extranet access.
Hybrid	Hybrid systems could be developed, allowing a company to build a private network to gain economies of scale and to exploit cheap fiber runs to higher density locations or sites where transmission facilities are reasonable priced. This network could be extended via a provider's IP-VPN or frame relay to reach remote sites.

option that works best in the context of its own. For example, a single service provider may work for smaller organizations that do not have the expertise or the resources to build its own telecomm infrastructure. However, one of the fallacies of obtaining a single source provider is that it may not be able to provide the required telecomm services needed by an organization. Therefore, organizations are forced to stitch together multiple service providers to ensure that all of their telecommunications needs are met.

An alternative strategy is that some companies may choose to roll their own telecommunications systems. There are cases when local exchange carriers are progressing slowly and are not up to speed with current market demands to make progress and improve performance on their networks. Reardon (2004) wrote:

For a total cost of $2.2 million and a year's worth of work, Douglas County traded its old 1.5 megabit per second leased system for a brand-new 10 gigabit per second network—enough capacity to consider selling the excess for a profit. The new network, which is capable of carrying everything from voice to video to data, has also eliminated roughly $320,000 per year in recurring data communications charges... (Reardon, 2004)

This option is expensive and requires considerable knowledge of telecommunications technology.

For companies that do not want to build their own network, working with other telecommunications companies to build/bridge a system is another option. The key is to link with providers that are reliable and to fully understand their capabilities and the extent of their footprint. However, a hybrid solution that employs a peer-to-peer concept using satellite transmission to communicate information, using wireless technology in remote areas and working with a single source in metropolitan areas, provides the most flexibility and allows organizations to develop a global strategy that best fits the need of that particular region.

Future Trends in Telecommunications

Voice Over IP (VOIP)

VOIP has positive attributes that make it the wave of the future for global businesses. It can substantially cut telecom costs by allowing access to voice and data using the same line, reduce long distance costs, and improve productivity. In a survey conducted by *InformationWeek* of 300 business-technology executives, more than 80% said their companies are using 29%, testing 18%, or planning to deploy 34% of the technology (Ewalt, 2004).

The most common VOIP applications in use are IP-based phone systems (71%); connections with satellite offices (68%); remote access to telephone features (63%); and phone-based productivity apps, including IP conferencing, unified messaging, and multimedia training (62%) (Ewalt, 2004). Although the use of VOIP is becoming more popular, there are concerns. Companies are concerned with the cost of installation, reliability of the voice component, and security. The handsets tend to fail more frequently than conventional telephones, and additional care must be taken to ensure that security patches and upgrades are applied across the VOIP system.

Wireless Implementation

Using wireless technology is another option for global communications. The Institute of Electronics and Electrical Engineers (IEEE) and Wireless Fidelity (Wi-Fi) alliance has completed the Robust Security Network that is designed to dramatically decrease attacks (Dornan, 2003). In addition, VISIONng, a non-profit consortium of telecom operations and Internet service providers (ISPs) promoting the creation of a global, multi-vendor IP telephony network has requested the International Telecommunications Union to establish a permanent global area code and prefix (878-10) for VOIP phone numbers registered with an electronic numbering service (Greenfield, 2003).

However, even with the right telecommunications solution, companies need to ensure that they are communicating effectively with the customer and providing product information back to the supply chain. An effective CRM enables companies to obtain order information while analyzing the trends and determining where the company's sales should be focused. Within the US, this process is challenging, because the correct solution is not always implemented, and stand-alone applications are used to evaluate this information. Developing a CRM solution that can be used globally is difficult. The subsequent section will review CRM, its challenges, advantages, and future trends in order for CRM to facilitate globalization.

Role of CRM in SCM Process

With the World Wide Web growing as a channel for global commerce, companies are trying to improve the way they communicate with their customers, obtain valuable marketing information, and increase customer loyalty. In the past, companies focused their marketing strategies on the areas of the world where they have a presence. In an effort to increase return on investment, companies use CRM software to identify target audiences and gather information about their spending habits and product use. The discussion that follows will focus on the challenges and opportunities of CRM in customer service, data management, and partnership management.

CRM Challenges and Opportunities

For companies globally marketing products on the Internet, the objective is to ensure that the company satisfies the three tenets of the customer relationship model (i.e., understanding consumer behavior, delivering personalized services, and earning customers' loyalty) (Hamid et al., 2004). Achieving each of these three tenets for global companies is a challenge. Although there are software vendors that provide customer relationship management software, additional developments are needed to increase effectiveness across the cultural markets and between the business-to-business (B2B) and business-to-consumer (B2C) customer relationships. An effective CRM is more than a software solution; it is about how customer information is used to create an ongoing relationship with the customer (Ragins et al., 2003). Companies are now seeking packages that can do the following:

- Allow for a multilingual order entry interface.
- Automate multilingual customer services.
- Allow for flexibility, depending on the way the customer prefers to shop (i.e., personal computer, wireless service, personal digital assistant (PDA), etc.).

Sergey Aityan, president of Huntington Beach Division, Paramon Technologies, said, "In a number of years, English will become the minority in the Internet world because the Internet is moving globally towards Asia and Europe" (Aityan, 2002). The US Census Bureau confirms Aityan's findings. There are more than 2.4 million Chinese-speakers, and four out of five of them prefer to speak Chinese at home. The number of Korean and Vietnamese speakers is also on the rise (Aityan, 2002). With B2C sales predicted to reach $100 billion in 2004 (Ragins et al., 2003), companies must find the right CRM solutions to fit their needs.

Business-to-Consumer Market

For B2C markets, the first challenge is to provide an interface that can be used universally across all ethnic channels and to ensure that accurate data is captured for market analysis. Second, businesses also will have to focus on providing B2C access services in the customer's preferred method of communication. Regardless of how a customer wants to access the Internet, the format must fit the various communication devices that are available. Finally, companies must ensure not only multilingual access to customer service, but also multilingual and multiple channels, such as customer initiated online chats, wireless access, or Web pages that provide the information the customer needs. Techniques that can foster ongoing dialog between marketers and their customers include CRM software, which integrates data from call centers and suggestion lines and develops customer profiles, personalized messages loyalty programs, special offerings, personalized Web pages, quarterly newsletters, and the formation of customer advisory councils. Other techniques might include chat-based online focus groups, Internet-based conferences, e-mail or Web- based customer surveys, and online customer panels (Ragins et al., 2003).

Business-to-Business Market

For companies whose primary customer base is the B2B market, finding the right CRM strategy is even more challenging, because the potential revenue loss an organization could experience from a substandard CRM strategy could negatively impact the relationship and discourage new customers from seeking their services. The CRM must allow sales representatives around the globe to access inventory from wherever they are in the world. The data must be updated in real time, and it must be converted easily from one language to another, allowing users to access the data in their preferred language. Gary Moore, vice-president of Global Business Development for mySAP, said, "If you've got a guy in Japan, and entering a (sales) opportunity and he's entering the text all in Japanese, it's not much use to anyone outside of Japan" (Aityan, 2002). Companies also can use future trends in CRM to meet their customers' demands and to help them achieve globalization. For companies that have B2C and B2B customers, there may be a need to have different software for the different relationships. "Effective CRM is more than a software solution; it is about how customer information is used to create an ongoing relationship with the customer" (Ragins et al., 2003).

Future Trends in CRM

Hosted CRM Solution

Although CRM software implementations are occurring within companies, several companies are turning to hosted customer relationship management solutions. For example, Polaroid has subscribed to CRM software from RightNow Technologies Inc. (McDougall, 2004). The hosted CRM solution approach has proven to be less expensive for companies than those that run CRM applications in-house. Hosted software allows companies to reduce IT complexity and to improve delivery and integration technologies. With the use of Web services, this concept is seriously being considered, because integration can be accomplished easily.

An effective CRM solution will enhance the ability of the supply chain management system by providing order data that the SCM can use to plan and schedule the manufacture of goods with minimal overruns. A global SCM uses data from every region of the world in the planning process, making it possible for companies to significantly reduce backorder occurrences. To achieve this, an organization should have a good telecomm strategy, along with an effective CRM solution to back it up.

Supply Chain Management

The process of implementing supply chain management solutions is slowly progressing among businesses. Major corporations such as Wal-Mart, Boeing, and Intel are investing in the tools because they recognize the fact that SCM solutions enable businesses to collaborate with their customers in order to meet their demands as well as to minimize the unnecessary production of goods. In short, the return on investment is greatly increased, once the proper SCM is implemented.

SCM Challenges and Opportunities

The companies that are implementing SCM solutions are implementing stand-alone components with the hope of integrating the software, once it is incorporated into their process. "All too often, they buy supply chain software on an ad hoc basis, gambling that each purchase will integrate with their prior acquisitions and deliver the promised benefits. This practice often creates more problems than it solves—and it generally leads to a poor return on investment (ROI)" (Taylor, 2004).

The major reasons why companies are not aggressively moving toward SCM process are:

- The pace of adopting new ways of doing business is slow.
- Demand information supplied by customers is not integrated into corporate planning.
- Demand management and supply management processes are not integrated and, hence, are unable to synchronize demand and supply.
- Lack of trust among trading partners to share pertinent information and to collaborate on decision making.
- The desire to partner but not to commit to executing the communicated plans.
- A common view that demands collaboration is a technology solution, and that current technology is too complex. (Crum et al., 2004)

Table 2. Logistics software implementation (Poirer et al., 2003)

Enterprise Resource Planning	63%
Inventory Planning and Optimization	53%
Web-Based Applications	52%
Advanced Planning and Scheduling	48%
E-Procurement Systems	47%
Warehouse Management Systems	42%
Business-to-Business	41%
Transportation Management Systems	30%
Customer Relationship Management	26%
CPFR	24%
Event Management	21%
Supplier Relationship Management	21%
Collaborative Product Design	13%
Enterprise Application Integration	13%

Even though companies are not quick to use technology, a survey conducted by Computer Sciences Corporation and Supply Chain Management Review of 142 businesses (Poirer et al., 2003) revealed that the companies that are using technology are implementing the following kinds of software listed in Table 2.

With the slow implementation of SCM software, companies realize the need for technology. However, they are reluctant to change processes, because they perceive that the cost and time associated with change is too great. Companies now are demanding that suppliers change their processes. This requires a paradigm shift where suppliers and customers have to share information, and each entity is truly a trading partner. Even if partnerships are developed, every discrete organization must select the software that best fits its needs. Taylor (2004) recommends one of the following four approaches:

- **Enterprise Resource Planning (ERP):** This approach focuses on planning and operations. It allows companies to feed the system with demand forecast and schedule production as late as possible. It does not assist in deciding where to place production facilities and warehouses and how to transport goods.

- **Advance Planning and Scheduling Systems (APS):** This approach focuses on managing a network of facilities and also scheduling production using mathematical equations.

- **Simulation Systems:** This approach focuses on predicting production and planning outcomes, based on the variables supplied by the end user. It enables companies to evaluate outcomes on a bell curve distribution and allows companies to plan accordingly.

- **Supply Chain Execution Packages:** This approach focuses on the integration of APS, simulation tools, ERP, CRM, supplier relationship management, and event management. (Taylor, 2004)

To increase the use of SCM software, vendors now are incorporating ERP software into their packages. This enables companies to streamline their processes, and it will provide them with the capability to manage sales activities as well as inventory planning. For example, Whirlpool is working with a single vendor that supplies ERP and SCM software in hopes that the software will ensure nearly every time a customer walks into a store to buy a Whirlpool product that the product is ready and waiting on the retailer's floor (Bacheldor, 2004).

Future Trends in SCM

Collaborative Relationships and Federated Approach

When discussing future trends for supply chain management, it is important to note that, while technology is evolving, most companies still lag behind in implementing it. Many

SCM research findings confirm that a good SCM process will yield ROI, but this only comes if the proper software selection is made and implemented. It is important for companies to understand thoroughly their processes before they can use software to enhance them and/or build collaborative relationships with customers to optimize results. "The most successful demand collaborative relationships are not brokered at the buyer-salesperson level but at the senior executive level of the trading partner organizations" (Crum, 2004). Both the supplier and the customer must agree to share information in order for both organizations to obtain what they need. "Reaching consensus on a single demand plan that is used by both the customer and supplier organizations to drive management and financial planning is a best practice. However trust is an issue here. Today, demand plans communicated between trading partners are usually just numbers. As a result, the demand plans are not well understood and thus lack credibility" (Crum, 2004).

For companies that have settled on an SCM strategy, they are striving to find ways to continue to reduce costs. One of the ways companies are achieving this is by providing customers with data regarding suppliers and subcontractors. These coordination efforts allow the customer, the supplier, and the supplier's supplier to plan resources more efficiently. Supply chain coordination is not new to leading companies like Wal-Mart and McDonald's. Their influence in the marketplace gives them a great advantage over their suppliers. For companies that may not have the same influence but want to achieve the same results, the federated approach to planning may be best. "The federated planning model does not depend upon a utopian dream that ignores the inherent conflicts between supply chain partners (such as the need to maximize returns to their separate shareholders). ... federated planning accepts that each will ultimately optimize alone which allows supply chain partners to collaborate"(Laseter et al., 2004). For example, if a group of companies combined its warehousing for like items, it could reduce warehousing and production costs by having the supplier provide services to all of the companies under one organization.

SCM Standards

Software will allow businesses to better plan their resources and reduce costs. With the use of standards, Jones et al. (2002) believe that it will improve communications among trading partners. In their study of the retail industry, they found that standardizing the processes would improve globalization. In fact, there is a global commerce initiative that endorsed standards that were developed to facilitate national and international communication among all trading partners participating in any supply chain, including raw material suppliers, manufacturers, wholesalers, distributors, retailers, hospitals, and final clients or consumers.

Implementing standards will assist in the following processes:

- A global approach will result in less diversity in communication among existing trading partners and thereby reduce overhead and facilitate cross-regional trading. This uniformity will enable better collaboration on non-competitive processes.

- A global approach will provide synergies within organizations that operate across regions. Reporting and information sharing will be more consistent, and certain services can be centralized.
- Currently, there are local standards and proprietary systems. Providing uniform standards improves the processes (Jones et al., 2002).

Peoplesoft has assisted the health care industry to implement standards by incorporating three initiatives from the Coalition for Healthcare Standards (CHeS) into its enterprise resource planning system in order to help health organizations automate supply chain functionality (Berman, 2003). With approximately 80% of the health care providers represented by CHeS, this software implementation will allow suppliers and distributors to transact business online and in a unified manner.

Recommendations

The following recommendations will help the organization achieve globalization:

- Create an SCM system that encompasses the required components and produces reports that are useful to all functional areas.
- Ensure the system is dynamic enough to allow for quick modifications (e.g., adding suppliers, changing portal information, product configurations, etc.).
- Use Web services to communicate information in real time.
- Create a hybrid telephony system that will enable the company to use carriers where they exist and develop wireless means of communications where there is no fiber.
- Consider hosted CRM services in regions where cultural differences exist.

With the integration of ERP applications into SCM software packages, vendors are recognizing that they can provide an integrated solution that will allow companies to achieve their supply chain goals. Companies that are using this software or creating their own processes and systems to address both global and domestic market needs also are realizing that they may need assistance and are outsourcing parts of the business that are too expensive to maintain. Regardless of the model used, as long as companies determine their strategy and work toward achieving or exceeding customer and supplier expectations, it is likely that whichever software or telecommunications solution is selected, it will enable the company to acquire global markets.

Conclusion

In this chapter, we have attempted to describe the steps needed to achieve globalization. We have also demonstrated that it is possible for companies to develop systems that will meet customer expectations, regardless of the customer's locale. The real challenge for organizations is how to create a system that streamlines operations and delivers, based on customer and supplier expectations while ensuring ROI in the shortest amount of time. Since functional departments within organizations traditionally have worked in isolation to create systems that work best for their area of expertise, it is necessary to consider key factors and prerequisites, if an organization wants to effectively penetrate global markets. First, organizations need to identify their strategic objectives. If the goal is to globalize, then an organization needs to develop a technology that supports this vision. Second, an organization needs to assess its current software capabilities and begin to meet with the various departments in the organization in order to understand their current demands and future needs. Third, it is imperative that an organization map all processes to show the interdependencies of each functional area in order to include the role each trading partner plays in the process. Finally, an organization must ensure buy-in from senior level management about the technological model that will be pursued. Once these steps have been implemented, the following recommendations will help the company achieve globalization.

- Create an SCM system that encompasses the following components and produces reports that are useful to all functional areas of the organization:
  - CRM
  - ERP
  - APS
  - Supplier Relationship Management (SRM)
  - WHMS (Warehouse Management System)
  - Event Management
  - Simulation Tools
- Ensure the system is dynamic enough to allow for quick modifications (e.g., adding suppliers, changing portal information, product configurations, etc.).
- Use Web services to communicate information in real time.
- Create a hybrid telephony system that will enable the company to use carriers where they exist and develop wireless means of communications where there is no fiber.
- Consider hosted CRM services in areas where cultural differences exist.

With the integration of ERP applications into SCM software packages, vendors are recognizing that they can provide an integrated solution that will allow companies to achieve their supply chain goals. Companies that are using software or creating their own processes and systems to address both global and domestic market needs also are realizing that they may need assistance and are outsourcing parts of the business that are too expensive to maintain. Regardless of the model used, as long as organizations plan and implement their strategy that meets or exceeds customer/supplier/stakeholder expectations, it is most likely that the software or telecommunications solution selected will serve as a catalyst and/or facilitate its globalization initiatives.

References

Aityan, S. (2002). CRM must speak many tongues. *Computing Canada*.

Bacheldor, B. (2004). Supply-chain economics. *Information Week, 979,* 32-42.

Berman, J. (2003). Peoplesoft adds CHeS standards for supply chain efficiency. *HealthŸIT World*. Retrieved April 5, 2004, from *http://www.health-itworld.com/enewsarchive/e_article000181909.cfm*

Choudrie, J., Papazafeiropoulou, A., & Lee, H. (2003). A web of stakeholders and strategies: A case of broadband diffusion in South Korea. *Journal of Information Technology, 18,*(4).

Crum, C., & Palmatier, G. (2004). Demand collaboration: What's holding us back? *Supply Chain Management Review, 8*(1), 54-61.

D'Avanzo, R. (2003). The reward of supply-chain excellence. *Optimize.* Retrieved January 26, 2004, from *http://www.optimizemag.com/printer/026/pr_financial.html*

Dolinov, M.L. (2003). Wi-Fi: Questions and answers for execs. *Forrester Research Inc.* Wholeview TechStrategy Research.

Dornan, A. (2003). Emerging technology: Wireless security—Is protected access enough? Retrieved March 10, 2004, from *http://www.networkmagazine.com/shared/article/showArticle.jhtml?articleID=15201417*

Ewalt, D.M. (2004). The new voice choice. *InformationWeek, 978,* 34-44.

Greenfield, D. (2003). Global Watch. *Network Magazine*. Retrieved March 10, 2004, from *http://www.networkmagine.com/shared/article/showArticle.jhtml?articleID=15201423*

Hamid, N.R.A., & Kassim, N. (2004). Internet technology as a tool in customer relationship management. *The Journal of American Academy of Business, 4*(1/2), 103-108.

Jones, R.H, & Green, M.D. (2002). Streamlining the supply chain. *Chain Store Age, 78*(12), 47-54.

Kaarst-Brown, M., & Wang, C. (2003). Doing business in paradise: How small, information intensive firms cope with uncertain infrastructure in a developing island nation (TCI). *Journal of Global Information Management, 11*(4), 37-57.

Laseter, T., & Oliver, K. (2003). When will supply chain management grow up? *strategy+business*. Retrieved April 6, 2004, from *http://www.strategy-business.com/press/article/03304?pg=0*

McDougall, P.(2004). Hosted software gains more converts. *Informationweek, 979,* 30.

Pankaj, M. (2003). *Asia Computer Weekly*.

Passmore, D. (2003). Network architect. *Business Communications Review, 33*(10), 14.

Poirier, C., & Quinn, F. (2003). A survey of supply chain progress. *Supply Chain Management Review*. Retrieved March 8, 2004, from *http://www.manufacturing.net/scm/index.asp?layout=articlePrint&articleID=CA323602*

Ragins, E.J., & Greco, A.J. (2003). Customer relationship management and e-business: More than a software solution. *Review of Business*, *24*(1), 25-31.

Reardon, M. (2004). A network of one's own. *C|net News.com*. Retrieved April 13, 2004, from *http://news.com.com/2100-1033_3-5166813.html?tag=st_pop*

Taylor, D.A. (2004). A master plan for software selection. *Supply Chain Management Review, 8*(1), 20-27.

Thought Leadership Summit on Digital Strategies. (2002). Real-time profit optimization: Coordinating demand and supply chain management.

Wresch, W. (2003). Initial e-commerce efforts in nine least developed countries: A review of national infrastructure, business approaches and product selection. *Journal of Global Information Management, 11*(2), 67-78.

Chapter III

Demand Forecasting for the Net Age:
From Thought to Fulfillment in One Click

Edward D'Souza
eSymbiosys Inc., Canada

Ed White
Bayer Canada Inc., Canada

Abstract

Picture this. The year is 2025. A customer is watching a new razor blade advertisement on interactive TV. The customer clicks to approve the purchase. When the order is received by the vendor, demand forecasting systems match customer experience data and integrate parameters—frequency of usage, preference of color, style of hand grip, language spoken by the customer, font style for customer's name to be engraved on the razor, and so forth—into the Global Integrated Supply Chain Systems (GISCS) process. The next interaction is the customer receiving the order with a six-month supply of blades in the shortest possible time at a very affordable price. This will truly represent the process of thought to fulfillment in one click. This chapter explores the role played by demand forecasting for the net age—an age where customers can be anywhere and wants to have their needs addressed the moment they think about them. The organization that can fulfill the needs of these individuals in the easiest, fastest, and most cost-effective way will win their business. Such organizations will win over their competition and, in the process, reap profits. Any error in the thought to the fulfillment of the supply chain will result in a dissatisfied customer and, in all probability, loss of future business to the competition. Meeting the demands of an anywhere-anytime environment requires more than just-in-time Supply Chain Management (SCM). It needs to move to the next level to what we call just-in-mind SCM. Demand forecasting for just-in-mind SCM requires the organization to do global thinking and local linking. The global thinking helps to forecast the demand, and local linking helps to fulfill it. The chapter helps the reader to understand the challenges faced by organizations in forecasting demand in the net age, gives real-life examples of these challenges, provides solutions for addressing them, and takes a look into the future.

Introduction

Why do businesses forecast demand requirements? They forecast demand requirements so that they make or acquire the right material in the right quantities at the right time. This allows them to keep costs low, customers happy, and their company profitable. The problem with this is that all forecasts, by their very nature, are inaccurate. If you knew exactly what you would sell and when, then it wouldn't be a forecast anymore; it would be a requirement. Even in businesses where they are selling 100% of their capacity, there is a need to forecast, so they can determine the most profitable mix on which to use that capacity and as a justification for increased capacity. If there is only 10% more business available, it does not make a lot of sense to increase capacity by 100%, although you might want to consider growing the capacity slowly as demand grows. When forecasting, it is also necessary to consider the variability of the demand. For example, in a city with 1,000,000 people, you can make a basic assumption that something in the neighborhood of 1,000,000 breakfasts will be consumed every morning. The problem with forecasting those breakfasts is that it will not be 1,000,000 servings of the exact same breakfast. Some people will have one type of breakfast; others will have something different. Some people will have large servings, while others will have small servings. To make the situation even more complicated, the amount of variability will change dramatically, based on time of year, region, economic conditions, or even religious events. This means that even if you developed an algorithm that worked in one city, you may not be able to extrapolate it to any other city or even to the same city at a different time of year. So, with such uncertainty in the breakfast market, is forecasting a waste of time? Absolutely not! As long as you realize there are inherent inaccuracies and pay attention to how inaccurate any given forecast is likely to be, it can be an extremely useful tool to help any organization in both its long- and short-term planning. This is a truism that has been recognized by most organizations, and, hence, forecasting has become an integral part of business planning in all organizations. Admittedly, some organizations are a little more informal in how they forecast than others, but even the most informal organization makes daily decisions on what is about to happen within the organization based on someone's best guess or forecast about the future. The question we need to ask is, how will this process of forecasting the demands of a company's product or services change in the future (new age), based on economic, sociological, and technological changes in the environment? In order to answer that question, one must first anticipate and study the sort of changes that are expected in both the short term and long term and then consider how best to forecast business demand, followed by the manner in which the demand will be fulfilled. Let's look at each of these environmental changes and then try to tie everything together at the end.

Changes in the Economic Environment

The most obvious and overwhelming trend in the economic environment is the rapid and ongoing industrialization of the developing nations. As these countries, primarily in Asia, Africa and Latin America, develop their economies, they have a huge impact on each other and on the current developed countries. These impacts will be all the larger when you consider that they are not trying to imitate current developed countries, but rather to take those things that work for them, develop new methodologies where necessary, and remain true to their own cultures in the process. For example, the North American model is based primarily on a wide-open, competitive marketplace in an open, democratic environment. While there are undeniable benefits to this paradigm, there are also undeniable weaknesses, such as the tendency to only worry about the next quarter and to let the long term take care of itself. Some developing countries are trying to moderate the worst excesses of this wide-open, chaotic environment with various types of built-in controls. Admittedly, some of the economic experiments have shown more promise than others, but with so many cultures trying so many different methodologies, new and different conditions are bound to develop. How does this impact forecasting? On a micro level, very little, as individual local operations will continue to only worry about their little niche; but on a macro level, the effect is huge. As economies grow and change, the world becomes a smaller place so that many companies no longer only market their product locally or source their materials locally, but rather extend these requirements globally. As companies grow and network, they need to be cognizant of how local conditions in areas other than their home ground affect their business. They need to build products that appeal to their customers in different locations, usually through some form of niche marketing that requires some form of niche forecasting. They need to firmly understand how different economic conditions will affect the marketability of their products. For example, in many emerging countries, the newly developing middle class can afford to have maids who shop for product daily rather than the North American model of shopping weekly. This leads to a tendency to buy smaller packages more often rather than buying a size that would last all week. With this in mind, the organization needs to forecast larger, more evenly spaced sales of smaller containers rather than the larger container size and weekly cycle of the North American market with its distinct food store sales peak toward the end of each week. Another consideration with developing nations for the food industry is the spottiness of availability of electricity, occasionally interspersed with total unavailability. This means that many of the households either do not have access to refrigeration or are not willing to trust large stocks of food to the vagaries of electricity availability. Again, this leads to a tendency to shop more often and buy smaller, immediately consumable portions of food.

Changes in the
Sociological Environment

Just as many of the economic changes are driving sociological changes, so many sociological changes are driving economic changes, giving rise to a chicken-and-egg situation. Which came first? The economic or the sociological change? Fortunately, we do not need to deal with that issue here, but it is an important consideration, because the two types of changes will always maintain a sort of dynamic tension between them, where changes in one will invariably create offsetting changes in the other. This means that alert and successful organizations not only must be aware of changes in their environments, but they also must be able to accurately extrapolate what sort of further changes will be caused by this tension and plan for how they will affect their organizations and markets. Literature is littered with examples of many successful companies that failed to anticipate changes in their environments and are no longer around to talk about it. As companies begin, merge, diverge, and die in response to changes in the environment, they create their own effects on that environment. This affects how a company forecasts on both a micro and a macro level. Changes in the local environment must be tracked, anticipated, and corrected at a local level. Globally, organizations must maintain enough control to drive the organization, yet they need to leave enough autonomy at the local level to deal with local differences. For example, let's consider something as simple as the labeling requirements for your product. Different countries or regions often have different legal requirements; therefore, forecasting, manufacturing, and distribution processes must take this into consideration, as a labeled product may not be interchangeable, even if the product is identical. An example of this would be labeling of packaging in the province of Quebec in Canada. Due to a desire of the government to protect their French heritage in a largely Anglo-cultured country, they have enacted provincial legislation that requires all labels (and signs) to contain French with at least the same prominence and size as any English on the label. It many cases, the French must be larger and more prominent than the English. What this means is that product that can be distributed in the rest of the country may not be distributable in Quebec, while there are certain other areas in Canada where distributing a product with the Quebec label may risk annoying local customers, resulting in potentially lost sales in those areas. Another consideration with labels is color. In many Latin cultures, bright red and yellow colors are desirable and will enhance the product's image and, therefore, its sales. In many Oriental cultures, these colors are considered bad and would have the exact opposite effect on image and sales. This type of information must be taken into consideration when designing a product or a product packaging for distribution, as well as for the potential effects on the organizations forecast. Again, this is local autonomy with global governance.

If we look at an even more micro level, we need to consider individual people and their effect on an organization's forecast. Historically, the consumer was thought of and acted like big blocks of interchangeable components of the market, with them all buying the same thing. Think about the mindset of Henry Ford's alleged statement, "The customer can have any color they want, so long as they want black." In the new reality, individual consumers are becoming more discriminating and more demanding, which causes much more variability. People are very specific about what they want and are not willing to be dictated to by the supplier. Ian Morrison, the author of the book, *The Second Curve*, says, "The new consumer is a powerful enough force to change the types of products and services coming to market, and to transform the way products and services are sold" (Morrison, 1997, p. 8). This shows in ways such as less brand loyalty, although consumers will be very loyal to a company that provides what they want, when they want it, and at a price they can live with. Also, consumers are looking for the best value, not the cheapest price. Modern consumers *will* pay more to get exactly what they want but will react very negatively if they think the company is trying to gouge them. The key word again is *value*. This reality changes the forecast paradigm as much or perhaps even more than any technological changes. As manufacturing adopts lean methodology and moves to a "lot size of one," so demand planning must move to ever finer levels of distinction in forecasting. In the new net-enhanced environment, there always will be a balance of dynamic tensions between actual demand from consumers, based on the changes in their buying patterns, and the need and ability to accurately forecast this demand. The shift is away from maintaining large stocks of finished goods at various locations and toward lean manufacturing and distribution practices. This means that, as stocks are driven down and consumer expectations rise, it becomes ever more important not only to accurately forecast requirements, but also to monitor proactively those forecasts against real sales to quickly spot divergences before they can impact customer service. This means taking advantage of new technologies, such as Radio Frequency Identification (RFID), to monitor movement within the system, using early warning triggers to spot trends away from the official plan and a willingness of the new companies to take risks in responding to these potential issues before they can impact the customer. These technological changes mean that customers can be anywhere and want to have their needs addressed the moment they think about them. The organization that can fulfill the needs of these customers in the easiest, fastest, and most cost-effective way will win their business. Such organizations will win over their competition and, in the process, reap profits. Any error in the thought to fulfillment of the supply chain will result in a dissatisfied customer and, in all probability, loss of future business to the competition. Meeting the demands of an anywhere-anytime environment requires more than just-in-time Supply Chain Management (SCM). It needs to move to the next level, or what we call just-in-mind SCM. Demand forecasting for just-in-mind SCM requires the organization to do not just global thinking, but local linking, as well. Again, the organization must take advantage of the technological tools and advances available to it in order to adequately forecast, distribute, and monitor the interactions between the two in order to close the loop in the process and to have feedback for any deviations to the plan for appropriate reaction. To quote Jeffery C. Shuman and Janice M. Twombly (2000):

[T]he challenge...facing all entrepreneurs today, to disregard all their legacy thinking and start with a clean sheet of paper. Don't think about how you can change your business to function in the age of the Internet. Focusing on your business will just mire you in more legacy thinking. Focus instead on the consumer. Focus on the personalized set of needs and wants of your consumers and once you know what those desires are, structure whatever organization and business infrastructure you have to in order to satisfy those personal needs and want profitably.

Changes in the
Technological Environment

In the 21st century, people who are not online will have to wait in line. In a world where the rate of change is ever increasing, people who wait in line will get a lot less done compared to those who are online. As stated by Jeffery Krames (2003, p. 66), *What the Best CEOs Know*, Michael Dell says:

Over 90 percent of our supply-chain transactions are machine-to-machine transactions. Of course, you have to put some sort of human framework in there. But if all transactions were non-Internet individual purchases [that is, individual orders placed over the phone], the expense would be just enormous.

The increasing use of the Internet by today's buyers calls for a radical change in the way SCM systems are designed and implemented. Some of the reasons are as follows:

- **Disintermediation:** The Internet provides direct access to the customer anywhere, anytime. Organizations that use conventional channels for order booking and fulfillment are inefficient, resulting in increased costs, slower delivery, and missed opportunities. The net age allows for orders to be collected electronically as bits. The challenge, then, is to have a fulfillment system that optimizes the use of bits (i.e., easy-to-use Enterprise Application Integration [EAI] systems).

- **Channel Substitution vs. Channel Complement:** In many cases, the Internet is not a substitute but a complement to existing channels. When a major North American retailer launched its online shopping capability, it had anticipated it cannibalizing its existing retail shopping business. Instead, it saw its retail sales maintain their levels, and the Internet channel provided additional business. This was because most Internet buyers turned out to be individuals who could not go shopping during regular business hours, as they were working or had other higher priority things to do during that time. The anywhere-anytime aspect of Internet-based shopping made it easier for this group of individuals to shop when the retailer's stores were closed for business. By assuming channel substitution for forecasting demand, the retailer had problems managing its inventory.

- **Unpredictability of Customer Behavior:** Since the Internet is relatively new, in many cases, there is not enough historical data on how customers will respond and what aspects of the Internet will influence customer behavior.

The next section provides solutions for addressing some of the challenges of the Net Age environment.

Figure 1. Demand forecasting loop

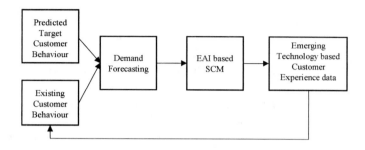

Solutions

In this new world of integrated systems and processes, it is impossible to consider demand forecasting without also considering the entire process up to and including the ultimate delivery to the customer. One of the keys to demand forecasting in the future will be building feedback mechanisms into the process design that will allow for timely corrections in errors made in forecasting. A simplified process map of such a process is shown in Figure 1.

It plays on the fact that, in addition to beginning with the end in mind, organizations also must end with the beginning in mind. In short, the end product must have the capability to provide feedback on customer behavior. For example, Gillette sells low-priced razors with the philosophy of 'give away the razor for the razor blade'. If Gillette embedded a feedback chip in the razor that provided the company with data on location of the customer and frequency of razor blade replacement, they would be in a better position to forecast the use of razor blades by their existing customer base. This information then could be used for efficient SCM.

The basis of the Dell model is an incredibly firm grasp on demand. Other companies, regardless of their size, can help themselves by doing a better job of forecasting demand and, in Michael Dell's words (Krames, 2003, p. 65), being "prepared for all possible instances of demand, whenever and wherever they may occur." Dell may never reach his stated goal of gathering 100% of his sales online, but remember that 90% of his supply-chain transactions are currently machine-to-machine. This may be unrealistic for many companies, but moving in this direction can lower transaction costs while freeing employees to get more involved with knowledge-based activities that can help the company in other ways (Krames, 2003, p. 67).

In order to better explore the details of this process, let's look at each of the boxes in Figure 1 in detail and then sew everything back together at the end.

Predicted Target Customer Behavior

For better forecasting, organizations will have to predict customer behavior by utilizing all the tools at hand; for example, by doing target customer polls over the wireless cell phone network or by using computer agents to do data mining throughout the Internet and reporting back with applicable information. But how does an organization define what is important or applicable?

In their book, *The Discipline of Market Leaders*, Michael Treacy and Fred Wiersema (1997) state that most organizations try to differentiate themselves by focusing most of their priorities on one of the three market disciplines: customer intimacy, product leadership, or operational excellence; or, put another way, better customer service, better product, or better production. There are many examples of each of these, but let's just look at one. Dell is world-renowned for its dedication to customer service and its many groundbreaking methods of receiving orders from the customer. It is this dedication to providing exactly what the customer wants that differentiates it from its competition. As Michael Dell says, "We're in the business of dramatically reducing the cost of distributing technology. To do that, we are going to get closer and closer to our suppliers and customers" (Krames, 2003, p. 62).

Some of the factors impacting the prediction of target customer behavior are shown in Figure 2. The more the collection of these factors is automated, the more time the decision makers will have to analyze target customer behavior and make increasingly accurate demand forecasts. This automation can be achieved by storing all relevant target customer behavior information in a data warehouse and by using data-mining software to extract analytics to help support the decision-making process. A data warehouse helps with the tracking of historical customer behavior, and the analytics help with understanding its relevance to current customer demand. This allows us to better predict the behavior of our target customers. Each of the factors shown in Figure 2 will have both direct and indirect impacts on customers' behaviors, which, in turn, will have direct and

Figure 2. Factors impacting prediction of target customer behavior

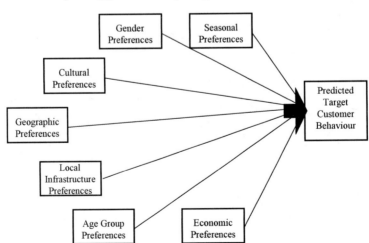

indirect impacts on their buying habits over time, and which, of course, will have an impact on the accuracy of any demand forecast we do. For instance, we talked earlier about cultural differences, such as how the colors red and yellow are perceived. If we do not consider this effect when predicting customer behavior in any particular environment, we run a substantial risk of inaccurate forecasts that would translate to misallocated resources, longer lead times, and lower profitability. In short, we would be less able to compete with other companies and ultimately risk the viability of our company's future.

As another example, let's consider the factor labeled *seasonal preferences*. This could be weather-related, such as when to stock snow blowers rather than lawn mowers in a country like Canada, or it could be event-based, such as the effect a holiday like Christmas would have on the buying patterns of any predominately Christian locality. Seasonality even can be time-based. An example of this would be expected customer patterns in a restaurant where they would expect to sell more food around the traditional lunch and dinner times then at other times during the day. It also is important to consider interactions between these factors. Using the example of the restaurant again, you would need to consider that different cultures have different eating habits in terms of timing and quantity. Gender preferences also would shade the choices, as would age-group preferences and even the time of year. All these factors need to be taken into consideration in order to optimize predicated target customer behavior.

Existing Customer Behavior

While it is important to pre-think all the factors that influence the demand for a product, it is equally important to consider the reality at the time the demand is being predicted. In other words, we can predict behavior, but how does the customer's actual behavior align with this prediction? As a company, we may feel that a particular product should appeal to a particular segment of the market, but when we check actual sales, we find that, in fact, the predicted customer is not there. We may find less than predicted sales, more than predicted sales, or even that an entirely different segment has bought this product. Fads would be almost impossible to predict but very easy to track. This makes it critical not only to be able to monitor actual customer behavior, but also to quickly react to any unpredicted customer behavior. The use of emerging technologies like RFID or smart chips can significantly ease the collection of factors that influence existing customer behavior. As illustrated in Figure 3, understanding existing behavior is influenced by information about the current customer environment, leading indicator information about the market environment, and the volume of existing orders.

One of the bigger questions companies have to answer is how can they access this information and organize it in a way that is useful (data vs. knowledge). While some of the information can be accessed through the company's internal information (sales orders, quotes, etc.), much of this information needs to come from external databases and creative interpretation of available information, such as popular literature or the Internet. In his book, *Being Digital*, Nicholas Negroponte (1996) speculates about changes in information sources, where people and their computer agents will pull the information

Figure 3. Tracking demand based on existing customer behavior

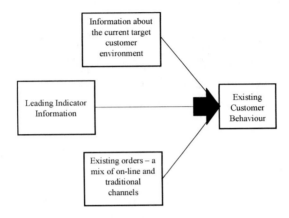

they want out of the information pool rather than having someone push the information to them in some sort of zine format. Keep in mind that this book was published in 1995, and we are just now seeing much of what he talked about starting to take place in everyday life. The information superhighway is, indeed, becoming a boutique where people only pull the information they need and ignore the rest. The question is, how does this concept affect forecasting? As the entire forecasting process goes global and digital, it becomes impossible for one person or even a group of people to adequately track the huge amounts of generated information. Instead, computer agents and warning signals will be used to allow the system (and its human overseer) to sort out (pull) only that information that is critical to the organization and allow non-critical information to be ignored. As a company, we can use automated agents to track predicted behavior against actual behavior and notify us of any developing significant divergences between actual and predicted behavior.

Ultimately, no matter what the predicted target customer behavior is, the key word to remember is *predicted*. In other words, this is forecasted behavior and, therefore, to a greater or lesser extent, is going to be wrong. In order to ensure the most effective response to our customers' needs, we need to monitor actual behavior and compare this to the predicted behavior. When there is variance or especially a trend away from the predicted behavior, it is critical that we modify our plans to stay in line with the customers' needs. Thinking back to our earlier statements about value, the customer is not terribly interested in what we think, only in what we offer. If they do not perceive value in our offerings, they will go where they do get the value they want and expect.

Demand Forecasting

The ultimate role of demand forecasting is its ability to help in decision support. The demand forecast information is the first step in enabling the making of sound business

Figure 4. Integrating demand data into a forecasting process

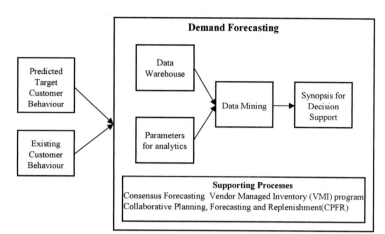

decisions that have a ripple effect on all strategic activities down the supply chain. Decision support efficiency can be achieved by storing all relevant target customer behavior information in a data warehouse and by using data-mining software to extract analytics to help decision support. A data warehouse helps with the tracking of historical customer behavior, and the analytics help with understanding its relevance to current customer demand.

As shown in Figure 4, for a successful implementation of demand forecasting, the system's activity must be supported by business processes, such as Consensus Forecasting, Vendor Managed Inventory (VMI) and Collaborative Planning, Forecasting and Replenishment (CPFR).

This will reflect a true implementation of an environment where the systems support the people and not vice versa. Those people who are the decision makers should ensure that the factors affecting demand forecasting are integrated into every subsequent process from design through manufacturing, supply chain, Customer Relationship Management (CRM) and even on to customer feedback. None of these support tools is new, and we don't propose to review them in this chapter; however, it is important to consider how they interact with new processes that are becoming available, as we move into the age of the Internet and advanced computer tools. Some changes and challenges are very obvious, and some are not so obvious. For now, let's just consider consensus forecasting, which, in its simplest terms, just means a forecast that has been agreed to by more than one party. Originally, this meant two or more people getting into the same room and talking until they agreed on a number. As various tools were developed, it became possible for the people to work from remote locations, at differing times, and even on different tools that then were able to transfer information back and forth. As we move into the future, the big change in consensus forecasting will be in how we take advantage of new communications tools on the Internet in order to enhance the forecasting process. As the overall processes become more and more complicated, it becomes more difficult for participants to stay abreast of the bigger picture. The bottom line of the consensus forecasting process is to gather various forecasts for the same things that are generated using different processes and then combine them to come up with a combined forecast to which all participants can agree. Most of the participants have real jobs to deal with and cannot spend large amounts of time forecasting. For example, a salesman's main (or real) job is to sell, and we need salesmen to be out doing that. While forecasting is important and does add great value to salesmen, there is a definite limit to how much time they can allocate to the process. However that time is not only necessary, but it is also critical to the accuracy of the overall forecasting process. The salesman is the one that is out talking to the customers and has the best feel for what is going to happen in the future with those customers. It is easy to statistically predict future sales based on past sales, but that is a lot like driving using only the rear-view mirror. So long as the road is straight, there is no problem, but at the first curve in the road, you will be in the ditch. When you try to forecast using only past sales, the ditch you run into might be only a slight inaccuracy, or you might drive right off a cliff, if there is a big enough change in the customer's behavior. The point is that everyone's opinion on future sales is important, and combining them together appropriately gives you a better chance at improving your accuracy.

So, what will the forecast process of the future look like? In a lot of ways, it will look much like the process of today but with many additional levels and tools involved in the process. If the virtual corporation is the model of the company of the future, then the virtual forecast is the model for demand planning. In the virtual corporation, you have many small groups or companies banding or networked together in order to accomplish some set goal. Each of the players brings something unique to the mix, with the actual combinations changing with time as the goals and needs change. Each of these small groups represents a node within the larger grouping. In virtual forecasting, you also have a nodal setup, with each node representing some logical subset within the larger context. For example, you could have a different node for each global region. Within these nodes could be subnodes for each country, and within these nodes could be subnodes for some specific grouping, such as customer groupings. As shown in Figure 5, each subnode would work independently of other subnodes to the point of potentially using different tools and processes to generate the required demand requirements.

This process is not all that different than the situation today. Where the difference comes in is in tying each of these different nodes together, using net technology to allow an organization to roll up the demand to get a holistic view of total requirements, then adding in feedback mechanisms in the actual sales and distribution levels to real-time monitor and modify the demand requirements forecast, based on what is actually happening rather than the best guess that the forecast represents. Those organizations that can spot and react most quickly to unanticipated changes in demand are the organizations that will have a competitive advantage in the modern global marketplace.

When thinking about nodal forecasting processes, keep in mind that the key to subnode forecasting is the communications linkage between each of these subnodes. It's like the old comparison among data, knowledge, and intelligence; the subnodes provide data, but without some way of making a synthesized whole or being able to easily find one specific piece of data, it is of no use. The problem, of course, quickly becomes a technological issue, when decisions need to be made on whether this gets controlled by one centralized processor or many little processors that communicate to each other.

Figure 5. Map of virtual forecasting process

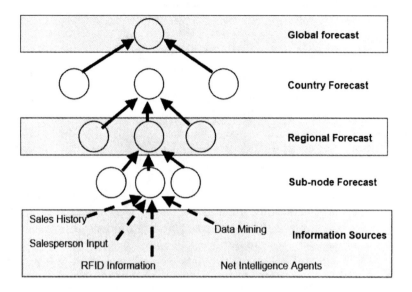

Obviously, in the early days of computers, the first inclination was to centralize everything, and this attitude still heavily influences much thought and practice today. With personal computers becoming more and more ubiquitous and ever more powerful, this may not be the ideal method anymore. Nicholas Negroponte (1996) talks about the concept of mass communication of many small processors in his book, *Being Digital*, where he makes the point of how much simpler it is to coordinate many small processes than most people would be willing to believe. By using a swarm of small computers to do the initial filtering and loading of data into the process, we gain far more information and far more useful information than we could with a single dedicated computer.

Another major factor in the forecasting process will be, again, at the subnode level, where new Web-based intelligence agents will be gathering information about target customers and factoring them into the overall forecast as an integral part of the consensus forecasting process. No longer will the consensus process be just people interpreting data and reaching a joint conclusion, but instead, you will have computers taking a larger role in the actual decision process, not just in the data gathering and sorting processes. Does this mean that computers will replace people in this process? Anything is possible, but until computers can be developed that have something equivalent to intuition, it is highly unlikely. While there is a large science component in forecasting, there is also a large art component, and it is this art component that still requires people in the process. What this means is that what the forecaster of the future does will change, as we take advantage of what computers do really well—crunch data. By that, we mean the computers and the new tools that are becoming available are really good at sorting through large databases, at doing many calculations, and at reporting information according to the directions they are given. What the forecaster will be concentrating on is supplying those directions to the system and interpreting the information, once the computer has presented it in a defined and understandable format.

EAI-Based GISCS

The accuracy of demand forecasting is related directly to the level of customer intimacy. It is the first step in improving the efficiency of the supply chain. Most importantly, it is the first step in knowing what will provide the most value for the target customer. Value has two sides to it—need and affordability. Demand forecasting captures the needs side of value. When this is followed by Enterprise Application Integration (EAI)-based SCM, it results in operational excellence (i.e., efficient Global Integrated Supply Chain Systems [GISCS]). A chain is as strong as its weakest link. EAI methodology helps in identifying the weak links, and its implementation helps in making them strong. The customer demand must be supported by an infrastructure that seamlessly integrates all stakeholders in the SCM process—product design, development, manufacturing, total quality management, packaging, suppliers, and delivery. Figure 6 shows the GISCS processes involved in the successful capture of customer order information, storing it in a tracking device like RFID, attaching the device seamlessly into the product, updating order fulfillment information in the device, and then delivering the product to the customer. For successful implementation, it must be noted that the process starts with the customer and ends with the customer.

The infrastructure used by customers, vendors, and suppliers is common to all—the Internet. Yet, its implementation in terms of Internet, intranet, and extranet will provide the necessary security and privacy boundaries required for a successful implementation. Organizations that use EAI to effectively integrate all their applications and improve the efficiency of the GISCS processes will be able to meet the demands of their customers in an affordable manner. By doing this, sharing the customer experience will not just be a buzz word, but it will be an integral part of the demand capture and fulfillment process.

Figure 6. EAI-based GISCS

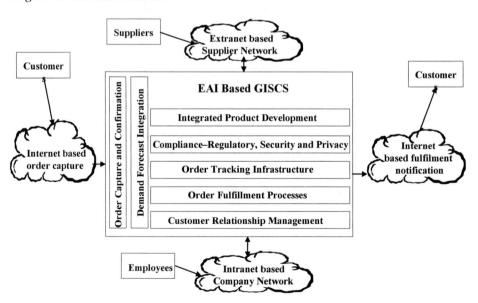

Figure 7. Customer experience capture

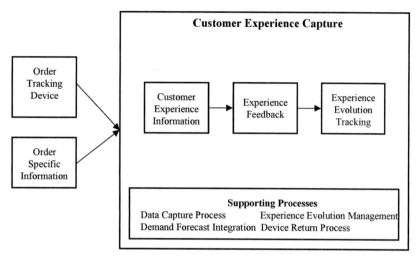

Capturing Customer Experience Data

So far, we have focused on demand forecasting as the first step—the beginning—in managing the capacity and efficiency of GISCS. To make it really work, it also must be the last step, the step that captures customers' usage patterns, maps them to initial expectations, analyzes the differences, records the evolutionary changes in customer behavior, and integrates the information into demand forecasting. It's like saying, "End with the beginning in mind." To be successful, the device used for data capture must be transparent to the consumer. To do this, the device will have to use mature technologies already used by the consumer in the environment in which the product is being used. If the product is the razor, then the device should have the ability to capture and transmit customer experience data from the wash-basin area—the environment in which the razor is being used.

To maintain continuity between the initial order placed by the customer and to capture the experience of the customer after the product has been delivered, the same device that stores the customer order and tracks its progress through the GISCS process will have to capture the customer experience data, as well. This technological solution will have to be supported by business processes that facilitate customer experience data capture, customer experience evolution management, demand forecast integration, and device return. This process is shown in Figure 7.

Issues that Need to Be Addressed

The international standards will have to address privacy issues about allowing customers to choose what data they would permit organizations to collect. The EAI systems will have to accommodate differences in needs due to cultural diversity, geographic environment, gender differences, and generation gaps.

- **Regulatory Issues:** As markets are becoming global, so are the reaches of regulatory compliance. Yet the difference in national preference will remain, for example, the requirement that all products have bilingual labels, English and French in Canada, or Arabic and English in the Middle East. At the same time, organizations will have to incorporate evolving international standards like Sarbanes-Oaxley into their demand forecasting processes and reporting.

- **Gender Differences:** Simple gender behaviors like ability to collect age information might challenge the accuracy of customer feedback. While males might not have an issue with providing their age in customer feedback, females might object to providing such information.

- **Generation Gaps:** While today's youth is entirely comfortable with online information access and feedback, the older generation might resist the use of emerging technology to provide customer feedback. This behavior will make the success of initial implementations of emerging technology-based customer feedback that much more challenging.

- **Geographic Environment Challenges:** Product design and, in turn, demand forecasting will have to address differences in parameters like weather in the geographic environment. A product that has to be sold in hot, humid environments in some parts of the Middle East might have to be packaged differently than when it is sold in the colder climate of Canada. Likewise, the variations in geographic climates will demand differencing tolerances in customer feedback tools, like smart chips that have to be embedded in the products.

- **Technological Challenges:** RFID and smart chip technologies still are evolving. The capabilities, accuracy, and reliability of these devices, while reasonably good, still is lagging behind mature infrastructures, like bar-code systems, in cost and accuracy (e.g., the 85% accuracy of current RFID systems with a low-end cost point of about a dollar is not impressive when compared with the over 99% accuracy and few cents in cost of bar-code-based systems.

Future Directions

Picture this. The year is 2025. A customer is watching a new razor blade advertisement on interactive TV. The customer clicks to approve the purchase. When the order is received by the vendor, demand forecasting systems match customer experience data and integrate parameters—frequency of usage, preference of color, style of hand grip, language spoken by the customer, font style for customer's name to be engraved on the razor, and so forth—into the Global Integrated Supply Chain Systems (GISCS) process. The next interaction is the customer receiving the order with a six-month supply of blades in the shortest possible time at a very affordable price. This will truly represent the process of thought to fulfillment in one click.

The behind-the-scenes technology will have embedded smart chips that could be used at all stages of SCM from the start of order fulfillment to assembly and shipment. In his book, *Only the Paranoid Survive*, Andrew Grove (1996) talks about the paradigm shift in the computer industry from a vertical solutions approach in the 1960s to a horizontal solutions approach in the 1980s. A similar paradigm shift is expected in the realm of demand forecasting. By developing appropriate international standards, residences and offices could be built with embedded chips that collect data for all items in the premises and send them to collection and distribution systems on a periodic basis. As shown in Figure 8, this will call for a sophisticated yet easy-to-use publish and subscribe information distribution model for management of customer experience data.

One of the possible ways to incorporate the data captured by smart chips into demand forecasting could be as one of the information sources for the bottom subnode level of the virtual forecast process, as discussed in the demand forecasting section. Effectively, this would be similar to current Point of Sale (POS) data that is currently used in some forecasting process. The difference is that POS tells you when something is bought, but embedded smart chips would tell you when something is used or needs to be replaced. Once the so-called smart housing starts to become more common, the house computer could track usage of tagged consumables within the house, feed anticipated require-ments (forecast) into a supplier's system, and, when needed, place a replacement order automatically with the supplier. Another example would be in the hospital environment. Currently, in most hospitals, new supplies are received into a central store, and, a couple of times a day, a technician will take a cart of supplies around to each ward to replenish stock. If there is not enough on the cart to complete the rounds, the technician needs to go back to the central store to get more. Now, consider an environment where each package or bundle of supplies is tagged with an RFID tag, and each ward has readers that are connected to the central computer. When the technician brings in a new set of supplies, the reader automatically notes and logs this arrival into the system. As the material is used up, the reader also notes this and keeps a running usage forecast supplied

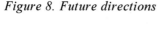

Figure 8. Future directions

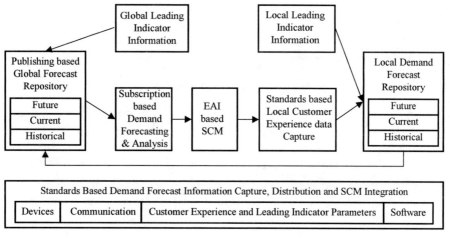

to central stores. When it is time for the technician to make the rounds, all the technician needs to do is to pull a pick list from the system of what is currently needed, gather the exact material from the storeroom, and deliver them to the appropriate ward. In addition, the readers in the storeroom also are noting movement of all materials, combining this with the running forecast from each of the ward's readers, maintaining its own forecast, and ordering conversations with the various suppliers that the hospital is using. Each of the wards has become a subnode in the storeroom forecasting process; the hospital is a node in its supplier's forecasting system; each of the suppliers is a node in its supplier's systems, and so forth. The technology to build this type of complete closed-loop forecasting and replenishment system exists now. What does not exist yet is the supporting infrastructure or the cost incentives to make it a reality, but both of these will exist in the not too distant future. In the meantime, the smart tag technology will continue to improve and get cheaper.

The initial implementation of smart-chip-based demand forecasting infrastructure will require customer-approved and customer-triggered feedback. It means that the customer will have the authority to decide whether to allow the product's experience information collector to capture data about customer experience. Subsequently, the customer will have to take the time and effort to provide the experience information to the collector. This could be as simple as the customer returning the current product in exchange for a new one or periodically sending information to the collector via the Internet, fax, or mail.

Future implementations could be based on customer-approved but device-triggered feedback. It means that once the customer has approved the collection of product experience information, the smart-chip-based device will automatically trigger relaying of customer experience information to the collector. One scenario would be the device using universally prevalent wireless networks to securely sign on to the collector's network using Public Key Infrastructure (PKI) and its unique device ID, and then transmitting the experience information to the collector. The experience information then could be integrated into demand forecasting for developing incentives for current product sales and suggesting enhancements for future product design. The device-triggered process also should increase the percentage of customer experience information collection approvals and the accuracy of information collected.

Conclusion

To summarize, the main points about demand forecasting for the Net Age are as follows:

- As the world grows smaller, the need for demand forecasting becomes a global endeavor.
- Yet the cultural, geographic, gender, and regulatory differences will remain.
- Organizations that incorporate these local differences into a global demand forecasting strategy will reap the benefit of satisfying their customers—anytime, anywhere.

- The capability of these organizations to integrate the global demand forecasting process into meeting local demands through efficient product design, global integrated SCM, and EAI will define their ability to have a sustainable competitive advantage.

- The use of smart chip technology to collect customer feedback for demand forecasting and use of RFID for integrating this feedback into customer fulfillment will be the enabler of this sustainable competitive advantage.

- Successful demand forecasting will depend on the ability of emerging technologies, GISCS, and EAI to capture a customer's thought and fulfill the demand in one click.

References

Dinning, M., & Schuster, E.W. (2003). *Fighting friction.* APICS The Performance Advantage.

Grove, A. (1996). *Only the paranoid survive.* New York: Bantam Doubleday Dell Publishing Group Inc.

Krames, J. (2003). *What the best CEOs know.* New York: McGraw-Hill.

Morrison, I. (1997). *The second curve.* New York: Ballantine Books.

Negroponte, N. (1996). *Being Digital.* New York: Vintage Books.

Proceedings of the Cardtech Securetch Conference. (2000). Chicago, Illinois.

Proceedings of the IBM—Architecting E-Business Solutions Conference. (2000). Toronto, Canada.

Reese, S. (2003, Winter). Reflections of an international forecaster. *The Journal of Business Forecasting, 22*(44), 23-28.

Schuman, J., & Twombly, J. (2000). Now Ford says … Any color you want. *Boston Business Journal,* October 20-26.

Treacy, M., & Wiersema, F. (1997). *The discipline of market leaders.* Boston: Addison-Wesley Longman.

Wright, C.M. (2004, March). Deep impact. *APICS The Performance Advantage, 14*(3), 18.

Chapter IV

The Future of Supply Chain Management:
Shifting from Logistics Driven to a Customer Driven Model

Ketan Vanjara
Microsoft, India

Abstract

This chapter initiates the concept of a customer-centric model in supply chain systems. It discusses various constraints of present-day supply chain systems resulting from their roots being in logistics management and suggests an alternative next-level paradigm of a customer-centric matrix model. This chapter further demonstrates how this model would add value to the customer by taking the example of a healthcare information management system. The chapter also delves into the limitations of and anticipated issues and challenges in implementing the suggested model. Finally, the chapter hints at some broad directions for future research and action in the field. Emergent behavior is what happens when an interconnected system of relatively simple elements begins to self-organize to form a more intelligent and more adaptive higher-level system (Johnson, 2001).

Introduction

Supply chain systems have come a long way from their initial days when their sole purpose was to support the inventory management function in terms of controlling inventory carrying and fulfillment costs, while making inventory management more efficient and effective. However, as the roots of Supply Chain Management (SCM) lie in managing supplies or inputs to a process or an enterprise, most of the developments (solutions, tools, and technologies) in this field obviously have been around effective management of supply chain toward better, faster, and more cost-effective fulfillment of customer demand.

While this focus on logistics and inventory management has certainly helped business, it still falls short of making the best use of the current tools and technologies for businesses. In order to provide this SCM advantage to businesses, the next level of evolution for the concept of supply chain would be to focus on the needs of the ultimate consumer in contrast to the needs of interim customers (i.e., manufacturers) that are the present-day focus. This chapter seeks to explore the possibilities of elevating the focus of SCM from a logistics-driven model to the next level of customer-driven model, thereby enhancing the value delivered to the end customer. The issues and challenges expected in the process also are delved into.

The chapter reviews some of the latest literature available on SCM, describes various models of supply chain since its origin, enumerates the limitations of the existing supply chain model, and suggests a customer-centric model. Furthermore, it goes on to discuss the challenges in the implementation of this model and the constraints of this model that will have to be addressed. Supply and procurement of healthcare services as well as a health care information management software developed by the author for the creation and management of virtual healthcare communities in line with the suggested customer-centric model is used as an illustration throughout the chapter.

Origins

As per one definition, SCM is the coordination of the demand and supply of products and services between a supplier's supplier and a customer's customer. It involves the flow of products, information, and money between the trading partners of a company's supply chain. The proactive improvement in the efficiency and effectiveness of the flow of goods, services, and knowledge across all stakeholders achieves the goal of reducing total costs and obtaining a competitive advantage for all parties.

Supply chain is the network of facilities (warehouses, factories, terminals, ports, stores, and homes), vehicles (trucks, trains, planes, and ocean vessels), and logistics information systems connected by an enterprise's suppliers' suppliers and its customers' customers. Supply chain flow is optimized when material, information, and money flow simultaneously in real time and without paper.[5]

SCM revolves around efficient integration of suppliers, manufacturers, warehouses, and stores. Other definitions are more comprehensive and detailed:

The challenge in supply chain integration is to co-ordinate activities across the supply chain encompassing these various players, whose systems are bound to be disparate right from the beginning. It is only with such integration that the enterprises can improve performance, reduce costs and increase their service levels to the end-user, the customer. These integration challenges are met not only by coordinating production, transportation, and inventory decisions but more generally by integrating the front-end of the supply chain, customer demand, to the back-end of the supply chain, the production and manufacturing portion of the supply chain. (Simchi-Levi et al., 2003)

As it can be seen from our discussion thus far and from the voluminous literature on supply chain, the focus is constantly on the network of facilities, logistics, supplies, and suppliers. This is due to two main reasons: (1) the origins of the concept of supply chain lie in logistics and in inventory. and (2) the supply chain is related mostly to manufacturing or tangible goods, and thereby, the developments in the services sector and in the knowledge economy are overlooked.

Some thoughts are emanating gradually on the use of supply chains for customer satisfaction. For instance, "efficient integration of suppliers, manufacturers, ... so that enterprise can increase service level" (Simchi-Levi et al., 2003) and "maximize customer service and minimize cost of the same" (Frazelle, 2002). The closest one gets to customer focus is in the following statement:

[A] supply chain consists of all parties involved, directly or indirectly, in fulfilling a customer request. The supply chain not only includes the manufacturer and suppliers, but also transporters, warehouses, retailers and customers themselves ... the customer is an integral part of the supply chain. The primary purpose for the existence of any supply chain is to satisfy customer needs. (Chopra & Meindl, 2004)

However, most of the integration referred to in most SCM literature is the vertical integration of suppliers, manufacturers, distributors and other business partners for the ultimate purpose of customer consumption and satisfaction. Thus, essentially, SCM has focused on vertical flow of goods and services toward order fulfillment, as described in Models A, B, and C in Figures 1, 2, and 3, respectively. But, as the delivery models of products and services become more complex (Model D), as shown in Figure 4, with the objective of fulfilling end-to-end requirements of a customer, supply chain systems will have to focus on integrating processes laterally, as well. The spread of such lateral processes across heterogeneous enterprises and geographical boundaries is becoming almost mandatory with the rapid globalization of enterprises, consequently adding to the challenge of managing supply chains.

Figure 1. Simple vertical model (1-1-1 relationship)

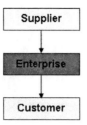

MODEL A: Simple Vertical Model (1-1-1 Relationship)

This model is based on an enterprise with a single product, single supplier, and single customer. Such a scenario exists in the case of contractual outsourcing or certain niche industries, products, or markets. Here, an enterprise fulfills the demands of its customer by adding value to the inputs from its supplier. The only contribution made by SCM in this model is the control of inventory-carrying costs, if at all. This is only a marginal improvisation over JIT (just-in-time) inventory systems.

MODEL B: Simple Vertical Model (Many-1-Many Relationships)

In this model, the enterprise still has a single product and phase of production but has many suppliers and customers. Many of the enterprises that are creating and/or providing goods and services (e.g., component manufacturers for automobiles or home appliances, PCB fabs, etc.) would fall under this category. Here, an enterprise fulfills the requirements of its (many) customers by adding value to the inputs from its (many) suppliers. The contributions made by SCM in this model are more than just control of inventory carrying costs. SCM contributes to the overall inventory management of an enterprise, depending on the level of integration among the systems of the suppliers and the enterprise.

Figure 2. MODEL B: Simple vertical model (many-1-many relationships)

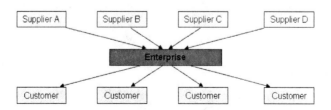

Figure 3. MODEL C: Complex vertical model (many-many-many relationships)

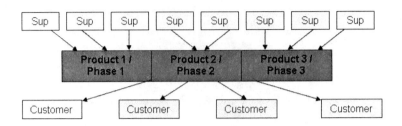

MODEL C: Complex Vertical Model (Many-Many-Many Relationships)

In this model, the enterprise has multiple products and phases of production and also has many suppliers and customers. A large number of enterprises that are creating and/or providing goods and services would fall under this category. This would include enterprises offering relatively complex products and services like white goods, home appliances, automobiles, IT and telecom equipment, real estate, banking, healthcare, and so forth.

Here, an enterprise either offers a variety of goods and/or services or has multiple phases of a complex production cycle that produces products to fulfill the requirements of its (many) customers by adding value to the inputs from its (many) suppliers. The contributions made by SCM in this model are enormous. A supply chain system in such a model is normally well-integrated with the inventory as well as with production planning and control systems of an enterprise and, thus, facilitates all the suppliers under the ambit of the SCM to support the inventory and PPC functions of the enterprise. Apart from controlling inventory-carrying and fulfillment costs, such an integrated approach also addresses issues related to timely deliveries (at different phases), quality of deliveries, exception handling, real-time changes in requirements, and so forth.

The Problem

While all the models mentioned earlier (A-C) contribute to customer satisfaction through reduced costs and faster deliveries, they add little direct value to the customer in terms of increased convenience, choice, or higher value for money. This is further compounded by the trends of globalization, restructuring of various industries, fragmentation of supply chain ownership, and the nature and structure of new industries evolving in the knowledge economy.

For a moment, let us step back to the physical world of goods and services as it existed a few decades ago. Taking the example of various services offered by governments to their citizens, a citizen had to go from pillar to post filling out various forms and documents for obtaining some service, and, after a few days if not weeks or months and a lot of agony, the citizen would get out of the bureaucratic maze with some positive result. This is quite akin to Model C with one major exception: the various stages of the process were not so efficiently integrated in case of a typical government organization.

To add to the convenience of their citizens, to introduce transparency into their work processes, and also to deliver faster positive results, many government organizations introduced the single-window system, whereby the end customer—the citizen—had to submit a set of documents only once at a window and collect deliverables in the form of some document, certificate, or money on a predetermined date or, sometimes, even instantaneously. As a result, the end customer could receive faster service with a lot of convenience. At the same time, the efficiency and effectiveness of various processes manned by specialist or expert bureaucrats was not compromised. It was either replaced with technology solutions or carried out in the back office without affecting the consumer.

Similar scenarios and examples exist today in services like travel and healthcare. The domain of healthcare services is replete with many of the issues and problems discussed earlier. For example, if a patient needs attention and requires the services of any of the healthcare service providers, at the very least, patients have to visit a doctor and a pharmacist. However, and more often than not, a number of visits to multiple service providers is required, especially if lab tests and diagnostic results are required. The prevailing bureaucratic governmental restrictions and the rigid health service practices add to the misery and suffering of patients by delaying their treatment. Typical stages of healthcare service procurement of a patient are shown in Figure 4.

As shown in Figure 4, the patient has to approach numerous service providers to get treated. Typically, the steps required are as follows:

- Patient visits the doctor.

- The doctor may suggest further diagnostic tests (the probability of this increases with the advancement of medical science).

Figure 4. Healthcare services procurement by a patient

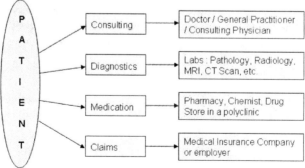

- Patient goes to the respective laboratory for getting the diagnostic tests done.
- Patient visits the laboratory again to collect the diagnostic reports.
- Patient visits the doctor again with the diagnostic reports.
- The doctor prescribes medication to the patient.
- Patient visits the pharmacy to buy the medication.
- Patient approaches the insurance company or concerned agency for reimbursement of medical expenses. Alternatively, the medical agencies (like the physician) approach the insurance company for reimbursement.

It is clear from this example that it is quite an exercise to move people and documents all over the place, sometimes in circles, to access one important and critical service most people require continuously. This is true for most of the service sector industries.

The ERPs, CRMs, and SCMs of today's world need to integrate and elevate to provide a single-window solution to the end customer in various areas, especially the service sector. One way of doing this is to offer all the products and services related to a solution through a single enterprise—creating a Web-based single window. The government services department example can be extended here. One also can think of travel service firms offering all related services, like hotel bookings, car bookings, and so forth, or hospitals and healthcare polyclinics providing all the healthcare services in one place.

However, there are some significant limitations to this approach:

- Such an integration of services may not be possible in all domains.
- Integrated offering of all services may result in a loss of focus for an enterprise and thereby inhibit the enterprise from developing expertise in any field. As a result, the end customer may not get the best possible service, may get it at a premium, or both.
- The end customer does not get multiple options—if customers want to avail of the single-window convenience, they will have to hire a car through the same travel agent who books their tickets, although there could be better options elsewhere.
- Such a solution also creates a constraint of physical proximity, especially with respect to services like banking and healthcare. The consumer always has to visit or transact with a particular single-window service provider (e.g., a hospital). Thus, after procuring a product or service from a vendor, if consumers move to some other location, they will have no or limited access to the products and services of that particular vendor. For instance, after getting treated at a hospital or polyclinic, when a patient moves to another place, the patient not only will be unable to avail of the services provided by that hospital but also will not have his or her medical history to get faster and better treatment from a hospital at the new location.

The Solution

As seen in the example of healthcare services, solutions and services in today's world are offered by a chain of multiple enterprises within an industry, and customers personally have to navigate through a mesh of network to procure an end-to-end solution to their requirements, which is obviously not very convenient. Since the mesh of network is the cause of the problem, a corresponding solution ought to be network-based.

MODEL D: Matrix Model (Many-Many-Many Relationships Spread Across Different Enterprises/ Geographical Locations)

One way of offering the single-window solution to the end customer is by creating virtual communities (mesh of network) of service providers on the Web. These communities can share and exchange data on a need-to-know basis and provide the single-window advantage to the consumer without any of the limitations discussed earlier.

The introduction of a horizontal flow of supply chain in addition to a vertical flow is of major significance in the matrix model. This assumes greater importance when subset products or services of the same set are offered either by different business units of the same enterprise spread across different geographies or by different enterprises all together.

Before getting into more details of the solution, let us also harp upon why such a solution is required. The reasons for such a shift are as follows:

- The changing method of product or service provisioning is one reason. With the globalization of almost every industry and the increasing quality-consciousness of the consumer, it is critically important to any industry to respond appropriately. One major response of many industries has been their focus on specialization and customization of customer requirements and needs. With this, the end-to-end solution is provided to the consumer by multiple enterprises—physical and virtual. In the absence of a comprehensive solution, consumers have to approach more than one enterprise to fulfill their requirements. This is also known as multiple funnel delivery.

- With the fragmentation of supply chain ownership, it is becoming increasingly difficult for the consumer to get the best value for money in a convenient manner. If at all, the consumer is required to put in considerable effort to get good value.

- Intangibles occupy a prominent position in the consumption and commerce that happens worldwide today. The dynamics of commerce and the consumption of intangibles are quite different from those of tangibles. So are the supply chains. This, too, necessitates a different solution.

Figure 5. MODEL D: Matrix model (Many-many-many vertical and horizontal relationships spread across different enterprises or geographical locations)

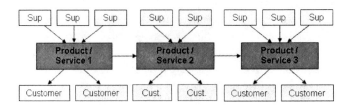

- With the growth of the Internet and other facilitating infrastructures, the customer expects 24/7 service based on a direct delivery model wherein services are delivered directly from the manufacturer or provider of services.

- Flexible pricing, product portfolio, promotions, and discrimination on service make the selection and procurement of a product or service a very complex decision for the consumer in the absence of an integrated solution.

- General expanse in the domain knowledge and increasing complexity in most domains of products and services add to the woes of the customer.

- An increasing number of alternatives in every sphere of products and services also compounds the problem.

All these and the primary requirement of providing the best value for money to the customer with utmost convenience create the need for a customer-centric SCM.

Virtual Communities

As mentioned earlier, the solution has to be network-based. A software solution created by the author for the formation and management of virtual communities for provisioning end-to-end healthcare services will be used as an example.

There are two potential solutions: (1) as mentioned earlier, hospitals and polyclinics (remember the single-window example); and (2) the creation of virtual communities of healthcare service providers, even globally.

While hospitals and polyclinics offer a viable solution, they are fraught with the limitations discussed earlier. Quite often, they also happen to be quite expensive. This necessitates the creation of a solution that would provide best services from distributed supply chains to the customer (here, the patient) with increased convenience.

The most compatible solution in such a scenario can be the creation of virtual communities of all the agencies involved in healthcare services provisioning. A virtual community is a collection of related individuals or organizations that connect with one another with the help of various communication media (e.g., the Internet) to fulfill a common objective or achieve a common goal. All are aware of different types of virtual communities like portals, newsgroups, chat groups, and so forth. However, most of them do not provide for transaction facility (if at all, it is permitted only within a closed user group), and most of them also are moderated or owned by an individual or an organization.

The virtual community proposed here is different on these two parameters. One, its primary function will be to facilitate transactions, and two; it will have shared moderation and ownership.

How will a virtual community help the customer?

- It becomes a one-stop shop for all the products and services in a particular segment.
- The customer can receive faster service.
- It is independent of location and, therefore, creates no physical proximity constraint. As the medical history of a patient is stored in the virtual space, a patient can obtain services from almost any part of the world.
- It reduces unnecessary physical movement of the customer (here, the patient).
- Customers can avail of the best services from the service provider of their choice.
- It can be integrated with various data-capturing tools, including equipment like those used for self-diagnostics.

Applying the matrix model to healthcare services provisioning, the flow would look like Figure 6.

This model certainly will enhance the convenience of the patient, since now, the various service providers also are interconnected. A meshed solution as follows (Figure 7) will create the maximum impact.

The networked model interconnects all the service providers who, in turn, can interact with one another on a need-to-know basis. For instance, after a patient has gone through the diagnostic tests, they do not have to revisit the laboratories to collect the reports;

Figure 6. Application of matrix model in healthcare services provisioning

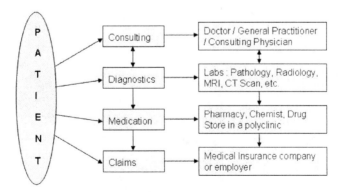

Figure 7. Networked model in health care services provisioning

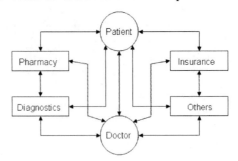

these can be collected by the patient as well as the doctor over the Web. Similarly, the medication also can be delivered to a patient's home by the nearest pharmacy, based on the prescription posted by the doctor on the Web and subsequently collected or received by the pharmacist.

This substantially reduces the number of steps that a patient has to go through to get treated. In most of the cases, only two steps are required:

1.   Patient visits the doctor for consultation.
2.   Patient visits diagnostic labs for tests.

How Does the Solution Work?

In a virtual community, as the suppliers of all the interrelated products and services are interconnected logically, in spite of being separate geographically (in the form of different locations of the same enterprise) or legally (in the form of different enterprises), they are able to provide an end-to-end solution to the consumer faster and with enhanced convenience.

In the example of healthcare services, the core engine of virtual communities takes care of most of the steps. Here is how it works:

• Patient visits the doctor for consultation.
• If diagnostics are required, the doctor submits a prescription of tests to be conducted to the intelligent engine and database of the virtual community, where it is picked up by the diagnostic lab chosen by the patient. If diagnostic tests are not required, a prescription of medicines is submitted.
• Patient visits the diagnostic lab of its choice for conducting the tests.
• The lab pulls the test prescription from the database of the virtual community to conduct tests. Patients are not required to worry about the prescription.

Figure 8. High-level architecture of customer-centric model for supply of healthcare services

- Diagnostic labs submit test reports to the same engine and database of the virtual community; where it is picked up by the doctor. The patient is spared a second visit to the lab.

- On receipt of test reports, the doctor submits a prescription of medicine. In most cases, patient will not have to visit the doctor again to obtain the prescription.

- The pharmacy of the patient's choice gets the prescription of the patient and manages to deliver the necessary medicines at the patient's doorstep. Again, this step does not require any movement on the part of the patient.

- Depending on the insurance plan, the doctor and/or patient can submit necessary documents electronically for claims processing and get paid by the insurance company directly into their bank account.

As all these steps happen over fiber (communication or Internet), the pace of transactions is much faster than physical movements of people and paper.

The availability of technologies like Web services and wireless networks not only make the solution feasible but make it even more capable.

The high-level architecture of such customer-centric model, wherein all the healthcare service providers can serve the patient by using the virtual healthcare community infrastructure through Web services, is shown in Figure 8.

Benefits of a Customer-Centric Model

A customer-centric model creates a win-win situation for all the stakeholders in the model. While it certainly benefits the customers and the suppliers involved in the model, it also creates some benefits at a higher level for the entire community. Some of the benefits generated by this model for various stakeholders are specified hereafter.

Generic Benefits

Greater value-add in the form of best price performance, procurement of end-to-end products and/or services, and greater customer convenience through provisioning of ease in the procurement of end-to-end products and services is the primary objective of the customer-driven model.

Be it supply of healthcare services or other services like travel, finance, and so forth, this enhanced supply chain model has certain inherent benefits for the customer as well as suppliers.

Benefits to Customers

- The community becomes a one-stop shop for all the interrelated products and services in a particular domain.
- The customer gets the best of both worlds—better and specialized services without the associated overheads of an integrated physical model.
- The customer also has the luxury of making choices among various service providers.
- There is no constraint of physical proximity. The customer can procure a product or service virtually anytime, anywhere.

Benefits to Suppliers

- Suppliers now can focus on their areas of specialization and yet offer their products and services at competitive prices to their customers.
- Depending on the nature of their product or service offering, suppliers need not be constrained by geographical proximity.
- In cases like pharmacies, suppliers can do away with physical stores altogether. Drugs can be shipped straight from their warehouse, based on prescriptions received.
- As participants of virtual community, suppliers can gain from mutual coordination and exchange of aggregated information

Benefits to Community

- The virtual community also creates quite a few extra benefits that can be shared by individual suppliers as well as customers. Such benefits are in the form of:
  - Creation of aggregated information and knowledge related to the industry.
  - Making the processes and workflows more efficient and effective, resulting into cost savings at individual entity levels.

- Providing a platform to conduct industry-related research. For instance, medical schools and colleges as well as pharmaceutical companies can use the virtual healthcare community to conduct industry-specific research on aggregated data.

Thus, a customer-centric SCM would be beneficial to all the stakeholders in the supply chain. As mentioned earlier, the supplies, especially information supplies, in this model would flow vertically as well as horizontally. In the example of healthcare services, for instance, the diagnosis reports would flow vertically to the patient as well as horizontally to the doctor. Similarly, a prescription would flow vertically to the patient and horizontally to the pharmacy.

In addition to forward integration with ERPs, the existing supply chain systems need to incorporate the horizontal flow of information in order to facilitate the creation of such virtual communities and thereby enable enhanced customer satisfaction.

Limitations of the Model

Like any good solution, this one also comes with a set of its own limitations. Some of the limitations of this solution are as follows:

- As the model is heavily dependent on information and communication technologies, any interruption in the availability of these in the form of communication media like the Internet and so forth can cause disruption in providing basic services like healthcare. Many people on the east coast of the US experienced such an inconvenience due to major power outages during late 2003. This happened due to people's heavy reliance on electricity as the major source of energy.

- While the model would deliver better products and services to the customer faster and at a reasonable price, on the downside, it can have a sociological impact on persons for whom a personal visit to any product or service provider also creates an opportunity for social interaction. For instance, many of the older people in Australia have been objecting to the installation of ATMs that lead to closure of several bank branches. Though ATMs provide better and faster service 24/7, a personal visit to the bank for cash withdrawals or deposits is a far more important opportunity, especially for the retired and elderly, from a social interaction standpoint.

- In services like healthcare, such a heavily automated model also can lead to the creation of some information gaps. Repeated interactions with the patient provide the doctor with quite a bit of relevant information that cannot be obtained through a structured approach.

- Also, in services like healthcare, a relationship of mutual trust and faith between the patient and the doctor is of vital importance. As repeated interactions have a bearing on the depth and expanse of such a relationship, the technology-based solution certainly would hamper that.

Issues and Challenges

Coordination among various partners in a supply chain is a huge challenge even today in the present state of SCM solutions. With the increased complexity of the solution, more issues and challenges are expected to arise.

According to Chopra et al. (2004), over the past several decades, most firms have become less vertically integrated. As companies have shed non-core functions, they have been able to take advantage of supplier customer competencies that they did not have. This new ownership structure also has made managing the supply chain more difficult. With the chain broken into many owners and each having its own policies and interests, the chain is more difficult to coordinate. In their book, Chopra and Meindl (2004) go on to list the causes of difficulties in coordination as well as the impact of lack of coordination in integrated supply chain models.

The following are two points to be noted: (1) reducing vertical integration with the new ownership structure and (2) increased difficulty in coordination.

The customer-centric model proposes horizontal integration of broken supply chain ownerships at a much higher level and spread across geographies, potentially making it a global solution.

Some of the challenges that can be anticipated for the customer-centric supply chain management system are listed hereafter. Wherever possible, potential solutions to challenges also are mentioned, together with the issues.

- **Diversity:** The model is an attempt to provide a universal solution that is independent of geographical constraints. In other words, it seeks to provide a uniform solution to diverse environments. The diversity could be in the form of the following:
  - **Standards:** Different countries follow different standards and codes pertaining to various industries like healthcare. Addressing all of these in a single solution could be a major challenge. Some ways of making this happen can be through the adoption of standards like HIPAA (Health Insurance Portability and Accountability Act) of the US by various countries or cooperative creation and implementation of global standards under the aegis of a UN body like WHO (World Health Organization), and so forth.
  - **Laws:** Laws related to the conduct of various industries like healthcare are widely different in various countries. These also need to be aligned at a broad level in order for a universal solution to work. While this is very difficult and far-fetched, if all the countries in the world can sign charters and conventions on pollution control, IPRs and many such issues, and create a common legal

framework at a higher level for the benefit of mankind (e.g., in the area of healthcare) this certainly can be made possible in the long term.

- **Language:** A global solution also has to address the need of multiplicity of languages. This, though, is the least of problems, as quite a few solutions (from Microsoft Windows to small accounting packages like Quickbooks and MYOB) already have addressed this issue. Unicode-based solutions also can be considered to address this issue.

- **Creation of a Common Framework:** Given the diversity of laws, standards, and many other practices related to an industry, creation of a universal solution or a framework in itself would pose an enormous challenge. However, good news is that common global XML standards are emerging in most of the industries, from news to banking to healthcare to entertainment. In the healthcare sector, for instance, HL7 is almost a universally accepted standard, and most of the software solutions created for healthcare industry (no matter who creates them where) are HL7 compliant. In fact, the author and his team have created a common software framework of reusable components that can be used to construct a global solution for the healthcare industry.

- **Ownership and Control of Virtual Communities:** While the components of a supply chain have a broken ownership, the solution that ties them up needs to have some command and control structure. This, too, would be a challenge to reckon with. To address this, one either can fall back upon the proven model of managing the Internet and assigning IP addresses and domain names (Internet Corporation for Assigned Names and Numbers [ICANN]) or attempt to create a new model, based on the paradigm of ant colonies. An emergent system is smarter than the sum of its parts. There is no master planner or executive branch—the overall group creates the intelligence and adaptability. Randomness is a key component. Almost all emergent systems are networks or grids. They tend to be flatter and more horizontal. Experimentation is another key component (Exact Software, 2004).

- **Data Trusteeship and Use:** Needless to say, a software solution that facilitates and manages such virtual communities in any industry will also create large databases of immense value to the industry. However, as the aggregated data would belong to the community as a whole and not to any individual participant in the community, it has to be held and maintained under trusteeship in order to prevent any leakage or misuse. This responsibility also can be undertaken by the same body that owns and controls the virtual communities on a distributed or centralized basis.

- **Data Sharing:** Another challenge pertaining to data would be sharing it among different entities of the community on authorization by the owner of the data. An interesting paradigm shift that happens here is the split between the owner and the possessor of data. Taking the example of healthcare, a patient's data in the form of medical history are currently possessed as well as owned by the doctor. Therefore, whenever a patient moves from one place to another, there is a rare chance that the patient or the doctor at the new place will have access to historical medical records of the patient. However, the customer-centric model can shift the ownership of data to patients, who then can provide access to the doctor or medical institution of their choice.

- **Security and Privacy:** Since the solution depends on information and communication technology, it also is prone to the security and privacy threats faced by such networks. The threat is all the more perceptible, given the sensitivity of certain types of data, like financial data, medical records, and so forth. However, this is a manageable challenge, given the number of high-quality encryption solutions available now.

Conclusion

This chapter has initiated the concept of a customer-centric model in supply chain systems. The chapter also has discussed how the model can work and how it addresses various constraints of the existing, essentially vertical supply chain systems by putting forward a matrix model. Apart from the global trends in various industries and supply chain that necessitate such a paradigm shift, the chapter seeks to ascertain the high value addition of the customer-centric model and how it will enhance the present-day supply chains to the next level. It further has enumerated the limitations of the new model and the issues and challenges that are anticipated in implementing the customer-centric supply chain model. While discussing the issues and challenges, the author has attempted to suggest some potential solutions to the challenges. Finally, the chapter has provided some directions for future research and action.

The Future

As discussed earlier in this chapter and also noted in the literature surveyed, there is a definite shift from vertical integration to matrix relationships among various partners in the supply chain. This, in conjunction with globalization, specialization, and broken ownerships of various components of the supply chain, certainly creates a need for a paradigm shift in the models and solutions of supply chain management conceived and practiced so far. In the opinion of the author, whether this paradigm shift will happen in the future probably is not a question; when it will happen is worth speculating and preparing for.

In the years to come, one can expect more aggressive initiatives toward this paradigm shift. This also throws up multiple business and research opportunities in a completely new direction. Such opportunities will be created in both areas—the respective domains of various industries as well as the domain of information and communication technology. Given the wide scope of the suggested solution, there could be opportunities in the areas of international relations and creation of global standards, as well.

Some specific opportunities for the immediate future are the following:

- Creation of globally acceptable standards related to operations, transactions, workflow, and information flow in various industries, especially in those belonging to the knowledge economy.

- Creation of software components, frameworks, and libraries that can facilitate the implementation of a customer-centric supply chain management system.

- Innovating new concepts to address the challenges around data management and sharing.

- Conceptualization of management models for ownership and control of virtual communities.

- Creation of a legal framework that would govern the working virtual communities.

Finally, I believe that mankind has all the necessary knowledge, tools, and technologies to make this happen. Does it have the will in the larger interest of mankind? Will we do it? Let time answer these questions.

References

Boeing SCOR case study. *Logistics of the Future.* Retrieved from *http://www.supply-chain.org/public/casestudiesboeing.asp*

Chopra, S., & Meindl, P. (2004). *Supply chain management:Strategy, planning, and operations.* Pearson.

Chorafas, D.N. (2001). *Integrating ERP, CRM, supply chain management and smart materials.* Averback.

Frazelle, E.H. (2002). *Supply chain strategy.* McGraw Hill

Hugos, M.H. (2002). *Essentials of supply chain management.* John Wiley & Sons.

Johnson, S. (2001). *Emergence—The connected lives of ants, brains, cities and software.* Touchstone.

Knolmayer, G., Mertens, P., & Zeier, A. (2002). *Supply chain management based on SAP sytems R/3 4.6, APO 3.0.* Springer.

Kubala, D. (2004). *Track, trace and control: The keys to collaborative supply chain execution.* Retrieved from *http://supplychain.ittoolbox.com/documents/document.asp?i=2632*

SCOR Basics. *http://www.supply-chain.org/public/scorbasics.asp*

Sengupta, S. (2004). The top ten supply chain mistakes. Retrieved from *http://www.manufacturing.net/scm/article/CA85844 .html?stt=%stt&pubdate=7%2F1%2F2004*

Simchi-Levi, D., Kaminsky, P., & Simchi-Levi, E. (2003). *Managing the supply chain.* McGraw Hill.

Stadtler, H., & Kilger, C. (2002). *SCM and advanced planning: Concepts, models, software and case studies*. Springer.

Suresh, H. (2004). *E-enabled supply chain management*.

Value cycle management: A "non-linear" approach to supply chain management. (2004). Exact Software. Retrieved from *http://supplychain.ittoolbox.com/ browse2.asp?c=WhitePaper&r=http://hosteddocs.ittoolbox.com/ VCMwpFinal.pdf*

Chapter V

Information Sharing in Supply Chain Systems

Lynn M. Batten
Deakin University, Australia

Ron Savage
Deakin University, Australia

Abstract

This chapter considers the importance of information-sharing techniques and strategies employed by industry sectors. Well-developed supply chain management often brings with it improved buyer-supplier communication processes, and we consider the impact of these not only from an intersector point of view, but also from a cross-sector viewpoint. The particular perspectives of the small business within a supply chain structure and of the supply chain customer are examined in detail. We conclude that information sharing is a critical component of business success both inside and outside the supply chain structure. However, while globally and at the large business level, both development and implementation of such technologies have mushroomed, smaller enterprises have tended to be left behind to cope as best they can with multiple pressures to conform.

Introduction

In Kannan and Tan (2002), the authors consider relationships between supplier management and improvements in business performance within several large US firms. In their study, they examine "relationships between the perceived importance of supplier selection and assessment criteria for items being used in production and business performance" (Kannan & Tan, 2002). Included in the study are several hard criteria such as price and quality, as well as a number of soft criteria such as management compatibility, integrity and buyer-supplier fit.

The authors conclude that "no evidence exists on the impact of supplier management on a buying firm's business performance" (Kannan & Tan, 2002). However, they identify one supplier assessment factor that correlates positively with all performance measures—a factor that also was considered to be least important by the group of respondents to the survey. This factor was information sharing. The authors conclude that "the results suggest the need for further study of buyer-supplier communication processes" (Kannan & Tan, 2002).

In this chapter, we discuss information-sharing mechanisms employed by industries in a number of sectors. In general, we restrict the discussion to those industry sectors in which supply chain management has been undertaken in an attempt to involve the entire sector. However, we also look at some of the sectors where it is evident that a lack of sector organization is causing major problems. Well-developed supply chain management often brings with it improved buyer-supplier communication processes, and we consider the impact of these not only from an intersector point of view, but also from a cross-sector viewpoint; not only within Australia, but also beyond national borders.

In a 2002 survey by the Center for Automotive Research (Frontline Solutions, 2002), it is reported that 47% of respondents expect adoption of e-business procedures as a supply chain tool to be a requirement for doing business with the automotive industry within two to three years. Additionally, the survey showed that a majority (81%) of suppliers anticipate a consolidation of the automotive supply chain in the near future and that, in consequence, customers will reduce their supply chain base all the way along the chain. A major result of these changes is likely to be a greatly increased information-sharing capability between the members of the supply chain.

An additional factor promoting information sharing is an industry sector's self-review process, which can reveal major inadequacies in operating methods. For instance, a report of the Australian Construction Industry Forum (PricewaterhouseCoopers, 2002) indicated that 30% of a construction project's total cost is the result of poor information management. The cost savings anticipated from rectifying such problems are a powerful motive for the adoption of new operating methods.

Information-Sharing Mechanisms

Bar coding is a major means of information sharing both within and between sectors and countries. The most prevalent bar coding system now used in Australia is the international EAN system. EAN recently has joined forces with the Uniform Code Council (UCC), which has taken a global leadership role in establishing and promoting multi-industry standards for product identification and related electronic communication with the goal of enhancing supply chain management. For instance, the meat and wool industries, which form significant components of the wholesale trade industry, have been persuaded to implement EAN bar code technology and have developed guidelines for the use of bar codes. Despite the huge and disparate nature of the wholesale and retail trade industries, much standardization has been achieved by adoption of the EAN•UCC numbering and bar coding system.

In his study of business-to-business e-commerce in Australia, Malone (1999) states, "the transport industry provides the logistical operations for Australian business through the movement of goods in the supply chain and to market. ... [I]ts adoption of eCommerce is likely to drive eCommerce uptake in the many sectors it services...with consequent benefits for those sectors". The implication is that the technology actually adopted will be shared by many components of the transport industry, which will promote interoperability and, hence, information sharing among several industry sectors, including those overseas.

The finance and insurance sector is worthy of special mention in that it already operates what is effectively a single mechanism for information sharing, managed by the SWIFT consortium, which has been in existence since 1977. SWIFT (http://www.swift.com) is an industry-owned, international cooperative (under Belgian law) supplying secure messaging services and interface software to 7,000 financial institutions in 200 countries. Such a broad grouping of parties shows just what is possible when information sharing is seen as a goal in its own right.

Despite the pressures for improved information-sharing mechanisms, information-based transaction methods have diverged along two paths. One of these is based on XML and the other on EDI. Significant incompatibilities between these two systems have forced people to choose one over the other, but more recent drivers for a single technology underlying business processes are resulting in a movement to one new system that combines the best of both.

Until the underlying technical issues are resolved, we will continue to see the problem of disparate or competing technologies as they exist worldwide in the health industry. In Australia, EDI was successfully implemented for orders and confirmations for manufacturers and distributors with supply chain reform pilots in some hospitals as a result of a nationwide government-sponsored special project that ran from 1996 to 2001 (The PECC Story, 2001). On the other hand, Global Health Exchange (http://www.ghx.com), based in Europe and North America, was founded in 2000 by five leading healthcare suppliers: J&J, GE Medical, Baxter, Abbot Labs, and Medtronic. It provides supply chain solutions based on customized code to bring together hospitals, manufacturers, and wholesalers. Yet a third consortium is HL7, which is based on a set of American National Standards Institute-approved standards, covering clinical documents and the sharing of medical knowledge, as well as administrative documents covering such items as intellectual property and ethics.

An industry that lags behind most others on the information-sharing front is construction. A report of the Australian Construction Industry Forum indicated that 30% of a construction project's total cost is the result of poor information management. Much of the problem is blamed on the failure of hardware and software solutions to meet operational requirements that include mobility of the workforce, diverse working conditions, and lack of a fixed infrastructure.

In January 2000, the Construction Industry Advisory Group BSITE (http://www.bsite.com.au) was formed. This was an amalgamation of 20 industry leaders from throughout the industry supply chain in Australia and New Zealand. BSITE uses technology already prevalent on construction sites, such as mobile phones and fax machines, to perform core functions, including job scheduling, time sheeting, activity logging and reporting, contract management, project workflow, and document revision. Thus, rather than being specifically a supply chain management consortium, BSITE focuses on workforce management and project collaboration. They have adopted various global standards for communication between the user and BSITE's software and simultaneously have used this arrangement to shield the customer completely from the implementation of that software (Batten & Savage, 2003).

Common standards adopted by a group of businesses can be seen to be of great convenience to those in the group. However, the standards themselves often are not a solution to the problem of sharing data at a more global level. This leads us to consider several questions in this chapter:

1. What is the effect on a single supply chain of forcing its companies to adopt a single system to guarantee interoperability?

2. In particular, what would be the impact of such a move on the small and medium suppliers within the supply chain?

3. What impact would it have on customers beyond the supply chain?

4. What are the global implications of single supply chains committing to a specific technology for information sharing?

These points are expanded one by one in the sections that follow.

Supply Chain Induced Systems

Suppliers often are not given a choice when it comes to the decision to join a supply chain or a similar consortium. Wal-Mart, for example, has demanded of its suppliers that they implement CRP (Continuous Replenishment Process) (Green & Shaw, 2003).

In discussing the impact on a single supply chain of forcing its companies to adopt a single system to guarantee interoperability, we note that this single new system already may be in use by some businesses in the supply chain, so adopting it actually may not incur a cost for them. On the other hand, those businesses who decide to move from an existing system to the proposed one will need to factor in the costs of discarding current physical resources and replacing them with new equipment, as well as the costs of retraining staff to use this new equipment.

We now consider the advantages and disadvantages to businesses.

Advantages

- **A1. A feeling of security in joining a group of similar organizations.**

  Joining such a group in effect is joining a community of like-minded entities, which can help suppliers reassure themselves that they have taken the correct decision. Such communities have become the norm, and, hence, suppliers now can concentrate on availing themselves of the advantages that result. In Shaw (2003), the author points out, "In running an e-business the Web-based supply chain model provides opportunities for several companies to work together and form a virtual enterprise" (p. 8). Such interactions then can be described as a *supply web* rather than just a supply chain.

- **A2. A reduction in the uncertainty surrounding the adoption of e-business in general and in the question of which system to adopt in particular.**

  The decision ends the uncertainty over what course of action to adopt and, hence, frees the supplier to focus on other matters. By choosing a specific system, the supplier's uncertainty is replaced by an expectation that concrete benefits will flow from the interoperability of the system.

- **A3. Saving (part of) the cost involved in committing some of the supplier's resources to investigating which system to choose.**

  Choosing a system being operated by other members of a supply chain means the supplier can stop expending resources on the decision process and, instead, concentrate on the implementation process. Choosing a system that is working for others means the supplier is utilizing the effort expended by those others in their investigation of which system to adopt. This saving can be achieved by a process that is quite informal. As explained in Tatnell & Burgess (2004), "In many instances a small business proprietor will adopt e-commerce because a friend is using it, or because they know a competitor is using it, or because a son or daughter learned about it at school" (p. 156).

- **A4. A greater likelihood of ongoing business with customers with whom the supplier is compatible.**

  Once an interoperable system is chosen, the supplier reasonably can expect that this will encourage others using the same system to want to do business with them, since the very interoperability means they can assume the effort involved will be less than it would have been otherwise. Of course, it is not normally the suppliers who are developing these systems, but other agencies. As with any software purchaser, the supplier must assume the agency developing the system they have chosen is aiming at goals that are shared by the supplier. For instance, "RosettaNet seeks to enable interoperability in a supply chain by developing modularized technical standards surrounding shared business processes between supply chain partners" (Nelson et al., 2003, p. 426). This explicitly stated goal is, of course, in accord with suppliers' expectations of what such systems ought to offer.

- **A5. A greater likelihood of ongoing business with other suppliers for whom the current supplier is a customer.**

  This is part of what is called the *virtual organization*, or the *extended enterprise*.

  Interoperability is a two-way street. With appropriate systems in place, a supplier more easily can become a supplier to new customers, where those customers are using compatible systems. In addition, the supplier more easily can become a customer to other suppliers, where those suppliers are also using compatible systems. "[B]uyer organizations should not only look to add more of their suppliers to the system, they should also motivate the suppliers' suppliers to join" (Subramanium & Shaw, 2003, p. 458).

- **A6. The reduced likelihood of similar changes again in the future now that the members of the supply chain have committed to a standard system.**

  Adopting a standard of any sort is a good excuse for conservatism. A supplier, having expended the resources to adopt such a system, is motivated to continue utilizing it, and all such suppliers and customers automatically become a block of like-minded entities with an investment in minimizing repeated expenditures of the same type. This, then, becomes a form of pressure helping to minimize changes in the standard and further helping to minimize the likelihood of changing to a new standard.

Disabled

Disadvantages

- **D1. Loss, or perceived loss, of independence in the supplier's decision-making processes.**

  Choosing a computer system is not an exact science. Hence, deciding what choice to make is going to be difficult for many suppliers. Most likely, the larger the organization, the more resources it can afford to dedicate to the selection process. But since, in Australia as elsewhere, the majority of organizations are small, many will be dependent on external parties to assess the alternatives.

  Joining a group and adopting the system(s) used by the group is saying, in effect, that the supplier adopts the decision-making process which led to the group's choice of system(s). Whether or not the supplier was involved in the decision-making process, it is obliged at the end of the day to accept the final outcome. Thus, the supplier may not actually have much influence either on the process or on the outcome, which could, in fact, leave its people feeling frustrated.

- **D2. The all-your-eggs-in-the-one-basket effect.**

  Having committed to this new system, the supplier may well find itself more dependent than before on one or very few customers, which means that if it loses those customers' business, it has fewer alternatives than before to turn to.

  Interoperability restricts a supplier to doing business with only those organizations using a compatible system. So, if one of its customers withdraws, the supplier is limited to its remaining customers or must try to convince other potential customers to convert to a new system.

- **D3. Redundancy of existing software and hardware and new hardware costs, if the new system does not run on the existing hardware.**

  A supplier, when considering a new system, has to take into account the depreciated value of its existing system. The less the value of the existing system, the more likely the supplier is to accept expenditure on a new system, and the more likely it will be to accept discarding the old system. Conversely, the more value remaining in the old system, the more incentive the supplier has to reject or delay the new system, and to continue utilizing the old one.

  Singh (2004) puts it, rather blandly, thus: "The costs of any modifications required to existing technology before e-business is adopted should also be assessed" (p. 8).

- **D4. Loss (or reduction) of business with customers who choose not to adopt the single system or who choose to delay implementation of it.**

  Another question faced by suppliers is this: Will they lose business by adopting a new system? This could happen when existing suppliers and/or customers are not in a position to interoperate with the supplier's new system. Clearly, this question must form part of the supplier's cost-benefit analysis undertaken before the decision is made to adopt a new system.

  The supplier may be faced with stark alternatives: choose a new system and lose old business, or maintain the old system in order to maintain old business but risk losing new business. It is plausible that this could lead to ambivalence on the part of the supplier, which may explain partially the observation in Coulthard, Castleman, & Batten (2004) that small businesses have not met expectations of B-2-B adoption.

- **D5. Increased costs if the supplier chooses to maintain old systems in parallel with the new system.**

  If the old system is to be maintained in parallel with the new one, it will be the supplier who bears the ongoing costs of such a choice. This also forms part of the cost-benefit analysis. Here is how Archer and Gebauer (2002) put it: "While sell-side systems allow selling organizations to interface with a multitude of customers, buying organizations may have to integrate their systems with multiple different solutions, depending on the number of suppliers. ... Still, suppliers wanting to participate in multiple buy-side solutions may have to deliver their data in multiple different formats, and adhere to multiple underlying business processes" (pp. 27, 29).

This can be construed as another aspect of Disadvantage 4 and serves to illustrate the fact that the adoption of new technology can be influenced by the very nature of the old technology.

- **D6. Transfer of the supplier's computer business away from its software and hardware supplier(s) to a new supplier (or set of suppliers) with consequent disruption in the (current) supplier's business processes.**

  Under this point, we are talking about the supplier's supplier of computer systems and, hence, a different supply chain, not the one (presumably) dealing with the goods and services normally transacted by the original supplier.

  Switching computer systems in order to gain or to enhance interoperability may involve switching computer suppliers, which can involve various types of additional expenditure over and above obtaining such a system from a computer supplier with whom the supplier already has a relationship. Beginning a new relationship with a supplier brings with it the usual teething problems of such a transition. So, in choosing a new system, the supplier is also accepting that it will have to undergo whatever difficulties arise during the transitional period. This can be yet another factor reinforcing the ambivalence and conservatism mentioned previously.

- **D7. Incompatibility with customers and suppliers who adopt apparently compatible systems from different vendors.**

  Although systems may be classified as meeting certain national or international standards, it is not uncommon for them to fail to interoperate.

  When suppliers are aware of such a possibility, it is understandable that they will be motivated to proceed with caution and, thus, will be unlikely to commit themselves when they are only partially convinced of the safe outcome of the changeover.

- **D8. Adopting the new system does not guarantee that the supplier will avoid losing business.**

  Business relationships change all the time. Existing customers and suppliers are not obligated to continue working with any particular supplier indefinitely.

  Gebauer et al. (2003) observe, "For example, in the area of office suppliers, Motorola used as many as 300 different suppliers for the same items (the number has since been cut down to one)."

  This implies that 299 suppliers lost some business with Motorola. We do not know how many of those also adopted systems compatible with Motorola's, but we can say that such adoption did not lead to a continuing relationship with Motorola.

- **D9. Staff, Training, Privacy, and Job Structure.**

  It may seem unusual at first to put these topics under disadvantages. Our intention here is merely to emphasize that handling such issues properly involves planning and ongoing effort. It is the expenditure of this effort that suppliers need to account for when considering (new) e-business systems.

Since interoperability will lead to more information flowing, not just more goods flowing, the staff may effectively be doing the same type of work after the adoption of e-business, but it will probably have to be trained to think differently about the process. Also, it is likely that the staff will have to be trained to use any new software that is introduced. Good methods of staff management suggest that staff be encouraged to do such training. Miller et al. (2003) state, "On this view, the new supply-chain management will shift its focus from old material flow to a combined flow of material, information and financials" (p. 80). But, despite the presence of computers, it will be the people who manage this flow, and it is the people who need to be trained.

For an extended discussion of this topic, see the section titled Sociotechnical Issues in Singh (2004).

Another aspect of staff training concerns privacy, since interoperability implies closer ties with other organizations and, hence, may shift the boundary of what is seen to be private (data); it is the people in each of the cooperating enterprises who have to become familiar with the legal requirements stemming from the relevant legislation. In Australia, this legislation is called the Privacy Amendment (Private Sector) Act 2000, which came into effect on December 21, 2001.

- **D10. Risk management.**

  Adopting a new computer system can be a risky undertaking for businesses large and small. However, large organizations often develop policies around the use of technology, which includes a risk assessment. Smaller businesses tend neither to have a policy nor to assess risk on a systematic basis. In fact, in Coulthard, Castleman, & Batten (2004), small and medium enterprises listed technical support problems and the lack of in-house skills as two areas of concern when asked about barriers to electronic trading; both of these impact the ability of an organization to manage trust.

In summary, although our list of advantages is shorter than the list of disadvantages, we do not want this to be taken to mean that we regard the advantages as a whole as being outweighed by the disadvantages.

Rather, the supplier is encouraged to assess the sum total of the advantages in terms of feeling more secure (A1), reducing uncertainty (A2), reducing some costs (A3), and the long-term consequences of interoperability (A4 to A6) (since standardization is hardly going to go away), to compare this with the effects of the diverse factors given here as disadvantages, and then to act on the result of that comparison.

Indeed, it may be better to describe these disadvantages as being more like complexities or complications that must be recognized and planned for rather than regarding them as disincentives. In this way, what appear to be negatives can be used to help formulate the plan of action that the supplier uses to handle the transition to a new system.

Impact on Small and Medium Suppliers

Small and medium suppliers (SMEs) are of particular interest to the supply chain issue, because, although as individual companies, they do not have the power of their large counterparts, as a group they constitute over 90% of all private business in most countries (Yellow Pages eBusiness Survey, 2003). However, because it relies extensively on its large customers, an SME tends not to think of itself as part of a large sector but in terms of its relationships with its customers. Indeed, this is generally how it is viewed from all sides (Batten et al., 2004). Survey results of Coulthard et al. (2004) determine that, for SMEs, e-business is not seen as a major strategy with which to meet business goals. They also point out that SMEs trading in multiple sectors rely on multiple transaction methods in order to maintain their business relationships.

The adoption of common information-sharing mechanisms in a supply chain within which an SME works would leave the SME with a major decision—move to the new system or leave the supply chain. Most SMEs faced with this decision likely would prefer to maintain the relationship with established supply chain customers. In fact, most SMEs would not have developed the expertise required to investigate such systems or make decisions on what to implement, so it is to their advantage to have the decision made on their behalf by better informed parties. Of course, these parties will be operating for their own commercial advantage, so any advice they offer to the suppliers often will take a specific viewpoint and may not be in the best interests of the smaller organizations within the supply chain. In addition, in order to work successfully, the supply chain must support all the components necessary to its operation and so must agree to maintain the less capable parts of the chain in the introduction of any new system.

Adopting a new system enhances the integration of an SME into one (or perhaps in some cases, more than one) supply chain but, at the same time, may well increase its processing costs. This can happen if the enterprise needs to upgrade an existing system, introduce a new one, or take on additional expertise to maintain its business systems. Hence, this adoption can be a factor in influencing them to put pressure on the members of other supply chains to adopt the same system and also to put pressure on themselves to cut ties with customers and suppliers who decline to adopt the new system.

Eikenbrook and Olsen (2002) agree with arguments in this direction and define e-business success as "the potential of value creation in e-business in four interrelated dimensions, which are efficiency, complementarities, lock-in, and novelty. ... The third dimension, lock-in, described the potential value in creating switching costs from arrangements that motivate customers and business partners to repeat and improve transactions and relationships" (p. 587).

Lock-in can have a domino effect and may well be a factor in the eventual widespread adoption of the new system. Each SME needs to decide for itself the cumulative effect of the four factors on its business and then whether to join in with a new system, to delay its adoption, or to reject it outright.

Impact on Customers
Beyond the Supply Chain

Simchi-Levi et al. (2004) cite a fascinating example of how the development of a supply chain by IBM in the early 1980s as a result of their decision to enter the PC market impacted the other customers of the supply chain members and, in the long run, adversely affected their own market share. "Rather than take the time to develop those capabilities, IBM outsourced almost all the major components. ...By 1985, IBM's market share was more than 40 percent....However, the downside to IBM's strategy soon became clear, as competitors such as Compaq were able to enter the market by using the same suppliers....By the end of 1995, IBM's market share had fallen to less than 8 percent" (Simchi-Levi et al., 2004).

It is unlikely in future that any large organization will make the same mistake as IBM. However, there are still opportunities for customers of supply chain organizations to benefit from the positive effects of supply chain involvement. Such benefits might include streamlining of the purchasing and delivery processes, improved product quality, as SMEs develop their expertise assisted by the larger community with which they work, shorter payment periods, and so improved cash flow.

Archer and Gebauer (2002) agree with this analysis. "The benefits include streamlined purchasing operations. ... This results in time and cost savings, and freeing purchasing and accounts payable personnel from clerical work for more strategic tasks. As information quality and market transparency is improved, maverick buying (end-user purchasing from non-standard suppliers) can be reduced, enabling more favourable contracts with fewer suppliers ... they [B2B electronic hubs] eliminate the need for market participants to link directly to their business partners. ... The savings from implementing only one interface to the intermediary instead of multiple interfaces to many suppliers or customers may in fact be quite substantial. Second, suppliers may deliver content in one standard format, while buyers access one integrated solution" (Archer & Gebauer, 2002, p. 31).

This leads to potential growth in the size of the supply chain, and it is interesting to note that if such growth occurred, it would be driven by the interoperability of the new system but would be independent of the precise nature (i.e., industry sector) of this new system.

Global Implications

There are interesting lessons to be learned from the history of the development of the personal computer. Initially, there were many manufacturers of the PC and its various components. PCs were based on different design configurations and were essentially incompatible, each having its own operating system. Each disk drive had to be configured for the specific PC into which the drive was installed (Allan, 2001).

Over time, with complaints that some major producers such as Xerox and Digital were not producing PCs that were compatible with IBM hardware, and with the realization that interoperability was both useful and cheaper for customers, components began to be standardized and often were interchangeable. The fact that IBM outsourced most of the PC component parts meant that there were supplier companies producing items that also could be bought by other PC manufacturers; thus, proprietary issues did not arise (Allan, 2001). This still left the market open for many manufacturers, but proprietary technology had given way to componentization. Hence, the hardware had to compete on capacity and price, because interoperability became a given.

With supply chains, something similar can be predicted. There are four major factors that influence the decision of supply chains to expand globally: the development of new markets; the minimization of costs; requirements to meet international standards, even in a national context; and the requirement for assessment and comparability.

In Handfield and Nichols (1999), the authors point out that "the trend toward global supply chains has been fuelled by needs for centralized research and development, the development of homogeneous markets and global products and global market segments for many products." Thus, those sectors with established supply chain alignments are confronted eventually with the need to go beyond this infrastructure in order to seek new markets.

In recent years, a demand on all industries to cut costs is reflected in the decisions made by many organizations in developed countries to offshore components of their business to less developed countries with a major wage differential. For example, "between 1998 and 2000, out-sourcing in the electronics industry increased from 15 percent of all components to 40 percent" (Simchi-Levi et al., 2004, p. 139).

This has had many side effects, including a move into new markets and pressures on governments to maintain low tariff barriers. Cisco employs the following strategy:

First, we have established manufacturing plants all over the world. We have also developed close arrangements with major suppliers, and if we do our job right, the customer cannot tell the difference between my own plants and my suppliers in Taiwan and elsewhere. (Simchi-Levi et al., 2004, p. 140)

The global move to standardization, especially in technology areas, has had a major impact on supply chains. As in the example of the PC, customer demand for interoperability has resulted in standardization; on the other hand, the introduction of standards is reflected in decisions at the research and development end of production, and products from various companies now tend to have components and modules with interoperable functions that can be used in many environments.

With supply chain provisioning software, in particular, becoming a commodity, SMEs should find it easier to pick and choose systems best suited to their business needs. For instance, those who do business by electronic mail have the option to choose an e-mail system that will safely export their data from the chosen system and import it into a client's different system. PocoMail is one such example, as it guarantees to import automatically all e-mail from Outlook Express and Eudora.

Radio Frequency Identification Technology (RFID), which uses smart tags to track products, is already heavily used in some supply chains and will enter many more industry sectors in the near future. According to Simchi-Levi et al. (2004):

[T]he impact of the RFID technology on supply chain performance cannot be overstated. It includes:

- *Improved service level by reducing store/shelf stockout rate.*
- *Reduction of the stockout level.*
- *Better utilization of store and warehouse space.*
- *Significant improvement in the ability to locate items at the store and in the backroom. (p. 257)*

Communication over the Internet has expanded into electronic shopping, the tracking of shipments, and collaboration among organizations. The year 2000 fears resulted in a major move on the part of many companies to replace their legacy systems with client-server-based enterprise resource planning (ERP) systems (Simchi-Levi et al., 2004). It is expected that ERPs will be integrated into supply chain management in the coming years.

In a different context, standards are applied to reporting company mechanisms by government and industry bodies. There has been a recent move, for example, of companies reporting their annual profit-and-loss sheets in XML, which, therefore, leads to simplification in the ease with which companies can be analyzed and compared.

The eXtensible Business Reporting Language (XBRL) consortium has gained rapid momentum over the past year. Projects to introduce XBRL are underway in a number of countries, and some US and Australian companies already are reporting their financials in it. Since it also is expected that regulators eventually will require companies to use the XML filing format, XBRL currently is producing a prototype.

In summary, supply chains seeking new markets beyond the national context will be obliged to think in global terms. The advantages may be greater market share along with reduced costs. In addition, the pressure to comply with global standards both at the product processing level and at the financial reporting level will position supply chain organizations to make the jump to global both easily and effectively.

Conclusion

Information sharing is a critical component of success both inside and outside the supply chain structure. Major innovations affecting industries globally include bar coding and RFID tracking, while within individual industry sectors, industry-specific technologies

(SWIFT, Global Health Exchange) often have been generated. Pressures to develop new markets have driven universal solutions such as XML and EDI.

For customers of supply chains, benefits have included improvements in market quality and transparency of transactions. For members of the supply chain, there are numerous advantages and disadvantages.

Small and medium enterprises are worthy of special note, as they form a significant part of the industry but do not act as a community in terms of implementing new business technologies. This makes them vulnerable to pressures from their clients to adopt certain technologies. As a result, many SMEs use several e-business methods of trading with their customers.

Information-sharing technologies and strategies are, thus, critical to the success of industry alliances, such as those in supply chains. While globally and at the large business level, development and implementation of such technologies have mushroomed, smaller enterprises have tended to be left behind to cope as best they can with multiple pressures to conform. It is this bottom end of the supply chain structure that will slow down rapid changes in information-sharing methods. Until the problems encountered by SMEs can be dealt with, it is difficult to see how growth can be optimized.

References

Allan, R.A. (2001). *A history of the personal computer*. Ontario, Canada: Allan Publishing.

Archer, N., & Gebauer, J. (2002). B2B applications to support business transactions. In M. Warkentin (Ed.), *Business to business electronic commerce: Challenges and solutions*. Hershey, PA: Idea Group.

Batten, L.M., Castleman, T., Chan, C., Coulthard, D., Savage, R., & Wilkins, L. (2004). Engaging suppliers in electronic trading across industry sectors: Multi-disciplinary solutions to industry and government's e-business challenges. *Proceedings of the IFIP WG8.4 Working Conference on E-Business* (pp. 182-199).

Batten, L.M., & Savage, R. (2003). eTransactions in the Australian supply chain setting. *Proceedings of the 3rd ICEB* (pp. 589-591).

Coulthard, D., Castleman, T., & Batten, L. (2004). eCommerce strategy in a multi-sector trading environment—Quandaries for SMEs. *Proceedings of the 17th Bled eCommerce Conference*, Bled, Slovenia (pp. 1-13).

Eikenbrook, T.R., & Olsen, D.H. (2002). Understanding e-business competencies in SMEs. In K.V. Andersen et al. (Eds.), *Seeking success in e-business: A multidisciplinary approach*. Kluwer Academic Press.

Frontline Solutions (2002). Auto suppliers focus on supply chain automation. *Center for Automotive Research, Duluth, 3*(11), 47-48.

Gebauer, J., Haacker, D., & Shaw, M.J. (2003). Global non-production procurement at Motorola: Managing the evolving enterprise infrastructure. In M.J. Shaw (Ed.), *E-business management: Integration of Web technologies with business models*. Kluwer Academic Press.

Grean, M., & Shaw, M.J. (2003). Supply-chain partnership between P&G and Wal-Mart. In *E-business management: Integration of Web Technologies with Business Models*. Kluwer Academic Press.

Handfield, R.B., & Nichols Jr., E.L. (1999). *Introduction to supply chain management*. Upper Saddle River, NJ: Prentice Hall.

Jamieson, R. (2002). Governance for e-business knowledge management systems. In K.V. Andersen, et al. (Eds.), *Seeking success in e-business: A multidisciplinary approach*. Kluwer Academic Press.

Kannan, V., & Tan, K.C. (2002). Supplier selection and assessment: Their impact on business performance. *The Journal of Supply Chain Management, 38*(4), 11-21.

Macquarie University Graduate School of Management Report. (2001). The PECC Story.

Malone, P. (1999). Business to business e-commerce case study. Retrieved September 2004, from *http://www.noie.gov.au/projects/ebusiness/Archive/trucks/presentation.htm*

Miller, T., Nelson, M.L., Shen, S.Y., & Shaw, M.J. (2003). e-Business management models: Services perspective from the Revere Group. In M.J. Shaw (Ed.), *E-business management: Integration of Web technologies with business models*. Kluwer Press Academic.

Nelson, M., et al. (2003). Modularized interoperability in supply-chains: A co-adoption study of RosettaNet's XML-based interorganizational systems. In M.J. Shaw (Ed.), *E-business management: Integration of Web technologies with business models*. Kluwer Academic Press.

PricewaterhouseCoopers. (2002). Innovation in the Australian building and construction industry. Report prepared for Australian Construction Industry Forum and the Department of Industry, Tourism and Resources.

Shaw, M.J. (2003). E-business management: A primer. In M.J. Shaw (Ed.), *E-business management: Integration of Web technologies with business models*. Kluwer Academic Press.

Simchi-Levi, D., Kaminsky, P., & Simchi-Levi, E. (2004). *Managing the supply chain*. New York: McGraw Hill.

Singh, M. (2004). Innovation and change management. In M. Singh & D. Waddell (Eds.), *E-business: Innovation and change management*. Hershey, PA: IRM Press.

Subramaniam, C., & Shaw, M.J. (2003). A study of the value of B2B e-commerce: The case of Web-based procurement. In M.J. Shaw (Ed.), *E-business management: Integration of Web technologies with business models*. Kluwer Academic Press.

Tatnell, A., & Burgess, S. (2004). Using actor-network theory to identify factors affecting the adoption of e-commerce. In M. Singh & D. Waddell (Eds.), *E-business: Innovation and change management*. Hershey, PA: IRM Press.

Yellow Pages eBusiness Survey. (2003). Sensis, Melbourne: 2003 Yellow Pages ® eBusiness Report.

Chapter VI

Global Integrated Supply Chain Implementation:
The Challenges of E-Procurement

Margaret L. Sheng
Hamline University, USA

Abstract

Supply chain functions must operate in an integrated manner in order to optimize performance. However, the dynamics of the organization and the market make this challenging. In particular, the procurement function is a crucial link between the sources of supply and the organization. With most organizations spending at least one-third of their overall budget to purchase goods and services, procurement holds significant business value. Emerging technologies, especially e-procurement, are promising to change the picture of traditional procurement processes. However, the implementation of e-procurement is facing significant reengineering and change management challenges. This study identifies four main challenges in e-procurement implementation: business process integration, technological issues, value creation, and change management. The major challenge among them is change management. Critically, leadership is one of the primary requirements to make the change successfully.

Introduction

The supply chain is a network of suppliers, factories, warehouses, distribution centers, and retailers through which raw materials are acquired, transformed, and delivered to the customers. Supply chain management is the strategic, tactical, and operational level decision making that optimizes supply chain performance. The strategic level defines the supply chain network (i.e., selection of suppliers, transportation routes, manufacturing facilities, production levels, warehouses, etc.). The tactical level plans and schedules the supply chain to meet actual demand. The operational level executes plans. Tactical and operational level decision-making functions are distributed across the supply chain.

In order to optimize performance, supply chain functions must operate in an integrated manner. However, the dynamics of the organization and the market make this challenging; materials do not arrive on time, production facilities fail, workers are ill, customers change or cancel orders, and so forth, causing deviations from the plan. In particular, the procurement function is a crucial link between the sources of supply and the organization. With most organizations spending at least one-third of their overall budget to purchase goods and services, procurement holds significant business value (Killen & Kamauff, 1995; Zenz & Thompson, 1994). Emerging technologies, especially Internet-based procurement, are bringing the promises to change the picture of costly, time-consuming, and inefficient procurement processes by enabling major improvements in terms of lower administrative overhead, better service quality, timely location and receiving of products, and increased flexibility. Meanwhile, growing pressures from increasingly competitive markets all around the world reinforce the need to reorganize and streamline inefficient procurement procedures.

The corporate procurement traditionally has been separated along two dimensions: the direct or production-oriented procurement and the indirect or non-production-oriented procurement. Direct procurement generally refers to the purchasing of items that immediately enter a manufacturing process, such as the parts that are assembled into a car or computer. Indirect procurement includes everything that is not covered by direct procurement; for instance, maintenance, repair, and operations (MRO) supplies that are consumed in the production process and required to keep up the manufacturing process. Indirect procurement also includes items as diverse as office supplies, computer equipment, promotional material, travel, and other services (Segev, Gebauer & Farber, 2000). Other researchers also include items in the indirect category such as training materials, accessories, temporary staff, public relationships, entertainment (Croom, 2000), and contract workers and consultants (Moozakis, 2001).

The direct procurement has been emphasized and treated differently than indirect procurement. Compared to direct procurement, indirect procurement covers a wider range of products and services that typically are involved with a larger number of buyers (possibly every employee) and is much less predictable with respect to buying volume and frequency. It often is not regarded as strategic relevance but rather as a clerical function. Thus, it comes at no surprise that businesses processes typically are not well standardized, most paper-based, and, as a result, inefficient and non-transparent (Gebauer & Segev, 2001).

Incidentally, the difference between direct and indirect procurement also shows in organizational charts; direct procurement often reports to a vice president of supply chain operations (or similar), while indirect procurement might fall into the responsibility of the finance function. The line of management for both areas only meets at the level of the chief executive officer. In the literature, the indirect products and services have received little attention, as by far the dominant focus of the purchasing literature has been the management of production item procurement. However, a multi-national company may spend millions of dollars of expenditure on indirect goods and services. Much of them may be carried out locally or divisionally, bypassing central guidelines. For example, a large manufacturer bought office supplies from as many as 300 suppliers regularly, more or less. Nobody was in control of the overall process, and each business unit had its own procedures in place. From a corporate perspective, the fragmented procurement resulted in slow and expensive processes and excessive product costs due to poor leverage of buying power (Nelson, Moody & Stegner, 2001). According to PricewaterhouseCoopers, a 10% reduction in purchase costs easily can lead to a 50% rise in profit margin.

IT-based tools have been introduced to support production procurement and supply chain operations. However, procurement activities in the non-production items have long been underestimated on an organizational level as well as with respect to the use of IT. Because of little process automation and a majority of manual activities, the non-production procurement is often an uncoordinated and non-valued activity (Croom, 2000; Gebauer & Segev, 2000). Available IT systems usually do not cover the full process or are very expensive to set up. Internet and Web-based applications promise alternatives that are less expensive and easier to set up. The new systems (i.e., e-procurement) allow employees to order goods directly from their PCs, either through an Intranet or a Web site. Orders are channeled automatically to suppliers, often via a hub that acts as a host for their online catalogs. The catalogs hold the companies negotiated prices as well as authorization rules that ensure the right people buy only what they are allowed to. When employees put the job out to tender, it will come back with a list of three or four suppliers. Operators of procurement hubs increasingly will scour the world for new low-cost suppliers in order to offer a better service for their purchasing customers. They will check out these suppliers for quality and integrity; if necessary, build catalogs for them; and plug them into their systems. E-procurement also allows employees to combine catalogs from several suppliers, check the availability of items, place and track orders, and initiate payment over the Internet. It does not mean just putting purchasing decisions online, but it also means linking suppliers into the purchasing network and broadening the range of employees who can carry out transactions. Therefore, e-procurement is not an example of computerizing the old manual process but of reengineering the process itself.

As a result of significant impact from the Internet, the traditional purchasing function is now facing substantial reengineering and change management challenges. The purpose of this study is to identify the challenges of e-procurement implementation, therefore enhancing its success.

Literature Review

Procurement vs. Purchasing

Procurement is distinct from purchasing. Procurement includes all activities involved in obtaining materials, transporting them, and moving them toward the production process (Segev, Gebauer & Beam, 1998). Purchasing is the act of buying and services, and represents a core element of procurement. Procurement processes take on many different forms in reality. Considering the types, uses, and value of the goods purchased, three categories of procurement have been distinguished (Hough & Ashley, 1992; Zenz & Thompson, 1994).

- Procurement of raw material and production goods usually is characterized by large quantities, high frequencies, and important and unique specifications; just in time is often critical.
- Procurement of maintenance, repair, and operation (MRO) supplies is characterized by low unit cost and high variety, but relatively high frequency; examples include office supplies.
- Procurement of capital goods means dealing with goods of high value at low frequency (e.g., new factories) and/or procuring items outside the regular purchasing process, often because of convenience or speed requirements.

Close supplier relationships are particularly relevant for direct procurement (raw materials or production goods), where the quality and availability of suppliers can be of critical importance (Lutz, 2001). A company typically spends several years establishing the relationship and ensuring that the supplier meets the high quality standards. The unknown suppliers are unthinkable in this context. For indirect procurement (MRO and capital goods), efforts to consolidate the supply base and to establish relationships with preferred suppliers often consider cost rather than quality and availability (Cousins, 1999). Buying firms expect better product prices and less cost to manage the supplier base.

These three types of procurements also involve three main categories of costs (Gebauer & Zagler, 2000). In the first category, the cost of procurement of raw materials is the product cost (and quality). To ensure consistent quality, the pre-selection of suppliers and active supplier management are critical activities of the sourcing cycle. The involvement of suppliers in target-costing activities and collaborative design has proven useful to limit total project cost. In the second category, the cost of procurement of MRO items is the process cost. In this category, the process costs may equal or even exceed the product cost. The third category is the technology cost for capital goods. Typically, the characteristics of capital goods are high complexity, innovation, and strategic relevance. Therefore, the range of available supplies is typically very limited (Brown, 2000).

Procurement activities also can be categorized: long-term-oriented strategic and short-term-oriented transactional activities (Segev, Gebauer & Beam, 1998). Long-term-oriented strategic tasks include sourcing activities, identifying vendors, and establishing and managing supplier relationships, as well as contract negotiation and management, but also the design and implementation of buying procedures and financial and asset management. Activities are long-term-oriented, and the resulting supplier relationships often last for many years. Short-term-oriented transactional tasks are mostly clerical order-related activities.

Many purchasing organizations distinguish between activities of sourcing and buying tasks (Dobler & Burt, 1996). Sourcing processes cover more than just one or a few individual buying operations and include market intelligence, demand forecast and planning, identification of suppliers, requests for quote and bidding, negotiation of terms of contract, selection of sources and finalizing of contract, and supplier management. Buying processes typically refer to single transactions only and include activities such as selection of product and supplier from catalog or other sources, submission of internal requests and management approval, submission of purchase orders to pre-approval supplies, delivery and payment, after-sales support, and customer service.

The Development of Internet-Based Procurement Systems

With procuring processes typically involving a large amount of information processing and communication, procurement is well suited for IT support and automation throughout all its steps.

Early initiatives to introduce Internet-based technologies to support procurement concentrated on the automation of highly structured processes. Desktop purchasing systems (DPS) extend traditional EDI systems with user-friendly, browser-based interfaces, increased flexibility, and automated workflow, which are well suited to facilitate end-user empowerment and self-service. Based on electronic catalogs as a central data repository, these systems are readily available and well suited to automate highly repetitive activities, as they prevail in the category of process cost-oriented procurement (low-unit value and high-variety items purchased at high frequencies, such as MRO items). In many cases, the operational gains from reduced process costs and lead times allowed procurement departments to reduce their administrative workloads, free time, and resources for strategic sourcing activities.

Recent developments are most prevalent in the area of Internet-based exchange, be they horizontal or industry specific (Kaplan & Sawhney, 2000; Phillips & Meeker, 2000). While horizontal exchanges connect market participants of the same function, such as automotive industry, exchanges provide information and services to all members of a particular industry. The other examples of trade exchange include MetalSite, e-STEEL, MetalSpectrum, GlobalNetExchange, WorldWideRetailExchange (retail), and E2Open (electronics). Although the boundaries are usually indistinct, exchanges tend to provide less automation than DPS but cover a wider area of products, typically procured at low frequency with a focus on product cost and quality. Also, solutions oftentimes support only a few aspects of the procurement process, such as supplier identification (supplier directories) or obtaining access to product information.

Supply Chain Management

Supply chain management (SCM) has been used to partner with suppliers and to integrate logistics functions and transportation providers to efficiently and effectively manage the value chain. Most of the recent literature on supply chain management focuses on manufacturers' attempts to integrate processes and form alliances with suppliers to more efficiently and effectively manage the purchasing and supply function.

The supply chain management philosophy expands the internally focused integrating activities of logistics by bringing multiple organizations along the supply chain, together with the common goals of efficiency and end-consumer satisfaction (Harwick, 1997). SCM creates a virtual organization of independent entities to efficiently and effectively manage the movement and transformation of materials, components, products, and services along the supply chain until final delivery to the end user (Croom, 2000). Thus, SCM integrates a number of key functions, including purchasing, demand management, manufacturing planning, and materials management throughout the supply chain.

The short-term objective of SCM is primarily to increase productivity and reduce inventory and cycle time. To realize this objective, all strategic partners must recognize that the purchasing function is an important link between the sources of supply and the organization. Indeed, the origin of SCM can be traced back to efforts to better manage the transportation and logistics function. In this respect, SCM is synonymous with integrated logistics systems that control the movement of goods from the suppliers to end customers (Ellram & Billington, 2001).

Integrated logistics systems seek to manage inventories through close relationships with suppliers and transportation, distribution, and delivery services. A goal is to replace inventory with frequent communication and sophisticated information systems to provide visibility and coordination. In this way, merchandise can be replenished quickly in small lot sizes and arrive where and when it is needed (Handfield, 1994).

Collaborative Commerce

The concept of collaborative commerce is defined as multiple companies working together to achieve better results than they could together. Clearly, the Internet is the key enabler of that. Corporate purchasing has been shaken by those collaborative activities. A new category of buy-side software from vendors like Ariba and CommerceOne appeared on the scene. This software allows companies to automate and streamline the purchase of indirect, everyday supplies that are not used in products. Then came net markets with their tantalizing promise of even greater cost saving in the purchase of direct products—the raw materials that actually go into a product.

Recently, several hundred independent exchanges have opened for business and announced plans to build their own Web-based marketplaces. These online markets create new ways of doing business in traditional industries, such as papers and chemicals, where the process is buying and selling commodity-like products. Buyers and sellers can meet on a virtual trading floor and transact quickly and efficiently.

We see that the first wave of Internet-enabled collaboration focused on the supply chain, as companies collaborated with their customers, suppliers, and intermediaries (Bowles, 2000). But the second wave is extending to enterprises with which a company previously had no relationship. Collaborative commerce rapidly is becoming the norm. Over the next years, increased business process integration will lead companies to a big payoff—a more synchronized supply chain that yields better customer service, higher quality products, lower inventory, and faster delivery.

Transaction Cost Theory

Economists have classified transaction among and within organizations as (a) those that support coordination between multiple buyers and sellers; that is, market transaction and (b) those that support coordination within the firm as well as the industry value chain (i.e., hierarchical transactions) (Wigand, 1997). Marketing hierarchy progressing from manufacturer to wholesaler, retailer, and consumer is associated with transaction costs. Transaction costs include the costs of searching, bargaining, coordinating, and monitoring, whicht companies incur when they exchange goods, services, and ideas (Benjamin & Wigand, 1995; Wigand, Picot & Reichwald, 1997).

The major force driving electronic commerce is the ability of networks to reduce transaction costs (Auger & Gallaugher, 1997; Garcia, 1997). Capitalism depends on information to allocate resources efficiently. When businesses can access the best available information at the most appropriate moment, they can reduce their costs and enhance their productivity. Similarly, when buyers and sellers can easily locate one another and have a good idea of what they can expect in terms of quality and prices, they are more likely to engage in trade. The ever-increasing and innovative use of the Internet or the Web to conduct business is a clear example of firms' desires to reduce transaction costs. Thanks to information technology, the evolution from separate databases within the firm to linked databases among firms to shared databases among firms, transaction costs, indeed, are falling rapidly (Wigand, 1997). Malone, Yates, and Benjamin (1987) also suggested that the communication effect via information technology and a tighter electronic linkage between buyers and sellers may lead to reduced transaction costs.

Strategic Networks

Strategic networks are defined as the long-range, deliberate, cooperative, and goal-oriented organizational forms among distinct but related organizations that enable such network member organizations to sustain competitive advantage vis-à-vis their competitors outside the network (Jarillo, 1993). Wingand, Picot, and Reichward (1997) emphasized strategic networks as a distinct organizational form; that is, separate from hierarchy and market.

Networks optimize communication, and a more efficient exchange of information becomes possible. As Powell (1990) stated, information passed through networks is less thick than information obtained in the market (since the price mechanism tends to treat information as a commodity and thus tries to make it as scarce as possible) and freer than communication in a hierarchy (since information is not filtered as clearly through power relationships). Therefore, network organizations combine the advantages of hierarchies, such as better control and coordination of actors, with the advantages of small, independent companies, who have more innovative abilities, tend to be in closer contact with the market and more flexible, with smaller staffs, fewer intermediaries, and lower overhead.

Malone et al. (1987) believe that the development of interorganizational electronic networks would increase the number of buyers and sellers. The use of open information systems may be seen to provide greater levels of information to buyers, thereby opening up greater competitiveness among providers. In addition, they argued that the use of electronic communication links between firms could reduce both the costs of coordinating economic transactions and the costs of coordinating production. As a result, the lowered coordination costs would encourage more outsourcing, enabling firms to buy goods and services less expensively than by producing them in house (Malone et al., 1987, 1989).

Challenges

This study addresses the challenges of e-procurement implementation, thereby providing significant information to executives and operational managers in industry to play a proactive role in global integrated supply chain processes. Overall, four main challenges come from business process integration, technology issues, value creation, and change management.

Business Process Integration

The premise of business process integration is that the rapid redesign of critical process of a company will generate improvements on the performance of the company and create the competitive advantage in the global marketplace.

- **Convergence Between Direct and Indirect Goods.** The division between direct and indirect goods is blurred. E-procurement encourages commoditization (brand details often are stripped from the catalogs), which means they will be ideal for standard production items (nuts, bolts, paper clips, etc.) as well as non-production, indirect goods. The real distinction is between purchases that can be commoditized and those that cannot. Traditionally, direct and indirect procurements have been separated. Convergence between them is a big change for an organization.

- **Back-Office Integration.** E-procurement systems need to integrate with purchasing, inventory, warehousing, invoicing, and the planning requirement departments. Also, the buyers and suppliers must determine the business process for document exchange, including product requisition, selection of order, issuance of RFQ, purchase order acknowledgement, evaluation of proposal, negotiation/award of contract, issuance of purchase order, fulfillment of orders, and payment of order.

- **Supply Base Reduction.** Small supplier bases go in reverse. This does not happen for critical components, where the need for ever-closer collaboration continues to shrink supplier numbers. But, if you are buying paper clips, why not cast your search as wide as possible? Reverse auctions allow you to spread the net far more widely, and the Internet is excellent at handling complexity. This is not to say that the end buyer will deal necessarily with more suppliers but will be dealing with a bigger supplier base. Organizations hope to spend less to manage many suppliers. The challenge appears in the consolidation of suppliers.

Technology Issues

Organizations are utilizing technology to integrate business processes. There are still several issues in information technology.

- **Security Concerns.** The issue of security is a major concern, especially in the context of electronic payments. The capability of any system to provide secure data transfer was regarded as a major criterion for both existing and potential users of e-procurement systems.

- **Inefficiencies in Locating Information.** This lack of interoperability and the lack of standards make it difficult to pull all buyers and suppliers together into a single protocol or a few market spaces for buying and selling. Despite its steady growth, the current use of Internet-based technologies has not yet reached critical mass.

- **Catalog Content Management.** The company must make sure that catalogs are properly maintained in a timely, accurate, and updated manner. Besides that, another challenge the buy-side community faces is when suppliers are not willing to share the information openly with all members of the supply chain by providing all information in the e-catalog. A buyer many be trapped in a situation when he or she compares products costs without knowing the details in the quality specification as well as a good delivery time option.

- **E-Bidding.** Writing up an electronic request for quote and submitting it to the electronic market space becomes easy for buying organizations. Suppliers are able to contact each other electronically, negotiate a team-based approach, and automatically respond to the request for quote. The challenge arises from multiple levels of negotiations on the Internet.

- **E-Auction.** The new generation MRO, electronic auctions, starts to play an important role. A prospective purchaser could dial in and see the spot price of paper, chairs, or office supplies and determine whether to purchase. In the future, next generation auctions also will feature more complex items and allow matching of supply and demand, not only with respect to price, but also for features such as service, quality, or speed of delivery.

Value Creation

The e-commerce world is value creation competition. More values created by e-procurement are toward faster, simpler, cheaper, more convenient, available anywhere, anytime, and by any means. Simplification, transparency, standardization, and automation of procurement processes always are challenging.

- **Empower Employees.** Now employees can check price, availability, and delivery time from their desktop. They can handle the entire procurement process by themselves. From a perspective of human resource, e-procurement can reduce training requirements. Because employees can purchase anytime and anywhere, crews' relocation also will be reduced. In addition to freeing up the procurement department, the finance, manufacturing, and logistics personnel also need to do more value-added activities by pushing purchasing decisions back to end users.

- **Increased Procurement Control.** A variety of MRO items consider difficulty in terms of developing specialist knowledge regarding product and service technical characteristics and supply market conditions. The ability to consolidate and categorize suppliers, services, and MRO goods is seen as an enabler in the move toward greater professional contribution to MRO procurement. In addition, the centralized purchasing function was able to exert greater control over sources of supply, purchase price, and inventory policy. Organizations should manage their MRO items in a more strategic manner through such actions as the establishment of single-source arrangements, consolidation of commodities and services, and increased buying power over the supply base.

Change Management

This is an age of accelerated changes characterized by the globalization of markets, ubiquitous presence of information technology, and integration of business process and enterprises. It will not be the brightest or the strongest who will survive, but those who are most adaptive to change. E-procurement implementation needs several changes.

- **Role Change in Purchasing Department.** There will be changes to business practices and organizational structures over the next years, as e-commerce solutions become more mature and more widespread. As a general development, we see the role change between end users and purchasing departments (i.e., new procurement system continues either to automate purchasing operations or to help push them down to the end user, allowing the purchasing department to concentrate more on strategic and managerial tasks, such as partnership relationships and long-term supply contract). Since employees can purchase directly through their Web access, purchasers no longer need to process orders, invoices, or chase delivery. As a result, purchasing departments become composed of mostly managers and less of clerks, secretarial staff, and administrative support. Additionally, the determining factor of geography reduces, freeing organizations to obtain the best deal and the most appropriate products from anywhere around the globe.

- **Staff Resistance.** The purchasing staff resists online solutions because, although not unreasonable, they detect a threat to their job security. Organizations no longer rely extensively on interpersonal communication (telephone, face-to-face negotiation, fax, etc.). In fact, their roles change dramatically, because they are freed from burdensome clerical labor that takes up 70% of their time in manual systems, and they are allowed to put their real skills into practice by negotiating contracts, monitoring supplier performance, and building relationships.

- **Lack of Top Management Support and Vision.** This is understandable, because not even researchers and market analysts are sure yet of the exact direction in which electronic procurement will move. There is a long road from friction-free e-procurement to reality. However, successful e-procurement is a top-down process that requires a champion and a visionary at the board room table, who can grasp the strategic potential of the procurement issue. Technology changes rapidly. To create sustainable competitive advantage, organizations need to consider their Internet plan as part of a larger strategy-oriented picture. Revolutionary changes happen much more slowly than anticipated, as many hurdles have to be overcome. Being aware of these hindering factors is just as essential as knowing about the opportunities that new technologies present.

Future Trends

The consolidation of suppliers shows that increasing integration will continue within organizations and among enterprises. Existing evidence in increasing new generations of e-auction and e-bidding at the industry level also indicates that increases in investment in information technology are associated with a decline in the average firm size and a rise in the number of firms. It may be expected that greater information availability will lead firms to encourage their level of outsourcing or global sourcing. As a consequence, an increase in the proportion of bought-out goods and services will place an increased strategic emphasis on the purchasing process.

With the widespread wireless, the future trend will involve mobile e-procurement. Substantial investments have been made to advance mobile technologies and applications, and already there are signs that developments have progressed more slowly than anticipated (e.g., the bidding for UMTS licenses in Europe that still have to pay off telecommunications companies). To date, mobile technologies primarily have been applied in consumer-oriented areas, while the business world still awaits large-scale usage. At present, the use of mobile technologies primarily concerns voice communication rather than the wireless transfer of data, thus effectively replacing (wired) telephone lines rather than desktop computers.

Conclusion

In spite of the value that e-procurement creates, the challenges of implementing this application do exist. Lessons learned from a few companies that have embarked on the e-procurement endeavor indicate that factors such as incompetent infrastructure, human resistance to change, and conflicting policies and standards pose immense pressure for the companies to move forward. The biggest challenge among them is change management. E-procurement is not about the introduction of software; it is about the change of business processes and the change of human habits. Moving people from their comfort zones means moving from the familiar, secure, and controllable to the unfamiliar, insecure, and uncontrollable. Sometimes, it is about the shifts in power and influence, such as loss or change of roles in the organization.

The applications were easy; the people issues were tougher. Essential elements such as preparing the organization for change, developing a sense of the scope of the change, communicating the motivation and need to change, and training are much more difficult to accomplish than finding technology that works and getting it all plugged in and interfaced (which is not to say technology integration is easy). The hard parts are management tasks. Building organizational support is harder than building identification and communication systems. It is really tough to do, unless management gets involved. Initiating change from the top creates a culture that embraces change and a shared vision that energizes the organization. The major organization transformation is not the job of middle management. Rather, the CEO and senior management team need to establish the context of change. Change, therefore, is primarily about leadership. A senior management team needs to communicate the vision of change throughout the organization. A frequent and consistent manner is a key component of that communication.

While change initiatives often arise out of crisis and are driven by dedicated leaders, research indicates that change also can be triggered in response to opportunity and organization growth. Change is not just about reducing costs or improving profitability but about the invention of strategies and management processes. Performance evaluations, rewards, career management, and operations all must change. Starting with standardized goods, especially MRO procurement, letting employees shop on their own will leave the procurement department to focus on strategic tasks (i.e., establishing and maintaining close relationships with suppliers and business partners, eventually leading to streamlined processes and leveraged buying power. Also, the company has employees participate in the software upgrade; the company is able to combine training with installation. Employees felt really empowered by the experience and were much comfortable with new interface and software. Furthermore, two organizations have created flatter structures with more empowered employees who are trusted more, expected to conform to shared values, and encouraged to be more entrepreneurial and innovative. Those accelerate change processes.

Selling generates revenues; buying right generates profits. E-procurement needs to be viewed as a way of doing business, not as a set of software applications that need to be installed and run. That is why the organization must be prepared for change. The demise of companies will come from a lack of competitive adaptiveness; essentially, most of these companies will not survive, because they are too slow to keep up with the pace of change.

References

Auger, P., & Gallaugher, J.M. (1997). Internet-based sales presence for small business. *The Information Society, 13*(1), 55-74.

Benjamin. R., & Wigand, R. (1995). Electronic markets and virtual value chains on the information superhighway. *Sloan Management Review, 36*(2), 62-72.

Bowles, J. (2000). E-procurement. *Forbes, 166*(3), 189-216.

Brown, R. (2000). *Bechtel's approach to e-procurement.* Berkely: Haas School of Business, University of California, Berkeley.

Brynjolffson, E., Malone, T., Gurbaxani, V., & Kambil, A. (1993). *Does information technology lead to smaller firms?* Cambridge, MA: MIT.

Cash, J.I., & Konsynski, B.R. (1985). IS redraws competitive boundaries. *Harvard Business Review, 2*, 134-142.

Cousins, P.D. (1999). Supply base rationalization: Myth or reality? *European Journal of Purchasing and Supply Management, 5*(3/4), 143-155.

Croom, S.R. (2000). The impact of Web-based procurement on the management of operating resources supply. *The Journal of Supply Chain Management, 36*(1), 4-11.

Dobler, D.W., & Burt, D.N. (1996). *Purchasing and supply management.* New York: McGraw Hill.

Ellram, L., & Billington, C. (2001). Purchase leverage considerations in the outsourcing decision. *European Journal of Purchasing and Supply Management, 7*, 15-27.

Garcia, D.L. (1997). Networked commerce. *The Information Society, 13*(1), 9-41.

Gebauer, J., & Segev, A. (2000). Emerging technologies to support indirect procurement: Two case studies from the petroleum industry. *Information Technology and Management, 1*, 107-128.

Gebauer, J., & Segev, A. (2001). *Changing shapes of supply chains—How the Internet could lead to a more integrated procurement function.* Berkeley: Haas School of Business, University of California, Berkeley.

Hammer, M. & Champy, J. (1993). *Reengineering the corporation: A manifesto for business revolution.* New York: Harper Business.

Handfield, R. B. (1994). U.S. global sourcing: Patterns of development. *International Journal of Operations and Production Management, 14*(6), 40-51.

Harwick, T. (1997). Optimal decision-making for the supply chain. *APICS-The Performance Advantage, 7*(1), 42-44.

Hough, H. E. & Ashley, J. M. (1992). *Handbook of buying and purchasing management.* Englewood Cliffs, NJ: Prentice-Hall.

Jarillo, J. C. (1993). *Strategic networks: Creating the borderless organization.* Jordan Hill, UK: Butterworth-Heinemann.

Johnston, H. R. & Vitale, M. R. (1988). Creating competitive advantage with Inter-organizational information systems. *MIS Quarterly, 12*(2), 153-165.

Kaplan, S. & Sawhney, M. (2000). E-hubs: The new B2B marketplaces. *Harvard Business Review, 78*(3), 97.

Killen, K. H. & Kamauff, J. W. (1995). *Managing purchasing: Making the supply team work.* New York: McGraw Hill.

Lutz, J. (2001). *Procurement strategies for eBusiness.* Haas School of Business, University of California, Berkeley.

Malone, T. W., Yates, J., & Benjamin, R. I. (1987). Electronic markets and electronic hierarchies. *Communication of the ACM, 30*(6), 484-497.

Malone, T. W., Yates, J., & Benjamin, R. I. (1989). The logic of electronic markets. *Harvard Business Review, 67*(3), 166-170.

Moozakis, C. (2001). E-procurement for services-Texas Instruments uses Clarity to better manage contract workers. *InternetWeek, 876,* 17-18.

Nelson, D., Moody, P. E., & Stegner, J. (2001). *The purchasing machine: How the top ten companies use best practices to manage their supply chains.* New York: Free Press.

Phillips, C. & Meeker, M. (2000). *The B2B Internet report: Collaborative Commerce.*

Powell, W. W. (1990). Neither market or hierarchy: Network form of organization. In B. M. Staw & L. L. Cummings (Eds.), *Research in organizational behavior* (vol. 12, pp. 295-336). Greenwich, CT: JAI Press Inc.

Ramsdell, G. (2000). The real business of B2B. *McKinsey Quarterly*, (3), 174.

Segev, A., Gebauer, J., & Beam, C. (1998). *Procurement in the Internet Age-Current practices and emerging trend.* Haas School of Business, University of California, Berkeley.

Segev, A., Gebauer, J., & Farber, F. (2000). *The market for Internet-based procurement systems.* Haas School of Business, University of California, Berkeley.

Wigand, R. T. (1997). Electronic commerce: Definition, theory, and context. *The Information Society, 13*(1), 43-54.

Wigand, R. T., Picot, A., & Reichwald, R. (1997). *Information, organization and management: Expanding markets and corporate boundaries.* Chichester, UK: Wiley.

Zenz, G., Thompson, G. H. (1994). *Purchasing and the management of materials* (7th ed.). New York: Wiley & Sons.

Chapter VII

Designing Integrated Supply Chains

Chean Lee
Methodscience.com, Australia

Abstract

This chapter introduces the concept of Supply Chain Management (SCM). It provides a broad definition of supply chain, the drivers for integrated supply chains design, and current challenges in global supply chains. More importantly, this chapter provides the reader an insight into aligning corporate strategy, people mindset, process design, and technology in designing an integrated supply chain. A real-life example in the health care industry is provided. The example aims to give readers the identification of supply chain bottlenecks, the right methodology to map the AS IS processes, and the redesign of simplified supply chain processes. Finally, the guidelines for supply chain management implementation issues, such as vendor selections and team building, are addressed.

Introduction

We live and breathe in a world of supply chains. Consider, for example, how we buy bread from retail stores. The ingredients come from various sources, dispersed physically.

Wheat and rice are grown by farmers. The flour or rice mill manufacturer processes the wheat into flour. It is distributed to the bakery to turn the raw material (flour) into breads of different shapes, sizes, or flavors. Then, the wholesaler packs the breads into different packages and sells them to retail stores. Increasingly, we expect information technology and systems to enable integration and delivery of such a supply chain. Needless to say, in order for businesses to fulfill the daily demand of customers, a well-designed supply chain is crucial. More importantly, though, this is becoming extremely significant in the context of business, where supply chains are an integral part of globalization.

The main objectives of this chapter are to:

- Address the concept and definition of supply chain.
- Analyze the current issues in the global supply chain.
- Identify the bottlenecks in the current supply chain design.
- Establish an urgency of aligning people, strategy, processes, and technology in a supply chain design.
- Provide a sensible and measurable approach in designing integrated supply chains in order to reduce risks.
- Provide recommendations in supply chain application, vendors, and partner selection during supply chain implementation.
- Address future trends in integrated supply chains.

Background

Considering a simple bread-buying process at the outset of this chapter, it is clear that businesses, suppliers, and consumers are involved in supply chain relationships. The entire supply chain encompasses demand planning, purchasing of raw materials, production planning, and delivery of finished products, as well as after-sales service. However, let us start this discussion by considering what we mean by supply chain management.

According to the Supply Chain Council (Bolstorff & Rosenbaum, 2003), supply chain management is defined as the art and science of managing the movement of product and services from businesses to end customers. The definition also varies on the motivation and interest of different parties. For example, business application and software vendors described SCM as APS (Advance Planning and Scheduling) tools to streamline business processes.

These definitions can be applied to create what would be a supply chain model (see Figure 1) to explain the supply chain management and integrated supply chain.

Based on the model, supply chain management consists of five core processes: Plan, Source, Manufacture, Deliver, and Service. Planning involves activities like sales forecasting, customer segmentation, material planning, and so forth; Source includes purchasing from suppliers; Manufacture deals with production; Delivery is the physical

Figure 1. Supply chain management (Based on the supply chain operations reference model created by the supply chain council, 2001)

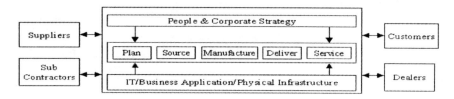

movement of goods to consumers; and Service refers to after-sale services like maintenance, warranty, and returns. A company or organization board, management team, managers, and executives support these five core processes (see Figure 1) by defining business strategy, goals, and objectives. The application and IT infrastructure also supports components for managing the entire supply chain. All these components are integrated with suppliers, customers, agents, and dealers, which eventually results in what is considered supply chain management and integrated supply chains. The question to ask, then, is do we need to design an integrated supply chain? According to research conducted by Accenture (world's leading management and IT consulting firm), INSEAD, and Stanford University of 3,000 companies in 24 different industries worldwide, there is a strong and consistent relationship between supply chain excellence and financial performance. Based on the finding, we can conclude that supply chain management's best practitioners are strong in inventory turnover, cost of goods sold, and returns on assets.

According to the research, Zara, an international clothing manufacturer and retailer, sped up its new fashion style delivery process from five months to three to six weeks using handheld technology in 450 Zara's stores to collect customers' feedback and send it directly to fashion designers.

Based on the research and best practices from the supply chain mastery companies, the designing of an integrated supply chain operating model is crucial in order for businesses to reduce operating costs such as faster inventory movements, accurate demand forecasting, better customer service, and financial performance.

In the next section, we provide an insight into what drives the design of integrated supply chains in a global perspective and the opportunities for companies to focus and follow in designing an integrated supply chain. In addition, we compare and contrast supply chain operating models in North America and Asia.

Why Integrated Supply Chain?

From the previous section, we can conclude that high performance companies are gurus in integrated supply chain management. This is due to the fact that they have faster inventory turnover and speed in responding to customer demands, and they adapt to the frequently changing business climate and standardize processes in the organization. For example, the world's leading automotive manufacturer, Toyota's annual profit was $8.13 billion during March 2003, surpassing the combined earnings of GM, Chrysler, and Ford (Liker, 2004). The secret behind this was the lean manufacturing model that streamlined the entire supply chain process.

The lessons from Zara, Toyota, and other supply chain process-centric companies like Dell, Amazon, and GE have shown us the drivers for an integrated supply chain. It can be categorized into the following business- and technology-driven issues.

(a)   Business Drivers

- **Globalization Climate:** The globalization trend has caused businesses to compete and distribute their products and services in different countries. In order to collaborate with international customers and partners, an integrated supply chain process is important in order for businesses to respond faster to market conditions.

- **The Demanding Customers and Suppliers:** Due to the overflow of information and low switching cost for products and services, customers require businesses to provide them faster, more reliable, and more excellent services. Second, suppliers require you to collaborate closely with them in providing customized product and services to customers.

- **Merger and Acquisition:** Merger activities triggered integration of best practices and processes in both companies' supply chains to eliminate process bottlenecks.

- **Increase in Operation Cost and Limited Working Capital:** Nowadays, working capital is scarce, and shareholders are often cautious with their investments; they talk about ROI (Return of Investment). As a result, businesses need to reduce their operating costs and fight for capital. For example, reducing inventories and WIP stocks are important for manufacturers and retailers.

- **Explosive Growth:** The expansion in your company requires management to integrate the supply chain process in order to eliminate repetition of work and wastage in production in order to cope with the customer's demand.

(b)   Technology Drivers

- **Explore New Technology Opportunities:** Businesses want to look into the opportunities of harnessing new technology, such as the Internet, Web services, and e-business, in order to improve their supply chain operating models as well as processes.

- **Applications and Software Replacement:** This is another technology driver whereby a company business application, such as the ERP (Enterprise Resource Planning) system not delivering measurable results for supply chain improvement. Second, businesses require add-value to their enterprise system by integrating the supply chain.

Challenges and Opportunities
for an Integrated Supply Chain

Before we start designing the integrated supply chain, we aim to define the potential challenges, threats, and opportunities that arise in the global supply chain.

(a)   **The Challenge Ahead:** We have looked previously into the areas where business and technology events triggered the needs for integrated supply chains. In this section, we identify the current challenges in the global integrated supply chain system by comparing and contrasting North American and Asian Pacific situations. These insights will assist us in tackling the opportunities in designing an integrated supply chain or even improving the supply chain process.

Table 1 provides a comparison between a supply chain operational scenario and challenges in Asia and North America as well as Europe. The summary is based on the

Table 1. Scenario and challenges for designing integrated supply chains

Challenges	Asia	North America and Europe
People's Mentality and Cultural Mindset	• Trust for designing an integrated supply chain for information sharing and collaboration is a main hindrance. • Partnership mentality is low, since competition perspective plays an important role in Asia.	• Partnership and collaboration is practiced among businesses, manufacturers, and customers. • Challenges in extending the partnership to Asia.
Supply Chain Management Skills	• Lack of supply chain design talents and still need time to learn.	• Excellent supply chain design skill and well-structured education system.
Organizational Model and Design	• Most companies in Asia are conglomerates. They dominate large market share. • Family-owned business and hierarchy decision making.	• Decline in conglomerate model. • Adopting outsourcing model to downsize the business and safe cost.
Supply Chain Complexity	• Regulatory and market conditions, such as tariffs, have caused complexity in supply chain network. • Multi-layer distribution channel.	• Simplicity and well-developed distribution channel and supply chain network.
Infrastructure and Information Technology	• Poor transportation and logistic infrastructure in less developed countries like Indonesia. • Challenges in IT readiness because some businesses in Southeast Asia don't even have LAN (Local Area Network) connection and ERP system.	• Good transportation, seaports, and logistic infrastructure. • Need to extend their supply chain system into an adaptive enterprise model by linking with global supply chain.

white paper, *Supply Chains in Asia: Challenges and Opportunities*, by Easton and Zhang (2003), published at Accenture's Web site.

Based on the comparison in Table 1, we can conclude that Asian countries are facing challenges in market diversity issues like distribution channel complexity, regulations, cultural mindset, and infrastructure for designing an integrated supply chain. For instance, Accenture's research shows that there are 16,000 wholesalers in the China pharmaceuticals industry, which causes complexity in supply chain design. As for North America and Europe, most companies have integrated their supply chains with B2B portals and marketplaces; however, there are still challenges in transforming the supply chain into an adaptive business network in order to respond to globalization challenges.

(b)   **The Opportunities:** In the previous insights of the challenges in the global supply chain, it is clear that the moving toward an integrated supply chain system or improvements in the value chain design is not an easy task for businesses. However, businesses can achieve the goal toward an integrated supply chain by looking at the following five opportunities proposed by Easton and Zhang (2003) in "Supply Chain in Asia: Challenges and Opportunities." These opportunities can be implemented by stages or even as a whole by considering the supply chain design objectives for the company. Figure 2 shows the supply chain model we discussed in the earlier section of the chapter.

1. **Strategize the Supply Chain:** Companies should determine the real benefits and outcomes that they need to achieve in the supply chain design. It is measured by strategic issues, such as streamlining process (i.e., reduce manufacturing setup or changeover, or eliminate waste), differentiation (i.e., speed up order fulfillment process to build up corporate or product brands), or even improving collaboration and customer relationships.

2. **Improve Process Functions:** This option provides opportunity for companies to focus on the supply chain process from plan, source, manufacture, deliver, and service (see Figure 2). For example, companies can improve the manufacturing process by introducing best practices like lean manufacturing and six sigma.

3. **Enterprise System and Application Integration:** This is another area whereby companies will consolidate or standardize their processes by integrating their internal business application, such as MRP or ERP, warehouse management system, and others, for better data integrity and information management. It also can be extended to front-office functions like CRM integration in order to provide a seamless operating environment.

4. **Outsourcing:** It involves the outsourcing of non-strategic functions and processes to enable businesses to focus on the core supply chain process. For example, companies like Nokia, Motorola, Procter & Gamble, and Hewlett-Packard have outsourced some of their Asian supply chain operations (Bowman, 2000).

5. **Transform the Supply Chain:** This is an advance level for companies to transform their supply chain model to an adaptive enterprise by leveraging the

Figure 2. Integrated supply chain opportunities (Based on the supply chain opportunity areas for Asia, Easton & Zhang, 2001)

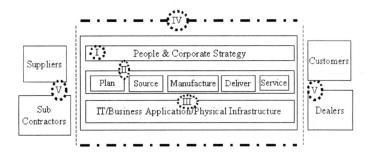

capabilities of collaboration with global suppliers and customers and to achieve better responsiveness to market changes with accurate demand and supply planning.

Aligning People, Strategy, Process, and Technology

We have identified all the challenges and opportunities, but how are we going to seize the opportunities that arise in designing an integrated supply chain? To simplify the illustration, Figure 3 provides four levels of best practices for companies to adopt as the pathway in integrated supply chain design.

Based on Figure 3, we noticed that the alignment of people, strategy, process and technology emphasized the integration of the internal functions from top-down and vice versa; it also extends to the interaction with external customers and suppliers by

Figure 3. The supply chain design methodology

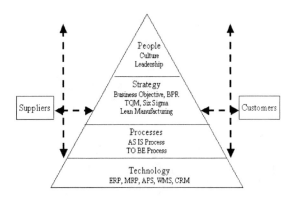

integrating with their business vocabulary and processes. This model is recommended in order to reduce the gap between businesses and external customers or suppliers, since most of the BPR or TQM projects in the late 1980s to early 1990s emphasized more improving internal processes rather than the whole supply chain. Now, let us summarize the four elements in the pyramid.

- **Level 1 – People:** It encompasses the educating of internal employees, customers, and suppliers toward the need of integrating the supply chain. It includes knowledge management, the promoting of process culture, management of change, as well as utilizing the principles of TQM and Kaizen within the workforce to improve the supply chain process.

- **Level 2 – Strategy:** Outlines the actions to be taken on a strategic level for designing an integrated supply chain (e.g., supply chain flexibility, efficiency, responsiveness, etc.). It also aims to provide a roadmap for companies to transform the supply chain to an adaptive business model.

- **Level 3 – Process:** Provides illustrations on the overall process and workflow of the supply chain. Wastage and bottlenecks need to be tackled for an integration design in order to eliminate the wastage and drawbacks in the supply chain process.

- **Level 4 – Technology:** In order to execute the integration of the supply chain, the technology infrastructure segment aims to assist decision makers in the various business applications suite from enterprise system vendors like SAP (www.sap.com), Manugistics (www.maugistics.com), i2 (www.i2.com), and others. The platform or framework, such as B2B marketplace or Web services, needs to be taken into consideration in order to standardize the supply chain process.

In summary, the supply chain design model (see Figure 3) aims to align the decision makers (people), business strategy, and processes with technology in order to reduce the gap between business objectives and technical feasibility. In the next section, we will drill down into details to describe each level of the model and analyze their importance for an integrated supply chain design project.

Level 1 (People):
Empower Your People to Create Value

People are the most valuable asset for every business and organization. Supply chain excellence-driven companies like Toyota, Dell, Amazon, Wal-Mart, and others emphasize grooming their workforce to be customer focused, innovative, and cross-functional-driven in the supply chain execution.

The preparation of companies' workforces and partners for the spinoff of an integrated supply chain is the foundation to the success of a supply chain project. Figure 4 provides a spiral model for developing a supply chain driven workforce.

Figure 4 shows four important processes in preparing the workforce and partners in marching toward an integrated supply chain. It encompasses Define Vision, Culture Development, Promote Leadership, and Execution Ability. To prepare people for these four steps, change management, knowledge management and key performance index are three major ingredients in the spiral model. Let's summarize all the elements.

(a) **Define Vision:** The definition of vision in integrating value chains comes from the executive management team, the company board, as well as the shareholders. A CEO recognized the needs of designing the integrated supply chain in order to serve the customer better. The CEO defined the roadmap and the vision to transform the supply chain after having a meeting with the board and the management team.

(b) **Culture Development:** We have set our vision, the creating of a corporate culture that is able to transform the supply chain. These cultures include the following:

- Focus on customers. Educate your organization on putting the customers in first place by improving your supply chain in terms of shorter lead-time, better sales forecasting, and after-sales service.

- Build a culture that focuses on quality and getting things right at the beginning. For example, Toyota focuses on controlling the quality at every stage of the production; stopping the whole process to solve problems before moving into the next stage is developed in the automotive manufacturer organization (Liker, 2004).

- Build a process culture in order to realize the integrated supply chain vision. A company is described as a process-centric company when all business processes are embedded in the daily operation, such as strategic planning, thinking, and the way employees carry out their tasks. Process culture also involves continuously innovating and improving the supply chain.

- Finally, a continuous learning and problem-solving philosophy is also an integral part in corporate culture development. It involves mutual respect, trust, and knowledge sharing among employees and partners throughout the marketing channels.

(c) **Promote Leadership:** To realize the integrated supply chain, a company needs to grow leaders that act as the role of evangelist—a person who understands the concept of the supply chain; has experience and working knowledge of designing the supply chain and project; has the ability to sell the concept to upper management, employees, and channel partners; and has project management as well as human skills.

(d) **Execution Ability:** It refers to the competencies of a company's employees and partners to turn supply chain strategic planning into actions (e.g., the forming of a project committee, team building, allocation of budget and resources).

(e) **Change Management, Knowledge Management, and Key Performance Measurement:** Based on Figure 4, we notice that managing change, knowledge management, and continuous key performance measurement are important in managing the workforce to move toward an integrated supply chain environment.

Figure 4. Developing your people for designing integrated supply chain

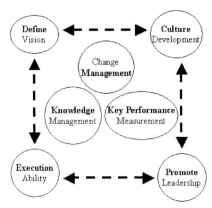

In the first place, managing change includes the managing of shifts in job functions and new responsibilities as well as new processes in the supply chain. During supply chain integration, new job positions, like project managers, B2B specialists, analysts or solutions architects, will be born in the organization (Lofts, 2002). It also creates changes in the order fulfillment, planning, purchasing, manufacturing, and customer service. Integration creates collaboration of all parties instead of performing the process as a single entity. Thus, managing change is important in supply chain design.

Second, knowledge management is another element that supports the model of getting the right people to kick-start the supply chain integration. Knowledge management is about making use of employees' and partners' knowledge in order to gain supply chain competitive advantage and turn ideas and innovation into execution.

Finally, it is recommended that a key performance index needs to be established in order to monitor the performance of the organization at each level, from bottom-line functions, like sales and marketing, logistic operations, production, IT infrastructure, and financial, to supply chain strategy planning. It helps a company to identify areas for improvements in people's performances.

To conclude, getting the right people is the first step in designing an integrated supply chain. It involves how companies prepare their workforce to transform the supply chain by adopting the jigsaws, such as creating leadership, promoting process culture, managing change, and so forth.

Level 2 (Strategy): Determine the Metrics and Roadmap

We have discussed workforce and supplier readiness for an integrated supply chain kickoff. Now, it is time to determine the overall business and supply chain strategy to get everything right from the beginning. In the strategic plan for supply chain integration, several steps are outlined:

- Step 1: Define objectives and strategy.
- Step 2: Conduct a SWOT analysis.
- Step 3: Conduct a gap analysis.
- Step 4: Finalize the integration roadmap.

(a) **Step 1:** Define Objectives and Strategy—When we start our supply chain integration design, a clear business objective needs to be developed; for example, improving response to customer queries and complaints, reducing defects in manufacturing, and so forth. A clear business objective assists us in further developing a business case. A business case determines how the new supply chain system resolves the current challenges in the supply chain. For example, the new APS (Advance Planning and Scheduling) system is expected to improve inventory turnover by 20%. When we have sets of business objectives and cases developed, then we have a clear visual clue of the overall project objectives and outcome to be delivered.

Table 2. Supply chain design metrics

Supply Chain Design Objectives	Design and Measurement Metrics	Supply Chain Management Methodologies	Applications and Technology Standards
Streamlining the Supply Chain	• Eliminate wastage • Improve production process and yield.	• TQM • Six Sigma • TOC	• ERP • MRP I and II • APS • Manufacturing scorecards.
Collaboration	• Enterprise-wide integration	• BPR • BPI	• PLM • APS • SRM • ERP
Supply Chain Responsiveness	• Order fulfillment lead time	• BPR and BPI	• APS • ERP • SRM • CRM
Supply Chain Synchronization and Flexibility	• Flexible production • Response time	• BPR • Lean manufacturing • Adaptive manufacturing	• APS • ERP • SRM • CRM
Reliability	• Excellent fulfillment cycle • Perfect delivery time	• JIT or Kanban	• APS • ERP • WMS • CRM • LMS
Supply Chain Profitability	• Inventory turnover • Reduction of production wastage • Return on asset	• Lean manufacturing • Kanban or JIT • Adaptive manufacturing	• APS • ERP • WMS • Manufacturing scorecard

When we get our business objectives, business cases, and project goals right, we can look at supply chain best practices to be considered in our integration design. In order to select the right supply chain integration metrics, companies need to understand the manufacturing practices with which they are involved (e.g., make-to-stock in the soft drinks industry, assemble-to-order in electronic circuit boards, and make-to-order for the high-end automotive sector).

After an understanding of the nature of manufacturing practices, Table 2 provides a template for businesses to select the metrics for their supply chain integration design according to their business objectives and requirements as well as organizational readiness. The following proposed template is further enhancement of the study conducted by a management consulting firm, AT Kearney, during 2003, in white paper, "Managing Supply Chains in 21st Century".

The template in Table 2 proposes common best practices to focus on in supply chain integration. There are six main focuses for businesses to consider in supply chain design. Businesses also can combine these practices, based on their business objectives.

1. **Streamlining the Supply Chain:** This category focuses on streamlining the internal supply chain process, especially in the manufacturing process. The core focus is to eliminate wastage in production, such as overproduction, excess inventory, defects in machinery, and failure in resource utilization. Main measurement is based on how to increase the performance yield to reduce the waste. It is supplemented with efficiency initiatives like total quality management (TQM), six sigma, and e-tools like material requirements planning (MRP) in order to make it happen. We will elaborate on supply chain management methodologies later and the technology issue in Level 4 (see Figure 4).

2. **Collaboration:** Collaboration practice refers to forming a partnership with major suppliers and contract manufacturers in product design. Collaboration aims to create a value chain to tie up all parties in the supply chain in order to share information, decision making, and planning to serve customers better. It is often supplemented with business process integration (BPI) and applications like product lifecycle management (PLM).

3. **Supply Chain Responsiveness:** Refers to the time where businesses produce the product and deliver it to the end customers. The key measurement metric is the lead time, where the end product reaches the customer.

4. **Supply Chain Synchronization and Flexibility:** Refers to the abilities and competencies of an organization's response to market changes, such as the rise of raw material cost and financial crisis. It also refers to how businesses provide order promises to customers using methods like available to promise or stock replenishment.

5. **Reliability:** The reliability practice often refers to the ability of companies to deliver the right product with the correct quantity and specifications to the customers at the right time and right place.

6. **Supply Chain Profitability:** In a manufacturing point of view, supply chain profitability focuses on how to reduce the wastage as well as increase the inventory

turnover. The overproduction or overstock of raw material, work-in-progress (WIP), stocks, and finished goods are considered a financial burden for manufacturers. The return on asset (ROA) is a measurement of profit margin and asset turn by enhancing the throughput in the shop floor, which increases the speed of product to the market (Bolstorff & Rosenbaum, 2003).

We have insight into the supply chain integration design practices and measurement metrics. However, we need formulas like BPR, JIT, TQM, and others to realize the vision. The following provides a brief definition of the terminology.

- **Total Quality Management (TQM):** A business initiative that focuses on improving the product and services to the customers while reducing the production cost. It emphasizes the continuous improvements and breakthroughs with development cycle within organizations (Integrated Quality Dynamics Inc., 2001).

- **Six Sigma:** The extension of TQM. The successful process improvement methodology that was implemented at General Electric (GE). It encompasses six steps in process improvement: Define, Measure, Analyze, Improve, and Control (Bolstorff & Rosenbaum, 2003). It measures and improves the manufacturing process by applying a statistical calculation method.

- **Theory of Constraint (TOC):** Improves the production process by eliminating defects and bottlenecks. It is developed by Eliyahu M. Goldratt in his book, *The Goal*.

- **Business Process Reengineering (BPR):** A business tool that helps a company to improve its organizational efficiency, reduce process duplication, and create standardization in order to serve customers better.

- **Lean Manufacturing and Adaptive Manufacturing:** The lean concept emphasizes a push on manufacturing; it runs production when there is a trigger of sale. It adopts the one-piece flow concept in manufacturing. Adaptive manufacturing emphasizes the competencies of responding to change and is able to sense and learn among manufacturers, suppliers, and customers.

- **Just-In-Time (JIT) / Kanban:** A method used in lean manufacturing for reducing production wastage and improving responsiveness.

The template we identified in Table 2 is sets of best practices and supply chain metrics for businesses to consider in a supply chain integration project. These methodologies need to be analyzed further, based on the corporate competencies and feasibility for execution. As a result, SWOT analysis is the next step in our supply chain strategy formulation.

(b) **Conduct a SWOT Analysis:** The supply chain integration best practices and metrics are ready; now it is crucial for businesses to conduct a SWOT (Strength, Weakness, Opportunities, and Threats) to evaluate their corporate competencies in terms of internal resources and external factors in order to jump-start the supply chain integration project.

1. **Strengths:** It refers to the internal competencies of a company, which sets it apart from its peers (e.g., brand image, excellent customer service, and product quality).

2. **Weaknesses:** The drawbacks of a company in the supply chain. For example, inconsistency in delivery performance; lack of an enterprise resource planning (ERP) system for internal processes like production, material control, and so forth; loose collaboration among suppliers and the company.

3. **Opportunities:** The availability of external factors, such as the availability of technology in order for the company to operate and manage its supply chain in a low-cost manner.

4. **Threats:** External pressure, such as limited capital, competition, and scare resources that caused the company to redesign the supply chain.

The SWOT analysis aims to provide an overview for businesses to have a broad picture of the organization's capability in a supply chain integration project.

(c) **Conduct a Gap Analysis:** After the SWOT analysis, we can start to study the gap between the actual company supply chain performance and the competitive requirement. For instance, the gap between an order fulfillment is 76%, and the competitive requirement of 88% is 12%. The aim of this analysis is to turn the negative percentage into a profit potential. This method also can apply to the supply chain process performance gap as well as the technology gap between new and old business applications. It gives us the opportunity to improve the overall supply chain performance.

(d) **Finalize the Integration Roadmap:** The supply chain best practices and metrics are defined; SWOT analysis provides insight to the company's competencies in supply chain integration or transformation; we also have the gap analysis on the target we should achieve in the supply chain. What's next? It is time to draw out a roadmap for the supply chain gluing journey. Figure 5 shows the road to supply-chain richness.

Figure 5 proposes that the success of supply chain integration relies on four major steps: Published, Accessible, Integration, and Transformation. The X-axis shows the degree of difficulty in supply chain integration based on time, human skills, cost, and technical implementation. The Y-axis shows the values that create an impact on businesses due to supply chain integration and transformation. These are measured in terms of return on investment, return on asset, elimination of production wastage, reduction of over-stock, and others. Thus, when companies move from informative supply chain to transformation, they are expected to create more business impacts. Table 3 summarizes the characteristics and objectives of each stage.

Figure 5. Steps to the supply chain success (Based on Adapt or Die: Transforming your Supply Chain into an Adaptive Business Network, *Heinrich, C. with Betts, B., 2003)*

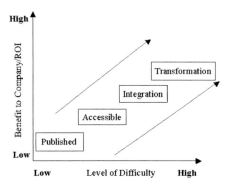

Table 3. Road to supply chain success (Based on adapt or die: Transforming your supply chain into an adaptive business network, Heinrich, C. with Betts, B., 2003)

	Published	Accessible	Integration	Transformation
Supply Chain Objectives	Achieve the information and data visibility.	Provides multi channel interaction for employees, partners and customers.	Linking and integrating the supply chain to streamline the workflow.	Extent the integration to adaptive supply chains that able to response to rapid changes.
Inputs & efforts	Publish information such as stock level, sales orders, pricing, production scheduling, delivery order and sales forecasting to employees & close suppliers.	Generate a community among users in accessing information like stock level by providing multiple access points.	Defined the business processes from planning, souring, manufacturing, deliver and servicing to be integrated. Link up the multiple interaction points with back-end system.	Add in new channel partners and all parties like customers and suppliers are able to participate in product design through collaboration.
Possible Technology Platform	Portal/extranet. E-mail. Excel spreadsheet.	Portal/extranet. Mobile sales force automation. Wireless devices. Inventory tracking system. MRP system. CRM.	Portal/extranet. ERP. MRP. EAI & Web Services. Available to Promise system.	B2B Marketplace with seamless integration. Integration of APS, MRP, ERP, CRM. Balance scorecard.
Timeframe	1-2 months	3-4 months	6-8 months	1-2 years
Outcomes & Supply Chain experience	• Better communication. • Information sharing. • Automate basic business processes. • Improve accuracy on stock level, job scheduling and delivery planning.	• Ease of information access. • Speed in customer order fulfillment. • Increase if stock turn over. • Real time material control. • Organizational change.	• Reengineered the whole supply chain processes. • Moving towards lean and flexible manufacturing. • Reduced wastage in production. • Excellent fulfillment. • Knowledge management.	• Able to sense market changes and response fast. • Supply chain reliability and flexibility. • Achieve the adaptive manufacturing model. • Continuous learning and improving business processes.

Level 3 (Process):
Redesign the Supply Chain Workflow

Now that our supply chain design strategy is ready, this section aims to provide a process to improve the current bottleneck or disconnect points in the entire supply chain process: Plan, Source, Manufacture, Delivery, and Service. We recommended the followings for the supply chain reengineering, based on the foundation of the SCOR model:

- Understand the bottlenecks in the supply chain process.
- Identify opportunities.
- Brainstorm.
- Analyze cause and effect.
- Prioritize the opportunities.
- Define the as-is process and design the to-be workflow.

(a) **Understand the Bottlenecks:** This step starts with the initial meeting within various departments in the company to define the bottlenecks in the supply chain process. For example, the sales department tackles the reasons for inconsistency of the customer order fulfillment cycle; the inventory/warehouse department discovers the excess inventory problem in the warehouse; the production manager finds out the problem of wastage due to inefficient resources allocation. Given this situation, it is recommended that all departments have a participative theater to act out their daily process like order fulfillment in a meeting room.

(b) **Identify Opportunities:** Based on the results from the life theater, executives in various departments start documenting the supply chain processes from plan, source, manufacture, delivery, and service. The discovery of opportunities for improvements is executed.

(c) **Brainstorm:** A brainstorming session is recommended at this stage. All senior managers from departments like sales, customer service, production, warehouse, and logistics are involved in supply chain improvement design and collaborate to tackle the disconnect points in the entire supply chain. Questions and answers review are released for further analysis and process redesign execution.

(d) **Analyze Cause and Effect:** After struggling in the brainstorming exercise, we adopt the cause and effect analysis model to analyze the supply chain process bottlenecks. In this case, we provide supply chain challenges in the pharmaceutical and health care industry as an illustration. ABC Pharmaceutical Manufacturing produces medicine, personal care, and health products. The company has a strong brand with the penetration of 70% of the retail shelves for major chemist outlets around the world. However, the company faces inconsistency in customer order fulfillment in the distribution of finished goods to chemist outlets and distributors around the world. Figure 6 shows the cause-and-effect analysis diagram from ABC Pharmaceutical Manufacturing.

The cause-and-effect chart in Figure 6 shows the main problem, which is inconsistent in customer order fulfillment. The main problem is further analyzed with the identification of causes as well as subproblems in the chart (Figure 6).

(e)   **Prioritize Opportunities:** Figure 7 provides the prioritization matrix for the order fulfillment process redesign. It is divided into four different cells.

Figure 6. ABC pharmaceutical manufactoring cause and effect analysis diagram

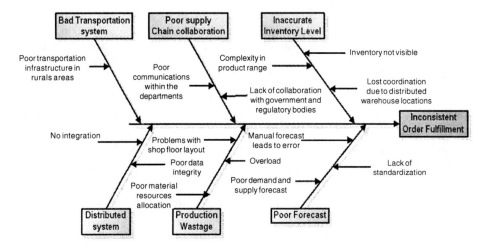

Figure 7. ABC pharmaceutical manufacturing supply chain prioritization matrix (Based on the Boston Consulting Group Matrix)

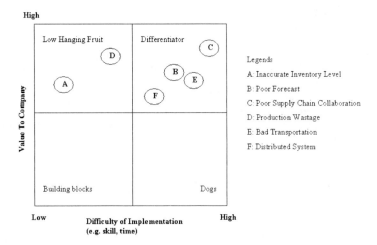

The low-hanging fruit cell presents improvements that need to be carried out at top speed, since they create high value and ease of implementation to ABC Pharmaceutical. The differentiator cell shows that the redesign initiatives enable the company to set itself apart from its rivals and create high value to company performance. However, it should be implemented with good long-run planning, given the complex nature of time, skills, and cost. The building blocks cell shows that project initiative is low in value, although it can be implemented easily. It should be chosen carefully without wasting company efforts. Finally, the dogs segment shows the unrealistic supply chain improvement initiative; ot should be avoided due to low return and high risks.

Based on the cause-and-effect analysis, we found the reasons for inconsistency in order fulfillment. We plot the solving of inaccurate inventory level (A) and production wastage (D) as low-hanging fruits, since ABC Pharmaceutical can design a portal Web site to show the inventory level. While resolving, poor forecast (B), supply chain collaboration (C), bad transportation system (E), and distributed system (F) need time, financial investment, and skills from ABC Pharmaceutical, distributors, suppliers, and regulatory bodies. However, it creates a high competitive advantage to the supply chain.

(f)   **Define the As-Is Process and Design the To-Be Workflow:** Figure 8 showcases the current customer order fulfillment process that happens at ABC Pharmaceutical Manufacturing. There are several potential bottlenecks in this entire process:

- Poor collaboration between retail outlets, manufacturer, suppliers, and regulatory bodies due to linear supply chain design.

Figure 8. ABC pharmaceutical manufactoring AS IS customer order fulfillment process (Based on SAP Pharmaceuticals Solution Map, Edition 2004)

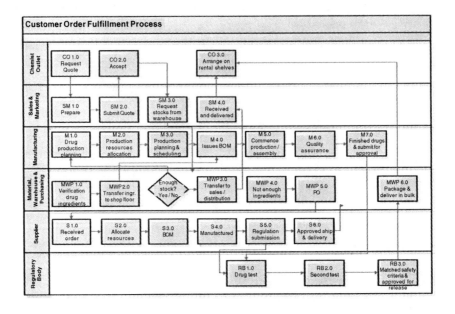

- The risk of overstocks of medicine, drugs, and health care products, since there is no sharing of information, such as inventory level, poor scheduling, and forecasting. It also will make the lead time longer to reach customers, due to non-standardized forecasting. The main reason for poor forecasting is inaccurate information on disease incidents, which causes inaccurate production in drugs and medicine.

- The adopted manufacturing model is much more an assembly mode, whereby all working cells will keep on moving, although there is a problem in one of the manufacturing parts, since quality inspection is placed in the end.

- Risk of wastage in production due to waiting unnecessarily for transfer, overprocessing, defects, and excess stock.

Now, let us look at the new design workflow in Figure 9. There are improvements in the entire customer order fulfillment process, due to the following reengineering efforts:

- Stock, delivery, quotation, and job scheduling visibility via a portal and improvement of flow of information throughout the organization.

- Better supply chain planning, demand planning, and forecasting, due to the MRP system that shows in process 2. In addition, ABC Pharmaceutical Manufacturing even can go a step further with an advance planning and scheduling system for more accurate forecast and collaboration with drug ingredients suppliers and government regulatory bodies.

Figure 9. ABC pharmaceutical manufacturing TO BE customer order fulfillment process

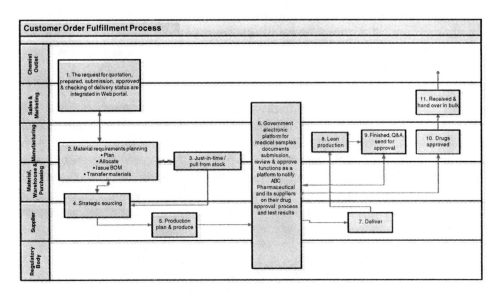

- The reduction of inventory level and working capital, due to the just-in-time method, whereby the company is moving from the push method to the pull stock replenishment. Materials and resources are utilized, once they are needed for production.

- Strategic sourcing enables the company to reduce its purchase cost, since electronic procurement enables it to allocate the most competitive pricing from suppliers.

- The lean manufacturing concept that stresses one-piece flow in the shop floor dramatically reduces wastage, as shown in the as-is process flow, due to better utilization of resources like manpower, materials, machines, and time. Thus, the overall fulfillment cycle is reduced, and ABC Pharmaceutical Manufacturing will enjoy return on investment and asset for their supply chain integration project.

To sum up, the definition of bottlenecks in the supply chain process, prioritizing the opportunities for improvements, and the visualization of the as-is and to-be processes play an important part in a supply chain integration design. It is very important for decision makers to look at the overall processes before investing in a supply chain application.

Level 4 (Technology): An Integrated Supply Chain System

In the previous section, we designed the to-be business process and workflow; now it is time to embed these processes in supported technology and applications. Figure 10 provides a high-level integrated supply chain management system architecture to streamline the value chain of ABC Pharmaceutical Manufacturing with its customers and suppliers as well as regulatory bodies (Figure 10).

Based on this architecture, we provide further discussions on the applications of supply chain management.

(a) **Rich Portal UI (User Interface):** Portal is the presentation layer to present information, such as order forms, stock level, pricing, and delivery scheduling information for customers, or even suppliers and dealers. The portal also functions as a collaboration point between ABC Pharmaceutical and its suppliers.

(b) **CRM (Customer Relationship Management:** An integrated system that automates the company interaction process with customers. It consists of several combinations: sales force automation, with functions like contact management, salesperson management, quotation tracking, and sales forecasting; marketing automation, which functions as a campaign management tool for promotion, discounts, and advertising; field service automation, which manages service requests from customers; order management, tracking, and tracing customers' orders.

Figure 10. Based on SAP Netweaver Architecture (For more information visit http://www.sap.com/solutions/netweaver/index.epx)

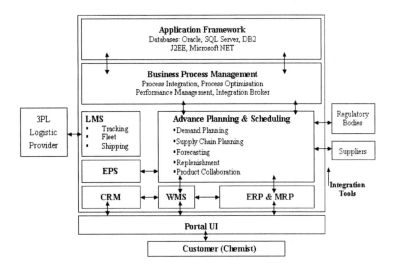

(c) **WMS (Warehouse Management System):** Manages the warehouse stock levels such as raw materials, WIP stocks, and finished goods turnover. It also keeps tracks of warehouse stock movements. It also can be integrated into a bar-code system or RFID (Radio Frequency Identification).

(d) **MRP (Material Requirements Planning) and ERP (Enterprise Resource Planning):** MRP refers to a software system that helps businesses and suppliers to allocate or configure the products or raw materials that are needed for production. It also determines the sequence of material to be consumed in manufacturing. ERP is an integrated system that assists a company in streamlining its internal process, such as purchasing, sales, production, stock control, HR, and others. Nowadays, ERP also combines the function of MRP.

(e) **EPS (Electronic Procurement System):** A system that helps ABC Pharmaceutical to conduct the spending analysis on procurement, sourcing, purchasing, and bidding of materials with suppliers in the electronic marketplace.

(f) **APS (Advance Planning and Scheduling System):** A system that assists businesses in collaborating resources, stock, and materials to serve the demand of the customers. It includes functions like demand planning, supply chain planning, sales forecasting, replenishment, and product collaboration.

(g) **LMS (Logistic Management System):** Software that integrates with third-party logistic providers to track and trace the goods movements, shipping status, and requests, as well as fleet management.

(h) **Business Process Management Tools:** Application that provides functions for the supply chain process integration, optimization, and visual monitoring of the process performance. It also includes the integration broker components.

(i)   **Application Framework:** The heart or foundation of the integrated supplies chain system. It performs all the business logic of the supply chain system and provides interactions with back-end databases, such as customer master data that run on database applications like Oracle or MS SQL Server. The application can be built on popular frameworks like J2EE (Java 2 Enterprise Edition) and Microsoft.NET Framework.

(j)   **Integration Tools:** Sets of EAI (Enterprise Application Integration) standards and middleware that link up ABC Pharmaceutical's internal system with suppliers. It includes middleware like WebMethods, data exchange standards like XML (Extensive Markup Language), or Web services standards like SOAP (Simple Object Access Protocol).

In summary, in order to integrate the entire supply chain, companies need to implement all pieces of applications to provide a seamless integration in order to serve customers better.

Implementation and Deployment

The supply chain implementation consists of two parts: project team organization and selection of vendors.

(a)   Project Team Organization: Supply chain integration is a serious task throughout an organization. Given its significance, it is important to organize a supply chain project team to kick-start the integration task. In the previous sections, we discussed supply chain integration, which involves the readiness of people; setting of business objectives and supply chain design metrics; and the definition of the to-be supply chain process flow and the high-level of technical architecture design and analysis. In this section, we provide recommendations for the organizing of team members' roles in the supply chain integration project. The following team members are outlined in the supply chain design:

- Executive Sponsor
- Steering Committee
- Project Manager
- Business Strategy/Process Lead
- Solution Architect
- Business Analyst
- Systems Integrator

Table 4. Team members' roles for supply chain integration

Team Members	Major Responsibilities	Skill Requirements
Executive Sponsor (Project Chairman)	• Stakeholder of the program or project • Monitor the details of the design and implementation • Conduct regular meetings	• Human and organizational skills • Problem and conflict solving • Change management • Supply chain experience and knowledge
Steering Committee	• Group of departmental heads like VP and senior managers that review the progress of the project	• Detailed understanding of departmental functions • Management skills
Project Manager	• Launch the project • Monitor project timeline, budget, objectives, and team members • Report to executive sponsor and steering committee	• Project management • Human and communication skills • Supply chain strategy planning • Supply chain analysis and design • Technical integration skills
Business Strategy/ Process Lead	• Lead a group of business analysts or business process analysts • Develop supply chain execution strategy • Identify the bottlenecks of the current supply chain • Define the area of process improvements • Report to the project manager • Collaborate with technical team	• Project management • Human and communication skills • Supply chain strategy planning • Supply chain analysis and design • Technical integration skills
Solution Architect	• Lead the system integration team • Access viability of the system architect and construct the supply chain system architecture • Architectural analysis and design • Define the design elements and incorporate with existing design • Collaborate with business team and project manager	• Technical and integration experiences and skills • Software project management • Sound business process and workflow knowledge • Human and organizing skills
Business Analyst	• Identify the stakeholder or process owner in the supply chain • Manage the stakeholders' business requirements • Designs supply chain business model • Identify supply chain process bottlenecks • Design new business process • Conduct user acceptance test and user training • Managing the process quality	• Strong business and supply chain acumen • Business process and workflow design skills • Understand human psychology • Change management • Analytical skills
System Integrator	• Implement the supply chain management software suite • Customization and system integration • Testing and debugging • Develop database	• Strong technical implementation skills • Programming languages and middleware skills • Basic business process knowledge • Balancing the business and technical constraints

Table 4 presents a summary of team members' roles in the supply chain integration project. It is proposed, based on the foundations of the SCOR model and the Rational Unified Process (RUP), a methodology for software and system development.

Table 4 summarizes the basic requirements for a supply chain integration team. It is crucial for businesses to allocate the right people with the right skills for supply chain design.

(b)   Vendor Selection: The market for supply chain management application is developing rapidly, and it is heading toward a maturity stage due to industry consolidation, such as mergers and acquisition between business application vendors (e.g., the merger between enterprise software vendor PeopleSoft with JD Edwads). However, vendors for the supply chain management system are still in the process of adding more functional capabilities, such as deploying Web services architecture to enhance the robustness and ease of integration of the supply chain suite. In addition, vendors such as IBM also create value-added services to clients by aligning the business strategy, process, and outsourcing services of the existing enterprise system package with the acquisition of the management consulting firm, PriceWaterHouse Consulting. These market movements create more options and rational approaches for businesses in consideration of vendors' selection for their supply chain implementation.

This section aims to classify supply chain management vendors to assist businesses in evaluating vendors based on matching their supply chain goals, strategies, and business processes. Before the vendor selection, there are several steps that need preparation.

- A clearly defined supply chain goal and objective.
- The availability of supply chain transformation metrics and performance measurement metrics.
- The education of employees and suppliers for the change initiative. Training and workshops need to be conducted to get the company ready for supply chain integration.
- The documenting of supply chain process bottlenecks and the new design process to improve the supply chain.
- Groups of project teams that are committed full-time to the project.

After these things are ready, the following are the key criteria for supply chain management vendor selection.

- Agreement on the supply chain strategy, metrics, design requirements, and business processes.
- Make sure the vendors understand the nature of industry in which the business is involved (e.g., the manufacturing process and unique business requirements).
- The supply chain application offers by the vendor, whether or not they can be embedded within the company's business processes.

- The maintenance, upgrade, troubleshooting, and other related after-sales services offered by the vendor. It is also important to evaluate the terms and conditions in the software service maintenance contract before the selection.

- The review of the supply chain suite system architecture, whether it is easily implemented without complex customization and also whether it is expandable for future company growth.

- Always ask for client references from the vendor in order to call its existing customers that use the system to evaluate the product and services as well as the vendor track records in the industry.

- Make sure the implementation is budget-wise feasible.

After we align the business objectives with technology and the selection criteria are ready, Table 5 provides the classification for supply chain management vendors.

There is no absolute answer for which vendor's solution is the best supply chain suite for integrating the value chain. The most important part of designing an integrating supply chain is to get the employee ready for change, develop a feasible supply chain strategy and improvement metric, define the to-be process flow, and design the technical architecture before selecting the vendor.

Table 5. Supply chain management solution providers

Vendor Category	Definition
Supply Chain Specialist	These solution providers are pure players in the supply chain management software market. They provide end-to-end supply chain suite, including demand planning, order fulfillment, warehouse and inventory management, sourcing, logistic management ,and delivery. Some of the leading vendors are i2 Technologies and Manugistics.
Enterprise Business Application Providers	These solution providers start their business by providing other business applications such as MRP and ERP systems for manufacturing and retailing companies. They jump on the bandwagon of providing supply chain management systems after they recognize the market needs (e.g., SAP AG, PeopleSoft, Oracle and SSA Global).
Niche Specialist	These solution providers focus on certain components of the whole supply chain suite, such as procurement and sourcing, or even B2B marketplace (e.g., Ariba, CommerceOne, and EXE (now part of SSA Global).
Middleware Vendor	These solution providers focus on providing Middleware, business process integration, and monitoring applications for supply chain integration. They are capable of utilizing Web services standards like XML, .NET, and J2EE in their application (e.g., WebMethods, SeeBeyond and Tibco).
Management and Technology Consulting Firms	These solution providers align business and supply chain consulting services with technical application implementation for clients. They have in-depth experience and expertise in vertical industries, and sometime they also provide business process outsourcing for clients (e.g., Accenture, IBM Business Consulting, EDS, and AT Kearney).
3PL Logistic Providers	These solution providers add value to their physical logistic services by providing logistic outsourcing solutions to clients in the areas of warehouse management, fulfillment, and inventory handling (e.g., UPS Supply Chain and FedEx).

Future Implications
of Supply Chain Management

Supply chain management is a kind of business management and art; it will gain its importance in the coming years and continue to develop as part of the corporate strategy. Its importance will create an impact on any industry, whether it is a manufacturing focus company, a retail store, or even a service line. Here are some predictions for future supply chain integration.

- A business starts to learn from previous bad practices and failures in the supply chain system investment. They will start to adopt a sensible approach by incorporating supply chain investment strategies with best methodologies like JIT, lean manufacturing, and six sigma; the combination with an effective business process redesign will grow important before the SCM system implementation.

- Businesses in North America will continue to embrace outsourcing of certain supply chain processes. On the other hand, the outsourcing of non-core supply chain processes will gain momentum in Asia Pacific.

- The adaptive manufacturing model will realize this, due to the emergence of new integration standards like XML and Web services. Adaptive manufacturing will help companies to have better planning of their manufacturing processes by taking into consideration the operating margins, material availability, shop-floor design, and so forth. Based on these capabilities, businesses will be able to sense and respond to these rapid changes and provide better services to customers' demands and improve decision making. It will reduce the working capital and inventory cost of manufacturing companies.

- There will be real-time information flow, such as inventory, production scheduling, and delivery schedule visibility throughout the organization, suppliers, and customers. The sea of information will contribute to continuous knowledge management and learning culture among employees and partners.

- More consolidation activities, such as mergers and acquisitions, will take place in supply chain management application markets. Vendors will benefit from mergers by combining the strengths of each party to provide better solutions for the companies.

- More technology standards and frameworks will be developed by vendors in order to realize the vision of supply chain transformation to an adaptive business model. For example, SAP developed its NetWeaver Platform for ease of enterprise application integration and development.

- The wireless and smart devices are new emerging gadgets for improving the supply chain management. For example, RFID will improve the data management in the areas of inventory management and movements.

- Businesses will gain benefits from adaptive business networks, since they are operating in a flexible mode.

- The thoughts and insights in this chapter are not definitive; there will be continuous writing on this chapter, Designing Integrated Supply Chains.

Conclusion

In conclusion, the design of integrating supply chains is not an easy task; it includes hard work to reach the goal. It is important for businesses to seize the opportunities available. Second, we must grow leaders in organizations by educating them on the importance of supply chain excellence, which contributes to company performance. We must promote the culture of continuous learning in companies and prepare employees for change. When implementing supply chain integration projects, it is important for companies to have the supply chain strategy ready, to construct the best practices metrics, to align them with a business formula like lean manufacturing or TQM, and to redesign the business processes and embed them in appropriate applications and technologies.

Finally, we must invest in people and have a full-time project implementation team that is committed to the project. The supply chain integration is a must in order for businesses to move toward an adaptive enterprise and to implement change quickly; otherwise, businesses will lose their competitive advantage.

References

Anderson, D.L., & Delattre, A.J. (2003). *Supply chain innovations: Five big, bold trends.* Accenture.

Bolstorff, P., & Rosenbaum, R. (2003). *Supply chain excellence: A handbook for dramatic improvement using the SCOR model.* New York: AMACOM.

Cross, K.F. (2004). *Quick hits: 10 key surgical strike actions to improve business process performance.* New York: AMACOM.

Easton, R.J., & Zhang, T.B. (2003). *Supply Chains in Asia: Challenges and Opportunities.* Accenture.

Heinrich, C., & Betts, B. (2003). *Adapt or die: Transforming your supply chain into an adaptive business network.* Hoboken, NJ: John Wiley & Sons.

Kearney, A.T. (2003a). *Managing supply chains in the 21st century.* Executive Agenda.

Kearney, A.T. (2003b). *Unlocking value from e-supply management.* Technology Watch, Executive Agenda.

Kearney, A.T. (2004a). *Healing Mexico's health-care system.* Executive Agenda.

Kearney, A.T. (2004b). *Shifting your supply chain into reverse.* Executive Agenda.

Liker, J.K. (2004). *The Toyota way: 14 management principles from the world's greatest manufacturer*. New York: McGraw-Hill.

Lofts, N. (2002). *Process visualization: An executive guide to business process design*. Ontario, Canada: John Wiley & Sons Canada Ltd.

The promise of purchasing software. (2003). *McKinsey Quarterly, 4*.

Smart tags for your supply chain. (2003). *McKinsey Quarterly, 4*.

The unexpected return of B2B. (2002). *McKinsey Quarterly, 3*.

Chapter VIII

A Framework for Analyzing Information Systems in an Integrated Supply Chain Environment:
The Interaction Approach

Christopher Van Eenoo
University of Western Sydney, Australia

Abstract

The concept and study of supply chains are nothing new. The concept of integrated supply chain environments (ISCE), however, has received increased study as of late. Technology has become the enabling factor for corporations to share information externally and to improve material flow within the supply chain. Many benefits can be realized from an integrated supply chain environment, including improved customer relations, cost reductions, and increased competitive advantage. Despite the potential benefits, there are many factors that lead to failed integrated supply chain implementations. Many of the major factors that lead to failure are not due to technological reasons but rather to the failure of the project team to recognize the complexities of the implementations of integrated supply chains. This chapter introduces the Interaction Approach methodology as a framework for analyzing supply chains in the hope of improving the design, development, and implementation of integrated supply chain environments.

Introduction

In today's economy, information and information technology seem to drive the supply chain to new requirements and dimensions (Evans & Wurster, 2000). This inevitably leads to the integration of supply chains across organizations. Integration allows entities within a supply chain to operate in a coordinated manner and, therefore, in an economical manner. As the economy becomes global, enterprises will be forced to exploit integration techniques in order to stay competitive.

Despite the many benefits advertised by supply chain management software vendors, there still exists major issues when implementing an integrated system, including the failure to correctly assess the implications and complexities of supply chain systems integration during the analysis phase (Lan, 2003).

This chapter will begin by presenting a review of the current literature concerned with the integration of supply chains through information technology. Four major technologies will be presented and discussed. Next, integrated supply chains will be defined, and the benefits of integration will be presented. After the benefits are presented, the chapter will explore current issues that hinder the implementation of integrated systems and cause projects to fail. In response to the issues, a new methodology for analyzing information systems in supply chains will be presented. The methodology provides a framework for analysis, which lends itself to object-oriented, agent-oriented, or structured design and development approaches.

Literature Review

There is much research aimed at and study conducted on the integration of supply chains using information technology. There are many approaches used for the integration, each exploring and exploiting a different technology. The following literature review presents work related to the major prevalent integration technologies, which includes EDI and XML, Internet and Web-based, and Intelligent Agents and Fuzzy Logic.

EDI and XML

Nurmilaasko, Kettunen, and Seilonen's (2002) research focuses on the implementation of an XML-based integration system. Their study outlines cases in which XML is more suited toward integration efforts than traditional EDI. They conclude that, because XML enables customized business documents and because integration systems are Internet based, the XML prototype is more flexible to implement and operate than EDI. They find that XML is a cost-effective alternative to EDI, despite the recent slowdown in adoption of XML technologies.

In a more recent research, Nurmilaasko (2002) teamed with Kotinurmi (2004) to analyze and explore various e-business frameworks of supply chains, such as document-centric, cross-industry, industry-specific, and process-centric, and to evaluate the impact that XML technologies can have on the integration of the supply chain. They argue that a comparison from XML to EDI is difficult and that XML alone will not solve all integration problems; however, XML is a cost-effective solution when compared to inflexible EDI. They feel that a shared understanding of business documents and processes is necessary for true supply chain integration.

von Mevius and Pibernik (2004) propose a new approach to supply chain process management, based on a new high-level Petri-net called XML-net. XML-nets consist of supply chain data objects and physical supply chain object documents. XML-nets support the exchange of intra- and interorganization data and offer superior supply chain process modeling capabilities.

Internet

Knoblock and Minton (1999) present the Ariadne system, which can be used to quickly provide access to data sources of new suppliers and requires only that the suppliers' data are available on the Web. Ariadne makes it easier and cheaper to rapidly assemble dynamic supply chains by providing a quickly produced wrapper for non- or semi-structured Web sources. Their approach does not require reengineering of individual systems and includes the conversion of semi-structured data into structured data, query planning techniques, fast access to slow Web sources, and solutions for solving inconsistencies across data sources.

Vanharanta and Breite (2003) examine the supply chain from a systemic view in order to understand if small- to medium-sized businesses can take advantage of Internet technology. They explore the effect that information technology has on the embedded value chain and the value that internal information technology can have on external customers. In doing so, they have identified general properties of the supply and value chains that can be used to characterize business environments. These properties can indicate the technological position of a company and the commercial potential of a company in a specific industrial sector. Vanharanta and Breite's (2003) research suggests that, since supply and value chains exist in all businesses, it is possible to find new ways to implement Internet technology into the business.

Intelligent Agents, Neural-Networks, and Fuzzy Logic

Berkstresser et al. (1998) are researching support models which use fuzzy mathematics, neural networks, genetic algorithms, and other efficient soft computing methodologies to provide intelligent, responsive knowledge support for optimizing integrated supply chain management decisions. The method that they propose will be used to extract fuzzy rules for guiding decision making from input-performance pairs generated from supply chains.

Fox et al. (2000) investigate the issues and solutions with regard to the construction of an agent-based software architecture. They describe an agent as an "autonomous, goal-oriented software process that operates asynchronously, communicating and coordinating with other agents as needed" (Fox et al., 2000, p. 2). They feel that, when situations in the supply chain change are not locally contained, agents can help the organization achieve the level of coordination necessary to manage information, decisions, and actions across the enterprise and the supply chain. They propose a model that enables the complex coordination and conversation of agents.

The current literature reveals many interesting issues facing supply chain integration. EDI appears to be falling by the wayside, and XML is being touted as a cheaper, more flexible alternative. Internet and Web-based integration using common browsers and portals is receiving less attention by researchers. It seems that Internet integration has not lived up to its own hype. An exciting new area of research looks at the use of autonomous agents to integrate the supply chain. This research has implications in boundless other business areas, as well.

Integrated Supply Chain Environments

Before the benefits of and issues facing integrated supply chain environments are presented, a formal definition is required. A supply chain is defined by Benita Beamon (1998) as:

an integrated process wherein a number of various business entities (i.e., suppliers, manufacturers, distributors, and retailers) work together in an effort to: (1) acquire raw materials, (2) convert these raw materials into specified final products, and (3) deliver these final products to retailers. (p. 2)

It can be argued that Beamon's (19998) definition should be expanded to include end customers and consumers, as well.

In regard to information technology in supply chains, Mark Fox, et al. (2000) argue that an organization's ability to manage the tactical and operational levels of the supply chain so that there is timely dissemination of information, accurate coordination of decisions, and management of actions of people, ultimately determines the efficient, coordinated achievement of the organization's goals.

Integration of the supply chain through the use of information technology can be beneficial, as the next section describes.

Benefits of ISCEs

There are many benefits that a corporation can realize from the successful integration of the supply chain. Not only does the immediate internal corporation benefit from integration, but so do external players.

van der Velde and Meijer (2002) list three major benefits to improving supply chain management and integration. Lan (2003) expands on each of the benefits.

- **Improving customer service.** This can lead to better customer retention and behavior. By improving the internal organization's capability to promise, customers can plan more accurately their own business functions.

- **Achieving the necessary balance between costs and service.** Integration can lead to cost reduction and more reliable and timely financial information.

- **Giving the corporation a competitive advantage.** Inventory management and efficiency is achieved as a result of increased planning and streamlined production capabilities. This gives the corporation the ability to remain competitive.

These items illustrate the impact that true integration can have on the supply chain environment. Notwithstanding the benefits, there are still issues that face the successful integration of the supply chain.

Barriers of ISCEs

According to various enterprise technology surveys, roughly 70% of all IT projects fail, and among those projects, supply chain management implementations fail with equal frequency (Southgate, 2003). The improper management of supply chains and their integration can be shattering to an organization's success. In May 2001, Nike announced that its sales were $100 million lower than expected because of problems with their supply chain. Shortly after, Cisco announced a $2.2 billion inventory write-down because of problems in its supply chain (Taylor, 2003).

Supply chain management and integration projects fail for many reasons. Mike Hugos lists three reasons why supply chain projects fail: (1) projects are ill-conceived; (2) projects fail to identify real benefits; and (3) projects have a tendency toward over complexity (Southgate, 2003).

Ballard (2003) augments Hugos' list with two more reasons for failure: (1) projects are overly ambitious in their scope; and (2) companies fail to prepare their infrastructure and fundamental business systems before the project begins. Supply-chain.com clarifies the second point by adding that when available software products force a company to modify its supply-chain processes to fit default criteria, implementations can fail to address the (supply-chain) problems at hand (www.supply-chain.org, n.d.). If an organization's employees do not agree to the methods embedded in the software, they will resist using the software or want to make customizations. Customizations make the software more unstable and harder to maintain (Koch, 2003). Despite this fact, companies must realize that changing the software is still easier than changing employees' habits and should endeavor to modify the software to suit the processes in order to succeed (Koch, 2003).

Supply-chain.com offers that, in order to properly improve the supply chain, organizations must identify non-competitive areas of the supply chain, understand where customer needs are not being met, set improvement goals, and quickly implement the improvements to the supply chain (www.supply-chain.org, n.d.).

Given the huge costs involved in integrating the supply-chain and the even bigger potential losses should the integration fail, it is paramount that proper steps be taken early in the project phase to correctly identify the weaknesses of the supply chain with respect to its actors, elements, and interactions.

ISCE IT Analysis Framework

Integrated supply chains are concerned heavily with the relationships or interactions between the entities or actors within the supply chain. The following methodology provides a framework for analyzing the supply chain, which focuses on the actors, data elements, and interactions within the supply chain environment. The framework consists of the following seven phases:

1. Actor Identification and Classification
2. Data Element Requirement Identification
3. Identification of Interactions
4. Review
5. Design
6. Development
7. Implementation

Figure 1. Interaction approach methodology conceptual model

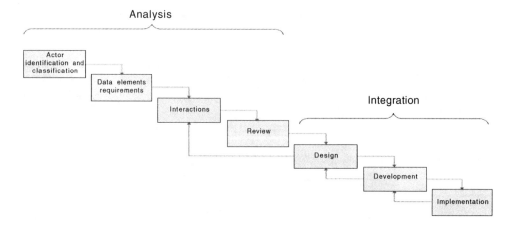

Figure 1 shows a conceptual model of the proposed Interaction Approach methodology. The phases of the framework are divided into two major stages of analysis and integration.

Actor Identification and Classification

Supply chains are very much involved with the interaction of suppliers, manufacturers, transporters/logistics, distributors, retailers, and end customers. Each of these actors plays a crucial role in the supply chain and should be recognized and identified early on in the analysis phase. The first phase in the process of analyzing an ISCE is to identify the actors. There are several major reasons for this, which include:

- The recent trend toward agent-oriented development.
- To lay the groundwork for intelligent agent integration.
- Allows for a strategic outside focus of systems development (Lan, 2003).
- To define the language, location, culture, and so forth of each actor.

The phase sees every possible actor identified and a list created. For each actor, the location, language, and other cultural or regulatory notes should be recorded. Lan (2003) suggests that language and cultural issues can be inhibiting factors to the integration of ISCEs. The identification of the non-technical characteristics (location, language, culture, etc.) will aid in the following interaction, review, and design phases. Because it is not always possible to list or recognize all actors, generalities can and should be used when the possibility of actors exists. For example, analysis may never uncover the exact number or names of all of the third-tier suppliers, but at least one entry into the list of actors should be made for third-tier suppliers.

The actor list is then examined for possible groupings or categorizations in a reiterative bottom-up approach with respect to data and information requirements. (Data requirements gathering is introduced in the next phase.) For example, suppliers that supply semi-assembled goods could be grouped together. Likewise, second-tier retailers could be grouped together. In the case where one actor plays two or more roles in the supply chain, the actors should be placed into all appropriate groups. The groups are then reexamined for possibilities of further grouping. For example, all first-tier suppliers could be grouped together. This process continues until every actor in the supply chain has been placed into one the following general, high-level groups: suppliers, manufacturers, transporters/logistics, distributors, retailers, and end customers. It should be noted that these could be grouped into a final Supply Chain Actors group, which would sit at the top of the actor hierarchy. Figure 2 shows an abbreviated actor hierarchy expanded on the supplier node only. Note that Thompson is a first-tier supplier and also provides transport services.

Finally, mark the suppliers that account for 80% of all outgoing expenses and the customers that are responsible for 80% of all income. This data will be used during the review phase.

Figure 2. Actor hierarchy

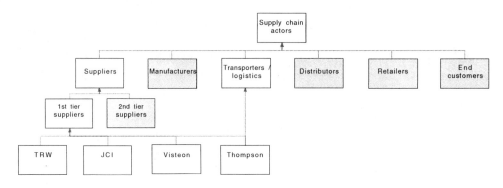

Data Element Requirements Identification

Once all of the supply chain actors have been identified, the next step is to identify the data requirements of each. This second phase in the framework is concerned with identifying the information elements required by each actor and the information flow of each element. In the traditional supply chain model, there were two types of flows: product flow and data flow. Product flow was considered upstream, whereas data flow was considered to flow downstream (Hughes et al., 1999). In today's technology-enabled world, data must flow in all directions.

Data element requirements analysis may begin by collecting all reports that are printed and made visible to external actors. These reports can include formal reports, invoices, sales orders, purchase orders, and so forth, and could be in the form of printed mail, fax, e-mail, EDI, XML, and so forth. Analysis continues by examining all methods of data exchange within the supply chain. If there are existing Web portals, the information elements accessible by these portals are collected, as well. If it is possible to identify where the data elements ultimately are used, either upstream or downstream, then attempts should be made to capture this data, as well. The objective of this phase is to identify and collect all internal information or data elements that currently are visible to external actors. In a similar fashion, all external data elements received and processed by internal actors also should be identified.

By identifying the data that flows in and out, a clear picture can be made of the overall requirements of data sharing in an integrated supply chain environment. The data element requirements list is used in the next phase of the framework.

Figure 3. Interaction matrix

			Bill of Material	Purchase Orders	Delivery Schedule
Supply Chain Actors					
	Suppliers				
		1st Tier Suppliers			
			TRW		EDI-Out English	
			JCI		**FAX-Out German**	
			Visteon		Web-portal-Out English	
			Thompson		Web-portal-Out English	
		2nd Tier Suppliers			
	Manufacturers				
	Transporters/Logistics				
		Thompson				Web-portal-Out English
	Distributors				
	Retailers				
	End-Customers				

Identification of Interactions

The Interactions phase of the framework combines the work products of the two previous phases to produce an Interaction Matrix. The Interaction Matrix defines the relationships of the actors and the data elements.

The Interaction Matrix lists the actors defined in the first phase of analysis along the y-axis. The entries should reflect the same hierarchy defined in the grouping step of the first phase. Again, if necessary, the same actor may appear more than once in the list. Figure 3 shows an abbreviated example of an Interaction Matrix.

The data elements defined in the second phase are recorded along the x-axis. Similar data elements may be grouped together, if access to those data elements by external or internal actors will be the same. If certain data elements contained within a group of elements will be visible only to certain actors or groups of actors, then the data elements within the entire group must be listed individually.

The grid or data portion of the Interaction Matrix contains the current method of access by the actors to each of the data elements. The grid portion also lists the way in which the data flows, either in or out. It is also beneficial at this point to list the language in which the data elements are viewed, entered, or transmitted. The actors that were identified as major actors (80% of expenses or income) should be highlighted in the matrix. Interactions that are known to be problem areas should be marked in bold for easy identification in the next phase.

The Interaction Matrix will be large in scale, so it is recommended that a spreadsheet be used to manage it. Using a spreadsheet to manage the matrix also will allow for easy resorting of the matrix, which may prove useful in the next phase.

Review

The Interaction Matrix developed in the previous phase provides the basis for the Review phase. The Review phase is interested in examining the actors and the roles that they play in the supply chain and serves as a critical step before the Design phase can begin. The Review phase consists of several steps:

- **Review the Interaction Matrix for patterns or opportunities for improvement:** By reviewing the matrix, the analysis team may uncover problem areas that could be improved. For example, analysis may reveal that some first-tier suppliers are using EDI to transmit invoices, while others are using XML, and one or two are using a Web portal. The analysis team may find that because the Web portal already exists, it would take minimal effort to move the other suppliers to the Web portal, as well. In another example, analysis may reveal that certain retailers have restricted rights to certain data elements, while others do not. Examination of the data elements may uncover that the restricted data does not necessarily need to be restricted, and the restriction can be removed. The review of the matrix can lead to the creation of homogenized data groups that can be accessed by a greater number of actors. Homogenized data have the benefits of manageability and maintainability by both system developers and system users.

- **Create a new idealized Interaction Matrix:** The Interaction Matrix created in the third phase was very much a physical representation of the supply chain, as it currently exists. After review of the matrix in the previous step, a new idealized Interaction Matrix can be created.

  This new matrix should incorporate all of the opportunities for improvements identified in the previous step. The new matrix should see groups of actors having the same access to the same data elements and accessing those elements in the same fashion. If necessary, the matrix can be reorganized. Actors or data elements can be regrouped, as necessary, to create streamlined interaction.

- **Prioritize the development of new processes, technologies, and interactions:** The new idealized matrix will include many suggestions for changes to processes, technology, and/or interactions. It is not possible to implement all of the changes at once, and, for that reason, the suggested improvements should be prioritized for both design and development.

  First consideration should be given to the changes that affect the actors who account for the majority of expenses and income. At the same time, consideration should be given to the problematic interactions. Perhaps there will be a greater return by correcting those first, even if those interactions account for less of the business.

It is also at this point that the project plan and timeline should be updated to include new priorities and the estimated design and development efforts. The stakeholders will need the project plan to assess their support of the project.

- **Reaffirm stakeholder buy-in to the project:** A critical step in the Review phase is to reassess the project and reaffirm stakeholder buy-in. The idealized interaction matrix, along with the prioritizations and an updated project plan, is presented to the stakeholders for evaluation. This checkpoint in the process also serves as a critical communication step between the project team and the project stakeholders. The stakeholders at this point may wish to modify the prioritizations and/or project timing.

Design

Once the review has been completed and the prioritizations for design and development have been approved, the design of the new interactions can begin, based on the prioritizations set in the previous step. The Design phase should include progressive refinements of the data structures, architectures, interfaces, and procedural detail (Pressman, 2001) required to support the interactions of the supply chain. The Design phase is iterative in nature, in that design will be ongoing as increments are released to the Development phase.

Because of the way in which the actors, data elements, and interactions were analyzed in the first three phases, there are various possible methods of design that may be employed. Object-oriented, agent-oriented, and even structured design models can be produced with the data acquired from the first three phases.

During the Design phase, consideration should be given to the existing technologies and infrastructure within the supply chain. Analysis should indicate whether the existing infrastructure should be used, retooled, or rebuilt to support the integration efforts.

The Design phase will see the beginning of communications with the external actors that will be affected by the endeavor to integrate the supply chain. The internal design and development teams will need to work closely, not only with the design and development teams of the external actors to ensure smooth project delivery, but also with the external operators affected by the business process changes.

Development

The Design phase will release incremental designs to the Development phase so that development may begin as early as possible. In some cases, where only processes are to be changed, the design can proceed directly through to implementation.

Development may take the form of software development in the case where new applications are needed to address the idealized interaction framework, or development may be in the form of hardware technical solutions.

Much like the Design phase, the Development phase will be releasing developed increments to the Implementation phase so that implementation can begin as soon as possible.

Implementation

The Implementation phase will see the implementation of the changes to the interactions of the supply chain. The actual integration and streamlining of the supply chain environment happens at this stage.

As processes, technologies, and interactions are being implemented, the implementation team should be open to feedback from the internal and external actors and should relay this information in a timely fashion to the design and development teams. The implementation team serves as the eyes and ears of the project when it comes to dealing with the internal and external actors.

Given the sheer size and complexity of an ISCE, implementation will not happen overnight, but incremental changes to the actor interactions will continue to steadily move the supply chain toward true integration, thus maximizing all of the benefits that ISCEs boast.

Conclusion

As supply chain environments become more integrated and the information flow is streamlined, actors within the supply chain begin to realize real benefits to processes, time, and cost.

There are many obstacles that corporations face when integrating the supply chain. The major barriers to successful integration and implementation of supply chains are failure to properly identify goals and scope, overly complex projects, and projects that fail to properly address changes to the internal business processes. Steve Banker, Director of Supply Chain Solutions for the ARC Advisory Group says, "Integration issues are one of the prime reasons we see for implementations that fail to achieve the expected results. Given the emerging importance of supply chain wide initiatives such as visibility and event management, integration issues are becoming even more critical (www.redprairie.com, 2003)."

In response to the issues presented, this chapter proposed a seven-phase Interaction Approach methodology as a framework for analyzing and developing ISCEs. The framework focused on the actors, data elements, and interactions within the supply chain environment. The framework makes itself available to object-oriented, agent-oriented, or traditional design and development approaches.

As today's world becomes local and organizations become global, the level of integration of an organization's supply chain will be the critical factor of an organization's success.

References

Ballard, M. (2003). Preparation is key to supply chain management. Retrieved April 17, 2004, from *http://www.vnunet.com/Features/1144012*

Beamon, B. (1998). Supply chain design and analysis. *International Journal of Production Economics, 55*(3), 281-294.

Berkstresser, B., et al. (2004). Integrated supply chain analysis and decision support. *198-S1*, 1-10.

Evans, P., & Wurster, T. (2000). Getting blown to bits. In H. Vanharanta & R. Breite (2003), *A supply and value chain management methodology for the Internet environment* (pp. 1-42). Pori, Finland: Tampere University of Technology.

Fox, M., Barbuceanu, M., & Teigen, R. (2000). Agent-oriented supply-chain management. In H. Vanharanta & R. Breite (2003), *A supply and value chain management methodology for the Internet environment* (pp. 1-42). Pori, Finland: Tampere University of Technology.

Knoblock, C., & Minton, S. (1999). *Building agents for Internet-based supply chain integration.* Los Angeles: University of Southern California.

Koch, C. (2003). *The ABCs of ERP.* Retrieved April 17, 2004 from, *http://www.cio.com/research/erp/edit/erpbasics.html*

Lan, Y. (2003). A methodology for developing an integrated supply chain management system. *Proceedings of the Third International Conference on Electronic Business*, National University of Singapore (pp. 580-582).

Nurmilaasko, J., Kettunen, J., & Seilonen, I. (2002). XML-based supply chain integration: A case study. *Integrated Manufacturing Systems, 13*(8), 586-595.

Nurmilaasko, J., & Kotinurmi, P. (2004). *A review of XML-based supply chain integration.* Espoo, Finland: Helsinki University of Technology.

Pressman, R. (2001). *Software engineering: A practitioner's approach.* New York: McGraw-Hill.

Southgate, D. (2003). Making supply chain management work. Retrieved April 17, 2003, from *http://itmanagement.earthweb.com/cio/article.php/2214561*

Supply chain FAQs. (n.d.). Retrieved April 17, 2004, from *http://www.supply-chain.org/Resources/faq.htm*

System integration. (n.d.). Retrieved April 17, 2004, from *http://www.redprairie.com/Services/sysint.htm*

Taylor, D. (2003). Supply chain vs. supply chain. Retrieved April 17, 2004, from *http://www.computerworld.com/softwaretopics/erp/story/0,10801,86908,00.html?nas=ERP-86908*

van der Velde, L., & Meijer, B. (2002). *A system approach to supply chain design with a multinational for colour and coating.* The Netherlands: Delft University of Technology.

Vanharanta, H., & Breite, R. (2003). *A supply and value chain management methodology for the Internet environment*. Pori, Finland: Tampere University of Technology.

von Mevius, M., & Pibernik, R. (2004). Process management in supply chains—A new petri-net based approach. *Proceedings of the 37th Hawaii International Conference on System Sciences*, January 5-8, Big Island, Hawaii.

Chapter IX

Evaluation of the SCM Performance in Using of Global Logistics Information Technologies:
A Research Study in Hong Kong

Pui Yuk Chan
Hong Kong Baptist University, Hong Kong

Xinping Shi
Hong Kong Baptist University, Hong Kong

Abstract

This chapter explores and evaluates the performance of supply chain management (SCM) (i.e., effectiveness and efficiency) in using global logistics information technologies (GIST) (i.e., information technology [IT] and information systems [IS]) in Hong Kong firms. This chapter is organized as follows. First, previous research on the role of functional information systems for supply chain management is discussed. Next, the characteristics of information systems utilized for supply chain management are identified, based on factor analysis of sample data from 71 Hong Kong firms. Third, a conceptual model and hypothesis relating to utilization of information systems, information technology, and SCM performance will be identified. Discussion and recommendations are explained, based on the results.

Introduction

General Background

Many firms today are effective in the management of logistics and supply chain activities both as a prerequisite to overall cost efficiency and as a key to ensuring their ability to competitively price their products and services. Information systems (IS) and information technology (IT) are being used by leading-edge firms to increase competitiveness and to develop a sustainable competitive advantage (Bowersox, Donald & Daughtery, 1995). Although capabilities relating to information systems and information technology traditionally have been regarded also as key strategic resources, expertise in these areas is now thought to be among the most valuable and essential of all corporate resources.

In previous studies, the introduction of information technology by a firm for integrated supply chain management could lead to better efficiency and effectiveness (Goldhar & Lei, 1991). Integrated supply chain management utilizing information systems can enable a company to identify optimal inventory levels, reduce warehouse space, and increase inventory turnover (Kaeli, 1990; Kaplan, 1986; Shull, 1987). Porter and Millar (1985) suggested that the utilization of IT has a significant influence on the relationship among value chain activities, and Porter and Millar believe that management of information systems focus on cost reduction.

IS must have a potential to be a strategic weapon for improving supply chain management performances. In Hong Kong, a great number of companies focus their efforts on value-added activities, such as international marketing, product planning, product R&D, so forth. Hong Kong companies also are concerned about how information technology/ information systems can enhance the competitiveness and efficiency of the supply chain (Lee, 2000).

This chapter is organized as follows. First, previous research on the role of functional information systems for supply chain management is discussed. Next, the characteristics of information systems utilized for supply chain management are identified, based on factor analysis of sample data from 71 Hong Kong firms. Third, a conceptual model and hypothesis relating to utilization of information systems and supply chain management (SCM) performance are tested using path analysis. Discussions and recommendations are explained, based on the results.

Objectives of the Study

The objectives of the study are (1) to test a research model of organizational factors with IT/IS utilization in SCM performance; (2) to develop recommendations for companies in Hong Kong to establish an IT/IS utilization strategy for SCM performance; (3) to find out the critical factors of IT/IS in SCM; and (4) to establish the performance measurement criteria for using IT/IS in SCM.

Literature Review

Supply Chain Management

Supply Chain Management (SCM) deals with control of material and information flows, structural and infrastructural processes relating to transformation of the materials into value added products, and delivery of finished products through suitable channels to customers in order to maximize customer value and satisfaction (Narasimhan & Kim, 2001). As the Council of Logistics Management noted, logistics is that part of the supply chain process that plans, implements, and controls the efficient, effective forward and reverse flow and storage of goods, services, and related information between the point of origin and the point of consumption in order to meet customers' requirements. (Mentzer et al., 2001). By integration of internal functions within an organization (e.g., marketing, manufacturing, product design, and development) and effectively linking them between suppliers and customers, SCM can help to enhance competitive performances and meet the customers' requirements. (Narasimhan & Kim, 2001). The benefits of SCM can be obtained through the information linkage among various supply chain activities utilizing information technology and construction of integrated supply chain information systems (Bowersox, Donald & Daughtery, 1995).

Global Logistics Information Technology and its Role in SCM

Information systems in the logistics and supply chain can be defined as an interacting structure of people, equipment, and procedures that together make relevant, timely, and accurate information available to a logistics manager for the purpose of planning, implementation, and control (Kolter, 1986; Stenger, 1986).

According to Computer Sciences Corporation (2000), the highest priorities of critical current issues in information systems are on customers, productivity, and performances. These issues show that they can affect the use and function of information systems in SCM. Information systems were viewed as providing infrastructural support to the value chain and having an impact on competitiveness of products. Companies started to utilize information systems to directly influence the processes comprising the value chain (Rushton & Oxley, 1994; Williams, Nibbs, Irby & Finley, 1997).

Earl (1989) classified the scope of information technology into the following categories, according to whether information technology is widely used in the value chain or used only for information processing and whether it is applied to value creation or applied to the connection of the following value chain activities: (1) information technology (IT) that automates or improves every activity; (2) IT is used for connecting each value activity; (3) information systems facilities support, management, and implementation of value chain activities; and (4) information systems optimize or adjust the connection of each value activity. Earl can be applicable to the internal value chain but also be extended to the company's supply chain.

Porter and Millar (1985) suggested that utilization of IT has a significant influence on the relationship among value chain activities as well as on the physical aspects of individual value chain activities. The following propositions can be made: (1) Competitiveness comes from creating customer value; (2) value creating activities are interdependent in the value chain; (3) firms can optimize or integrate their value chain through IT to improve their competitiveness and efficiency. Porter and Millar (1985) suggested that proper use of information minimizes the costs while it maximizes the value, optimizing value chain activities and improving efficiency.

From the work of Earl (1989), Porter, and Millar (1985), the utilization of information systems shows the enhancement of competitiveness and improving efficiency in the value chain. To better understand the utilization of IS, general research questions should be considered. How can IS applications support, through information processing, value creation management for improving the value activities and logistics operation connection of activities? What are the performance measures for proving that IS influences the supply chain? Porter and Millar (1985) believe that management of information systems focus on cost reduction. The ability to pursue the cost reduction should be the criterion of IS utilization.

Performance Management

Apart from cost reduction, performance measures can be used to indicate the SCM performance in order to illustrate the IS utilization influence. According to the University of Tennessee Logistics Survey (1998), a list of measures varies the degrees of utilization among companies. Outbound freight cost, inventory count accuracy, and order fill are the highest three priorities for performance measures captured on a regular basis within the company. Logistics metrics suggested the use of measuring the performances with logistics key performance indicators (LKPI) (Frazelle, 2000). The logistics metric was divided into four categories: finance (cost), productivity, quality, and response time.

Organizational Factors

The role of individual and organizational factors also may play a part in the benefits of SCM. These factors highlight the importance of an organization's experience to implement information systems in order to enhance the competitive advantages and efficiency (Legare, 2002). A creativity framework adapted from organizational literature will be used to illustrate the implementation effort of IS in the company. The individual and organizational characteristics are used to improve the implementation of IS (Woodman, Sawyer & Griffin 1993). Amabile (1979, 1983, 1988, 1990, 1993) conceptualizes individual creativity from the framework. The framework includes three major components: domain relevant skills (task knowledge); creativity (cognitive abilities); and task motivation (intrinsic and extrinsic). Intrinsic motivation is an individual baseline attitude toward the task, and extrinsic motivation is individual perceptions of undertaking the task in a given instance. Organizational characteristics create the contextual influences that operate organization members to influence creativity. Organizational creativity is a group of creativity influences, such as leadership, reward, availability of information, and so forth (Woodman, Sawyer & Griffin, 1993). Kartz and Allen (1985) indicated that the importance of leadership and management is influenced the interaction of other components of the organization and acquisitions of resources. Another way to improve organizational creativity is through the structure and culture (Burgelman, 1983, 1984; Nislen & Hisrich, 1985). More organic structure, lack of formalization, and high levels of complexity establish a linkage between high levels of organizational creativity.

Global Logistics Information Technologies in SCM in Hong Kong

In Hong Kong, a large number of companies focus their efforts on value-added activities, such as international marketing, product planning, product R&D, so forth. Hong Kong companies also are concerned about how information technology/information systems can enhance the competitiveness and efficiency of a supply chain (Bowersox et al., 1995). In the meantime, Hong Kong SAR Government proposed the development of Digital Trade and Transportation Network (DTTN) for companies, which provides a neutral e-platform and IS for facilitating information flow and service integration locally and globally.

In summary, the influence of IS utilization (i.e., effectiveness and efficiency) can be shown through different roles of IS applications in supply chain value-creation management, logistics operation, and infrastructural support through using different performance measures, such as financial and non-financial indicators.

Research Model, Hypothesis and Methodology

Research Model

The research model is comprised of three parts. The first part relates to the relationship among the three different IS functions utilized in a supply chain. The second part demonstrates the relationship between IS utilization and supply chain performance. The third part relates to the relationship between organizational factors and different roles of IS utilization.

Hypothesis

This research model is derived from prior studies discussed in the literature review section (Closs, 1994; McFarlan, Warren & Mckenney, 1984; Porter & Millar, 1985). Information systems for information processing provide the basis for establishing strategic competitive advantage. IS utilization makes it possible to achieve strategic competitive advantage. IS plays the role of infrastructural support for direct IS utilization in supply chain functions.

> **H1:** IS/IT utilization for infrastructural support has a direct influence on IS use for value creation management.
>
> **H2:** IS/IT utilization for infrastructural support has a direct influence on IS use for logistics operation.

Prior research on the process of supply chain integration illustrate that internal integration with the company should precede external connection with suppliers and customers. (Bowersox, Donald & Daughtery, 1995). To identify the casual relationship between IS for values creation management and IS for logistics operation, we should consider the reciprocal relationships between two variables.

> **H3:** IS/IT utilization for value creation management has a direct influence on IS use for logistical operation.
>
> **H4:** IS/IT utilization for logistical operation has a direct influence on IS use for value creation management.

The previous studies introduce the relationship between IS/IT utilization and IS/IT in value chain processes, which would eventually enhance the company's supply chain activities. (Bowersox et al., 1995; Closs, 1994; McFarlan et al., 1984; Porter & Millar, 1985). The focus of IS utilization should shift from information processing to value creation and value connection. The change of IS/IT utilization focus would make it possible for IS/IT utilization to have a direct effect on supply chain competitiveness and efficiency.

> **H5:** IS/IT utilization for value creation management has a direct influence on supply chain performance.
>
> **H6:** IS/IT utilization for logistical operations has a direct influence on supply chain performance.

According to Legare (2002), organizational factors contribute to the implementation of IS/IT in order to enhance competitiveness and efficiency of work. Organizational factor is contributed by individual characteristics and organization characteristics within an organization (Woodman, Sawyer & Griffin, 1993). Therefore, the following hypothesis can be assumed:

H7: Organizational factors for an organization has a direct influence on IS/IT infrastructural support.

H8: Organizational factors for an organization has a direct influence on IS/IT utilization for value creation management.

H9: Organizational factors for an organization has a direct influence on IS/IT utilization for logistics operations.

Measurement

IS/IT Utilization Level

Based on prior research (Narasimhan & Kim, 2001) that classifies logistics activities in integrated supply chain management and functional information systems for logistics management, 12 traditional uses for information systems in supply chain management were identified: plant and warehouse location selection, order processing, resource management, production plan and process control, inventory and warehouse management, distribution and transportation management, sales and price management, consumer service and customer management, forecasting, network planning and design system, office information system, and accounting information system.

SCM Performance Management

The approach to measuring SCM performance has been used by previous researchers (Bowersox et al., 1995; Frazelle, 2002). Measures (Birou, Laura, Fawceet & Magan, 1998; Frazelle, 2002; Tan, Kannan & Handheld, 1998; Zaheer, Akbar, McEvily & Perrone, 1998) consisted of cost reduction, cycle time reduction, on-time delivery of materials from suppliers and customers, product quality, response time for customers and suppliers, the speed of suppliers' order processing, the reduction degree of response time of suppliers and customers, the accuracy of order processing for customers, the speed of order handling, and perfect order fulfillment.

Organizational Factors

The measurement is based on the vision, sense of business urgency, authority and responsibility, reward, skill knowledge, cognitive abilities, motivation, resources, structure, and culture (Legare, 2002; Woodman, Sawyer & Griffin, 1993). Knowledge, cognitive abilities, and motivation are items for individuals, while resources, structure, and culture are items for the organization.

Questionnaire Design

The questionnaire is composed of two parts. Part I consisted of three general questions. First, respondents were asked whether they have had experience using information systems in logistics before. Second, respondents would answer the current business type for their company. Finally, the respondents answered what positions they held. Part II consisted of 36 measurement items that were used to measure the extent to which items described are information systems application, organizational issue, and supply chain management performance. The scale ranged from Strongly Disagree (1) to Strongly Agree (7). Respondents needed to rank them.

Sampling

Target corporations to be sampled were small, medium, and large corporations that can carry out or provide value-added activities in a supply chain to other company in Hong Kong. The data were collected through questionnaires sent to supply chain managers. In order to raise the reliability of measurement, respondents were requested to consult with others in the SCM department or functional executives to answer the questions.

The group of respondents was randomly selected from companies under the Web directory and company directory in Hong Kong Trade Development Council's official Web site.

Data Collection

For the replied respondents, 72 copies of paper questionnaires were collected from a total of 200 copies distributed (36% response rate); one of them was invalid due to missing data (35.5% usable response rate); so the sample size of respondents was 71.

Research Findings

Descriptive Analysis

Of the 71 questionnaires from the respondents' companies, all of them had experience using information systems applications in logistics. In the current business type, one quarter (25%) of them was logistics service providers, 22.5% of them were distribution and transportation, nearly 20% of them were retailers. In the current position of respondents, nearly half of them (49.3%) were information technology or information systems managers, while nearly 41% of them were operation managers. Less than 10% of them were general managers. None of them was a chairman or chief executive officer. In organizational factors, authority, responsibility, and policies have higher means in the factors. In SCM performance, perfect order fulfillment, accuracy of order processing, and reduction of response time from customers have higher means in the factors.

Factor Analysis

Factor analysis by Varimax rotation was used to assess the constructs of 12 measured degrees of functional IS utilizations. According to Bryman and Cramer, factors that have eigen values greater than one were selected and extracted for further analysis. As a result, three factors were extracted, with 68.417% of total variance.

All 12 variables were found to be loaded on one of three factors with factor loading greater than 0.5, which is considered significant.

Table 1. Convergence/divergence of extracted factors

	Components (Extracted Factors)		
	1	2	3
Distribution and transportation management	.904		
Resource management	.870		
Forecasting	.848		
Order processing	.810		
Plant and warehouse	.707		
Accounting		.895	
Networking planning and design system		.827	
Office management		.784	
Sales and price management			.743
Inventory and warehouse management			.722
Service and customer management			.703
Production plan and process control			.650
Cronbach Alpha	0.8991	0.8149	0.7299
Eigen value	4.357	2.414	1.439
Cumulative variance %	36.309	56.428	68.417

The 12 functions identified can be divided into three major utilization areas. The detailed discussion about classification of characteristics of IS for supply chain management will be found in the discussion part.

Reliability

The reliability test result shows that the alphas of factors 1 to 3 are already greater than the reliability ratio (0.7).

Path Analysis

The multiple regression analysis technique was used to model the interrelationship among the latent variables. The R^2 are shown in Table 2.

To conclude, organizational factors do not have a significant direct effect on IS for Infrastructural support, Value Creation Management, and Logistics Operations. IS for Infrastructural support has a significant direct effect on the IS for Value Creation Management. IS for Value Creation Management has a significant direct effect on IS for Logistics Operations and SCM Performance. IS for Logistics Operations has a significant effect on IS for Value Creation Management.

After that, the total effect of each variable was calculated by the sum of the direct effect and indirect effect of variables. So, the total effect of IS for Value Creation Management was 0.560 (0.227+0.333 = 0.560). The total effect of IS for Logistics Operations was 0.550 (0.448+ 0.448 x 0.227=0.555). The total effect of SCM performance was 0.694 (0.445 + 0.227 x 0.445 +0.333x 0.445 =0.6942).

Table 2. Path coefficients of all variables

Variables	IS for Infrastructural Support	IS for Value Creation Management	IS for Logistics Operations	SCM Performance
Organizational Factors	1.868x10-2	0.199	-2.756x10-2	---
IS for Infrastructural Support	---	0.227*	-3.422x10-3	---
IS for Value Creation Management	---	---	0.448*	0.445*
IS for Logistics Operations	---	0.333*	---	-6.660x10-2
R2	0.00	0.260	0.180	0.180

Discussions and Implications

Discussion

The Classification of the Characteristics of IS/IT Utilized for Supply Chain Management

The 12 functions identified can be divided into three major utilization areas. The first is the IS/IT utilization for logistics operations that focuses on the connection among value chain activities within and outside of a corporation (plant/warehouse location, resource management, order processing, distribution and transportation management, and forecasting). The second is IS/IT utilization for value creation management that focuses on automation and improvement of the physical aspects of individual value chain activities (product/process control, inventory/warehouse management, sales/price management, and consumer service/customer management). The third is the IS/IT utilization for infrastructural support, which provides infrastructural foundation for the effective operation of value chain activities (network planning/design system, office information system, accounting information system).

The above classification into three clusters of utilization areas has validity in light of the previous studies on the classification of logistics activities and functional information systems for logistics management (Ballou, 1985; Bowersox et al., 1995; Cooper & Ellram, 1993; Gustin, 1994; Mentzer et al., 2001; Robeson & House, 1985; Stenger, 1986). The functional information systems comprising the same factor have high-level factor loadings on the factor, thus a high validity.

The results from the research model confirm H1, H3, H4, and H5 but do not lend support for H2, H6, H7, H8, and H9.

IS/IT for Infrastructural Support

First, IS/IT for infrastructural support does not have a direct effect on SCM performance. However, IS/IT utilization for infrastructural support has a direct effect on IS/IT utilization for value creation management, and IS utilization for value creation management has a direct effect on supply chain management performance. This means that IS/IT utilization for infrastructural support may have an indirect effect in enhancing supply chain management performance through IS/IT utilization for value creation management. It can be served as the foundations for IS/IT utilization for infrastructural support and provides the basis for establishing strategic linkages that direct IS/IT application to value chain activities, which can help increase the supply chain performance and consequently gain competitive advantage (Closs, 1994; Daugthery, 1994; Earl, 1989; Porter & Millar, 1985).

IS/IT for Value Creation Management

Second, It is about the structural relationship among the three IS/IT latent variables showing IS/IT utilization in a supply chain. The paths that are statistically significant indicate the structural relationship: infrastructural support → value creation management → logistics operations. This implies that IS for infrastructural support enhances the utilization level of IS for value creation management and brings about the use of IS/IT for logistics operations. The result shows that IS utilization for value creation management is a precondition for the utilization of IS/IT for logistics operations. In other words, IS/IT utilization for value creation management should be established in order to make sure that utilization of IS for logistics operations works properly. This coincides with the previous studies, which emphasize that improvements of each internal function should precede the external connection with suppliers and customers. IS/IT utilization strategy should be step-by-step in the processes.

IS/IT for Logistics Operations

Third, there is a relationship between the use of IS/IT for logistics operations and supply chain management performance. The result shows that the path coefficient is not statistically significant. This can suggest that benefits of IS/IT for logistics operations on supply chain management performances are not supported in the study sample. Partial explanation for this result was shown in the previous studies. The majority of the items related to the aspect of supply chain over which the logistics function does not exercise direct control. Another explanation could be that IS/IT utilization for logistics operations and its influence could be related to the firm's stage of supply chain integration. That means that it can be speculated that IS/IT utilization for logistics operations is more beneficial in firms that are pursuing external integration than in firms that are pursuing internal integration (Steven, 1989).

Fourth, there is a relationship between the utilization of IS/IT for logistics operations and IS/IT for value creation management. The relationship was not shown in the previous studies, especially utilization of IS for logistics operations → IS for value creation management. The path coefficient is statistically significant on these utilizations. This situation can be explained that the logistics operations in several areas, such as order processing, resource management, and distribution management, can support IS/IT for value creation management. Functional support of logistics operations serve as a factor for value creation management, such as inventory and sales, which provide value-added service to customers. The recursive relationship between utilization of IS/IT for logistics operations and IS/IT for value creation management shows that both functions of IS should not be ignored in the supply chain activities and should be well established in order to utilize both functions. Although the relationship between the use of IS for logistics operations and supply chain management performance is not valid, IS/IT for logistics operations can be served as an indirect effect on supply chain performance, so the logistics operations have some degrees of effect on the performance, such as time and costs.

Organizational Factors

Finally, there is a relationship of organizational factors with IS utilization of infrastructural support, IS for value creation management, and IS for logistics operations. There are no statistically significant effects on these IS utilizations. Some reasons can be explained in the following:

First of all, the respondents were mainly small and medium enterprises in Hong Kong. The size and structure of the organization are small. The functions of IS and IT are limited for their current business. Functions of IS and IT can be accepted, if the sales and revenues can be generated and recover the revenue. The functions and scope of IS and IT are limited due to the size of the organization and the amount of investments. A small group of staff is responsible for all functions in the business. Organizational factors, such as leadership, motivation, policies, skills, and knowledge may not be utilized fully, which concerned top managements in the companies.

Second, the respondents are from different businesses in Hong Kong, and, from the descriptive analysis, there is no dominated business groups in the study, so no clear dominated organizational factors can be found in the study. This may minimize the effect of organizational factors to different functions of IS utilization.

SCM Performance

From data analysis, respondents are mainly concerned about supply chain performance. Perfect order fulfillment, accuracy, and reduction of response time have a higher ranking, which mainly concerns the management in the company. The major concerns for the company are customer-orientated measurement.

To conclude, the companies are mainly concerned about customer-oriented performance measurement, because customers are sources for generating revenue and sales. Because of limited customer resources for small and medium enterprises, if they lose customers, they suffer the loss in sales and profits. This can motivate them to provide an excellent customer service with IS utilizations to gain their competitive advantages.

Implications

First of all, this research develops and validates a measurement scale for SCM performance on IS utilization in Hong Kong enterprises. This scale will give a preliminary foundation for facilitating research and analysis on SCM performance in Hong Kong and examines its casual relationship and its effect on SCM performances. The research model adapted by previous studies will enrich current findings and clarify the IS influences on SCM performances, thus enabling the further studies and theory development.

Second, this research provides empirically justified studies so that Hong Kong companies can understand that IS utilization has a likely effect on SCM performance. From the results of data analysis, ISIT for infrastructaral support and logistics operation has an indirect effect on SCM performance through value creation management, while value creation management has a direct effect on SCM performance. This gives an insight that IS value creation management is supported by infrastructural support and logistics operations in IS/IT functions in order to provide improved SCM performances.

Finally, knowledge of IS/IT utilization and organizational factors can be contributed to their consideration and planning for IS/IT strategy and adoption. IS strategy requires system preparations in term of gathering information about supply chain processes organization, environments, and user and customer requirements (Daugherty, 1994). Through these processes, companies can understand the user requirements and customer requirements on IS/IT functions in order to utilize fully the systems and improve SCM performances (i.e., efficiency and effectiveness of supply chain activities).

Recommendations

Supply Chain Integration

In order to utilize fully the information systems in the supply chain management, top management should consider developing an integration of supply chains. The existing study on supply chain management emphasizes that supply chain integration should be accomplished sequentially from internal integration to external integration. (Stevens, 1989). In a sense, Stevens presents the integration process of supply chain management comprehensively, starting with the integration of related functions to internal integration and on to external integration. Internal integration is characterized by full system visibility with a focus on tactical rather than strategic issues and an emphasis on efficiency rather effectiveness. External integration is characterized by completely sharing information on products, processes, and specification changes; technology exchange and design support; a focus on strategic rather than tactical issues and long-term planning. Management should have operational, tactical, and strategic issues in the process and IT development.

Continuous Support on IS/IT Development

Government and SMEs should cooperate together for continuous development of IT/IS in Hong Kong. According to the Hong Kong Logistics Council, the Digital Trade and Transportation Network study completed in December 2002 confirmed the strategic value of the initiative and the importance of jump-starting the project in order to enhance Hong Kong's competitiveness as an international logistics hub. It is a kind of e-platform for logistics systems to facilitate information flow and sharing among the trade and logistics industry stakeholders. These features can be suggested for implementation through the Digital Trade and Transportation Network in Hong Kong for SMEs provided by Hong Kong SAR Government. This can increase the efficiency and effectiveness of processes and organizations, which can enhance the competitiveness and SCM performance of the company.

Considerations of Implementing the IS Utilization

The utilization of IS actually can have an effect on SCM performance, but how can we make sure that IS can be fully utilized? Several suggestions can be raised as consideration before implementing IS utilization that fulfills the organizational requirements and performance requirements (Coyle, Bardi & Langley, 2002).

(a)   It is important to have a scientific and an intuitive understanding of customer and supplier requirements, as well as all supply chain participants. Information systems and technologies should be flexible and adaptable, depending on specific sets of needs.

(b)   It is important to see that logistics organizational strategies move from a functional to a process orientation. Emphasis on the latter assures a more meaningful measurement of relevant processes and assures more timely and accurate process feedback and process knowledge.

(c)   It is necessary for firms to create opportunities for interaction and team efforts among logistics managers and those others most knowledgeable about information technologies. Logistics managers need to know more information systems, and information specialists must develop greater insight into types of problems faced on a daily basis involving management of the logistics process.

(d)   Financial resources are needed to assure a smooth, full implementation. The employees' cooperation and use of the systems also are very critical.

Conclusion

This research empirically justifies that IT/IS for infrastructural support and logistics operations has indirect effects on SCM performance through value creation management. This gives an insight that IT/IS is fundamental for organizational value management, through value creation and growth and SCM performance, and further organizational performance can be enhanced. Finally, knowledge of IT/IS utilization and organizational factors can be contributed to their consideration and planning for IT/IS strategy and adoption.

Recommendations for further research and organizational IT/IS strategy are suggested, based on these outcomes, such as supply chain integration and consideration for implementation of IT/IS. IT/IS utilizations with strategic planning are believed to be more efficient and effective in SCM performances for organizations.

References

Amabile, T.M. (1979). Effects of external evaluation on artistic creativity. *Journal of Personality, 37,* 221-233.

Amabile, T.M. (1983). *The social psychology of creativity.* New York: Springer-Verlag.

Amabile, T.M. (1988). A model of creativity and innovation in organizations. *Res. Organ. Behav., 10,* 123-167.

Amabile, T.M. (1990). Within you, within you: The social psychology of creativity and beyond. In M.A. Runco & R.S. Albert (Eds.), *Theories of creativity.* Newbury Park, CA: Sage.

Amabile, T.M. (1996). *Creativity in context.* Boulder, CO: Westview Press, Inc.

Ballou, R.A. (1985). *Business logistics management.* Englewood Cliffs, NJ: Prentice Hall.

Baroudi, J.J., & Orlikowski, W.J. (1998). A short-form measure of user information satisfaction: A psychometric evaluation and notes on use. *Journal of Management Information Systems, 4*(4), 50.

Birou, L.M., Fawceet, S.E., & Magan, G.M. (1998). The product life cycle: A tool for functional strategic alignment. *Internal Journal of Purchasing and Material Management, 34*(2), 37-51.

Bowersox, D.J., & Daughtery, P.J. (1995). Logistics paradigm: The impact of information technology. *Journal of Business Logistics, 16*(1), 65-80.

Burgelman, R. (1983). A model of interaction of strategic behavior, corporate context, and the concept of strategy. *Academic Management Review, 3*(10), 61-69.

Burgelman, R. (1984). Designs for corporate entrepreneurship in established firms. *California Management Review, 26,* 154-166.

Byrne, P.M., & Markham, W.J. (1991). *Improving quality and productivity in the logistics processes: Achieving customer satisfaction breakthroughs.* Oak Brook, IL: Council of Logistics Management.

Closs, D.J. (1994). *Positioning information in logistics: The logistics handbook.* New York: The Free Press.

Computer Sciences Corporation. (2000). *13th annual critical issue of information systems management survey.* Cambridge, MA: Computer Sciences Corporation.

Cooper, M.C., & Ellram, L.M. (1993). Characterisitcs of supply chain management and implications for purchase and logistics strategy. *The International Journal of Logistics Management, 4*(2), 13-22.

Coyle, J.J., Bardi, E.J., & Langley Jr., C.J. (2002). *The management of business logistics: A supply chain perspectives.* Mason, OH: SouthWesten Thomson Learning.

Daugherty, P.J. (1994). *Strategic information linkage: The logistics handbook.* New York: The Free Press.

Earl, M.J. (1989). *Management strategies for information technology.* Englewood Cliffs, NJ: Prentice Hall.

Ellram, L.M. (1992). Partner in international alliances. *Journal of Business Logistics*, *13*(1), 1-25.

Frazelle, E.J. (2002). *Supply chain strategy: The logistics of supply chain management.* New York: McGraw-Hill.

Goldhar, J.D., & Lei, D. (1991). The shape of twenty-first century global manufacturing. *The Journal of Business Strategy, 12*(2), 37-41.

Gustin, C.M. (1994). *Distribution information system: The distribution management handbook.* New York: McGraw-Hill.

Kaeli, J.K. (1990). A company wide perspective to identify, evaluate, and rank the potential for CIM. *Industrial Engineering, 22*(7), 23-26.

Kaplan, R.S. (1986). Must CIM be justified by faith alone? *Harvard Business Review, 64*(2), 27-29.

Kartz, R, & Allen, T.J. (1985). Project performance and locus of influence in the R&D matrix. *Acadmeic Management Journal, 28*, 67-87.

Keebler, J.S., Manrodt, K.B., Durtsche, D.A., & Ledyard, D.M. (1999). *Keep Score.* Oak Brook, IL: Council of Logistics Management.

Kolter, P. (1986). *Principles of marketing.* Englewood Cliffs, NJ: Prentice Hall.

Lee, H.Y.H. (2000). Manufacturing support for Hong Kong manufacturing industries in southern China. *Journal of Supply Chain Management, 36*(1), 35-44.

Legare, T.L. (2002). The role of organizational factors in realizing ERP benefits. *Information Systems Management, 19*(4), 21-42.

Lummus, R.R., Vokurka, R.J., & Alber, K.L. (1998). Strategic supply chain planning. *Production and Inventory Management Journal, 39*(3), 49-58.

McFarlan, F.W., & McKenney, J.L. (1984). Information technology changes the way you compete. *Harvard Business Review, 62*(5), 98-103.

Mentzer, J.T., Schuster, C.P., & Roberts, D.J. (1990). Microcomputer versus mainframe usage in logistics. *Logistics and Transportation Review, 26*(2), 115-132.

Mentzer, J.T., et al. (2001). Defining supply chain management. *Journal of Business Logistics*, 22(2), 1-26.

Nislen, R., Peters, M., & Hisrich, R. (1985). Intrapreneurship strategy for internal markets—Cooperate, non-profit and government institution case. *Strategic Management Journal, 6*, 181-189.

Porter, M.E., & Millar, V.E. (1985). How information gives you competitive advantage. *Harvard Business Review*, 63(4), 149-160.

Ram, N., & Kim, S.W. (2001). Information system utilization strategy for supply chain integration. *Journal of Business Logistics,* 22(2), 51-75.

Robeson, J.R., & House, R.G. (1985). *The distribution handbook.* New York: Free Press.

Rushton, A., & Oxley, J. (1994). *Handbook of logistics and distribution management.* London: Kogan Page Ltd.

Shull, D.H. (1987). Migrating toward CIM. *Control Engineering, 34*, 161-164.

Stenger, A.J. (1986). Information systems in logistics management: Past, present and future. *Transportation Journal, 26*(1), 65-82.

Stevens, G.C. (1989). Integrating the supply chain. *International Journal of Physical Distribution and Material Management, 19*(8), 3-8.

Sullivan Jr., C.H. (1985). System planning in information age. *Sloan Management Review, 26*(2), 3-11.

Tan, K.C., Kannan, V.R., & Handheld, R.B. (1998). Supply chain management: Supplier performance and firm performance. *International Journal of Purchasing and Materials Management, 34*(3), 2-9.

University of Tennessee logistics survey. (1998). Council of Logistics Management. TN: University of Tennessee, Knoxville.

Williams, L.R., Nibbs, A., Irby, D., & Finley, T. (1997). Logistics integration: The effect of information technology, team composition, and corporate competitive positioning. *Journal of Business Logistics, 18*(2), 31-41.

Woodman, R.W., Sawyer, J.E., & Griffin, R.W. (1993). Toward a theory of creativity. *Academic Management Review, 18*, 293-232.

Zaheer, A., McEvily, B., & Perrone, V. (1998). The strategic value of buyer-supplier relationships. *International Journal of Purchasing and Materials, 36*(3), 20-26.

Chapter X

Supply Chain Management in China

Wei Liu
Nanjing University of Traditional Chinese Medicine, China

Wu Dan
Nanjing University of Traditional Chinese Medicine, China

Chen Xiao
Nanjing University of Traditional Chinese Medicine, China

Abstract

China, a high-developing country, is facing reform in the 21ˢᵗ century. Almost every company in China is undergoing some form of transformation in order to reduce costs and to maximize profits. It is easy to understand the position of the supply chain in a Chinese company, because taking good control of a supply chain means acquiring quality materials at lower costs, so that the cost of unit products will be dramatically reduced, and maximum profits will be made. However, in China, this is easier said than done. This chapter discusses the current status of supply chain management (SCM), challenges and solutions to SCM critical issues, and the role of technology used in SCM in China.

An Overview of SCM in China

Definition of Supply Chain Management

The theory behind the supply chain began to surface by the end of the 1980s, when global manufacturing was increasingly gaining popularity around the world. This is why supply chains were widely and mostly used in the manufacturing industry; before, it had evolved to become a new mode of management. Although the full potential of Supply Chain Management (SCM) had not been in place for very long, it is fair to say that SCM is being broadly accepted and highly regarded by many people in the industry. However, to some people, logistics and the supply chain are all the same. This misconception is gradually disintegrating due to the fact that we have begun to understand more about the supply chain for its close tie to e-commerce and to logistics. Meanwhile, SCM is becoming a worldwide issue. In China today, SCM is gradually being accepted and applied in logistics and in electronic commerce companies.

At present, because of the different applications of SCM, groups of organizations tend to have their own versions of the SCM definition; each is based on its own comprehension and experience. However, regardless of how different the terminology is or how the experience or the approach may vary; they all carry the fundamentals of the SCM at heart. In China, according to Tsinghua University, a modern management research center defines supply chain as the network that is made up of retailers, suppliers, manufacturers, and other business partners that reciprocally supply each other with raw materials,

Figure 1. A sample of supply chain

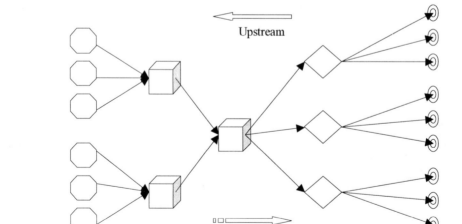

Figure 2. Value chain activities

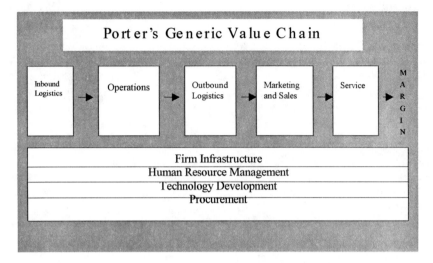

accessories, products, and service. Based on this definition, SCM brings all operation units in an enterprise into a supply chain that is managed as a whole. These operation units may include ordering, stocking, inventory, scheduling, production, transportation, marketing, selling, serving, finance, human resource management, and so forth. Figure 1 shows an example of a supply chain. Materials flow downstream, from raw material sources through a manufacturing level, transforming the raw materials into intermediate products (also referred to as components or parts). These are assembled at the next level to form products. The products then are shipped to distribution centers and then to retailers and customers.

This brings us to an important theory that is intimately related to the supply chain and SCM concepts: the Value Chain theory (Michael Porter theory). A Chinese professor describes the value chain theory as the latest development to SCM, because it brings the customer into management. ABC Technologies, an American company, and the Value Chain Authority defined the value chain as a high-level model of how businesses receive raw material as input, add value to them through various processes, and then sell the finished product to end customers. Its content starts from raw material investment and ends as final products sold to customers with different processes. At each process or activity, value is added to the product. These value-added activities are the components that build up the value chain. From Figure 2, we can see the primary activities and the support activities.

Current SCM Status in China

Supply chain management only recently (10 or more years ago) has been introduced and accepted in China. Therefore, it has not been applied at a large scale. At present, SCM has been adopted by several key industries, such as manufacturing, pharmaceutical, tobacco, and commerce.

Nowadays, competition among enterprises is forcing organizations to consider moving toward supply chains. SCM systems are becoming more common in today's expanding market to reach enterprise partners. A professional investigation has found that the majority of Chinese companies do not make use of SCM systems yet, but the potential is huge. According to this investigation, only a few enterprises own integrated supply chain systems. However, nearly 60% of enterprises that were investigated expressed that they were very interested in SCM or were in the process of implementing it.

In modern competition, each enterprise will adopt the most suitable way to achieve its goals when implementing an SCM approach. This is why there is no uniform way or a standardized approach for the implementation of an SCM system. However, when P&G and Wal-Mart successfully realized the importance of business cooperation by creating a supply chain in 1987, four cooperation concepts became the basic principles of the modern SCM standard. The concepts are collaboration, planning, forecasting, and replenishment. Collaboration enables business partners to create a win-win situation all around. Planning requires that all business partners coordinate scheduling issues related to the supply chain. Forecasting implies that all business partners of a supply chain share forecast information that is vital to the decision-making process. Replenishment provides members of a supply chain with the flexibility to plan for and to deal with emergency situations and other contingencies.

As the business world is continuously changing its ways of doing business, so are the rules of organizations competing for a slice of the market. It is no longer a race between discrete organizations; it's more like a supply chain competing with another supply chain for its share of the pie. Therefore, it is becoming crucial for an organization to review and to improve its management model, and to consider adopting SCM approaches tailored to its needs. Porter, the famous professor of strategic management at Harvard Business School, once indicated that SCM systems support manufacturing managers in making decisions that optimize the tradeoff between capital tied up in stocks and inventories vs. the ability to deliver goods at price and delivery dates agreed with customers.

There are two modes of a supply chain: promotion, the traditional supply chain mode, which means that salespersons promote products to customers designed according to product inventory condition; and demand drive, which is gaining popularity as more organizations are adopting it. Just as its name implies, this supply chain mode roots from customer demand, and the customer is the fundamental drive of all the operation issues in the supply chain. In demand drive mode, retailers gather relevant product information that customers purchase using POS systems. The data collected are analyzed and then sent to manufacturers. This allows manufacturers to prepare for the next consignment and to adjust delivery and stocking schedules accordingly. This also can influence manufacturers to update their manufacturing process schedules. As a result, raw material suppliers also can reschedule their processes, based on that same information.

Chinese SCM Market in 2003

It was reported (Zhao, 2003) that software sales in the Chinese market in the first quarter of 2003 were 75 million RMB, moderately increasing by 11.3% compared to the first quarter of 2002, while sales in the second quarter of 2003 were 82 million RMB, decreasing by 10.6% compared to the second quarter of 2002. This may be due to a 20% decrease in advanced SCM software (full-range capability).

Generally speaking, China's application of SCM software has not yet reached maturity. Most SCM systems are applied within medium to large organizations and enterprises, mainly in manufacturing, circulation, and energy sources. There is no evidence that suggests any use of SCM software by any government body or by any academic sector in any way.

Problems Chinese Companies Need to Solve

A survey shows that, although SCM in China has made remarkable progress in the past few years, it is still too soon to predict or even to speculate on how widely it will be accepted and embraced by the majority of Chinese businesses. It is typical for almost every Chinese company, whether private or public, to invest heavily in technologies such as Enterprise Resource Planning (ERP), but not in SCM technologies. The reason is that businesses in China would not see the value of switching to a new concept or a new technology; while existing technologies (e.g., ERP) can still deliver and satisfy their immediate business needs. Therefore, it is typical of Chinese decision makers to breathe life into a dying technology, so long as it achieves their goals. Therefore, millions of dollars simply are wasted on ERP, which is not suitable for every company and does not help most Chinese companies achieve their financial desires. So, in this view, we think that the first thing Chinese decision makers should do is to sit down and to take a clear view of their companies and their positions, and then decide how to lower costs and to increase revenue.

It is obvious that there is an abundance of SCM issues in China. The following are some major issues for Chinese decision makers to consider:

- The high cost of a supply chain implementation, about 5%-20% of net sales revenue.
- The high cost of inventory level. It is common for a Chinese company to keep stock for three to five months.
- The conflict between planning and actual capacity.
- Problems of product life cycle and R&D.
- External competition and other uncertain factors.
- The gap between customers' needs and the ability to meet demand.

Figure 3. SCM improvement cycle

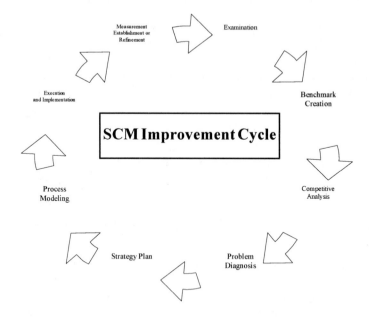

Some companies have found alternative ways to go around the conventional implementation of SCM to solve their supply problems. These companies have invested in information technologies (IT) to assemble an SCM platform. For example, some companies have set up Web sites to advertise demand of particular raw materials and to allow suppliers to bid for the sale; they also have made use of advanced technologies and software to manage their inventory levels of raw materials and products. As a result, companies that made use of IT to manage the supply chain reported remarkable cost reduction, maximum profits, and better work environment. China's Lenovo Group is one good example of such a company, as we demonstrate in the following section.

Successful Cases of SCM in China

Successful Cases with Electronic SCM—Lenovo Group Limited Company (Formerly Legend Group Limited)

Brief Introduction of the Company

Lenovo Group Limited, formerly Legend Group Limited, is a famous information technology (IT) corporation in the People's Republic of China (PRC). The company develops and markets its own Legend brand of personal computer (PC). Besides manufacturing and selling PCs, the company manufactures handheld devices, mobile handsets, and motherboards, and provides IT consulting services.

General View of Lenovo's SCM

Lenovo has established an integral system of SCM. The system has optimized the manufacturing process by transmitting the latest supply and demand information from sales to headquarters and to manufacturing, which has resulted in automatic adjustment of the overall product manufacturing process that is dynamically evaluated according to market demand. The SCM system also adjusts the supply and stock of hardware and groupware; it adjusts the manufacturing planning process to ensure on-time delivery and just-in-time access to the market. Lenovo's SCM system adopts Lenovo Wanquan* server, based on Intel® frame, and i2* SCM software. Based on these, Lenovo has constructed an excellent SCM project.

Factors that Affected the Development of Lenovo's SCM

Lenovo is the largest IT corporation in the PRC. Its own brand PC has been the country's best seller since 1997 and had a market share of about 27.0% in 2003, according to International Data Corporation.

From 1996 to 1999, Lenovo was able to establish its own in-house SCM system that led to the creation of its primary electronic SCM system. In 2000, Lenovo adopted an ERP system in order to be able to integrate the full range of its information systems. The reason was that Lenovo couldn't meet the continually changing demands of its consumers, if it was to rely solely on its centralized system, while its major operations wee distributed throughout China. Lenovo is not only a PC manufacturing company, it is also the largest IT corporation in PRC. Lenovo's business performance has proved that the group has deep insight into the PRC IT market and a clear grasp of user needs. The company engages in the manufacture and sales of desktop PCs, notebook computers, mobile handsets, servers, peripherals, and so forth. The product line of Lenovo's desktop PCs, notebook, and servers are arranged in Beijing, Shanghai, and Huiyang, and independently in Guangdong. Sales and retail branches have been established in almost every city. It is clearly apparent, given the nature of Lenovo business activities, that SCM had not only helped Lenovo to satisfy its customer demands, but also its SCM model is becoming a benchmark for competitive organizations to adopt.

A critical factor that led Lenovo to implement an SCM system is that the traditional sales model of purchasing raw materials, manufacturing products, marketing, and selling to the end customers had proved inefficient. This model had to be replaced in order to stay one step ahead of the competition in China's developing market. Lenovo's SCM system can now manufacture and deliver to end consumers, based on information gathered and analyzed according to customer demand. This SCM model enabled Lenovo to dramatically reduce costs, maximize its profits, and deliver the goods to end customers in less than half the time that it took under the traditional model.

Organizations should be able to dynamically adjust production levels and distribution channels according to current market environments and customer demand. This is particularly essential when organizations today strive to personalize services to accommodate for individual customer needs to achieve consumer loyalty.

In 2001, Lenovo began the testing and evaluation process of its SCM system. By June 2002, the system was successfully implemented and was able to manage three main product lines: desktop PCs, notebooks, and servers. According to an independent (zone) research, the SCM system was able to integrate the systems of Lenovo raw material suppliers, hardware and groupware providers, manufacturers, distributors, and, last but not least, the Chinese Academy of Sciences. The system provides the ability to gather consumer information for research to analyze and for manufacturing to adjust the production process, based on the given information. For instance, based on sales projection and figures, suppliers are notified automatically of any increase or decrease to the amount of supplies needed. It takes a few hours for the process to configure hundreds of products and thousands of material types and to coordinate with hundreds of suppliers. Products are shipped directly from manufacturing to franchisers, automatically by the system, which helps to reduce the inventory level and shorten stock time. For example, from 1995 to 1996, the stock time at Lenovo was shortened from 30 to 70 days down to 20 days, which shortened the average time of supplying product to 4.5 days, which, in turn, improved the rate of punctual consignment to 90%.

In China's current aggressive and highly competitive PC market, shorter stock time means more effective capital flow and faster feedback. For example, manufacturing at Lenovo receives more than 2,000 orders per day; the system can process the orders and create plans for manufacturing in a very short time.

Technical Platform of Lenovo's SCM: SCM Infrastructure

It is critically important for Lenovo to implement its system within a platform that is flexible, effective, and steady, and that allows for future expansion. Since Lenovo has been a rising star since its creation, progress and expansion at Lenovo is a process on its own. Every decision made at any location in Lenovo's vastly distributed enterprise can affect the overall operation of business. The complex nature of Lenovo's operations is inherited by its SCM system. Therefore, it is common for Lenovo to drop excess components and/or to add newly created modules whenever expansion is needed. Without a flexible platform, this can be cost ineffective and an agonizing exercise. Until 2002, Lenovo had adopted 10 modules of i2* software, and it will add more modules to accommodate for new requirements and/or expansion plans.

Lenovo chose Intel® as one of its strategic partners. The decision was strictly business. Intel had a proven record of successful implementations at Lenovo. Another reason to decide on Intel was the ease and flexibility of Intel platforms. To Lenovo, using Intel-based technologies meant plenty of support and expertise. For example, for future maintenance, Lenovo easily would find IT experts that are highly specialized in Intel technologies, while many other platforms lack such a feature. By using Intel platform based on Intel® frame, it only took 10 months for 30 engineers to complete the SCM system at Lenovo. Today, there are only 10 engineers that respond to maintenance and other technical issues.

A Vision for SCM Development in China

SCM Software Market in the Next Five Years

Experts predict that in the next five years, the SCM software market in China will keep increasing, due to the boom of the current Chinese economy. Total sales will increase from 409 million RMB currently to 954 million RMB in 2007. This is less than the 42.5% increase from 2003 to 2004. The reason is that, according to marketing experts, by 2005, while the Chinese market is heading toward maturity, a decrease to 10% is inevitable.

Future trends and projections indicate that large organizations and enterprises will still occupy the principal part of the SCM software market; the number of participants first will increase and then will tend to decline due to various reasons, including unsuccessful implementation of SCM systems. However, SME (small to medium enterprise) will show an interesting increase in the number of organizations that will implement SCM or include it as part of their future strategic plans. Manufacturing, circulation, and energy resources will still be ahead, and the leaders of the SCM software market will take up 80% of the market.

As the focus is shifting from the traditional supply-to-stock approach into supply-on-demand, SCM will include the following four characteristics:

- Real-time collaboration throughout the supply chain.
- Flexibility in choosing the supply and supplier.
- Responsibility that focuses on personalized customer service and on reducing the time required for delivering the goods to end consumers.
- New products will continue to be introduced to the market according to market trends and consumer desire.

At this stage in China, it is appropriate to say that, although the utilization of SCM technologies has made its mark and gained a remarkable acceptance by the business community, it is far from complete. SCM systems still need to keep up with upcoming new technologies. Capabilities such as real-time collaboration and event management have not reached full maturity yet. Seamless integration is the dream of all organizations; supply chains in China are striving to achieve this goal within the next five years, as we've demonstrated earlier.

How to Develop SCM Systems in China

Nowadays, competition between enterprises is becoming the strife between supply chains. SCM also is important for Chinese enterprises, although the development of SCM is in its primary phase.

Focus on the Essence of SCM: Cooperation and Long-Term Alliance Relationship

Instability, information systems propriety and compatibility integration issues, and the complex nature of the continuous change of user/system specific requirements are the root causes of SCM problems, which is why cooperation is the essence of SCM. The SCM market in China has not matured yet; so, it is important to strengthen the holistic stability of the SCM system through alliance. The establishment of an SCM system needs the participation of all partners in the supply chain. It was reported that cooperation among members of the supply chain had improved the performance level of the overall system by 40%, had reduced stock/inventory levels by 15%, had improved reliability and accountability by 15%, had reduced expenditure by 20%-30%, and had reduced logistics costs by 3%-5%.

Understand/Study the Chinese Environment

When developing SCM systems in China, Chinese enterprises should not copy the SCM modules from foreign enterprises, simply because the Chinese market has its own actual identity and its own requirements. Chinese enterprises should develop their own modules, based on research of the current economic atmosphere and by extracting or duplicating, in part, foreign models that can fit the Chinese market requirements. In addition, organizations in China should not duplicate other successful Chinese organizations, because each has its own requirements and identity.

Gradual and Incremental SCM System Development Approach

As we've pointed out earlier, the Chinese SCM market has not yet reached maturity. Therefore, Chinese organizations should adopt the step-by-step approach in implementing SCM systems. It is essentially important for Chinese organizations to research, study, and comprehensively understand SCM's different approaches and methodologies. Any SCM initiative should start from the inside out; it doesn't make sense for an organization to integrate or to cooperate with its business partners in the supply chain, if it cannot effectively and efficiently communicate within its own borders. It's also helpful and appropriate to start implementing SCM at the bottom, and then work your way up. Start with the less complex processes, such as warehousing and EIP management, and leave the complex processes to the last.

How Electronic Technology Can Be Used in SCM Development

SCM deployment involves new applications that require the integration of diverse business functions similar to enterprise resource planning (ERP) applications. The integration of all systems must start from inside the organization in order to be able to successfully integrate its external partner systems. To meet the demands for server availability, application performance, and quality of service in such an environment, IT departments must optimize the server architecture as well as the LAN, WAN, and extranet infrastructures.

Whether a business deploys a pre-packaged back-end application or a custom-built enterprise SCM system, three primary technical issues must be considered in the planning, design, and implementation process.

Availability

Performance and value of the SCM solution depends first and foremost on continuous application availability. Locating servers in a secure, central location and equipping them with redundant gigabite ethernet network connections can help to maximize the availability of critical application and database servers. Redundant backbone network components with dual gigabite ethernet uplinks virtually can eliminate performance degradation or outages due to heavy network traffic or equipment failure.

Quality of Service

Another important aspect of application performance is network quality of service (QoS), which ensures that high-priority or delay-sensitive traffic receives preference across the network. The network hardware should support advanced QoS features, including the IEEE 802.1p standard, which enables prioritization of ethernet traffic. Switches should allow administrators to designate priority on a per-port basis, and intelligent client devices should work with the switches to ensure that high-priority traffic retains preferred treatment.

Security Issue

The unprecedented external access to corporate data inherent in an SCM solution makes security a primary concern. Firewall security, VPN technologies, policy-based authentication capabilities and access control, and isolation between ports are essential to protect both sensitive data resources and sensitive traffic.

Mobile SCM in China

It is clear that, in the following years, MT (mobile technology) will affect the development of SCM. As mobile technology is on the rise, the utilization of its capabilities and services by businesses is endless. SCM is one of the candidates that is yet to see how it can take advantage of mobility. Anywhere-anytime will be commonplace to business. This means easy and instant connection to suppliers and purchasers; cost will be lowered dramatically, and efficiency will be increased exponentially. But the question remains: Is it still a long way for Chinese companies to go mobile? The answer is obviously *no*. Today, there are two major operators in china—China Mobile and China Unicom—who provide customers with various mobile services, including SMS, MMS, WAP, GPRS, and so forth, which provide the confidence and incentives for Chinese companies to invest and to maximize their technology. There is already a number of organizations that use SMS, WAP, and various mobile technologies to communicate. For those companies to fully consider using mobile technologies in their SCM systems is not out of reach.

Furthermore, in today's time-driven environments, time means money; the quicker an organization can access information, the quicker it gets ahead of the competition. It was

Figure 4. Mobile SCM platform

Figure 5. Mobile model of ChannelOK

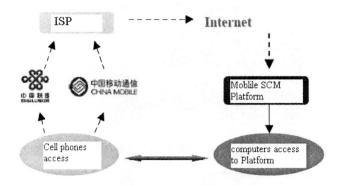

reported (Zhao, 2002) that almost two people out of 10 in China use mobile technologies, such as laptops and cell phones. So, applied MT in China does not seem to be an impossible mission. Connection facilities, standards, and protocols are needed to ensure successful SCM implementation.

One mobile SCM platform called ChannelOK (QuDaoTong) has been developed by Stateline SCM Research Center, Shanghai. This production facility uses cell phones to send, receive, process, and customize orders to end consumers. The order is sent as an SMS and is received by a system that promptly processes the information and then sends it to the supplier for confirmation. The supplier responds to the sender and decides to act, based on orders instructions and specifications.

Conclusion

SCM is a new concept in China, as we demonstrated throughout this chapter. It will be a while before the Chinese marketplace can fully adopt the full range and capabilities of the different approaches of SCM. In this chapter, we discussed SCM as a concept and a tool that provide businesses with easy access to needed information for making decisions. Customer satisfaction and expectations are met by building quality products at a price and delivering them on time. This is achieved by implementing a successful supply chain. We outlined the challenges and issues surrounding SCM in China. We also pointed out that understanding the current Chinese environment is essential to successful SCM initiatives. We believe that China is changing and eventually will reach IT maturity sooner than we expect.

References

Berger, A.J., & Gattorna, J.L. (2002). *Supply chain cyber mastery: Building high performance supply chain of the future*. China: Publishing House of Electronic Industry.

Christopher, M. (2000). The agile supply chain—Competing in volatile markets. *Industrial Marketing Management*.

Copper, M.C., Ellram, L.M., Gradner, J.T., & Hanks, A.M. (1998). Meshing multiple alliance. *Journal of Business Logistics*.

Hewitt, F. (1994). Supply chain management redesign. *International Journal of Logistics Management*.

Kuang, K.W., & Wang, X.M. (1999). *Information system analysis and design*. Beijing: University of Tsinghua Press.

Persson, F., & Olhager, J. (2002). Performance simulation of supply chain designs. *International Journal of Logistics Management*.

Song, H. (2001). *Cases of modern logistics and supply chain management*. Beijing: Economics and Management Press.

Stateline SCM Research Center. (2003a). *The electronic platform of supply chain management*. China Machine Press.

Stateline SCM Research Center. (2003b). *Definition of supply chain management*. Beijing: China Machine Press.

Stock, G.N., Greis, N.P., & Kasarda, J.D. (2000). Enterprise logistics and supply chain structure: The role of fit. *Journal of Operational Management*.

Wang, Y.J. (2001). *Methods of prototyping supply chain management and data*. Beijing: University of Tsinghua Press.

Wu, M. (2003). *Building electronic platform for supply chain management*. Stateline SCM Research Center

Zhang, C., & Huang, X.Y. (2002). Optimise supply chain management in modeling.

Zhao, D.J. (2003). Value created from supply chain management. Stateline SCM Research Center.

Zhao, L.D. (2002). Supply chain management in modern age.

Zhao, L.D. (2003). *Practice and theory of supply chain management*. Beijing: China Machine Press.

Chapter XI

A Multi-Objective Model for Taiwan Notebook Computer Distribution Problem

Ling-Lang Tang
Yuan-Ze University, Taiwan

Yei-Chun Kuo
Vanung University, Taiwan

E. Stanley Lee
Kansas State University, USA

Abstract

A multi-objective model of global distribution for the Taiwan notebook computer industry is proposed. The proposed two-stage approach involves a mixed integer linear programming model and the fuzzy analytic hierarchy process (AHP) approach. The analytic method provides quantitative assessment of the relationships between manufacturers and customer service. To show the effectiveness of the proposed approach, a Taiwan notebook computer model is solved. The results of this multi-objective model show some dynamic characteristics among various performance criteria of the outbound logistics.

Research Background and Objective

Today's global economic environment is causing profound changes in how companies manage their operations and logistic activities. Empirical evidence suggests that vertical integration along the supply chain, modeled earlier by General Motors and Compaq, is not adequate. More and more companies are replacing vertical integration with vertical coordination and are developing long-term arrangements with outside suppliers. This phenomenon forces corporations to modify their logistics organization and invent fresh solutions; that is, alternative means of transportation, new sites for warehouses, or reallocation of inventory. In response to these infrastructure problems, companies must change their operating approaches by considering (1) increasing the procurement areas by implementing international sourcing policies, (2) pursuing wider geographical spread and greater mobility of production facilities, and (3) implementing worldwide distribution for marketing (Dornier, Ernst, Fender & Kouvelis, 1998).

Another aspect is the change in economic conditions on international trade. Taiwan, for example, had been a preferred site for offshore assembly in the semi-conductor and other assembly-required industries because of cheap labor. However, following local currency (NT) appreciation, labor was no longer cheap, and startup costs became much larger. As a result, industries moved the assembly function offshore, while Taiwan moved toward high-tech industries. In general, companies have three options for focusing their facility networks. These include focusing by market, by product, and by process. Successfully locating offshore also requires a commitment to strategic planning.

In order to carry out the above-mentioned changes and to obtain an efficient global network, the use of multi-objective optimization is ideally suited. The objectives of the logistic network are to meet the competitive priorities of the various products at various markets. Some of the priorities are cost, quality, service, and flexibility. These priorities often are incommensurate, both quantitatively and qualitatively, and carry different weights of importance. This leads to a complex problem of trade-off using the decision maker's utility or preference function. Reliable construction of a utility function, however, may be too complex, unrealistic, or impractical (Zeleny, 1982). Thus, the set of non-dominated solutions, which are not the optimum, are used frequently. To overcome this difficulty, a fuzzy set approach is used in this investigation.

In order to optimize this multi-objective global network and to help the CEO to balance between cost and customer service by selecting manufacturers, warehouse locations (Hubs), and customer assignments, we propose a combined multi-objective and fuzzy analytical hierarchy process (AHP) approach. In addition to the fuzzy aspects, the multi-objective optimization is carried out by the use of a mixed integer linear programming. The logistic problems of the computer industry and fuzzy AHP are discussed in the next two sections. The next section introduces the mathematical model, which is then used to model and to solve a typical problem; namely, a Taiwan notebook computer example in the second to last section. The final section discusses some conclusions and suggests areas for further research.

Logistic Problems of Notebook Computer Industry

In reacting to market conditions, most of the notebook industrial is to improve or shorten the delivery lead time and to reduce the inventory, but not to reduce production quantity (Rutherford & Wilhelm, 1999). Thus, shortened delivery time is the key to success for the notebook industry. A product produced at one point has no value to the prospective customer, unless it is moved to the point where it will be consumed. Transportation achieves this movement, which, across space or distance, creates value or utility. Time utility mostly is created or added by the use of a warehouse to store the product until it is needed. If a product is not available at the precise time it is needed, expensive repercussions, such as lost sales, customer dissatisfaction, and production downtime, may occur (Lambert & Stock, 1993).

Another aspect is customer satisfaction, which can significantly influence a firm's success and overall sales. Distribution is closely related to customer service, so the logistic department plays an important role in the establishment of customer service goals and objectives (Johnson, Wood, Wardlow & Murphy, 1999). Logistic managers must be aware that the goals and objectives that they want to establish are related to cost. Relatively small increases in the overall level of customer service can increase the costs substantially.

The Dell Company's direct business model eliminated the cost of inventory and the cost of reselling. This company used information and technology to blur the traditional boundaries in the supply chain among suppliers, manufacturers, and end users. This blur of the boundaries has been named *virtual integration*. Technology enhances the economic incentives to collaborate, because it makes it possible to share among the various entities the design databases and methodologies, and thus, the product can speed to the market with shortened time. As Simchi-Levi, et al. (2000) pointed out, the whole idea behind virtual integration is that it lets you meet customers' needs faster and more efficiently than any other model. While Compaq, IBM, and Hewlett-Packard all announced plans in 1998 to emulate portions of Dell's business model with various build-to-order (BTO) plans, all of them had difficulty making the transition. Many of them are

Figure 1. A framework of global logistics for a notebook computer company

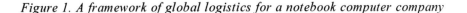
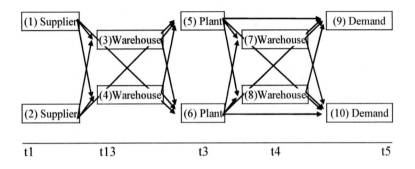

moving to a target inventory level of four weeks, while Dell maintains just eight days of inventory, which allows Dell to turn over inventory 46 times a year.

Tang and Yu (2000) developed algorithms based on these models in order to compare the operational cost by adopting different BTO or configuration-to-order (BTO) logistic models (see Figure 1). They applied BTO/CTO logistic models to analyze the interactive relationships among the computer firms, the material suppliers, the distribution centers, and the customers. Based on this analysis, these authors built various mathematical models to represent the logistic distribution systems. Although this research has investigated different logistic systems, it only considered cost and ignored other objectives. In this chapter, we will use a multi-objective networking with the consideration of time and service to simulate and to optimize the logistic models.

Fuzzy AHP Approach

To obtain the most appropriate supply chain structure, one must assess the trade-off between cost and service. Services are influenced by delivery time and service rating. Thus, three criteria (i.e., total cost, delivery time, and service rating) will be considered. However, these criteria are frequently in conflict. For example, shorter delivery time most probably will require the opening of more warehouses and, hence, higher operating costs. Furthermore, the relationships between delivery time and service rating and between total cost and service rating may not be known a priori (Tyagi & Das, 1997).

Because of the complexity of the logistic model and the existence of unknown and difficult to define factors, information frequently is expressed linguistically. For example, service quality can be expressed as *very good, good, average, bad,* and *very bad* (Lee & Li, 1993). These linguistic expressions can be represented by fuzzy membership functions. The use of fuzzy data can be incorporated into the AHP. Thus, the model can be classified according to the type of information (crisp or fuzzy data), the number of decision makers (single or multiple), and the number of criteria (single or multiple). Qualitative, linguistic data should be converted into quantitative data by the use of fuzzy sets.

Figure 2. A hierarchical system

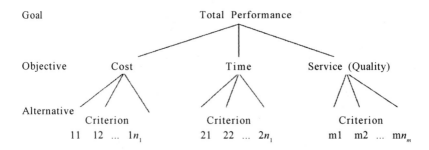

The interrelationships among the various objectives are best expressed by the use of a hierarchical structure, as illustrated in Figure 2. Under this type of hierarchical structure, only the performance criteria in the bottom level are given by the experts; performance of the other criteria not in the bottom level can be obtained by the use of aggregation (Lee & Shih, 2001).

The major advantage of hierarchical performance structure is as followings:

1. To express the interrelationships among all the criteria in a brief and clear form.
2. To cluster criteria into a category according to their characteristics and to allocate them in a suitable position such that we can identify and review the criteria performance within and between each category.
3. To obtain the performance level by level; the evaluation results can give the actual achievement for each criterion, which can be used to improve the system.

AHP can be used to determine the comparative weightings of the various criteria. It can decompose a complicated system into a well-organized structure, based on the hierarchy. By the use of pair-wise comparison between the various criteria, a more credible and more objective criterion weighting can be obtained. The quantifying scales for pair-wise comparison can be separated into five levels where:

- '1' represents equal importance;
- '3' represents weak importance;
- '5' represents strong importance;
- '7' represents demonstrated importance; and
- '9' represents absolute importance.

The intermediate values 2, 4, 6, and 8 represent the values between the two adjacent judgments (Saaty, 1980). For more detailed fuzzy AHP, the reader can consult the paper of Hon, Tang & Peng (2001).

The Mathematical Problem and Solution Approach

Various investigators have studied the time-cost trade-off problem. For example, Kanda and Rao (1984) investigated penalty costs for delaying certain events by treating the problem as a network flow problem. Hamacher and Tufekci (1984) transformed the problem treated by Kanda and Rao (1984) into a sequence of algebraic flow problems that have the ability to handle different objective functions.

Tyagi, et al. (1997) considered the location-distribution problem of a wholesaler and developed a procedure that can be adapted to a given wholesaler's business environment. A multi-objective approach was proposed to solve the wholesale's procurement and distribution problem. The three performance measures are cost, delivery time, and customer service rating. A mixed-integer linear programming model was developed to generate the alternatives, which were then evaluated by the AHP.

In this chapter, we formulate the time-cost trade-off problem as a multi-step, multi-objective decision problem by the combined use of mixed integer linear programming, fuzzy sets, and AHP. We assume that the decision maker ranks the criteria based on their relative importance and specifies the minimal acceptable levels, which would represent the minimum standards that must be fulfilled. These minimal levels can be obtained by considering the competitive environment. The mixed integer linear program is solved first for the objective of the top-ranking criteria. Next, the objective functions for the lower-ranking criteria are solved successively. While solving the lower-ranking objectives, a pre-specified percentage of sacrifice of the top-ranking criteria is allowed by the use of a suitable additional constraint.

Instead of obtaining one solution with a fixed set of weights, a number of alternative solutions using different weights or priority were obtained. The decision maker can subjectively select the most satisfactory solution among these alternatives.

The nomenclature of the different symbols is listed in the following:

TC	Total cost
C_j	Unit processing cost of node j, $j \in N$
C_{ij}	Unit transportation cost of path ij, $ij \in A$
t_{ij}	Time of transportation from node i to node j, $ij \in A$
B	A large positive number
D_m	Demand of customer m, $m \in M$
$\hat{T}$	Maximum acceptable delivery time
t_j	Processing time of node j
$\hat{V}_i$	Maximum capacity of warehouse or plant i, $i \in N$
$\delta_{im,p}$	=1 if path im fall in the pth route; =0, otherwise, $im \in A, p \in P$
$\delta_{ij,p}$	=1, if path ij fall in the pth route; =0, otherwise, $ij \in A, p \in P$
V_i	Capacity of plant or warehouse i, $i \in N$
X_{ij}	Amount shipped from node i to node j, $ij \in A$
y_p	=1, time of path p ≤ maximum acceptable delivery time; =0, otherwise
f_p	Amount in path p
R	Average service rating
r_{im}	Service rating of node i with respect to customer m

Objective

a) Min $TC=\Sigma_i\Sigma_jC_{ij}X_{ij}+\Sigma_jC_jV_j$ (Minimize total cost)   (1)

b) Min $DT=\Sigma_j\delta_{ij,p}\,(t_{ij}+t_j)\,y_p$ (Minimize delivery time)   (2)

c) Max $R=\Sigma_m\Sigma j(\delta_{im,p}+\delta_{ij,p})r_{im}D_m/\Sigma_mD_m$ (Maximize average service rate) (3)

s.t.

$\Sigma_p\delta_{ij,p}f_p=X_{ij}$ $\forall\,ij\in A$ (4)

$f_p\leq B\,y_p*\delta_{ij,p}$ $\forall\,p\in P$ (5)

$\Sigma_j\delta_{ij,p}\,(t_{ij}+t_j)\,y_p\leq\hat{T}$ $\forall\,p\in P$ (6)

$\Sigma_j\Sigma_p\delta_{ij,p}f_p=V_1$ $\forall\,i\in N$ (7)

$V_i\leq\hat{V}i$ $\forall\,m\in M$ (8)

$\Sigma_i\Sigma_p\delta_{im,p}f_p\geq D_m$ $\forall\,p\in P$ (9)

$f_p\geq0$ $\forall\,p\in P$ (10)

$y_p\in\{0,\,1\}$ $\forall\,p\in P$ (11)

$\delta_{ij,p}\in\{0,\,1\}$ $\forall\,p\in P$ (12)

The outbound logistics problem is an NP competed problem. In this chapter, LINDO software will be used to solve it.

An Example of a Taiwan Notebook Computer Company

In the notebook computer industry, orders for key components must be placed months in advance. Furthermore, the order quantity subsequently can be changed by only limited amounts. Because technologies quickly become obsolete, suppliers are reluctant to make the investments necessary to provide sufficient production capacity to allow manufacturers more flexibility. This means that manufacturers must decide months in advance which models to produce and in what quantities. A firm's ability to change production levels to react to unforeseen demand is tightly constrained. For example, to increase the production of one model by 10% within one month requires that every supplier be able to increase deliveries by that amount within that time. This increase is not always possible.

To illustrate the proposed approach, a problem with two raw material warehouses, two plants, two finished-product warehouses and two demand points is solved. For the details of the data used, the reader is referred to the paper by Tang and Yu (2000).

Generation of Optimization-Based Alternative Solutions

- **Step 1:** Specify the lowest acceptable levels of delivery time and service rating. Total cost is the most important criterion. Delivery time is the next ranked criterion with 10 days as the maximum permissible delivery time to any customer. Average service rating, the third criterion, must be maintained at no less than 60%.

- **Step 2:** Since the total cost (TC) is the most important criterion, optimize it subject to the acceptable levels of all criteria. For this example, there is a feasible solution, and the objective function value of this problem, NT$294,630,300, is regarded as the target cost.

- **Step 3:** Generate the first alternative as follows: add a constraint $TC \leq 294,630,300$ to keep the total cost at the target value, and minimize T in order to optimize the next ranking criterion, delivery time. The optimum value of T is 5.5 days. Now, maintaining delivery time at 5.5 days, maximize R, the service rating. The optimized value of R is 71.79%. The alternative routes are shown in the last row of Table 1. The route 1-5-9 means that the demand from Taiwan is 230 sets; it is manufactured by Taiwan plant (node 5) with the materials procurement from the Japan supplier (node 1). The other one, route 7-10, is 13,908 sets from a U.S. customer, which is supplied by the finished-product warehouse in Taiwan (node 7).

- **Step 4:** Generate the second alternative by allowing TC to be added to NT$319,912,500. Repeat Step 3 first to optimize the delivery time (five days), and then to optimize the service rating (69.15%).

- **Step 5:** Generate three more alternatives with allowable cost increasing; the criteria values and the route selections for these alternatives are shown in Table 1 and in Figure 3.

Table 1. Generating five alternatives of the example

Alternative	Actual Cost	Delivery Time (days)	Service Rating (%)	Selected Route
A1	294,630,300	5.5	71.79	1-5-9 7-10
A2	319,912,500	5	69.15	1-5-9 3-5-10
A3	320,517,200	4	71.58	3-5-9 3-5-10
A4	465,125,200	3	73.80	3-5-9 8-10
A5	475,802,500	1	77.52	7-9 7-10

Note: The number of route is location of node

Figure 3. Delivery time (days) vs. allowable cost

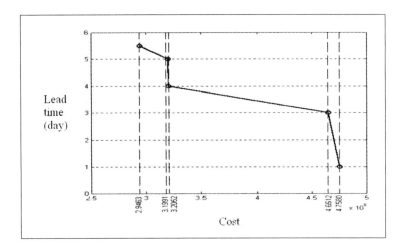

Evaluation of the Alternatives by Analytic Hierarchy Process

In this chapter, we assume that the service ratings for all warehouse-customer pairs are expressed as a score between zero and 100 to reflect the overall quality of service expected or perceived by a customer.

- **Step 1:** Let us assume that the decision maker has specified the relative weights of total cost, delivery time, and service rating to be 50%, 30%, and 20%. These weights should be determined by using the comparative importance of various criteria in Section 3.

- **Step 2:** We now illustrate the process of assigning the relative preferences of the five alternatives for each criterion. In AHP (Saaty, 1994), the alternatives must be compared with each other on a ratio scale of 1 to 9, with 1 representing equal preference and 9 representing extreme preference of one alternative over the other (see Table 2).

- **Step 3:** To rank the five alternatives, we use Expert Choice to develop the composite weights. The ranking of the alternatives is summarized in Table 3; alternative A1 is the best alternative.

To illustrate the trade-offs made in the example, delivery time and service rating have been plotted as a function of the corresponding allowable cost of the five alternatives in Figures 3 and 4. It may be observed that, as the allowable cost increases, the delivery time decreases. This trend is predictable, since higher costs should result in improved measure of delivery time due to a direct trade-off between the two criteria. However, no

Table 2. The preference for five alternatives

<table>
<tr><td rowspan="2">Cost</td><td>Alternative</td><td>T1</td><td>T2</td><td>T3</td><td>T4</td><td>T5</td></tr>
<tr><td>MNTD</td><td>294.630</td><td>319.913</td><td>320.517</td><td>965.125</td><td>975.803</td></tr>
<tr><td></td><td>Preference</td><td>9</td><td>8</td><td>3</td><td>2</td><td>1</td></tr>
<tr><td rowspan="3">Time</td><td>Alternative</td><td>D1</td><td>D2</td><td>D3</td><td>D4</td><td>D5</td></tr>
<tr><td>Days</td><td>5.5</td><td>5</td><td>4</td><td>3</td><td>1</td></tr>
<tr><td>Preference</td><td>1</td><td>2</td><td>4</td><td>6</td><td>9</td></tr>
<tr><td rowspan="3">Service</td><td>Alternative</td><td>S1</td><td>S2</td><td>S3</td><td>S4</td><td>S5</td></tr>
<tr><td>Rating %</td><td>71.79</td><td>69.15</td><td>71.58</td><td>73.80</td><td>77.52</td></tr>
<tr><td>Preference</td><td>3</td><td>1</td><td>2</td><td>5</td><td>9</td></tr>
</table>

Table 3. AHP ranking for five alternatives

Alternative	Composite Weight Calculation for each alternative	Composite Weight
A1	$(0.5)(9)/(9+8+3+2+1)+(0.3)(1)/$ $(1+2+4+6+9)+(0.2)(3)/(3+1+2+5+9)$	0.37
A2	$(0.5)(8)/(9+8+3+2+1)+(0.3)(2)/$ $(1+2+4+6+9)+(0.2)(1)/(3+1+2+5+9)$	0.054
A3	$(0.5)(3)/(9+8+3+2+1)+(0.3)(4)/$ $(1+2+4+6+9)+(0.2)(2)/(3+1+2+5+9)$	0.14
A4	$(0.5)(2)/(9+8+3+2+1)+(0.3)(6)/$ $(1+2+4+6+9)+(0.2)(5)/(3+1+2+5+9)$	0.175
A5	$(0.5)(1)/(9+8+3+2+1)+(0.3)(9)/$ $(1+2+4+6+9)+(0.2)(9)/(3+1+2+5+9)$	0.232

such consistent improvement trend is observed for service rating, due to a lack of direct trade-off between cost and service rating. Since service rating is the lowest ranking criteria in our example, it is allowed to be optimized only after the delivery time first is optimized for the allowable cost. Hence, if a different ranking is assigned to the previously discussed criterion, a different set of alternatives should be generated.

When the total cost is NT$294,630,300, the solution with the delivery time 5.5 days and service rating 71.79% is obtained. When the total cost increases to NT$320,517,200, the delivery time decreases to four days, and the service rating decreases to 71.58%. If minimum total cost is the only target, the single objective solution of TC obtained is NT$283,348,400. It is lower than alternative A1 solution with delivery time of 6.5 days and service rating of 67.49%. It is different between a multi-objective approach and single objection programming.

Figure 4. Service rating vs. allowable cost

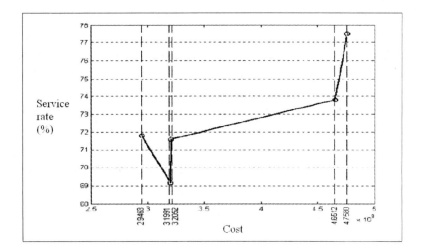

Conclusion

In the area of logistics and supply chain management, a large amount of literature exists to investigate and to discuss warehouse location selection and the assignment of distribution route. Most of these studies use single objective programming to generate the maximum or minimum solution. However, for almost all company decision makers, it is necessary to consider more than one criterion. Some of these criteria are cost, delivery time, service, demand, profit, and so forth.

In this chapter, we develop a multi-objective decision process to help the decision maker to select the material supplier, plant, and warehouse locations in order to obtain the best trade-offs between cost and customer service.

The proposed analytic method provides quantitative assessment of the relationships between manufacturers and customer services. Computation results of the multi-objective model show some dynamic characteristics among various performance criteria of outbound logistics.

References

Dornier, P.P., Ernst, R., Fender, M., & Kouvelis, P. (1998). *Global operations and logistics—Text and case*s. New York: John Wiley & Sons.

Hamacher, H.W., & Tufekci, S. (1984). Algebraic flow and time-cost trade-off problems. *Annals of Discrete Mathematics, 19*, 165-182.

Hon, C.C., Tang, L.L., & Peng, T.K. (2001). Quantitative and qualitative analysis of criteria grading and weight setting in performance evaluation system under group decision making and fuzzy data. *Proceeding of the 6th Annual International Conference on Industrial Engineering Theory, Applications and Practice,* San Francisco.

Johnson, J.C., Wood, D.F., Wardlow, D.L., & Murphy Jr., P.R. (1999). *Contemporary logistics.* Prentice Hall.

Kanda, A., & Rao, U.R.K. (1984). A network flow procedure for project crashing with penalty nodes. *European Journal of Operational Research, 16,* 174-182.

Lambert, D.M., & Stock, J.R. (1993). *Strategic logistics management.* Homewood, IL: Irwin.

Lee, E.S., & Li, R.J. (1993). Fuzzy multi-objective programming and compromise programming with Pareto Optimum. *Fuzzy Sets and Systems, 53,* 275-288.

Lee, E.S., & Shih, H.S. (2001). *Fuzzy and multi-level decision making—An interactive computational approach.* London: Springer-Verlag.

Rutherford, D.P., & Wilhelm, W.E. (1999). Forecasting notebook computer price as a function of constituent features. *Computers & Industrial Engineering, 37,* 823-845.

Saaty, T.L. (1980). *The analytic hierarchical process.* New York: McGraw-Hill.

Saaty, T.L. (1994). How to make a decision: The analytic hierarchy process. *Interfaces, 24*(6), 19-43.

Simchi-Levi, D., Kaminsky, P., & Simchi-Levi, E. (2000). *Designing and managing the supply chain—Concepts, strategies, and case studies.* Boston: Irwin/McGraw-Hill.

Tang, L.L., & Yu, J.C. (2000). The comparison of different logistic models for Taiwan notebook computer industry. *Proceedings of the 5th Annual International Conference on Industrial Engineering Theory, Applications and Practice,* Taiwan.

Tyagi, R., & Das, C. (1997). A methodology for cost versus service trade-offs in wholesale location-distribution using mathematical programming and analytic hierarchy process. *Journal of Business Logistics, 18*(2), 77-99.

Zeleny, M. (1982). *Multiple criteria decision making.* New York: McGraw-Hill.

Chapter XII

Inter-Enterprise Process Integration for E-Supply Chain Business Practices

Chian-Hsueng Chao
National University of Kaohsiung, Taiwan

Abstract

For every industry, the demands for optimization and greater efficiency become particularly urgent when the flow of business information goes beyond the borders of organizations. Driven by the need to attain even greater corporate competitive advantages, many organizations already have reengineered their internal processes, and the focus has shifted to their trading partners. With network connectivity, supply chain integration is now the core strategic competence that enables many companies to act as one. he development of an integrated supply chain by way of the Internet is one of the most important business trends in today's e-business practices. This chapter focuses on the development of an object-oriented enterprise business blueprint for e-supply chain inter-enterprise process integration. The approach described here will illustrate how the enterprise applications can be developed and woven into the very fabric of business practices by using object-oriented techniques. In contrast to an isolated IT system, this approach allows business processes to permeate different organizations, and communication in this system becomes process-to-process oriented.

Introduction

The globalization of markets and the subsequent volatile competitions are driving enterprises to optimize their business strategies and operations constantly. Many enterprises already have reengineered their internal processes, and now the focus has shifted to their trading partners. With network connectivity, supply chain integration is the core strategic competence that enables many companies to act as one. This supply chain represents the cross-functional integration of activities that span the borders of organizations and companies. he issues involved in selecting e-supply chain partners extend beyond choosing a trading partner or a contractor and must include configuring business-to-business collaboration among trading partners. Today, every industry is an information-intensive industry. Information and communication have always played a major role in organizations' competitiveness and growth. The development of an integrated supply chain by way of the Internet is one of the most important business trends in today's e-business practices. This chapter focuses on the development of an object-oriented enterprise business blueprint for e-supply chain inter-enterprise process integration. The approach described here will illustrate how the enterprise applications can be developed and woven into the very fabric of business practices by using object-oriented techniques. The goal can be accomplished through the following steps: (a) examination of the current state of general business practices and theories of organizational structures; (b) classification of several business modules and combining them as a whole for enterprise business applications; (c) application of several modeling principles in the concept of creating an object-oriented environment for business; and (d) development of an object-oriented supply chain blueprint for e-business practices.

The New Dimension of Channel Integration

In order to compete in today's real-time economy, every business must be able to identify and respond quickly to changing market conditions and customer needs. Enterprises need to adapt a new type of agile and responsive organizational structure in order to fit into the global spectrum of business. New market players in today's e-economy gain diverse skills of workers through alliances, and a flat managerial hierarchy enables them to collaborate on a virtual basis that produces flexible products to meet customers' needs. This places the global economy as a whole in a continual restructuring mode, putting pressure on every industry. The situation is intensified by rapid advances in Information Technology (IT), which have drastically shortened the adaptation periods for organizational changes that used to be comparatively long. Hammer (1990) suggested that enterprises use IT to reengineer their existing business processes in order to achieve strategic outcomes and improve competitiveness. Reengineering is critical to an organization's survival during certain periods when there are major economic upheavals that threaten the organization's existence, and many organizations that do not reinvent themselves are doomed to become part of business history.

Today, many companies have "reengineered" changes in their organizational structures, business functions, and business processes in order to achieve more agility, flexibility, and responsiveness in their operations. With the maturity of Internet technologies, organizations readily perform certain business functions that go beyond organizational boundaries. E-commerce practices today have demonstrated the power of this "virtual organization", that integrates business processes from the front office to the back office through the Internet. Due to these paradigm shifts, the traditional business partnership scheme has changed, and the focus has now shifted to their business partners. Today, companies can achieve a business advantage by leveraging networking technology and the principles of supply chain integration. With network connectivity, supply chain integration is now the core strategic competence that enables many companies to act as one. This feature is very important for every industry, because many firms need to cooperate/collaborate intensively throughout a project life cycle. Today, every industry is an information-intensive industry. Information and communication have always played a major role in their competitiveness and growth. In the future, the supply chains, rather than the enterprises (designer, manufacturer, and supplier), will compete with each other. An increase in horizontal integration synchronizes the output of the entire supply chain. There will be no isolated islands of automation (Hannus, 1998), and those who best define and reengineer their business processes in the e-supply chain partnership likely will be the most successful in this industry.

Customer-Centric Supply Chain Management

E-business is a complex fusion of business processes, enterprise applications, and organizational structure necessary to create a new high-performance business model. The issues of e-business often include business-to-business process automations. Ordering, selling, outsourcing, production, shipping, logistics, billing, and payment are typical examples. These processes, by definition, almost always go beyond enterprise boundaries, and there are many other e-business service environments where Internet technologies are being utilized by enterprises, end users, and other parties that wish to do business over the Internet. Structure changes caused by these shifts impact the boundaries of enterprises. Indeed, without transition to an e-business foundation, e-commerce cannot be executed effectively, and no e-business will be truly effective without interacting with all of its supply chain partners in an automated fashion.

Today, customers are in charge and make the rules. Consumers are demanding solutions customized to meet their specific interests. Consequently, the challenge is shifting from product-centric marketing to customer-centric marketing. While technology is at the heart of the change that is revolutionizing our economic life, successful e-business is concerned with building new kinds of relationships with customers, employees, business partners, and all other participants in the business cycle. These relationships are termed the *supply ch*ain. Supply chain management (SCM) evolved several decades ago from a set of logistics performance tools to an inter-enterprise, and even channel-wide, operating philosophy. The growing dependence on the supply chain has been empha-sized by the following changes to traditional business practices: (a) the paradigm shift in the marketplace from the mass production of standardized products to flexible operations providing customized/personalized products that customers are demanding solutions designed to meet their specific needs; (b) the growth of more transparent information sharing between vendors and customers; (c) the rise of process-oriented team efforts replacing traditional divisional/departmental functions; and (d) increased trend of inter-enterprise processing and global outsourcing. All of these features are very important to today's industries, because many firms need to collaborate intensively throughout a project life cycle and the project team needs continuous access to business plans as the project proceeds.

In general, the supply chain involves procurement, enterprise resource planning (ERP), enterprise application integration (EAI), inter-enterprise processing, sharing, inventory management, logistics, feedbacks, and so forth. To be successful, members of the supply chain need to collaborate to help the enterprise reduce cost, utilize resources more effectively, and improve relationships with their stakeholders. The fundamental benefit of SCM is cooperation and collaboration among different stakeholders. The objectives and scope of work must be clearly stated and faithfully executed (Figure 1). Cooperation and collaboration are especially critical in the management of today's supply chain; these depend on enterprises' willingness to link their strategic objectives and fundamental business processes to create unique, seamless, enterprise-wide portals that are ready to

Figure 1. The virtual team in a supply chain scheme

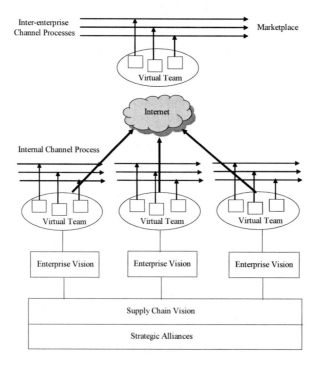

serve their customers These enterprises also are capable of quickly consolidating critical competencies and physical processes to gain competitive advantages. Therefore, issues related to e-supply chain integration include the internal and external core business processes, the development of close linkages between channel partners, and the management of production and information, as they move across organizational boundaries.

For example, the manufacturing process for materials or the production and distribution of equipment is transparent to all members in the supply chain. A supply chain is integrated in terms of people focused on processes that ultimately respond to customer demand, but its success requires technologies that can integrate and support every information exchange across the entire supply chain. Issues involved in selecting e-supply chain partners extend beyond choosing a trading partner or a contractor and must include configuring the business-to-business inter-enterprise processes among partners. The selection of processes and cooperation with supply chain partners are critical to the success of business.

Designing an E-Business Supply Chain Strategic Framework

In today's e-supply chain practices, all business data are transmitted over a variety of communication networks, and the essence of e-business is the communication of business data among organizations under a collaborative scheme in an entire supply chain. Data communication is critical for streamlining the entire supply chain business processes. However, the difficulty is that management has not yet examined these issues from any perspective, nor is there much effort to target the issue of transforming e-business practices into an inter-enterprise collaboration supply chain scheme. A typical project involves the coordination of multi-disciplinary work efforts by different organizations. Although participants may share a common goal of completing a project satisfactorily, their specific objectives are different, and their degree of participation depends on their organizational strategies. Thus, the need for integration of trading partners, especially integration of the supply chain and managerial functions, becomes a strategic vision for the future of business practices in the e-business era, and the major parts of the supply chain inter-enterprise processing design concepts are presented here.

Value Chain Thinking

To design a supply chain solution, one must start by examining the basic framework of an enterprise's major business activities, which are considered competitive factors derived from Porter's value chain (Porter, 1985). The value chain divides the organization into a set of generic functional areas, which can be further divided into a series of value activities. In the value chain, there are two distinct types of functional areas: primary and

Figure 2. Value and value activities (after Porter, 1985, modified)

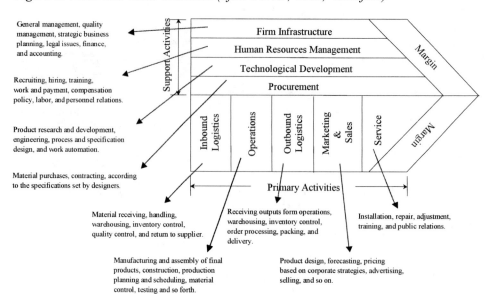

General management, quality management, strategic business planning, legal issues, finance, and accounting.

Recruiting, hiring, training, work and payment, compensation policy, labor, and personnel relations.

Product research and development, engineering, process and specification design, and work automation.

Material purchases, contracting, according to the specifications set by designers.

Material receiving, handling, warehousing, inventory control, quality control, and return to supplier.

Receiving outputs form operations, warehousing, inventory control, order processing, packing, and delivery.

Installation, repair, adjustment, training, and public relations.

Manufacturing and assembly of final products, construction, production planning and scheduling, material control, testing and so forth.

Product design, forecasting, pricing based on corporate strategies, advertising, selling, and so on.

support (Figure 2). Primary activities are concerned with the direct flow of production (such as inbound logistics, operations, outbound logistics, marketing, sales, and service), whereas support activities (firm infrastructure, human resource management, technology, and procurement) support the primary activities and each other. Starting with its generic value chain categories, a firm can subdivide into discrete activities, categorizing those activities that contribute best to its competitive advantage. Porter's version of supply chain management is called a value chain, because it focuses on value. The value is measured by the amount customers are willing to pay for an organization's product or service. Primary and support activities are called value activities, and an enterprise will be profitable as long as it creates more value than the cost of performing its value activities (Kuglin, 1998). In this way, a value chain is defined, and a better organizational structure and business process can be created around those value activities that can most improve an organization's competitive advantage (Curran, Ladd & Keller, 2000).

Porter also recognized linkages outside the enterprise, as they relate to the customer's perception of value. This provides the possibility that one value chain could be linked to another value chain, because one business partner could be the other's customer. This interconnected value chain system can act as a supply chain that encompasses the modern business world, and participating organizations readily can extend their technologies to their partners. The "extended enterprise" aspect enables supply chain integration, more effective outsourcing, and self-service solutions for both internal and external stakeholders (Curran, Ladd, & Keller, 2000). This extended enterprise allows for the sophisticated interweaving of online business processes across trading partners and with other internal and external information sources. The following section will illustrate a typical integrated e-supply chain solution for the inter-enterprise business practices.

Figure 3. Typical purchase order and payment process

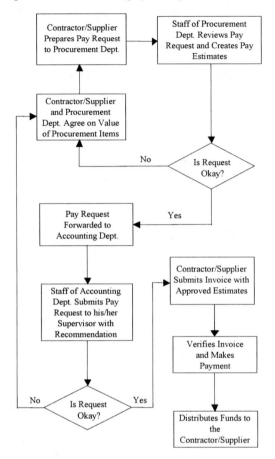

The Business Blue Print

Consider the following purchase order and payment example. A purchase payment is a requested pay estimate to the accounting department for quantities of any procurement (see Figure 3). The staff of the accounting department reviews the pay request to ascertain that the indicated items comply with the actual quantity; the staff then forwards it to a supervisor with a recommendation. If the request is approved, an account will be established, and funds will be distributed to the contractor or suppler. If the request is rejected, the procedure will revert or roll back to the settlement between the procurement department and the contractor on the value of the work in place. To determine whether or not payment is justified, the accounting department reviews the scope of the procurement and identifies its control objective.

According to the value chain concept, everything that a company does can be categorized in primary and support activities. In the progress payment scenario, the activities include (a) operational and execution functions of procurement and communication; (b) contractor/supplier integration to accounting and quantity systems; and (c) automated workflow and document management, all of which are incorporated into the value chain scenario for procurement logistics. The value chain depicts the subsequent workflow of converting the proposed supply plan for purchased items/works into commercial arrangements with the contractor/supplier, monitoring the status of these purchases, and receiving the procurement items. The purchase order and payment are typical business processes that follows business rules and policies in every industry.

General Business Services

Based on a value chain analysis, several general base business activities are identified, and a series of decomposing efforts will render more detailed sub-processes. On the other hand, effective management involves many managerial functions, such as scheduling, budgeting, quality control, resource management, and so forth. The ultimate purpose of these management functions is to allocate resources (manpower, equipment, material, etc.) and then monitor, control, and keep all processes on track during every stage of the project cycle. Many business managements share many of the same business activities as derived from the value chain, because Porter's value chain activity is the backbone of every type of organization in every type of industry. Here, the transformation process and object view of the enterprise for inter-enterprise processing are summarized in Figure 4 and Figure 5.

Object Orientation

In this study, an object-oriented approach is used to map the corporate business process with the information system in terms of a series of reusable business objects, that

Figure 4. Transformation process for inter-enterprise processing

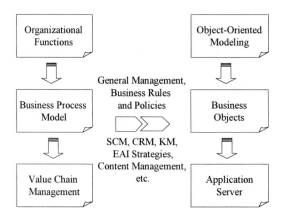

Figure 5. The object view of enterprise

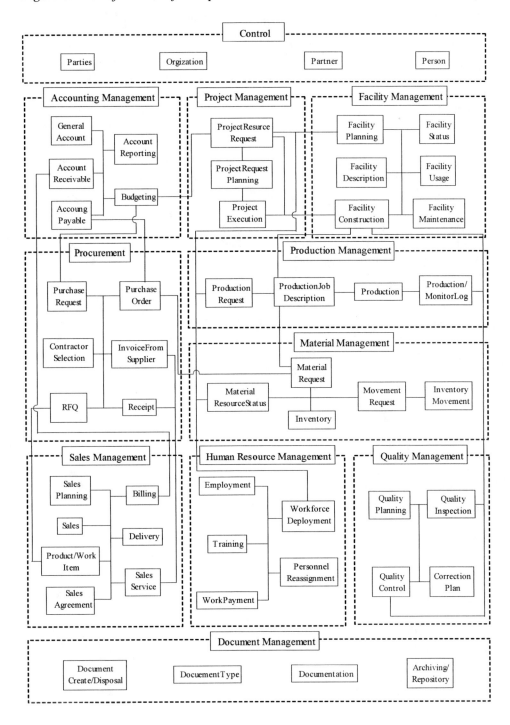

encapsulate complex business rules. Accordingly, (a) the tedious redesign efforts of information systems can be circumvented, and the corporate information system can become very adaptive; (b) the applications can run on different platforms through network connectivity; and (c) this schematic business blueprint not only fits a given enterprise, but it also can be viewed as an open architecture that links to trading partners. From a process-oriented point of view, this blueprint allows many organizations to share the same business components (or database) in a network and to participate in the business practices of the strategic alliance supply chain. In contrast to an isolated IT system, this approach allows the organization business process to permeate different organizations, and communication in this system becomes process-to-process oriented.

The Unified Modeling Language (UML) is an object-oriented modeling technique that provides a comprehensive methodology for designing object-oriented applications in a logical, structured manner, and it is available for the development of three-tier client/ server distributed applications. A basic core set of diagrams (using case models, interaction diagrams, class diagrams, and activity diagrams) is used in the development process to refine the design and ultimately define the business objects, after which the class diagrams are coded and mapped into the organizational information system (Figure 6). The Unified Modeling Language (UML) developed by Grady Booch, James Rumbaugh, and Ivar Jacobson is a systematic analysis methodology, that visually expresses system models and designs in an object-oriented fashion. With the UML approach, the designer will be able to express the execution of the system's business logic in terms of UML models. Also, with this reference model, the IT architecture also is easily deployable. For example, some of the business logics can be executed by logics can be executed by traditional server-side objects and components, such as middle-tier components, trans-action-processing, data storage three-tier -architecture, and so on. Some of the objects and components are handled by Web -elements, such as browsers and client-side scripts, depending on deployment strategies. Therefore, the UML is suitable for expressing Web application design. For the UML modeling technique, one can refer to Ivar Jacobson's books with more detail.

By applying the object modeling methodology, these business component relationships can be transformed into object-based interactions. The purpose of the Object Modeling Technique (OMT) is to select certain business functions as business objects to be coded

Figure 6. The UML design process

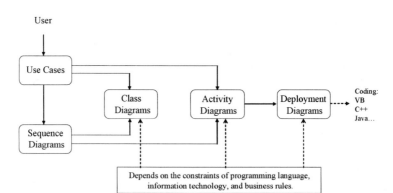

into business applications. The use case method (Jacobson, 1994) can help to identify business objects by using descriptive statements of the procedures and functions of particular business scenarios (e.g., purchase and payment). In this context, the pay estimate, pay request, staff of procurement, staff of accounting, work items, contractor, and so forth all may be viewed as business objects, and a three-tier approach can be used to map the business applications and relationships with the company information system (Figure 7). The business objects located in the middle of Figure 7 actually reside in the application server of the IT system; on the left side is a user services layer representing the client interface that a user may need to access the system; and the data service layer on the right side represents the data storage module that corresponds to each business object.

Wielding the Solution

These tools and theories now can be combined to provide an inter-enterprise processing scheme for e-supply chain practices. The first step is to transform a functional organizational structure into a process-based structure, based on the value chain model and business process reengineering. The second step is to use the UML to build an object view (class diagrams) of business operations that follows the organizational business rules, policies, and business process scenario (Figure 7). The third step is to translate

Figure 7. Object-oriented approach of progress payment in three-tier architecture

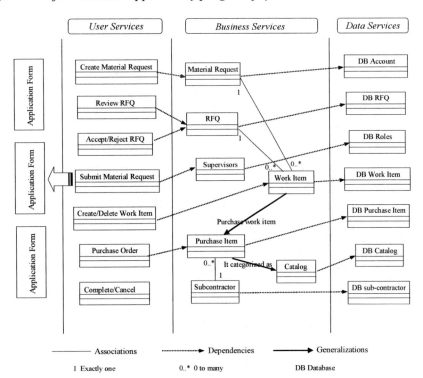

Figure 8. The adaptive business information system

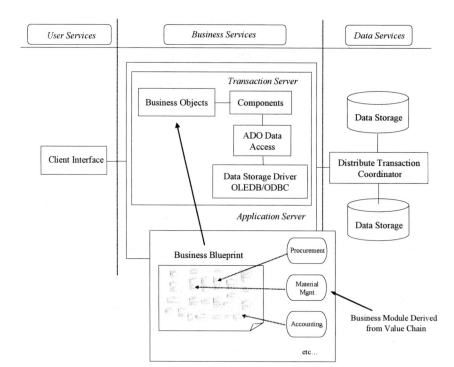

the object-oriented blueprint of the enterprise processes model into machine recognizable codes that can be compiled into a series of reusable business objects. Several programming languages (such as C++, Java, and Visual Basic) can be used in this transformation. The fourth step is to migrate these business objects into a transaction-processing system that has Internet/intranet capabilities (e.g., Microsoft Transaction server or the SAP R/3 Enterprise Resource Planning Transaction Server). The business objects can reside on the   project team's information system and "talk" to each other using the Common Object Request Broker Architecture (CORBA) scheme to perform over the Internet certain business functions that go beyond organizational boundaries. Regardless of location, users can participate in team coordination/collaboration and share their "collective intelligence" within a virtual corporation. Figure 8 is a schematic diagram of a three-tier information system that stores business objects in order to perform certain tasks for the organization. This global information networking and inter-enterprise process offers enormous benefits to many industries. The business objects presented thus far depict business services, in that each represents an artifact that is encountered or produced in the daily business routine. Each module in the user services part of the model actually relates to a single use case statement, which, in code terms, actually would have to be divided into a number of distinct routines. These routines deal with the methods and properties of the business objects in the business services tier, and the user interface uses these objects to display needed information and feed user input into the system. The business objects, in turn, use objects in the data services layer to get their data. In this way the user interface could change without impacting the underlying way in which the application dealt with the business, and the database could be replaced with a new database without affecting the rest of the system. As long as the interface to the data service objects remains intact, the rest of the code will compile and run properly.

The E-Supply Chain Inter-Enterprise Application Integration

As mentioned previously, most business plans are unique, complex, extensive, expensive, and subject to tight schedules and budgets. The teams for any given project includes some combination of staffs, engineers, contractors, materials suppliers, equipment providers, and even inspectors, and thus, the team normally will be different for each business project. All of the complexities inherent to different project situations are an inherent part of business practices. As a consequence, managing a business project may require extensive interdisciplinary professional skills to achieve optimum performance. From the supply chain point of view, project members must collaborate to synchronize the output of the entire supply chain in order to fulfill a particular job. The project partnership in the supply chain becomes a strategic alliance wherein contractors must align their business processes and information systems to support inter-enterprise processes and decision-making. Configuring business-to-business operations among trading partners is very important, because the supply chain represents the cross-functional integration of all activities that cross the borders of the participating organizations. Using the value chain concept to identify an enterprise's competitive advantages and then reengineering its core business processes accordingly is the best way to make an enterprise more process-aware, and that is the beginning of inter-enterprise processes.

E-business solutions should be built on an Internet computing architecture that leverages standard Internet communication protocols and company intranets, extranets, and the global Internet to provide low-cost and universal access to all members of the e-business supply chain. With new Web technologies, such as XML, Internet-based systems can offer functionality and information to users through a standard Web browser, thereby eliminating requirements for traditional Electronic Data Interchange (EDI) or client-based software and reducing IT implementation and maintenance costs, cycles, and burdens. The winners in the Internet economy will be those companies that can respond most rapidly and efficiently to the customer's demands. As a result, an e-business supply chain solution must provide support for the capture and communication of customer demand, as well as enable this demand to automatically trigger business events and initiate process workflow (i.e., launching manufacturing runs, starting business tasks, and issuing purchase requests within the enterprise and across the supply chain). This supply chain also needs a common data model, because in order to be effective, an e-business supply chain solution will need to deliver an accurate and common view of customer demand data, as well as any subsequent events, plans, or other business data.   This new "e-supply chain" offers virtually unlimited business opportunities in the alignment of processes and technologies. A well-designed and well-integrated supply chain will improve upon existing cost-responsive processes and have organizational agility in the event of change.

The Information Processing Network and Value Chain

The information processing view of an organization has been considered one of the most influential contributions to the contingency literature (Wang, 2003). In this philosophy, an information-processing network provides the channels for exchange and processing of information in a global system. The primary system objective of the information-processing network is to provide a communication backbone for information exchange among its subsystem, the information processing nodes. The information-processing nodes within the network are responsible for receiving, using, selecting, producing, sending, and communicating (i.e., exchange information) with other information processing nodes. As a result, the lattice of channels between the various information-processing nodes forms a physical communication infrastructure called an information-processing network.

The characteristics of information-processing nodes are much like the business components, but they conduct the actual exchange of information. The business components

Figure 9. Information processing view of shared component inter-enterprise processing

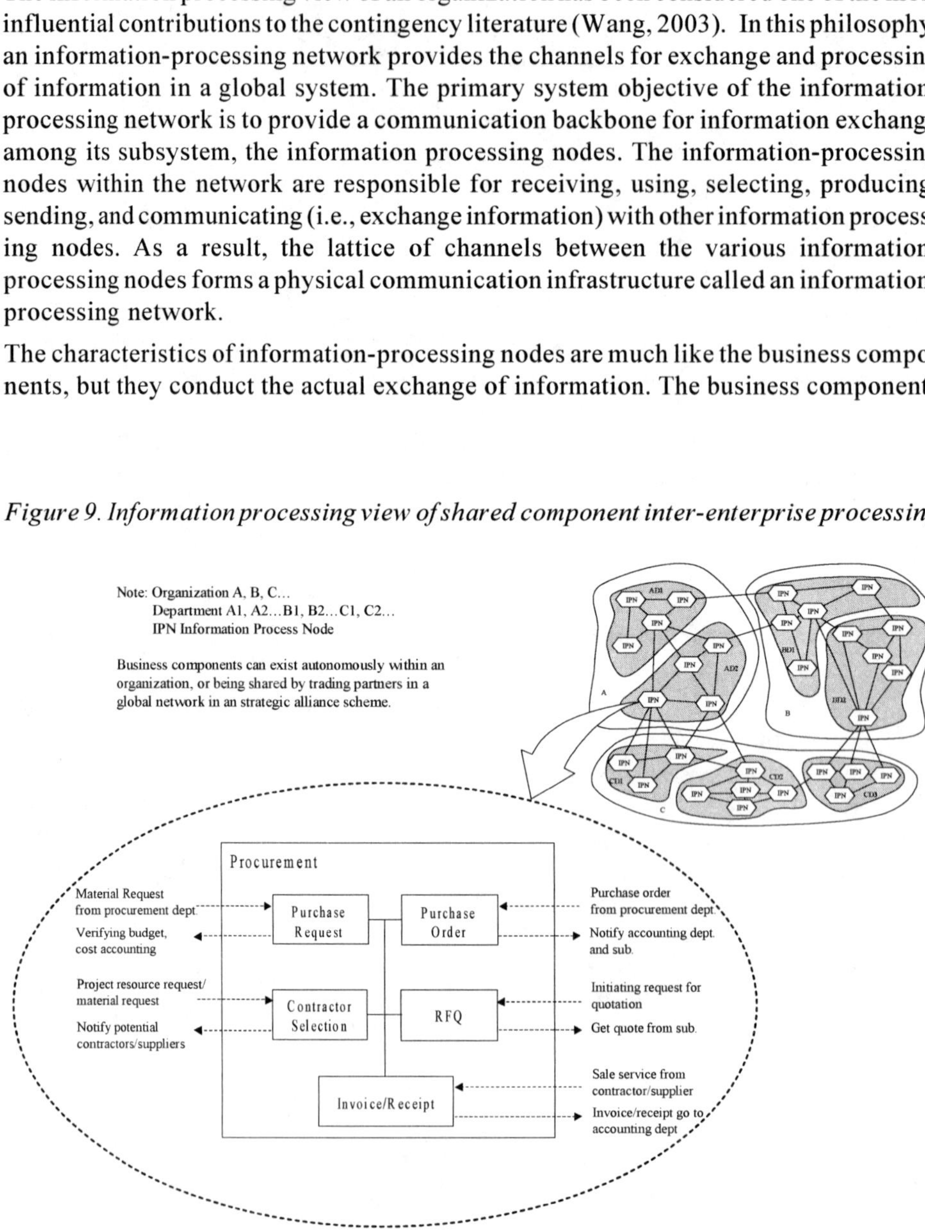

of the organization include people, processes, events, machines, and information that interact and combine to produce the products or output of the organization. People and information-processing machines, such as computers, are in this category. An enterprise operates as an information-processing system in a global information-processing network. Because it is an open structure, the network can be developed in a fractal pattern. The information-processing network can be expanded and connected to other enterprises' information-processing networks (Figure 9). The information-processing nodes within each network in either organization can work collaboratively to achieve strategic goals in the newly joined network. To this point, we also concluded that one value chain can be linked to another value chain. This interconnected value chain system can act like a supply chain that encompasses the modern business world, and participating organizations readily can extend their technologies to their partners.

Conclusion

The challenges of the global marketplace are increasingly forcing today's process-centered organizations to utilize more fully the skills, knowledge, competencies, and resources found in their integrated supply chain networks. Parallel, rather than serial optimization is the key to supply chain management, and companies must acknowledge that adaptivity is increasingly becoming a measure upon which its productivity will be evaluated. This adaptivity requires enhancing communication among all team members and aligning their actions toward a common project goal, and IT will be a key "enabler" for this transformation effort.

The explosion of strategic alliances and partnerships on a global scale has brought about the formation of inter-enterprise virtual organizations capable of leveraging the skills, physical resources, and innovative knowledge that reside at different locations in a supply chain network (Figure 10). This chapter provides a broad discussion on the possible development of an EAI scheme for inter-enterprise processes that embraces all aspects of business practices, and creates multi-channel and multi-technology solutions, such as CRM, and partner relationship management (PRM) in a fast-moving and technologically indefinite environment. In business practices, information is the glue that unifies businesses partnerships. Many organizations use their information processing networks and strive to become knowledge-enabled organizations to ensure that all employees are able to locate, access, and utilize the knowledge and skills they need to meet their individual and corporate goals. A common data model also will be needed for the entire supply chain knowledge network, because the effectiveness of an e-business supply chain solution will depend largely on its ability to deliver an accurate and common view of customer demand data, as well as any subsequent events, plans, or other business data. This new "e-supply chain" offers unlimited business opportunities when enterprises fully integrated their knowledge, processes, and technology.

In today's customer relationship management, or selling chain management practices, the customer is in control, and a business must realign its value chain around the customer to eliminate inefficiencies, and custom information, products, and services.

Figure 10.   The knowledge-enabled supply chain

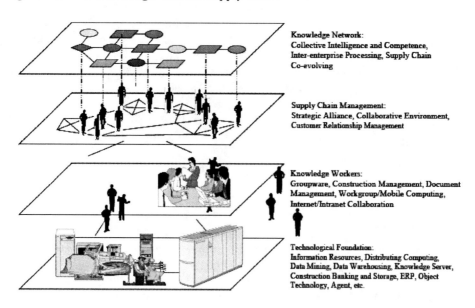

Knowledge Network:
Collective Intelligence and Competence,
Inter-enterprise Processing, Supply Chain
Co-evolving

Supply Chain Management:
Strategic Alliance, Collaborative Environment,
Customer Relationship Management

Knowledge Workers:
Groupware, Construction Management, Document
Management, Workgroup/Mobile Computing,
Internet/Intranet Collaboration

Technological Foundation:
Information Resources, Distributing Computing,
Data Mining, Data Warehousing, Knowledge Server,
Construction Banking and Storage, ERP, Object
Technology, Agent, etc.

Communication in the supply chain must be process-to-process oriented, and collaboration is the best way that trading partners can interact. Process integration across the supply chain becomes a new challenge for today's industries. Enterprises will need to learn that content communication is as important as technological infrastructure to the enterprise software application architecture. For example, the future mobile business will rely more heavily on content management than on software application.

Opportunity opens doors, but success requires walking through them.   With a new focus on process and supply chain management, traditional business partnerships will have to redesign their business strategies. The Collaborative Commerce (CC) e-supply chain scheme that enables a dynamic "virtual team" to fulfill many mission-critical business processes throughout a project life cycle undoubtedly will be the best business solution for the new millennium.

References

Curran, T.A., Ladd, A., & Keller, G. (2000). *SAP R/3 business blueprint: Understanding enterprise supply chain management.* Upper Saddle River, NJ: Prentice Hall.

Hammer, M. (1990, July/August). Reengineering work: Don't automate, obliterate. *Harvard Business Review, 68*(4), 104-112.

Hannus, M. (1998). Islands of automation. Technical Research Center of Finland. Retrieved from *http://www.vtt.fi/rte/projects/cic/ratas/islands.html*

Jacobson, I. (1994). Using objects to develop your business & IT support: The use case driven approach. *Proceedings of the SIGS Object Expo Conference,* June (pp. 6-10), New York.

Kuglin, F. A. (1998). *Customer-centered supply chain management: A link-by-link guide.* New York: AMACOM, a Division of American Management Association.

Porter, M. (1985). *Competitive advantage: Creating and sustaining superior performance.* New York: The Free Press.

Wang, T.G. E. (2003). Effect of the fit between information processing requirements and capacity on organizational performance. *International Journal of Information Management, 23,* 239-247.

Chapter XIII

LOSIMOPU:
Logistics Simulator on Policy Under Uncertainty

Hiroshi Tsuji
Osaka Prefecture University, Japan

Ryosuke Saga
Osaka Prefecture University, Japan

Takefumi Konzo
Osaka Prefecture University, Japan

Akihiro Koretsune
Osaka Prefecture University, Japan

Abstract

This chapter presents a software simulator called LOSIMOPU. LOSIMOPU allows users to build a supply chain model and analyze the sensitivity of logistics on assigned policy and capacity under uncertainty. LOSIMOPU consists of five kinds of participants (end-customer, intermediate supplier, end-supplier, transportation server, and electronic payment server) and an e-marketplace for the supply chain. Each participant is implemented as a distributed object so that it runs concurrently and has capacity and policy for playing its role. The e-marketplace defines the trade protocol for the workflow management and transaction analysis. LOSIMOPU visualizes expected indices of assigned parameters for decision support. This chapter discusses the background of the proposal, the goal of the simulator, the milestone, the technical issues for development, and the prototype system.

Introduction

Although individual business applications have been integrated into an ERP (Enterprise Resource Planning) system for constructing value chain, there is still a limit on business process restructuring, because one company activity has a relation to other companies. The management in a specific company is not always useful at global competition, and workflow controls for cooperating among companies are required.

One of the workflow control methods among companies is known as SCM (Supply Chain Management). Supply chains are an integrative philosophy to manage the total flow of a distribution channel from the suppliers to the ultimate customers (Coyle, 1996). Customers, vendors, manufacturers, and parts suppliers are players in supply chains. Although the term *chain* seems to be a single connected line, supply chain is a complex network. SCM is building the structure of the business model that promotes information sharing among players in order to eliminate lurking waste in operating processes and shortens the total lead time.

The purpose of SCM is to increase throughput and profits. In particular, a constraints theory on throughput (Goldratt, 1993) that requires the managers to detect the bottlenecks in the business process has impacted many industries. For SCM, there are two research approaches: (1) OR/MS technology, such as mathematical programming, which optimizes the objective function in order to allocate resources, such as persons, machines, and money (Karaesmen, 2002; Mine, 1966); and (2) IT technology, such as workflow management, information sharing, and electronic payment that integrates enterprise systems (Hammer, 1993; Knoshafian, 1995).

These researches have tackled the technical issues independently, not only to assess the risk and the chance of the business process reengineering, but also to evaluate the implementation issues; the SCM designers require the means that integrate both OR/MS (Operations Research/Management Science) technology and IT. Because there are so many factors in business activity, the supply chains are too complex to analyze mathematically. The followings are examples on complexness:

1. SCM is a time-variant and large-scale combinatorial problem. In a supply chain, there are several players, such as vender, manufacturer, and supplier. They also have competitors. Sometimes, one that was a competitor may become an alliance. Thus, the problem is time-variant. Furthermore, one's optimal policy under its constraints is not always optimal for the total supply chain. Therefore, it is difficult to decompose the static optimization problem.

2. There are uncertainties in a supply chain. In a supply chain, there are various uncertain factors, such as demand of product, supply capacity, lead time, and mechanical problems. For example, the lead time for delivery may take long because of traffic. Therefore, uncertainties make SCM more complex.

3. Evaluation measures differ in companies. There is a variety of evaluation measures for SCM. Cost, sales, profit, and lead time are examples. Then, the policy for increasing sales is different from the policy for decreasing cost. Therefore, it is difficult for the planner to formalize SCM as an optimization problem.

Therefore, a software simulator is an effective tool for solving these problems (Angerofer, 2000; Tian, 2003). Finding the bottleneck or the redundancy in the whole chain, the simulator shows the alternative for improving the performance of the whole chain. Given the probability distributions to uncertainties, the simulator should predict the risk indices. For a better forecasting method, system dynamics in a supply chain have been analyzed.

Although the conventional serial simulator is effective in a specific problem domain, it has the fault of recalculating a model when the composition of a chain is flexible. In fact, the serial simulator does not work well in the case where those players in a chain act asymmetrically.

In order to cope with these issues, we plan to develop a concurrent software simulator based on object-oriented technology, called LOSIMOPU (LOgistics SIMulator On Policy under Uncertainty) (Konzo, 2003; Koretsune, 2004; Saga, 2003; Tsuji, 2003). Object-oriented technology (Gomma, 2000) is the form in which the operating subject of the work, called *object*, carries out interaction and performs problem solutions. Class concept in object-oriented technology allows us to generalize players into some categories and to hide individual strategic data of the players, such as policy and capacity, inside certain objects. Therefore, to add or delete players and to change the policy and capacity of players are not program modifications but parameter adjustments.

This chapter describes the target, the system configuration, the design issues, and the prototype system of our LOSIMOPU. The remainder of this chapter is organized as follows: First we describe the role of LOSIMOPU, and then we present how a class object on players and e-marketplace works. Next, we will discuss the workflow among players in LOSIMOPU, especially trade protocol. Further, we will analyze uncertainty in SCM and finally describe our prototype system, including its limitations and future work.

Overview of LOSIMOPU

The basic concept of SCM is not brand new. In fact, most companies have been interested in managing a set of interrelated activities, including transportation, distribution, warehousing, inventory levels, and materials handling to ensure the efficient delivery of goods to customers.

Today, a number of external factors cause companies to handle complex decision parameters so that the final customer receives the right product at the right cost, at the right time, in the right condition, and in the right quantity. As shown in Figure 1, there are varieties of players, such as vendors and manufacturers, between customers and parts suppliers. Note that some are competitors and others are collaborators (Coyle, 1996).

To assign decision parameters precisely, most companies are interested in establishing the partnerships and alliances among players. If they establish partnerships and share information, such as inventory and customer demand, the throughput will be improved by dissolving bottleneck. However, trade-off between throughput improvement and

Figure 1. An example of supply chain

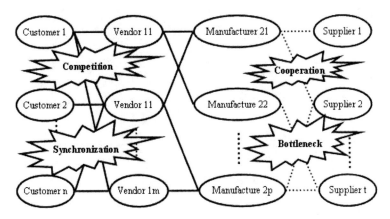

total cost is extended from one company to all companies. Then, it is not easy to assign decision parameters that optimize the whole supply chain. To support how to manage the total flow of a distribution channel from supplier to end customer, we propose software simulator LOSIMOPU.

Let us clarify the role of LOSIMOPU. In our framework, there are two worlds, as shown in Figure 2: real world and modeled world. In the real world, business is performed by two activities: observation on a supply chain and decision on policy and capacity. In the modeled world, our LOSIMOPU supports the user to model the supply chain and make a decision.

Once policy and capacity alternatives for the supply chain are given in the modeled world, LOSIMOPU simulates trade among players, such as customers and suppliers, and it visualizes the indices for the assigned policy and capacity. The visualized indices will suggest model modification and present policy and capacity alternatives.

If the expected indices are fine for the decision, the policy and capacity will be applied to the real world to support decision making. Observation on the supply chain will be updated after a period of time. Then, there is a chance for LOSIMOPU again. Generally, the simulation is a reasonable solution to understand the complicated system.

Next, let us discuss the features of LOSIMOPU. There are two kinds of functions, as follows:

1.   Policy and capacity assignment for a supply chain.
2.   Expected indices visualization.

For the former, it is important for LOSIMOPU to edit the whole supply chain. Bird's eye for the supply chain helps a user to understand what kinds of policy and capacity are parameters. The assigned parameters should be stored in LOSIMOPU as alternatives, and a part of alternative parameters can be modified for sensitivity analysis. In general,

Figure 2. Role of SCM simulator for decision support

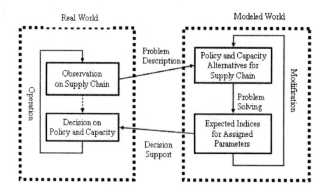

a product consists of multiple parts. Therefore, LOSIMOPU should manage part deployment in the supply chain.

For the latter, LOSIMOPU should visualize not only the simulation result but also the simulation process. For the simulation result, LOSIMOPU will present whole chain balance as well as each player's balance. For the simulation process, LOSIMOPU alarms the user if it finds a bottleneck in the supply chain. To allow the user to monitor the alarm, LOSIMOPU has a function to adjust simulation speed (if LOSIMOPU runs slowly, it is easy for the user to notice the alarm).

The development of LOSIMOPU is a grand project. It is not easy to develop in a short time. Therefore, we have three stages of milestones, as follows:

1.   First, we develop LOSIMOPU as the learning system that teaches general users what the supply chain management is and what policy affects the supply chain.

2.   Next, we enhance it as the research platform that the experts can include in the supplemental policy controllers and the special functions in the simulator.

3.   Finally, we expect it can be used in industry.

Systems Configuration of LOSIMOPU

Although the spreadsheet-based risk simulator is well known (Evans, 1998), it is difficult for the designer to express the concurrent and complex supply chain. As shown in Figure 3, the players in the supply chain have the common actions, as follows: request, reply, sell, buy, and manufacture. Of course, according to the core competence of the player, some activities should be added, and others should be omitted.

Figure 3. Usecase for intermediate supplier

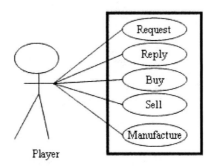

For example, the end customer does not have the function *sell*, while the end supplier does not have the function *buy*. Furthermore, each player has attributes such as name and the account data in time series. Thus, the participants are expressed as class/subclass relation.

Then, the distributed object-oriented modeling technology is suitable for the following reasons (Gomaa, 2000; Tsuji, 2003):

1.   Improved availability.
2.   Flexible configuratio.
3.   Localized control and management.
4.   Incremental system expansion.

There are five player subclasses in our simulator, as shown in Figure 4: (1) end customers; (2) intermediate suppliers, such as vendors and manufacturers; (3) end suppliers; (4) electronic payment servers; and (5) transportation servers.

Each player object in the supply chain runs concurrently. Note that the action strategies of players are different according to capacity and policy and are hidden in the object. The strategy often is designed by OR/MS technology, based on information sharing among players. Individual attributes are as follows (Konzo, 2003):

1.   **Intermediate Supplier Class:** It has attributes on components that constitute goods and those on capacity for manufacturing and inventory. Such attributes are used to control the inbound of the supply chain. It also has the mechanism for the economic order quantity and material requirement planning.

      On the other hand, it has attributes on sales logs and customer demand forecast that control the outbound of the supply chain. It also has mechanisms for customer relationship management. Further, it keeps management indices, such as cost, income, real estate, and so forth. Those are indispensable for calculating the interest, the throughput, and the sales loss.

Figure 4. Class diagram of players

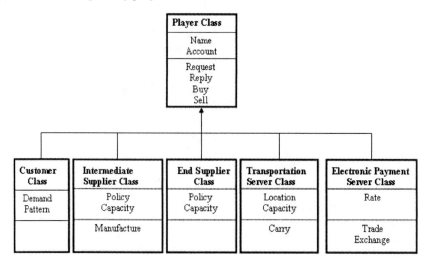

2.   **End Supplier Class:** In general, there are the competitors for the parts supply. It has price table and lead time on parts delivery as attributes. For LOSIMOPU, the latter is assigned as a stochastic variable.

3.   **End Customer Class:** It plays a role for a demander. The demand information includes goods identification, volumes, and time limit for the delivery. LOSIMOPU should allow the user to assign a variety of patterns for the customer order arrival: constant, impulse type sudden rise, steady growth, seasonality, short life cycle, and their combinations.

4.   **Electronic Payment Server Class:** It plays a role for the electronic payment among the players. It simulates the time delay on the account DB as a business process and charges the payment.

5.   **Transportation Server Class:** It delivers parts to the manufacturer and delivers goods to the customers. It has a price table as an attribute that is a function of transportation lots and distance.

In our premise, each player acts on e-marketplace. As shown in Figure 5, each player trades with other players, and e-marketplace plays a role in mediating players in LOSIMOPU.

Figure 5. Relationship among player and e-marketplace

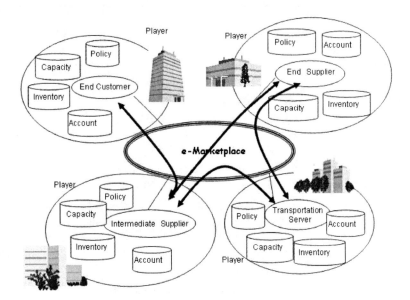

Workflow in LOSIMOPU

To describe the workflow in LOSIMOPU, let us classify requirements for e-marketplace as follows:

Flexibility of Participants

To evaluate the combination of participants, e-marketplace provides functions for adding and deleting player objects. This function allows player objects to join in and exit independently from e-marketplace. Once a player object is added to a player database in e-marketplace, the player object is managed by e-marketplace. To delete a player object from e-marketplace should be a simple operation and should not affect side effects on other objects.

Concurrent Simulation

While a player retrieves a transaction from its queue, other players may decide their actions concurrently. Thus, many players exist in LOSIMOPU and they trade in parallel at the same time. Therefore, the function should be provided for e-marketplace to deal with the transaction asynchronously. In addition, it also is necessary for each player to receive the data recurring asynchronously.

Status Control

To discover a bottleneck or redundant capacity, a transaction should be monitored and recorded. There are varieties of statuses in the transaction, from initial state to terminal state. Because these states depend on trades among players, they should be controlled by e-marketplace. Then, object flow and money flow also are expressed in the supply chain and should be managed by analyzing databases.

To satisfy the requirement, both player and e-marketplace should have queues for transaction. E-marketplace has (1) looping software with queue, called e-marketplace engine; (2) databases on throughput, audit/log, and player's information; and (3) trade protocol. Referring to the trade protocol, e-marketplace engine mediates every trade and updates the databases. The flow on e-marketplace with queues is depicted in Figure 6.

Let us next consider the workflow in LOSIMOPU. Each player receives the requests from its customers via e-Marketplace. Then, it makes a decision whether it accepts the request and replies to the requester. On the other hand, the e-marketplace engine receives the message from the players, records the audit, and transfers it to the other players.

Each transaction has the state in LOSIMOPU, and it starts as initial state. If the trade is established, the transaction finalizes as OK state, otherwise as NG state. In order to control the states between the initial state and the terminal state, e-marketplace should offer a trade protocol. Then, any transaction is in a specific state. Transaction path and time are recorded in the database, so that the statistics on trade can be analyzed.

Let us define the trade protocol as follows:

Figure 6. Flow on e-marketplace with queuse

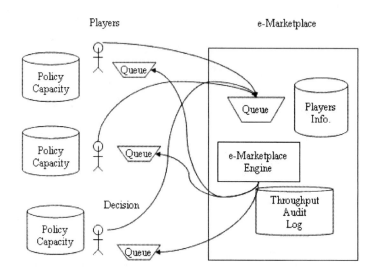

Figure 7. Trade protocol based on conversation for action model

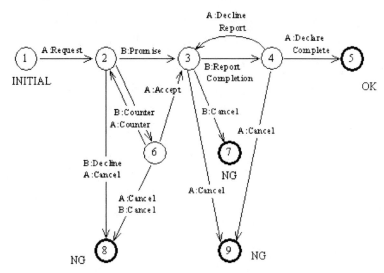

- The method is based on finite state-transition model,
- All transactions will be absorbed in either the agreement (OK) state or the disagreement (NG) state.

The basic idea for the trade protocol can be borrowed from the traditional conversation-for-action model shown in Figure 7 (Winograd, 1988). This model is expressed by state and state-transition, when player A asks player B for an action. This model is not only simple, but it is also powerful for conversation, because the transition is robust for the trade.

For example, in case player B is not satisfied with player A's request at state 2, player B counters the proposal for modifying A's request. Further, even if the promise is done once at state 3, there are chances for both player A and player B to cancel their trade before either of them agrees to the completion of the trade. How to modify the protocol is discussed elsewhere (Saga, 2003).

Prototype System

We are going to develop the prototype system for the first step. As described before, the target of the first step is to teach the general users what the supply chain management is and what policy affects the whole chain.

Although there are varieties of commerce types in the real world, let us classify commerce type into four patterns, as shown in Table 1. To simplify the implementation, current

Table 1. Classification of commerce type

Supplier \ Customer	Fixed	Selectable
Fixed	Established Relationship	Supplier-driven Market
Selectable	Customer-driven Market	Flexible Relationship

LOSIMOPU focuses on established relationships, while LOSIMOPU will support other patterns.

Let us discuss the features of patterns.

1. The relationship between customers and suppliers is established beforehand. For example, a supplier provides its products only for predefined customers. Conversely, a customer requests parts or product to predefined suppliers. Thus, in this pattern, there is no competition.

2. In order to sort out a supplier, a customer negotiates with suppliers. For example, the customer compares price and deadline of suppliers that manufacture the same product. A customer has a choice for suppliers, while a supplier does not select customers.

3. A supplier sorts out customers based on policy. For example, contrary to the previous feature, suppliers can look for the customers who buy products under better conditions. The auction is an example. A customer has to consider and bid for the other customer.

4. Either a supplier or a customer has chance to select each other. This commerce type is flexible for trade and also general. Negotiation and auction are found in this type of commerce.

Let us discuss the general scenario of LOSIMOPU. Figure 8 shows the activity diagram where there are six activities:

1. **Supply Chain Model Description:** Players in a supply chain and their relationships are registered in LOSIMOPU. LOSIMOPU requires their class and profile. Their relationships can be regarded as a bird's eye. If a player has controllable capacities, those are registered at this step. Figure 9, which shows that there are four players, is an example screen of bird's eye for a supply chain in our prototype.

2. **Product Specification Registration:** Product-related parameters are specified at this step. The parts composition example for a product is shown in Figure 10, where a product is made of two pieces, part A and part B.

Figure 8. Activity diagram for LOSIMOPU

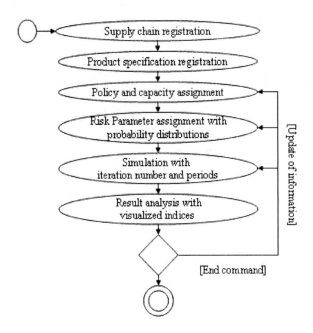

Figure 9. Bird's eye for supply chain

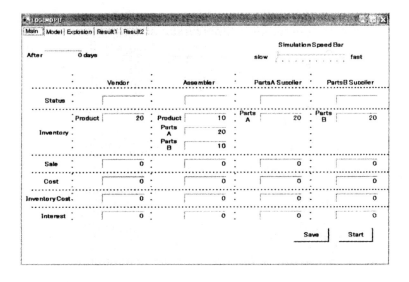

Figure 10. Product specification

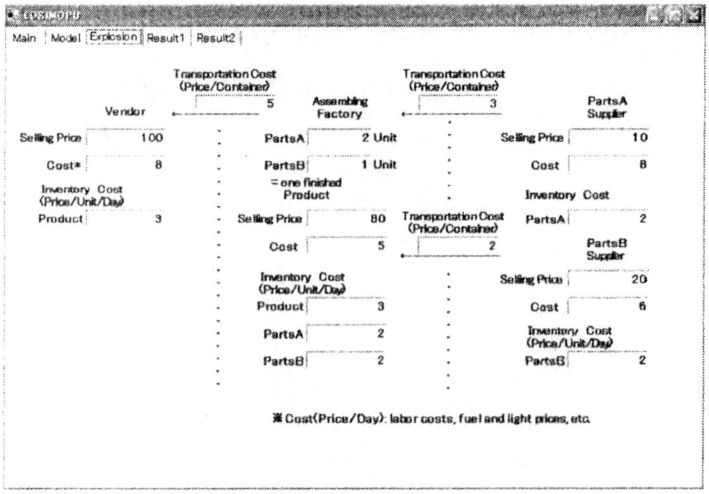

Figure 11. Player profile

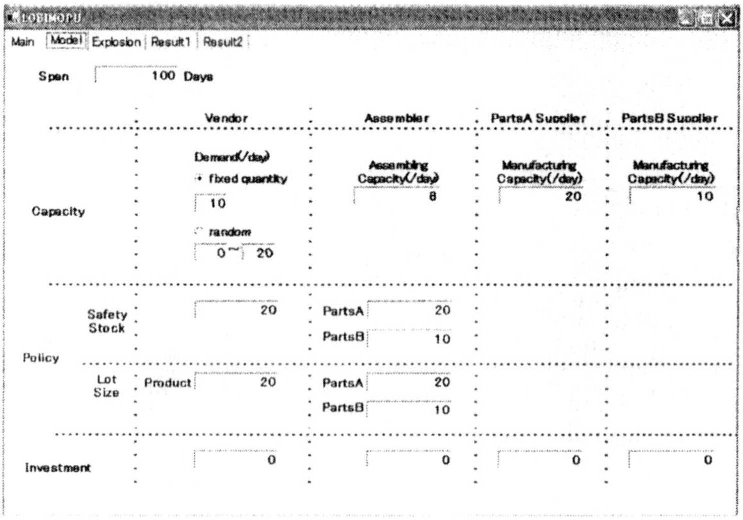

Figure 12. Monte Carlo type simulation in LOSIMOPU

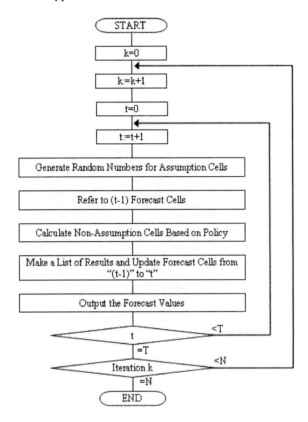

3.   **Policy and Capacity Assignment:** Assembly capability and manufacturing capacity are prepared for capacity items. Safe stock size and lot size are required to specify as policy items. Figure 11 is an example screen in our prototype.

4.   **Risk Parameter Assignment with Probability Distribution:** In case there are uncertainties in players' capacities, let us assign probability distribution at this phase.

5.   **Simulation Run:** According to the registered player profile and the product specification, LOSIMOPU simulates trades for a specified period. LOSIMOPU repeats the trade simulation when there are uncertainty factors, given probability distribution, until the related indices converge. The iteration flow following Monte Carlo type simulation is shown in Figure 12.

4.   **Result Analysis:** To allow the user to compare alternative scenarios, LOSIMOPU saves the simulation results. Arranging the alternatives in a screen, LOSIMOPU shows how policy modification or capacity modification changes the expected indices. As long as the user pursues another alternative, these activities are repeated.

Figure 13. Example model for validating prototype system

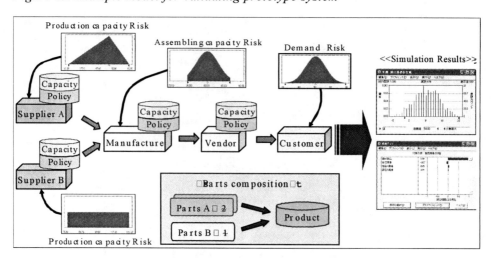

To validate the prototype system, we develop a simple supply chain model. The example model is summarized in Figure 13. There are five players: customer, vendor, manufacturer, supplier A and supplier B. Vender and manufacturer are intermediate suppliers, while there are two end suppliers. Final product is made from two pieces, part A and part B. There are five indices: inventory, sale, cost, inventory cost, and interest. Initial inventory is defined later.

Let us explain an example scenario in detail. There is an assembling capacity for manufacturer and producing capacity for arts suppliers. Note that the vendor has demand from the customer as a special capacity. LOSIMOPU should allow the vendor to assign demand patterns: constant, impulse type sudden rise, steady growth, seasonality, short life cycle, and their combinations. As a policy, there are safety stock and lot size. If current stock is less than safety stock, the player orders parts or products for lot size.

Simulation will be executed, if all parameters are assigned. The change of indices can be seen day by day. Our prototype system will not only present results visually, but it also will find bottlenecks or redundancies, as shown in Figure 14. Furthermore, any simulation result is saved by pushing the *save* button. The result screen allows comparing alternatives.

While our prototype is developed for the first step, there still remains a variety of subjects. Main issues are classified into three categories.

1.   **Commerce Type:** In the current LOSIMOPU, the commerce type corresponds, in case customers and suppliers are established beforehand. LOSIMOPU will support other commerce patterns in Table 1, step by step.

2.   **Logistics:** A transporter has not been implemented in the current LOSIMOPU, which is set up so that it may be delivered automatically one day after orders come. In order to be closer to the real world, we should create a transporter object with policy and capacity.

Figure 14. Screen example for finding bottlenecks

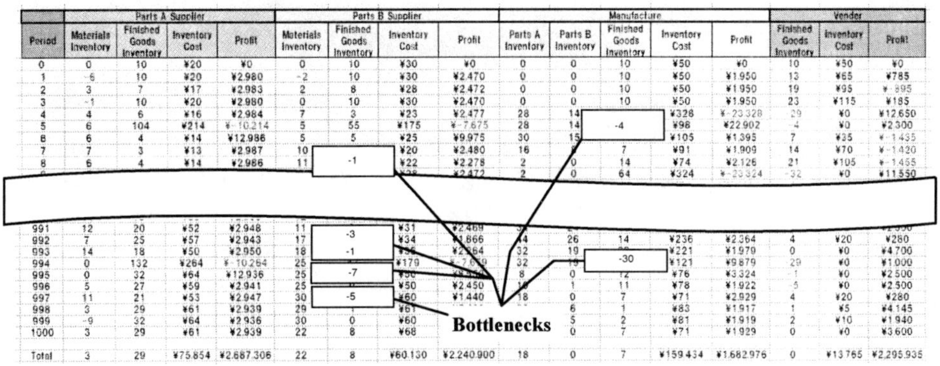

Period	Parts A Supplier				Parts B Supplier				Manufacture					Vendor		
	Materials Inventory	Finished Goods Inventory	Inventory Cost	Profit	Materials Inventory	Finished Goods Inventory	Inventory Cost	Profit	Parts A Inventory	Parts B Inventory	Finished Goods Inventory	Inventory Cost	Profit	Finished Goods Inventory	Inventory Cost	Profit
0	0	10	¥20	¥0	0	10	¥30	¥0	0	0	10	¥50	¥0	10	¥50	¥0
1	-5	10	¥20	¥2,980	-2	10	¥30	¥2,470	0	0	10	¥50	¥1,950	13	¥65	¥785
2	3	7	¥17	¥2,983	2	8	¥28	¥2,472	0	0	10	¥50	¥1,950	19	¥95	¥-895
3	-1	10	¥20	¥2,980	0	10	¥30	¥2,470	0	0	10	¥50	¥1,950	23	¥115	¥185
4	4	6	¥16	¥2,984	7	3	¥23	¥2,477	28	14		¥326	¥-23,328	29	¥0	¥12,650
5	6	104	¥214	¥-10,214	5	55	¥175	¥-7,675	28	14	-4	¥98	¥22,902	-4	¥0	¥2,300
6	6	4	¥14	¥12,986	5	5	¥25	¥9,975	30	15		¥105	¥1,395	7	¥35	¥-1,435
7	7	3	¥13	¥2,987	10		¥20	¥2,480	16		7	¥91	¥1,909	14	¥70	¥-1,420
8	6	4	¥14	¥2,986	11	-1	¥22	¥2,278	2	0	14	¥74	¥2,126	21	¥105	¥-1,455
								¥2,472	2	0	64	¥324	¥-23,324	-32	¥0	¥11,550
991	12	20	¥52	¥2,948	11	-3	¥31	¥2,469								
992	7	25	¥57	¥2,943	17		¥34	¥1,866	4	26	14	¥236	¥2,364	4	¥20	¥280
993	14	18	¥50	¥2,950	18	-1			32	19		¥221	¥1,979	0	¥0	¥4,700
994	0	132	¥284	¥-10,264	25		¥179		32		-30	¥121	¥9,879	29	¥0	¥1,000
995	0	32	¥64	¥12,936	25	-7				8		¥76	¥3,324	-1	¥0	¥2,500
996	5	27	¥59	¥2,941	25		¥50	¥2,450		1	11	¥78	¥1,922	-5	¥0	¥2,500
997	11	21	¥53	¥2,947	30	-5	¥60	¥1,440	8	0	7	¥71	¥2,929	4	¥20	¥280
998	3	29	¥61	¥2,939	29		¥6			6	1	¥83	¥1,917	1	¥5	¥4,145
999	-9	32	¥64	¥2,936	30	0	¥60			5	2	¥81	¥1,919	2	¥10	¥1,940
1000	3	29	¥61	¥2,939	22	8	¥68			0	7	¥71	¥1,929	0	¥0	¥3,600
Total	3	29	¥75,854	¥2,687,306	22	8	¥60,130	¥2,240,900	18	0	7	¥159,434	¥1,682,976	0	¥13,765	¥2,295,935

Bottlenecks

3. **Evaluation:** There is a variety of indices for evaluating capacity and policy. One approach is to apply DEA technique (Zhou, 2003).

Conclusion and Discussion

This chapter has described a concurrent supply chain simulator called LOSIMOPU. LOSIMOPU is designed for modeling and decision making under policy and capacity alternatives.

This chapter classifies players into five classes, where classification is based on business activity analysis. Player objects act concurrently for assigned policy and capacity. This chapter also shows the prototype system under established relationships among participants. The prototype system provides the function for policy and capacity assignment and indices visualization.

For future work, LOSIMOPU will simulate a wide range of supply chains, such as customer-driven market, supplier-driven market, and flexible relationships among players. Then, we will have the chance to use it as a research platform in which the experts can include the supplemental policy controllers and the special functions in the simulator.

References

Angerofer, B.J. (2000). System dynamics modeling in supply chain management: Research review. *Proceedings of the Winter Simulation Conference,* Orlando, FL.

Coyle, J., Bardi, E.J., & Langley, C.J. (1996). *The management of business logistics.* St. Paul, MN: West Publishing Company.

Evans, J.R., & Olson, D.L. (1998). *Introduction to simulation and risk analysis.* Englewood Cliffs, NJ: Prentice Hall, Inc.

Goldratt, E., & Cox, J. (1993). *Goal: A process of ongoing improvement.* Great Barrington, MA: Penguin Highbridge Audio Publisher.

Gomaa, H. (2000). *Designing concurrent, distributed, and real-time applications with UML.* Boston: Addison Wesley.

Hammer, M., & Champy, J. (1993). Reengineering the corporation: A manifesto for business revolution. *Harper Business.*

Karaesmen, F., Buzacott, J.A., & Dallery, Y. (1992). Integrating advance order information in make-to-stock production systems, *IIE Transactions, 34,* 649-662.

Knoshafian, S., & Buckiewica, M. (1995). *Introduction to groupware, workflow, and workgroup computing.* New York: John Wiley & Sons.

Konzo, T., Saga, R., Aoki, S., & Tsuji, H. (2003). Embedding policy and capacity in concurrent SCM simulator. *Proceedings of the IEEE International Conference on Systems, Man & Cybernetics,* Washington, DC.

Koretsune, A., Saga, R., Konzo, T., & Tsuji, H. (2004). SCM simulator with uncertain parameters. *Proceedings of the IEEE International Conference on Systems, Man & Cybernetics,* Hague, The Netherlands.

Mine, H. (1966). *Operations research.* Tokyo: Asakura-Shoten.

Saga, R., Konzo, T., Aoki, S., & Tsuji, H. (2003). Framework of e-marketplace for concurrent SCM simulator. *Proceedings of the IEEE International Conference on Systems, Man & Cybernetics,* Washington, DC.

Tian, C., et al. (2003). Enterprise collaborative system based on supply chain. *Proceedings of the IEEE International Conference on Systems, Man & Cybernetics,* Washington, DC.

Tsuji, H., Saga, R., & Konzo, T. (2003). Distributed object based simulator LOSIMOPU. *Proceedings of the IRMA (International Resource Management Associates) International Conference 2003,* Philadelphia, Pennsylvania.

Winograd, T. (1988). A language/action perspective on the design of cooperative work. In I. Grief (Ed.), *Computer supported cooperative work: A book of readings.* San Mateo, CA: Morgan Kaufmann.

Zhou, Y., & Chen, Y. (2003). DEA-based performance predictive design of complex dynamic system—Business process improvement. *Proceedings of the IEEE International Conference on Systems, Man & Cybernetics,* Washington, DC.

Chapter XIV

A Time-Dependent Supply Chain Network Equilibrium Problem

Huey-Kuo Chen
National Central University, Taiwan

Huey-Wen Chou
National Central University, Taiwan

Abstract

This chapter deals with a time-dependent supply chain network equilibrium (TD-SCNE) problem, which allows product flows to be distributed over a network, not only between two successive sectors in the same time period (a transaction), but also between two successive periods for the same agency (an inventory). Since product price and flow interactions are inherently embedded within it, the TD-SCNE problem is formulated as a variational inequality (VI) model. A three-loop-nested diagonalization method, along with a specially designed supernetwork representation, then is proposed and demonstrated with a numerical example. In equilibrium, for each time-dependent retailer agency or demand market, the product prices of transactions are the same and minimum, no matter when or where the product comes from, which is a realization of the Wardropian first principle. The proposed framework can be extended with minor modifications to other TD-SCNE-related equilibrium problems.

Introduction

Supply chain management is a major subject in economics (Hopp et al., 2000). A bundle of research topics in this area has been identified and elaborately explored, consisting of optimum buffer sizes, stock levels, and the dynamics and stability of supply chains, among other topics. This book covers a large variety of skills and techniques for analyzing and designing global integrated supply chain systems. Setting it apart from the other chapters, this chapter focuses on a highly technical, yet equally intriguing, topic— the time-dependent supply chain network equilibrium (TD-SCNE) problem. Since development of related models and algorithms is still in an embryonic stage, there is only a handful of relevant publications on the TD-SCNE problem.

The TD-SCNE problem is based largely on its time-independent counterpart, the supply chain network equilibrium (SCNE) problem. The SCNE describes how product flows distribute over a network and finally end up with product prices, which, in turn, affect the amount of product demands. The convective phenomenon between the product prices and demands will resonate. This problem first was formulated using the variational inequality (VI) approach and analytically solved with the modified projection method (Nagurney et al., 2002). Under the assumption that a vector function F enters the VI and is strictly monotone and *Lipschitz* continuous (and that a solution exists for it), the modified projection algorithm for the SCNE model is guaranteed to converge. This equilibrium model captures both the independent behavior of the various decision makers as well as the effect of their interactions, which, indeed, are essential components for closely representing a perfect competitive market. However, this model formulation (in the class of spatial price equilibrium problems) and its modified projection algorithm (consisting of two main algorithmic steps: computation and adaptation) have not really intrigued the transportation community, perhaps because the familiar concept of transportation networks and relevant solution algorithms has not been employed.

Generally speaking, transportation networks are characterized by link/path flow variables, and the corresponding link/path cost information is computed by cost functions based on the known flows. Compared with spatial price models such as the SCNE, transportation network models have been widely taught and applied. Yet, transforming the SCNE model into a corresponding transportation network model is not an easy task. The difficulty arises from the fact that the former is characterized essentially by the demand function in terms of price decision variables (called a price model formulation) and the latter by the quantity function (or the inverse of the demand function) with respect to quantity decision variables (called a quantity model formulation). Unless the inverse of the price model formulation exists and can be derived, the transformation of the SCNE problem into its corresponding transportation network model cannot be made. In fact, the inverse of a function can be derived only when that function is defined under a one-to-one mapping condition. To this end, the premise of the conversion between two types of model formulations relies on the understanding of and, moreover, on resolving the (asymmetric) link interactions embedded in the price model formulation.

Without knowing how to transform the price model formulation into the corresponding quantity model formulation, and by persisting with the quantity model, Chen, et al. (2004a) proposed a brute-force method or, more specifically, a trial-and-error solution algorithm, which iteratively solved a fixed demand traffic assignment problem for the SCNE problem. Though feasible, the trial-and-error method is not satisfactory, mainly due to the lack of sound theoretical foundation (and a rather low level of precision in the results). Nonetheless, these drawbacks inspired innovations in elaborating the link interactions of the demand functions upon which a corresponding quantity model was developed successfully (Chen et al., 2004b, 2005). Following the construction of the aforementioned quantity model, some other quantity interactions embedded in the remaining cost functions also were treated, yielding an optimization subproblem. A nested diagonalization (ND) method embedding the Frank-Wolfe algorithm, along with a supernetwork representation, was then proposed and validated with the same numerical example as that given in Nagurney et al. (2002). Since the dual variables associated with the flow conservation constraints for the retailers need not be explicitly included in their VI model, this new model formulation, hereafter referred to as the *basic model*, is more compact and, indeed, simpler than that of Nagurney et al. (2002).

This basic model constructs a core-to-price modeling and can pave the way to an enriched area of research in which many convenient, real features will be added to price models. In this regard, a feature of price models that need immediate treatment is the inventory flows between two successive time periods for a manufacturer and/or a retailer. Having an inventory is common and sometimes inevitable for an entrepreneur, regardless of whether a just-in-time operational policy is respected or not. The level of inventory affects the profitability of an entrepreneur. The first step, then, in making the SCNE problem more realistic is to model the inventory appropriately. Note that taking inventory flows into consideration requires no additional behavioral assumptions for achieving the equilibrium conditions. The only work, as shall be seen later, is incorporating the temporal dimension into the SCNE model, which will result in the TE-SCNE model. With this maneuver, the amount of inventory for each agency during each time period still will be governed, as experienced in the static SCNE model, by the so-called Wardropian first principle and automatically determined within the proposed solution procedure.

In the following, the TD-SCNE problem is introduced first, including its equilibrium conditions and corresponding VI-based model formulation. Second, after resolving the product price and flow interactions, a three-loop ND method, along with a specially designed supernetwork representation, is proposed and elaborated. Third, a small numerical example is validated. Finally, a few closing remarks are given in the end.

The Time-Dependent Supply Chain Network Equilibrium Problem

The TD-SCNE problem represents economic sectors in tiers over a number of time periods of interest; each tier/sector contains a number of its agencies, and each agency is denoted by a node. Some nodes between the two consecutive tiers are connected by links in which products can flow from one tier to their successive tier. The other nodes between the two consecutive periods for an agency are connected by links in which products can flow

Figure 1. Basic network representation of the TD-SCNE problem (before relaxation of link interactions)

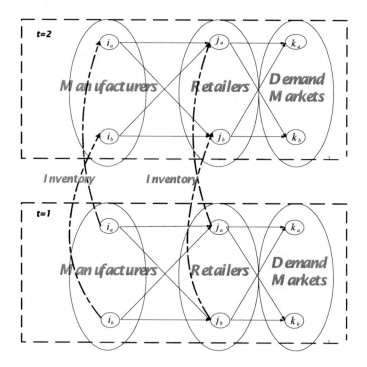

from one period to the next for the same agency. Three sectors (manufacturer, retailer, and demand markets) are of interest over $|T|$ time periods (indexed by t). For each specific period t, the products are produced first by the $|I|$ competitive manufacturers (indexed by i) and then shipped to the $|J|$ retailers (indexed by j) and, finally, cleared at the $|K|$ demand markets (indexed by k). The total amount of the product consumed (represented as the function of the product prices in the demand markets) is, in turn, produced by manufacturers and then transacted to retailers.

In each time period that the amount of the product manufactured or purchased at an agency is greater than that transacted out, the agency incurs an inventory. The product inventory incurred at an agency will be carried over from one period to the next through the newly added inventory link that is associated with inventory cost.

Let $\{q_{ijt}\}=Q_t^1$, $\{q_{jkt}\}=Q_t^2$, $\{q_{iit}\}$ and $\{q_{jjt}\}$ denote, respectively, the vector for product flows between manufacturer and retailer sectors during time period t, the vector for product flows between retailers and demand markets during time period t, the vector for product inventory incurred by a manufacturer during time period t and to be carried over to time period $t+1$, and the vector for product inventory incurred by a retailer during time period t and to be carried over to time period $t+1$.

We also assume that for each time period t, each manufacturer i is faced with a production cost $c_{it}(Q_t^1)$ (a node cost), inventory cost $c_{iit}(q_{iit})$ (a link cost), and a transaction cost $c_{ijt}(q_{ijt})$ between manufacturer i and retailer j (a link cost). The retailers must agree with the manufacturers on the volume of shipments, since the former are faced with the handling and storage cost $c_{jt}(Q_t^1)$ associated with having the product in their retail outlet (a node cost) and inventory cost $c_{jjt}(q_{jjt})$ (a link cost). Consumers in demand market k determine their optimal consumption levels at the various retailers, based both on the prices charged for the product and the cost $\hat{c}_{jkt}(Q_t^2)$ (a link cost) for conducting the transaction (which may include the cost of transportation associated with obtaining the product from the retailer).

To conserve product flows between sectors, the TD-SCNE model also requires that (1) the total amount of the product manufactured or left over from the previous time period either be shipped to the successive retailer sector or carried over to the next time period; (2) the total amount of the product purchased from the upstream manufacturer sector and those left over from the previous time period wither be shipped to the successive demand market or carried over to the next time period; and (3) all the product shipped to the demand markets must be cleared. If equilibrium is achieved, all shipments among the tiers of network agencies or among the time periods for the same agency will coincide.

Equilibrium Conditions

The equilibrium conditions for the TE-SCNE problem can be decomposed into two parts. One is associated with time-dependent product flows and the other with time-dependent product prices. The equilibrium conditions having to do with the time-dependent product flows are as follows. For a manufacturer i during interval t' (denoted as an origin it') and a demand k during time period t (denoted as a destination kt), the price charged for the product (mathematically equivalent to a cost on route p from manufacturer it' to demand market kt through a retailer j, denoted as $\hat{c}_p^{it',kt}$ in the network) is equal and minimal. In detail, for each time-dependent O-D pair (it',kt), if the product flows over route p are positive (i.e., $q_p^{it',kt*} > 0$), then the corresponding product route cost $\hat{c}_p^{it',kt}$ is minimal and, furthermore, essentially equal to the product price in the demand market k during time period t (i.e., ρ_{kt}). However, if no product flow occurs on route p (i.e., $q_p^{it',kt*} = 0$), the corresponding product route cost $\hat{c}_p^{it',kt}$ is at least as great as the product price ρ_{kt}. The corresponding equilibrium conditions can be expressed mathematically as follows:

$$\hat{c}_p^{it',kt*} \begin{cases} = \rho_{kt}^* & \text{if } q_p^{it',kt*} > 0 \\ \geq \rho_{kt}^* & \text{if } q_p^{it',kt*} = 0 \end{cases} \quad \forall i,t',k,t,p \tag{1}$$

Note that route p is comprised of several links in the network. The links could include production and/or inventory links in the manufacturer sector, handling and storage, and/or inventory links in the retailer sector; finally, the transaction links between manufacturer and retailer sectors and between the retailer sector and demand markets. This incidence notation between a link, $Link$, and a path, p, may be illustrated by the incidence index $\delta_{Link,p}^{it',kt}$. When a $Link$ is on route p, then the corresponding incidence index is realized as 1 (i.e., $\delta_{Link,p}^{it',kt}=1$); otherwise, $\delta_{Link,p}^{it',kt}=0$. With the above definition, the route cost $\hat{c}_p^{it',kt}$ is defined as the sum of link costs along route p, which readily can be calculated from the associated $Link$ costs, such as the marginal inventory cost of a manufacturer i from time period t to $t+1$, $\hat{c}_{iit}(q_{iit})$, the marginal production cost incurred by a manufacturer i during time period t, $\hat{c}_{it}(Q_t^1)$, the marginal transaction cost between a manufacturer i and a retailer j during time period t, $\hat{c}_{ijt}(q_{ijt})$, the marginal inventory cost of a retailer j during time period t, $\hat{c}_{jjt}(q_{jjt})$, the marginal handling and storage cost of a retailer j during time period t, $\hat{c}_{jt}(q_{jt})$, and the transaction cost between a retailer j and a demand market k during time period t, $\hat{c}_{jkt}(Q_t^2)$. The symbol "^" placed above a total cost function represents its derivative. Note that the time-dependent product cost $\hat{c}_{it}(Q_t^1)$ and time-dependent marginal handling and storage costs $\hat{c}_{jt}(q_{jt})$ are represented as node costs in Figure 1, which are not common in transportation network modeling and need to be suitably represented as link costs.

The other type of equilibrium conditions for the TE-SCNE problem have to do with product prices. In the case of product prices, if the equilibrium time-dependent price ρ_{kt}^*, which consumers are willing to pay for the product in the demand market k is positive, then the quantity produced for the demand market kt by all the manufacturers it' (i.e., $\sum_{(i,t')}q^{it',kt*}$), will be precisely equal to the demand for the product in that time-dependent demand market kt (i.e., $d_{kt}(\rho^*)$). Otherwise, the demand is less than or equal to the total amount of commodity available in that time-dependent demand market. (Note that when a supernetwork with the super-origin K is constructed, as will be discussed latter, the quantity $\sum_{(i,t')}q^{it',kt*}$ is regarded as the demand flow between super-origin K and destination kt (i.e., $q^{Kkt}=\sum_{(i,t')}q^{it',kt*}$)). These assumptions correspond to the following spatial price equilibrium conditions.

$$d_{kt}\left(\boldsymbol{\rho}_t^*\right) \begin{cases} = \sum\limits_{(i,t')} q^{it',kt*} & \text{if } \rho_{kt}^* > 0 \\[2mm] \leq \sum\limits_{(i,t')} q^{it',kt*} & \text{if } \rho_{kt}^* = 0 \end{cases} \qquad \forall k,t \tag{2}$$

Model Formulation

The equilibrium conditions (1)~(2) are equivalent to the solution of the following VI model defining the TD-SCNE problem

$$\sum_i \sum_t \left[\hat{c}_{it}\left(Q_t^{1*}\right)\right] \times \left[q_{it} - q_{it}^*\right] + \sum_i \sum_t \left[\hat{c}_{iit}\left(q_{iit}^*\right)\right] \times \left[q_{iit} - q_{iit}^*\right]$$

$$+ \sum_i \sum_j \sum_t \left[\hat{c}_{ijt}\left(q_{ijt}^*\right)\right] \times \left[q_{ijt} - q_{ijt}^*\right]$$

$$+ \sum_j \sum_t \left[\hat{c}_{jt}\left(Q_t^{1*}\right)\right] \times \left[q_{jt} - q_{jt}^*\right] \qquad \forall \left\{q_{iit}, Q_t^1, q_{ijt}, Q_t^2, \boldsymbol{\rho}_t\right\} \in \Omega$$

$$+ \sum_j \sum_t \left[\hat{c}_{jjt}\left(q_{jjt}^*\right)\right] \times \left[q_{jjt} - q_{jjt}^*\right] + \sum_j \sum_k \sum_t \left[\hat{c}_{jkt}\left(Q_t^{2*}\right)\right] \times \left[q_{jkt} - q_{jkt}^*\right] \tag{3}$$

$$+ \sum_k \sum_t \left[\sum_{(i,t')} q^{it',kt} - d_{kt}\left(\boldsymbol{\rho}_t^*\right)\right] \times \left[\rho_{kt} - \rho_{kt}^*\right] \geq 0$$

where the feasible region Ω is delineated by the following flow conservation: nonegativity and definitional constraints.

Flow conservation constraints:

$$q_{ii(t-1)} + q_{it} = \sum_j q_{ijt} + q_{iit} \qquad \forall i,t \tag{4}$$

$$q_{jj(t-1)} + \sum_i q_{ijt} = \sum_k q_{jkt} + q_{jjt} \qquad \forall j,t \tag{5}$$

$$d_{kt}\left(\boldsymbol{\rho}_t\right) = \sum_j q_{jkt} \qquad \forall k,t \tag{6}$$

Nonegativity constraints:

$$q_{it} \geq 0 \quad \forall i,t \tag{7}$$

$$q_{iit} \geq 0 \quad \forall i,t \tag{8}$$

$$q_{ijt} \geq 0 \quad \forall i,j,t \tag{9}$$

$$q_{jjt} \geq 0 \quad \forall j,t \tag{10}$$

$$q_{jkt} \geq 0 \quad \forall j,k,t \tag{11}$$

$$\rho_{kt} \geq 0 \quad \forall k,t \tag{12}$$

Definitional constraints:

$$\hat{c}_p^{it',kt} = \sum_{LINK \in p} \hat{c}_{LINK} \quad \forall i,t',k,t,p \tag{13}$$

$$q_{Link} = \sum_{(i,t')} \sum_{(k,t)} \sum_p q_p^{it',kt} \quad \forall Link \tag{14}$$

Eqns (4)~(5) conserve product flows at each time-dependent manufacturer and retailer, respectively. Eqn (4) states that for manufacturer I, the product inventory left over from the previous time period $q_{ii(t-1)}$ plus the time-dependent product production q_{it} is equal to the quantity $\sum_j q_{ijt}$ (which is sold to all the retailers during time period t) plus the inventory incurred in the current time period q_{iit}. Eqn (5) states that for retailer j, the product inventory left over from the previous time period $q_{jj(t-1)}$ plus the quantity $\sum_i q_{ijt}$ (the amount of the product purchased from all the manufacturers during time period t) is equal to the quantity $\sum_k q_{jkt}$ (shipped to all the demand markets during time period t) plus the inventory q_{jjt} incurred in the current time period. Eqn (6) indicates that the quantity $\sum_j q_{jkt}$ purchased of the product from the retailers will be precisely equal to the time-dependent demand $d_{kt}(\rho_t^*)$ for the product in that demand market during time period t. Eqns (7)~(12) require that the total amount of the time-dependent production by each manufacturer q_{it}, the time-dependent inventory for each manufacturer q_{iit}, the time-dependent transaction between each manufacturer-retailer pair q_{ijt}, the time-dependent transaction between each retailer-demand market pair q_{ijt}, the time-dependent inventory for each retailer q_{ikt}, and the time-dependent demand price in each demand market ρ_{kt} be non-negative. Eqn (13) defines a time-dependent route cost comprising several time-dependent link/node costs, such as the marginal production cost and inventory cost for each manufacturer, the marginal transaction cost for each manufacturer-retailer pair, the marginal handling and storage cost, the inventory cost for each retailer, and the transaction cost for each retailer-demand market pair. Eqn (14) expresses the link flows in terms of route flows.

For the sake of compactness, this chapter does not include the equivalent proof between the equilibrium conditions (1)~(2) and their corresponding TD-SCNE model (3). The interested reader may refer to Nagurney, et al. (2002) for a similar proof.

Solution Algorithm

Concept of the Proposed Solution Algorithm

The TD-SCNE problem inherits two types of asymmetric link interactions: (1) time-dependent price interactions in the demand functions $\{d_{kt}(\rho_t)\}$ and (2) time-dependent product flow interactions in the production cost functions $c_{it}(Q_t^1)$, the handling and storage cost functions $c_{jt}(Q_t^1)$, and the transaction cost function $\hat{c}_{jkt}(Q_t^2)$. Treatment of the first type of link interactions allows the transformation of the price model formulation into its corresponding quantity model formulation, which is more consistent with the conventions of transportation studies. Further treatment of the second type of link interactions will result in an optimization subproblem, to which many prevailing optimization solution algorithms can be applied. Resolving these two types of asymmetric link interactions naturally results in a three-loop ND method for solving the TD-SCNE problem. In the first loop, asymmetric price interactions are relaxed, resulting in a reduced VI subproblem (a quantity model formulation). In the second loop, product flow interactions embedded in the link cost functions are relaxed, yielding a separable optimization subproblem with variable demand. In the third loop, the resulting variable demand subproblem can be addressed (by way of a network presentation) as a fixed demand problem (Sheffi, 1985), and solved by any suitable optimization solution algorithm, such as the gradient projection (GP) algorithm (Jayakrishnan et al., 1994).

First Loop Operation (Relaxation of Price Interactions)

The quantity of a product being consumed in a market usually can be expressed as the demand function of several product prices shown in different markets and perhaps across different time periods. The inverse of this many-to-one demand function does not exist, which prevents us from transforming the original price formulation model into a quantity formulation model.

However, by way of a relaxation (i.e., $\left(\bar{\rho}_t \setminus \bar{\rho}_{kt}, \rho_{kt}\right), \forall k, t$), the time-dependent asymmetric demand functions can be diagonalized as $d_{kt}\left(\bar{\rho}_t \setminus \bar{\rho}_{kt}, \rho_{kt}\right)$ or simply denoted as $\{d_{kt}(\rho_{kt})\}$, which is essentially a one-to-one mapping function. Note that the diagonalized time-dependent demand functions $\{d_{kt}(\rho_{kt})\}$ now are separable, and, hence, the corresponding inverse demand functions $\left\{d_{kt}^{-1}\left(\sum_{(i,t')} q^{it',kt}\right)\right\}$ can be derived. With these inverse demand functions, the equilibrium conditions (2) subsequently can be rewritten as follows:

$$\rho_{kt}^* \begin{cases} = d_{kt}^{-1}\left(\displaystyle\sum_{(i,t')} q^{it',kt*}\right) & \text{if } \displaystyle\sum_{(i,t')} q^{it',kt*} > 0 \\[2ex] \geq d_{kt}^{-1}\left(\displaystyle\sum_{(i,t')} q^{it',kt*}\right) & \text{if } \displaystyle\sum_{(i,t')} q^{it',kt*} = 0 \end{cases} \qquad \forall k,t \qquad (15)$$

Eqn (15) states that if the total amount of product transacted in demand market k during time period t is positive (i.e., $\sum_{(i,t')} q^{it',kt*} > 0$), then the corresponding product price ρ_{kt}^* is equal to the time-dependent inverse demand function $d_{kt}^{-1}\left(\sum_{(i,t')} q^{it',kt*}\right)$. However, if no product is transacted in demand market k during time period t (i.e., $\sum_{(i,t')} q^{it',kt*} = 0$), then the corresponding time-dependent price ρ_{kt}^* is at least as great as the time-dependent inverse demand function $d_{kt}^{-1}\left(\sum_{(i,t')} q^{it',kt*}\right)$.

Corresponding with equilibrium conditions (1), (15), TD-SCNE problem (3) consequently is reduced to the following VI-based quantity submodel, which characterizes the time-dependent supply chain network equilibrium with diagonalized inverse variable demand and cost

$$\sum_i \sum_t [\hat{c}_{it}(Q_t^{1*})] \times [q_{it} - q_{it}^*] + \sum_i \sum_t [\hat{c}_{iit}(q_{iit}^*)] \times [q_{iit} - q_{iit}^*]$$

$$+ \sum_i \sum_j \sum_t [\hat{c}_{ijt}(q_{ijt}^*)] \times [q_{ijt} - q_{ijt}^*]$$

$$+ \sum_j \sum_t [\hat{c}_{jt}(Q_t^{1*})] \times [q_{jt} - q_{jt}^*] \qquad\qquad \forall \{q_{iit}, Q_t^1, q_{ijt}, Q_t^2\} \in \Omega_d$$

$$+ \sum_j \sum_t [\hat{c}_{jjt}(q_{jjt}^*)] \times [q_{jjt} - q_{jjt}^*] + \sum_j \sum_k \sum_t [\hat{c}_{jkt}(Q_t^{2*})] \times [q_{jkt} - q_{jkt}^*] \qquad (16)$$

$$- \sum_k \sum_t d_{kt}^{-1}\left(\sum_{(i,t')} q^{it',kt*}\right) \times \left[\sum_{(i,t')} q^{it',kt} - \sum_{(i,t')} q^{it',kt*}\right] \geq 0$$

functions, where Ω_d is the subset (with the diagonalized inverse variable demand functions) of the original feasible region Ω delineated by constraints (4)~(14). Note that when prices other than those in the subject demand market k during time period t are fixed temporarily at a certain level, Eqn (6) already has been changed to:

$$d_{kt}(\bar{\rho}_t \setminus \bar{\rho}_{kt}, \rho_{kt}) = \sum_j q_{jkt} \quad \forall k, t \qquad\qquad (17)$$

The reader may refer to Tobin (1986) for a similar equivalency proof among equilibrium conditions (1) and (15) and their corresponding subproblem (16).

Second Loop Operation (Relaxation of Product Flow Interactions)

The supply cost of a product often can be expressed as a cost function with respect to several interrelated time-dependent product flows. The effect of the time-dependent product flow in one market on the supply cost of another market often is not the same as the time-dependent product flow of the first market on the supply cost of the other market. In short, the product flow interactions embedded in the time-dependent cost functions are not parallel. However, time-dependent product flow interactions in the production cost functions $c_{it}(Q_t^1)$, the handling and storage cost functions $c_{jt}(Q_t^1)$, and the transaction cost function $\hat{c}_{jkt}(Q_t^2)$ can be relaxed by temporarily fixing the other time-dependent product flows at a certain level. By doing so, the above cost functions become

228 Chen & Chou

separable and can be simplified as $c_{it}\left(\overline{Q}_t^1 \setminus \overline{q}_{it}, q_{it}\right)$, $c_{jt}\left(\overline{Q}_t^1 \setminus \overline{q}_{jt}, q_{jt}\right)$, $\hat{c}_{jkt}\left(\overline{Q}_t^2 \setminus \overline{q}_{jkt}, q_{jkt}\right)$, respectively. As a consequence, according to Green's theorem, an optimization subproblem with variable demand can be yielded. We will treat this subproblem in the next subsection.

Third Loop Operation (Solving an Optimization Subproblem)

After the time-dependent price and flow interactions have been relaxed, an optimization subproblem with variable demand results as follows:

$$
\begin{aligned}
\min_{\mathbf{q} \in \Omega_d} & \sum_i \sum_t c_{it}\left(\overline{Q}_t^1 \setminus \overline{q}_{it}, q_{it}\right) + \sum_i \sum_t c_{iit}\left(q_{iit}\right) + \sum_i \sum_j \sum_t c_{ijt}\left(q_{ijt}\right) \\
& + \sum_j \sum_t c_{jt}\left(\overline{Q}_t^1 \setminus \overline{q}_{jt}, q_{jt}\right) + \sum_j \sum_t c_{jjt}\left(q_{jjt}\right) \\
& + \sum_j \sum_k \sum_t \int_0^{q_{jkt}} \hat{c}_{jkt}\left(\overline{Q}_t^2 \setminus \overline{q}_{jkt}, \varpi\right) d\varpi - \sum_k \sum_t \int_0^{\sum_{(t,t')} q^{it',kt}} d_{kt}^{-1}\left(\varpi\right) d\varpi
\end{aligned}
\tag{18}
$$

This variable demand problem (18) can be regarded (by way of a supernetwork representation) as a fixed demand problem by which optimization solution algorithms, such as the GP algorithm, can be applied.

Supernetwork Representation

The TD-SCNE problem can be illustrated by a meaningful network representation. However, the basic network graphed in Figure 1 is too aggregate for many essential ingredients of the TD-SCNE problem to be appropriately represented. Additions of dummy nodes and links thus are needed to address this issue.

1. The time-dependent marginal product cost $\hat{c}_{it}\left(Q_t^1\right)$ that is implicitly embedded in each manufacturer node in Figure 1 can be associated explicitly with a dummy link $K{\to}it$ for each manufacturer i during time period t, where K is a dummy super-origin node.

2. The time-dependent marginal handling and storage cost $\hat{c}_{jt}\left(Q_t^1\right)$ that is implicitly embedded in each retailer node in Figure 1 can be explicitly associated with a dummy link $j{\to}j'$ by duplicating a dummy node j' for each retailer j.

3. For each demand market k during time period t, the amount of product consumed may be produced from various manufacturers at different time periods, rather than only one. To conserve the product consumption in each demand market k during

time period t (i.e., $\sum_{(i,t')} q^{it',kt} = d_{kt}(\mathbf{\rho}_{kt})$), a dummy super-origin node $\check{s}$ that proceeds all manufacturers in different time periods is needed. Having done this, the assignment of the productions in the forward direction from the manufacturer sector to the demand markets via the retailer sector can be carried out readily.

4. Asymmetric price interactions make the time-dependent demand functions $\{d_{kt}(\rho_t)\}$ inseparable. However, by temporarily fixing the price interactions (i.e., by fixing the other product prices at a certain level), the diagonalized time-dependent demand function can be expressed as $d_{kt}(\rho_{kt}) = d_{kt}(\overline{\mathbf{\rho}}_t \setminus \overline{\rho}_{kt}, \rho_{kt}), \forall k, t$, which is separable with respect to the product prices and makes feasible the time-dependent inverse demand function $d_{kt}^{-1}\left(\sum_{(i,t')} q^{it',kt}\right) \forall k, t$. In the case of variable demand problems, a dummy link from time-independent super-origin $\check{s}$ to each destination k during time

Figure 2. Supernetwork representation of the TD-SCNE problem (after relaxations of link interactions)

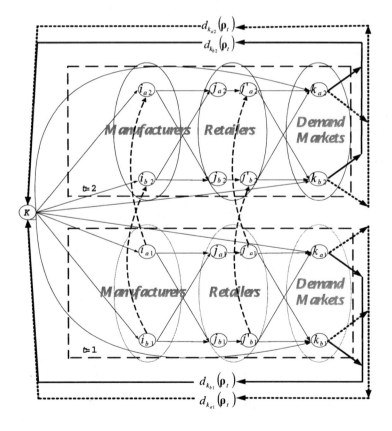

period t (associated with the cost of $d_{kt}^{-1}\left(\sum_{(i,t')} q^{it',kt}\right), \forall k,t$) usually is constructed to accommodate the excess demands (i.e., $q_{max}^{Kkt} - d_{kt}(\rho_{kt})$), where q_{max}^{Kkt} denotes the upper bound of demand in market k during time period t. Given the upper bound of demands in all markets in this supernetwork representation, the variable demand problem (18) can be treated as a fixed demand problem.

Following the addition of these dummy nodes and links, the end nodes of some links appearing in Figure 1 should be changed accordingly. The link j->k that is associated with the transaction cost between retailer j and demand market k during time period t should be changed to link j'->k with cost $\{c_{j'k}(Q_t^2)\}$. Additions of dummy links it->$i(t+1)$ for each manufacturer from time period t to $t+1$ and for each retailer from time period t to $t+1$ are necessary. Based on the preceding discussion, Figure 2 illustrates a new supernetwork for the TD-SCNE problem. Note that for each origin-destination pair (K, kt), a number of paths are possible; some are within a time period, whereas others may span different time periods.

Algorithmic Steps

In responding to the preceding detailed discussion, an ND method embedding the GP algorithm is proposed in order to solve the TD-SCNE problem. The main idea behind the diagonalization technique is that it fixes certain independent variables of the equilibrium problem in such a way so as to create its own variable or separable transportation cost and its own demand function. Separability makes the Jacobian matrices formed from these functions diagonal and, therefore, symmetric; hence, the name of the method. Each separable or diagonalized problem is solved, and its solution is used to create a new diagonalized problem. The sequence of flow/price/quantity patterns generated in this process will subsequently be shown to converge, in at least certain circumstances, to a unique equilibrium.

As shown in Figure 3, the schematic of the ND method includes three loop operations. In the first loop operation, product price interactions are diagonalized, and, consequently, a VI-based quantity submodel is formulated. In the second loop, product flow interactions are relaxed and, hence, separable, yielding a variable demand optimization subproblem. In the innermost loop, the variable demand subproblem is solved as an equivalent fixed demand subproblem by giving an upper bound of demand q_{max}^{Kkt} for each origin-destination pair (κ, kt). At an equilibrium, the excess demand $q_{max}^{Kkt} - d_{kt}(\rho_{kt})$ will be dumped onto the dummy link $\check{s}$->kt associated with link cost $d_{kt}^{-1}(q^{Kkt}), \forall k,t$. Next, the obtained product flows and prices are checked for convergence. If the convergence criterion has not been obtained, then, as necessary, the time-dependent product prices will be updated in the first loop operation; the time-dependent product flows will be updated in the second loop operation, and the variable demand problem (treated as an

Figure 3. Schematic of the nested diagonalization method

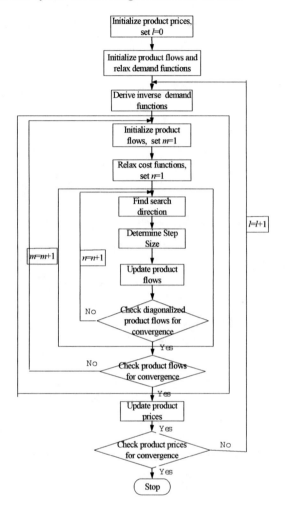

equivalent fixed demand problem) will be solved again. This procedure is continued until the convergence criteria are satisfied.

The algorithmic steps can now be stated as follows:

Step 0: Initialize time-dependent product prices.

Step 0.1: Set initial time-dependent product prices to zero, $\{\rho_{kt}\}^0 = \{0\}$. Set $l=0$.

Step 1: First loop operation (resulting in the VI-based quantity model formulation).

Step 1.1: Impose upper limits for the demand functions $q_{\max}^{Kkt} = d_{kt}(\boldsymbol{\rho}_t)$, $\forall k,t$. Construct the diagonalized time-dependent demand functions $d_{kt}(\rho_{kt}) = d_{kt}(\bar{\boldsymbol{\rho}}_t^l \setminus \bar{\rho}_{kt}^l, \rho_{kt}) \forall k,t$. Derive their inverse functions $\{d_{kt}^{-1}(q^{Kkt})\}$ and formulate the VI-based quantity submodel (16).

Step 2: Second loop operation (resulting in the variable demand optimization subproblem (a separable problem).

Step 2.1: Initialize time-dependent product flows. Find an initial feasible time-dependent flow pattern $\{q_{iit}\}^m$, $\{Q_t^1\}^m = \{q_{ijt}\}^m$, $\{q_{ijt}\}^m$, $\{Q_t^2\}^m = \{q_{ikt}\}^m$, $\{q^{Kkt}\}^m$ based on the $\hat{c}_{it}(0)$, $\hat{c}_{iit}(0)$, $\hat{c}_{ijt}(0)$, $\hat{c}_{jt}(0)$, $\hat{c}_{ijt}(0)$, $\hat{c}_{jkt}(0)$ and $d_{kt}^{-1}(0)$. Let $m=0$.

Step 2.2: For each link, fix the time-dependent product flows at the current level, except for the flow on the subject time-space link, yielding the variable demand optimization subproblem (18).

Step 3: Third loop operation (solving the variable demand subproblem by way of a network representation as an equivalent fixed demand subproblem).

Step 3.1: Initialize time-dependent product flows. For each O-D pair (K,kt), find initial feasible time-dependent path flows $\{q_p^{Kkt}\}^n$ and link flows $\{q_{Link}\}^n$ based on $\hat{c}_{it}(0)$, $\hat{c}_{iit}(0)$, $\hat{c}_{ijt}(0)$, $\hat{c}_{jt}(0)$, $\hat{c}_{ijt}(0)$, $\hat{c}_{jkt}(0)$ and $d_{kt}^{-1}(0)$, where $Link \in \{Kkt, Kit, ijt, jt, jjt, jkt\}$. Store path information into the shortest path set (i.e., Set $n=0$).

Step 3.2: Update the time-dependent marginal costs. Compute $\hat{c}_{it}(Q_t^1)^n$, $\hat{c}_{iit}(q_{iit})^n$, $\hat{c}_{ijt}(q_{ijt})^n$, $\hat{c}_{jt}(Q_t^1)^n$, $\hat{c}_{jjt}(q_{jjt})^n$, $\hat{c}_{jkt}(Q_t^2)^n$ and $d_{kt}^{-1}(q^{Kkt})^n$. For each O-D pair (K,kt), search for a shortest path over the time-dependent network. If the shortest path is different from all the paths in the path set $\mathbf{B}^{Kkt}$, denote this path as $\hat{p}$ and add it to $\mathbf{B}^{Kkt}$. Otherwise, discard the path and tag the shortest among the paths in $\mathbf{B}^{Kkt}$ as $\hat{p}$. (Note that equal route travel time can be used as a criterion to distinguish approximately two routes).

Step 3.3: Find descent direction.

For each O-D pair (K,kt), compute a search direction component, which is defined as the negative of the first derivative of the objective z with respect to route flow q_p^{Kkt}, as follows:

$$\frac{\partial z}{\partial q_p^{Kkt}} = \hat{c}_p^{Kkt} - \hat{c}_{\hat{p}}^{Kkt} \quad \forall k,t,p \tag{19}$$

Step 3.4: Determine step size. Assuming the step size modifier is set to 1, then the step size α_p^{Kkt} can be determined by the reciprocal of the second derivative below.

$$\alpha_p^{Kkt} = \left(\frac{\partial^2 z}{\partial q_p^{Kkt\,2}}\right)^{-1} = \frac{1}{\sum\limits_{Link \in A} \hat{c}'_{Link} + \sum\limits_{Link \in \hat{A}} \hat{c}'_{Link}} \qquad \forall k,t,p \tag{20}$$

where

$$A = \left\{ Link \in \left\{ \left(\bar{\delta}_{Link,p}^{Kkt} = 1\right) \wedge \left(\bar{\delta}_{Link,\hat{p}}^{Kkt} = 0\right) \right\} \right\} \tag{21}$$

$$\hat{A} = \left\{ Link \in \left\{ \left(\bar{\delta}_{Link,p}^{Kkt} = 0\right) \wedge \left(\bar{\delta}_{Link,\hat{p}}^{Kkt} = 1\right) \right\} \right\} \tag{22}$$

$$0 \leq \alpha_p^{Kkt} \leq \alpha_{max} \qquad \forall k,t,p \neq \hat{p} \tag{23}$$

Set A contains those time-dependent links in non-shortest path p (incidence index $\bar{\delta}_{Link,p}^{Kkt} = 1$) but not those in shortest path $\hat{p}$ (incidence index $\bar{\delta}_{Link,\hat{p}}^{Kkt} = 0$), while set $\hat{A}$ comprises those time-dependent links not in non-shortest path p (incidence index $\bar{\delta}_{Link,p}^{Kkt} = 0$) but in shortest path $\hat{p}$ (incidence index $\bar{\delta}_{Link,\hat{p}}^{Kkt} = 1$). $\hat{c}'_{Link}$ is the derivative of link cost function $\hat{c}_{Link}$.

Step 3.5: Update time-dependent product flows.

For each O-D pair (K,kt), update the time-dependent product path flows and associated link flows by the following formulas:

$$q_p^{Kkt^{n+1}} = \max\left\{0, q_p^{Kkt^n} + \alpha_p^{Kkt^n}\left(\hat{c}_{\hat{p}}^{Kkt^n} - \hat{c}_p^{Kkt^n}\right)\right\} \qquad \forall k,t,p \neq \hat{p} \tag{24}$$

$$q_{\hat{p}}^{Kkt^{n+1}} = q_{max}^{Kkt^{n+1}} - \sum\limits_{p \neq \hat{p}} q_p^{Kkt^{n+1}} \qquad \forall k,t \tag{25}$$

$$q_{Link}^{n+1} = \sum\limits_{kt}\sum\limits_{p} q_p^{Kkt^{n+1}} \bar{\delta}_{Link,p}^{Kkt} \qquad \forall Link \in \left\{ Kkt, Kit, iit, ijt, jt, jjt, jkt \right\} \tag{26}$$

Step 3.6: Convergence check.

If $\{q_{iit}\}^{n+1} \approx \{q_{iit}\}^n$, $\{Q_t^1\}^{n+1} \approx \{Q_t^1\}^n$, $\{q_{ijt}\}^{n+1} \approx \{q_{ijt}\}^n$ and $\{Q_t^2\}^{n+1} \approx \{Q_t^2\}^n$, continue. Otherwise, let $n=n+1$, go to step 3.2.

Step 4: Convergence check for the second loop operation.

Let $\{q_{iit}\}^{m+1} = \{q_{iit}\}^{n+1}$, $\{Q_t^1\}^{m+1} = \{Q_t^1\}^{n+1}$, $\{q_{ijt}\}^{m+1} = \{q_{ijt}\}^{n+1}$ and $\{Q_t^2\}^{m+1} = \{Q_t^2\}^{n+1}$. If $\{q_{iit}\}^{m+1} \approx \{q_{iit}\}^m$, $\{Q_t^1\}^{m+1} \approx \{Q_t^1\}^m$, $\{q_{ijt}\}^{m+1} \approx \{q_{ijt}\}^m$ and $\{Q_t^2\}^{m+1} \approx \{Q_t^2\}^m$, continue. Otherwise, set $m=m+1$ and go to Step 2.2.

Step 5: Convergence check for the first loop operation.

Let $\{\rho_{kt}\}^{l+1} = \{\rho_{kt}\}^{m+1}$. If $\max\limits_{k,t}\left\{\left\|\dfrac{\rho_{kt}^{l+1} - \rho_{kt}^l}{\rho_{kt}^{D^l}}\right\|\right\} \le \varepsilon$, stop. The current solution is optimal.

Otherwise, set $l=l+1$, go to Step 1.1.

Numerical Example

To demonstrate the TD-SCNE model, next we solve a numerical example modified from Nagurney et al. (2002). The test network consists of three sectors: manufacturers,

Table 1. Time-dependent Cost Functions

Time-dependent Cost Function		Production /Handling and Storage /Inventory Cost	Transaction Cost
M_t	$t=1$	$c_{it}(Q_t^1) = 1.75q_{it}^2 + q_{1t}q_{2t} + 2q_{it}$	$c_{ijt}(q_{ijt}) = 0.5q_{ijt}^2 + 3.5q_{ijt}$
	$t=2$	$c_{it}(Q_t^1) = 2.5q_{it}^2 + q_{1t}q_{2t} + 2q_{it}$	
M_t->M_{t+1}		$c_{iit}(q_{iit}) = 0.75q_{iit}^2$	-
R_t		$c_{jt}(q_{jt}) = 0.5(q_{jt})^2$	-
R_t->R_{t+1}		$c_{jjt}(q_{jjt}) = 1.5q_{jjt}^2$	-
D_t		-	$\hat{c}_{jkt}(Q_t^2) = q_{jkt} + 5$

"M_t" *denotes manufacturers during time period t, "R_t" retailers during time period t, "D_t" demand markets during time period t;*

"M_t->M_{t+1}" *inventory incurred by a manufacturer from time period t to t+1, and*

"R_t->R_{t+1}" *inventory of a retailer from time period t to t+1*

Table 2. Time-dependent demand functions

Time Period	Demand Function
t=1	$d_{ka1}(\mathbf{p}_1) = -2\rho_{ka1} - 1.5\rho_{kb1} + 884.9$
	$d_{kb1}(\mathbf{p}_1) = -2\rho_{kb1} - 1.5\rho_{ka1} + 884.9$
t=2	$d_{ka2}(\mathbf{p}_2) = -2\rho_{ka2} - 1.5\rho_{kb2} + 918.1$
	$d_{kb2}(\mathbf{p}_2) = -2\rho_{kb2} - 1.5\rho_{ka2} + 918.1$

retailers, and demand markets, spanned in two time periods. Each sector contains two agencies. The time-dependent cost functions associated with the three tiers of the test network are given in Table 1. Note that the product cost functions in the two time periods are different for the same manufacturer. This difference can be attributed to various positive and/or negative factors, such as increased labor cost, inadequate supply of raw materials, technology advancement, and a higher degree of automation.

Two time-dependent demand functions in two markets are assumed in Table 2. Note that the demand is expressed here as a function of several product prices during the same time period. However, it is implicitly influenced by some other product prices in different time periods through the flow propagation over the network.

The link flows and costs, by applying the proposed ND solution algorithm, are summarized in Table 3. A pattern of product flows (or route flows) and product prices (or route costs) is also summarized in Table 4. Combining these two tables, we found, not surprisingly, that the equilibrium conditions shown in Eqns (1) and (2) were fully

Table 3. Link results

Link		Link Flow	Link Cost	Head Node Cost (Product Price)
t=1	$K{\rightarrow}i_{a1}$	37.35	170.075	170.075
	$K{\rightarrow}i_{b1}$	37.35	170.075	170.075
	$i_{a1}{\rightarrow}j_{a1}$	16.6	20.1	190.175
	$i_{a1}{\rightarrow}j_{b1}$	16.6	20.1	190.175
	$i_{b1}{\rightarrow}j_{a1}$	16.6	20.1	190.175
	$i_{b1}{\rightarrow}j_{b1}$	16.6	20.1	190.175
	$j_{a1}{\rightarrow}j'_{a1}$	33.2	33.2	223.375
	$j_{b1}{\rightarrow}j'_{b1}$	33.2	33.2	223.375
	$j'_{a1}{\rightarrow}k_{a1}$	15.5625	20.5625	243.9375
	$j'_{a1}{\rightarrow}k_{b1}$	15.5625	20.5625	243.9375
	$j'_{b1}{\rightarrow}k_{a1}$	15.5625	20.5625	243.9375
	$j'_{b1}{\rightarrow}k_{b1}$	15.5625	20.5625	243.9375

Table 3. Link results (continued)

	K->i_{a2}	29.05	132.725	176.3
	K->i_{b2}	29.05	132.725	176.3
	i_{a1}->i_{a2}	4.15	6.225	176.3
	i_{b1}->i_{b2}	4.15	6.225	176.3
	i_{a2}->j_{a2}	16.6	20.1	196.4
	i_{a2}->j_{b2}	16.6	20.1	196.4
	i_{b2}->j_{a2}	16.6	20.1	196.4
$t=2$	i_{b2}->j_{b2}	16.6	20.1	196.4
	j_{a2}->j'_{a2}	33.2	33.2	229.6
	j_{b2}->j'_{b2}	33.2	33.2	229.6
	j'_{a1}->j'_{a2}	2.075	6.225	229.6
	j'_{b1}->j'_{b2}	2.075	6.225	229.6
	j'_{a2}->k_{a2}	17.6375	22.6375	252.2375
	j'_{a2}->k_{b2}	17.6375	22.6375	252.2375
	j'_{b2}->k_{a2}	17.6375	22.6375	252.2375
	j'_{b2}->k_{b2}	17.6375	22.6375	252.2375

Table 4. Time-dependent route flows and O-D product flows

Time-Dependent Route	Route Flows	O-D Product Flows (Demands)	Productions
K->i_{a1}->j_{a1}->j'_{a1}->k_{a1}	7.78125		
K->i_{a1}->j_{b1}->j'_{b1}->k_{a1}	7.78125		
K->i_{b1}->j_{a1}->j'_{a1}->k_{a1}	7.78125	(K, k_{a1}): 31.125	
K->i_{b1}->j_{b1}->j'_{b1}->k_{a1}	7.78125		
K->i_{a1}->j_{a1}->j'_{a1}->k_{b1}	7.78125		
K->i_{a1}->j_{b1}->j'_{b1}->k_{b1}	7.78125		(K, i_{a1}): 37.35
K->i_{b1}->j_{a1}->j'_{a1}->k_{b1}	7.78125	(K, k_{b1}): 31.125	(K, i_{b1}): 37.35
K->i_{b1}->j_{b1}->j'_{b1}->k_{b1}	7.78125		$(K, i_{?1})$: 74.7
K->i_{a1}->i_{a2}->j_{a2}->j'_{a2}->k_{a2}	1.0375		
K->i_{a1}->i_{a2}->j_{b2}->j'_{b2}->k_{a2}	1.0375	$(K, i_{?1}$->$i_{?2}, k_{a2})$:	
K->i_{b1}->i_{b2}->j_{a2}->j'_{a2}->k_{a2}	1.0375	4.15	
K->i_{b1}->i_{b2}->j_{b2}->j'_{b2}->k_{a2}	1.0375		
K->i_{a1}->j_{a1}->j'_{a1}->j'_{a2}->k_{a2}	0.51875		
K->i_{a1}->j_{b1}->j'_{b1}->j'_{b2}->k_{a2}	0.51875	$(K, j'_{?1}$->$j'_{?2},$	
K->i_{b1}->j_{a1}->j'_{a1}->j'_{a2}->k_{a2}	0.51875	$k_{a2})$: 2.075	
K->i_{b1}->j_{b1}->j'_{b1}->j'_{b2}->k_{a2}	0.51875		
K->i_{a1}->i_{a2}->j_{a2}->j'_{a2}->k_{b2}	1.0375		
K->i_{a1}->i_{a2}->j_{b2}->j'_{b2}->k_{b2}	1.0375	$(K, i_{?1}$->$i_{?2}, k_{b2})$:	
K->i_{b1}->i_{b2}->j_{a2}->j'_{a2}->k_{b2}	1.0375	4.15	
K->i_{b1}->i_{b2}->j_{b2}->j'_{b2}->k_{b2}	1.0375		
K->i_{a1}->j_{a1}->j'_{a1}->j'_{a2}->k_{b2}	0.51875		
K->i_{a1}->j_{b1}->j'_{b1}->j'_{b2}->k_{b2}	0.51875	$(K, j'_{?1}$->$j'_{?2},$	
K->i_{b1}->j_{a1}->j'_{a1}->j'_{a2}->k_{b2}	0.51875	$k_{b2})$: 2.075	
K->i_{b1}->j_{b1}->j'_{b1}->j'_{b2}->k_{b2}	0.51875		

Table 4. Time-dependent route flows and O-D product flows (continued)

Time-Dependent Route	Route Flows	O-D Product Flows (Demands)	Productions
$K\text{->}i_{a2}\text{->}j_{a2}\text{->}j'_{a2}\text{->}k_{a2}$	7.2625		
$K\text{->}i_{a2}\text{->}j_{b2}\text{->}j'_{b2}\text{->}k_{a2}$	7.2625	(K, k_{a2}): 29.05	
$K\text{->}i_{b2}\text{->}j_{a2}\text{->}j'_{a2}\text{->}k_{a2}$	7.2625		(K, i_{a2}): 29.05
$K\text{->}i_{b2}\text{->}j_{b2}\text{->}j'_{b2}\text{->}k_{a2}$	7.2625		(K, i_{b2}): 29.05
$K\text{->}i_{a2}\text{->}j_{a2}\text{->}j'_{a2}\text{->}k_{b2}$	7.2625		$(K, i_{?2})$: 58.1
$K\text{->}i_{a2}\text{->}j_{b2}\text{->}j'_{b2}\text{->}k_{b2}$	7.2625	(K, k_{b2}): 29.05	
$K\text{->}i_{b2}\text{->}j_{a2}\text{->}j'_{a2}\text{->}k_{b2}$	7.2625		
$K\text{->}i_{b2}\text{->}j_{b2}\text{->}j'_{b2}\text{->}k_{b2}$	7.2625		

Demands at various markets: k_{a1}: *31.125;* k_{b1}: *31.125;* k_{a2}: *35.275;* k_{b2}: *35.275*

Figure 4. Flow(s) vs. iteration

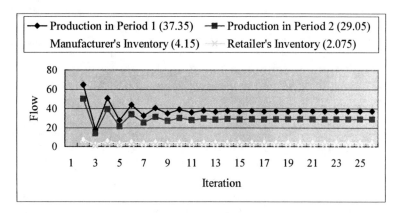

Figure 5. Product price(s) vs. iteration

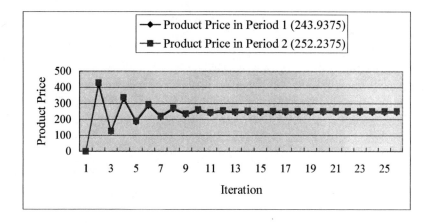

compliant. It is worth mentioning that, although not explicitly required in the model formulation, the equilibrium conditions for each retailer agency are satisfied automatically. In other words, the prices an agency is willing to pay for the product in its retailer outlet are equal and minimum. Note, furthermore, that in Table 4, four routes are available for each demand market during time period $t=1$. In contrast, eight routes are generated for each demand market during time period $t=2$, among which four of them are from the previous time period. It could mean that the demands in the latter periods may be more likely to be fulfilled.

For the reader's reference, the intermediate results of the first loop operation (which deals with the VI-based quantity subproblem) carried out 25 times were recorded. In Figure 4, we can observe that the time-dependent productions for two manufacturers gradually converge to 37.35 and 29.05, respectively, and inventories for the manufacturers and the retailers gradually converge to 4.15 and 2.075, respectively. In Figure 5, the product prices in two time periods asymptotically converge to 243.9375 and 252.2375, respectively.

Conclusion and Suggestions

This chapter studied the TD-SCNE problem and addressed it as a VI-based time-dependent transportation network model. The TD-SCNE problem essentially extends the basic SCNE model by taking the temporal dimension into consideration. No additional assumptions on distributional behavior are needed to make this extension. The inventory flows, in particular, were the focus of treatment. A supernetwork representation was drawn to better explain the model formulation and the subsequent solution algorithm. A three-loop ND method embedding the GP algorithm then was proposed. In the first loop, the time-dependent product price interactions were diagonalized, from which a simplified VI-based quantity subproblem resulted. In the second loop, the time-dependent product flow interactions were relaxed, and a variable demand optimization subproblem was yielded. In the third loop, the variable demand subproblem was regarded by way of a supernetwork representation as an equivalent fixed demand problem and solved with the GP solution algorithm. The results show that the time-dependent product prices and flows complied with the so-called Wardropian first principle at both retailer and demand market sectors. The proposed ND method can be equally applied to other TD-SCNE-related equilibrium problems to resolve the difficulty caused by the inherent asymmetric link interactions. In addition, many extensions of the current TD-SCNE problem, such as bi-level formulation in oligopoly markets; practical application to more realistic network structures and demand/cost functions; incorporation of scale capacity constraints; and treatment of stochastic/fuzzy input data, random demand analysis (Dong et al., 2004), and the influence of telecommunications are all possible and, indeed, attractive as subjects of future research.

Acknowledgments

The authors would like to thank the National Science Council, Taiwan, for financially supporting part of this work.

References

Chen, H.K. (1999). *Dynamic travel choice models: A variational inequality approach.* Berlin: Springer-Verlag.

Chen, H.K., & Chou, H.W. (2004a). A solution algorithm for the supply chain network equilibrium problem. *Proceedings of the Eighth Pacific-Asia Conference on Information Systems*, Shanghai, China.

Chen, H.K., & Chou, H.W. (2004b). Supply chain network equilibrium with asymmetric variable demand and cost functions. Submitted to the *Journal of Operations Research*.

Chen, H.K., & Chou, H.W. (2005). A capacitated supply chain equilibrium problem. *The 85th Annual Meeting of the Transportation Research Board*, Washington, DC.

Dong, J., Zhang, D., & Nagurney, A. (2004). Supply chain supernetworks with random demands. In D.H. Lee (Ed.), *Urban and regional transportation modeling: Essays in honor of David Boyce* (pp. 289-313). Edward Elgar Publishing Limited.

Hopp, W.J., & Spearman, M.L. (2000). *Factory physics.* McGraw-Hill.

Jayakrishnan, R., Tsai, W.K., Prashker, J.N., & Rajadhyaksha, S. (1994). A faster path-based algorithm for traffic assignment. *Proceedings of the 73rd Transportation Research Board Annual Meeting*, Washington, DC.

Nagurney, A., Dong, J., & Mokhtarian, P.L. (2003). A space-time network for telecommuting versus commuting decision-making. *Papers in Regional Science, 82*, 451-473.

Nagurney, A., Dong, J., & Zhang, D. (2002). A supply chain network equilibrium model. *Transportation Research Part E, 38*, 281-303.

Sheffi, Y. (1985). *Urban transportation networks: Equilibrium analysis with mathematical programming methods.* Englewood Cliffs, NJ: Prentice-Hall Inc.

Tobin, R.L. (1986). Sensitivity analysis for variational inequalities. *Journal of Optimization Theory and Applications, 48*(1), 191-204.

Notations

c_{it} : Production cost function associated with manufacturer i during time period t.

$\hat{c}_{it}$: Marginal production cost associated with manufacturer i during time period t (i.e.,

$$\frac{\partial c_{it}}{\partial q_{it}} = \hat{c}_{it}).$$

c_{iit} : Inventory cost function associated with manufacturer i from time period t to time period t+1.

$\hat{c}_{iit}$: Marginal inventory cost associated with manufacturer i from time period t to time

period t+1, i.e., $\dfrac{\partial c_{iit}}{\partial q_{iit}} = \hat{c}_{iit}$.

c_{ijt} : Transaction cost function for shipment from manufacturer i to retailer j during time period t.

$\hat{c}_{ijt}$: Marginal transaction cost function for shipment from manufacturer i to retailer j during time period t.

c_{jt} : Handling and storage cost associated with retailer j during time period t.

$\hat{c}_{jt}$: Marginal handling and storage cost associated with retailer j during time period t

(i.e., $\dfrac{\partial c_{jt}}{\partial q_{jt}} = \hat{c}_{jt}$).

c_{jjt} : Inventory cost function associated with retailer j from time period t to time period t+1.

$\hat{c}_{jjt}$: Marginal inventory cost associated with retailer j from time period t to time period

t+1 (i.e., $\dfrac{\partial c_{jjt}}{\partial q_{jjt}} = \hat{c}_{jjt}$).

$\hat{c}_{jkt}$: Transaction cost function for shipment from retailer j to demand market k during time period t.

$\hat{c}_p^{Kkt}$: Cost associated with a route p from super-origin $š$ to a demand market k during time period t.

$d_{kt}(\rho_t)$: Demand function in market k during time period t.

i: Manufacturer designation, $i \in I$; set $I = \{1,2,\cdots,i,\cdots,|I| \}$.

j: Retailer designation, $j \in J$; set $J = \{1,2,\cdots,j,\cdots,|J| \}$.

k: Demand market designation, $k \in K$; set $K = \{1,2,\cdots,k,\cdots,|K|\}$.

š: Super-origin designation.

Q_t^1:   Transaction between manufacturers and retailers during time period t, $Q_t^1 = \{q_{ijt}\}$.

Q_t^2:   Transaction between retailers and demand markets during time period t, $Q_t^2 = \{q_{jkt}\}$.

$(\overline{Q}_t^1 \setminus \overline{q}_{ijt}, q_{ijt})$: Product flows Q_t^1 between manufacturer and retailer sectors during time period t are temporarily fixed, except for the subject product flow q_{ijt}, at a certain level.

$(\overline{Q}_t^2 \setminus \overline{q}_{jkt}, q_{jkt})$: Product flows Q_t^2 between retailer sector and demand markets during time period t are temporarily fixed, except for the subject product flow q_{jkt}, at a certain level.

p: **Route designation.**

$\mathbf{q}_t$:   **Productions by all manufacturers during time period t.**

$q_p^{it',kt}$: Product demand between manufacturer i during time period t' and demand market k during time period t.

q_{it}:   Amount of productions by manufacturer i during time period t.

$(\overline{\mathbf{q}}_t \setminus \overline{q}_{it}, q_{it})$: Productions $\mathbf{q}_t$ by all manufacturers during time period t are temporarily fixed, except for the subject production q_{ij}, at a certain level.

q_{iit}:   Amount of inventory for manufacturer i from time period t to time period $t+1$.

q_{ijt}:   Amount of transactions between manufacturer i and retailer j during time period t.

q_{jt}:   Amount of product available at retailer j during time period t.

$(\overline{\mathbf{q}}_t \setminus \overline{q}_{jt}, q_{jt})$: Transactions $\mathbf{q}_t$ between retailer sector and demand markets during time period t are temporarily fixed, except for the subject transactions q_{ijt}, at a certain level.

q_{jjt}: Amount of inventory for retailer j from time period t to time period $t+1$.

q_{jkt}: Amount of transactions between retailer j and demand market k during time period t.

q^{Kkt}: Total amount of product shipped from super-origin $š$ to demand market k during time period t.

t: Time period designation.

α: Step size.

ρ_{kt}:   Product price in demand market k during time period t.

$\left(\overline{\mathbf{\rho}}_t \setminus \overline{\rho}_{kt}, \rho_{kt} \right)$: Product prices $\mathbf{\rho}_t$ in all demand markets during time period t are temporarily fixed, except for the price ρ_{kt} at demand market k, at a certain level.

Ω: Feasible region of the TD-SCNE problem (associated with asymmetric demand functions).

Ω_d: Feasible region of the TD-SCNE's subproblem (associated with diagonalized demand functions).

Endnotes

[1]   Professor, Dept. of Civil Engineering, National Central University, Taiwan (Address: No. 300, Jung-Da Road, Wu-Chuan Li, Jung-Li, Taoyuan 32054, Taiwan, Tel: +886-3-4227151 ext 34115, Fax: +886-3-4252960, E-mail: ncutone@cc.ncu.edu.tw)

[2]   Professor, Dept. of Information Management, National Central University, Taiwan (Address: No. 300, Jung-Da Road, Wu-Chuan Li, Jung-Li, Taoyuan 32054, Taiwan, Tel: +886-3-4267256, Fax: +886-3-4254604, E-mail: hwchou@mgt.ncu.edu.tw)

Chapter XV

An Agent-Based Collaborative Negotiation System for Global Manufacturing Supply Chain Management

Jianxin Jiao
Nanyang Technological University, Singapore

Xiao You
Nanyang Technological University, Singapore

Arun Kumar
Nanyang Technological University, Singapore

Abstract

This chapter applies the multi-agent system paradigm to collaborative negotiation in a global manufacturing supply chain network. Multi-agent computational environments are suitable for dealing with a broad class of coordination and negotiation issues involving multiple autonomous or semi-autonomous problem-solving agents. An agent-based multi-contract negotiation system is proposed for global manufacturing supply chain coordination. Also reported is a case study of mobile phone global manufacturing supply chain management.

Introduction

Economic and industrial communities worldwide are confronted with the increasing impact of competitive pressures resulting from the globalization of markets and supply chains for product fulfillment. More and more manufacturing enterprises are being driven to pursue a global manufacturing strategy that aims to transcend national boundaries in order to leverage capabilities and resources worldwide (Pontrandolfo & Okogbaa, 1999). Next generation manufacturing calls for new forms of manufacturing strategies, which are based on global networks of self-organizing, autonomous units (Anderson & Bunce, 2000). These units may be part of a single company located globally or several companies cooperating together to address customers' requirements coherently within extended and virtual enterprises (Bullinger et al., 2000). Since global manufacturing activities might be dispersed and carried out in diverse locations, coordination decisions have been identified as crucial for the successful implementation of global manufacturing strategies (Fawcett, 1992).

A global manufacturing supply chain is a network of suppliers, factories, subcontractors, warehouses, distribution centers, and retailers, through which raw materials are acquired, transformed, produced, and delivered to end customers (Fox et al., 2000; Ho et al., 2000). In a global manufacturing supply chain, a number of autonomous or semi-autonomous business entities are collectively responsible for procurement, manufacturing, and distribution activities associated with one or more families of related products (Pontrandolfo et al., 2002). Performance of any entity in a supply chain depends on the performance of others and their willingness and ability to coordinate and negotiate activities within the supply chain of product fulfillment (Swaminathan, 1996). A global manufacturing supply chain usually involves heterogeneous environments (Tso et al., 2000). Such a supply chain network is much more complex than that for the procurement, production, and delivery of a simple commodity, not only for the volume and complexity of transactions but also due to its dynamic and heterogeneous manufacturing environments (Gaonkar & Viswanadham, 2001).

The rapidly expanding Internet provides a promising networking medium, while the agent technology lends itself to the management of global supply chain networks within a distributed environment. An agent is a computer system situated in a certain kind of environment and is capable of autonomous action in order to meet its designed objectives (Jennings & Wooldidge, 1998). Moreover, a multi-agent system is a loosely coupled network of software agents that interact to solve problems that are beyond the individual capacities or knowledge of each problem solver (Barbuceanu & Fox, 1996). Agent-based technology has emerged as a new paradigm for conceptualizing, designing, and implementing software systems. Multi-agent systems (MAS) enhance overall system performance; in particular, along such dimensions as computational efficiency, reliability, extensibility, responsiveness, reuse, maintainability, and flexibility. They also are capable of solving the problem of matching supply to demand and allocating resources dynamically in real time by recognizing opportunities, trends, and potentials, as well as carrying out negotiations and coordination (Blecker & Graf, 2003).

In this regard, this chapter applies the multi-agent system paradigm to collaborative negotiation in a global manufacturing supply chain. Multi-agent computational environments are suitable for studying a broad class of coordination and negotiation issues involving multiple autonomous or semi-autonomous problem-solving agents. This study discusses an agent-based multi-contract negotiation system for global manufacturing supply chain coordination. A case study of mobile phone global manufacturing supply chain coordination also is reported.

Background Review

Various approaches to supply chain coordination have been reported in the literature. Cohen and Lee (1998) have developed a planning model to optimize material supply, production, and distribution processes. Arntzen et al. (1995) have proposed a resource allocation and planning model for global production and distribution networks. Most of the quantitative models seek overall efficiency of the entire supply chain (Li et al., 2001). In practice, different entities in a supply chain operate subject to different sets of constraints and objectives and, thus, are autonomous in nature (Swaminathan, 1996). In contrast to traditional centralized control and management systems, a supply chain network becomes a distributed paradigm, where different participants collaborate and negotiate with one another to achieve the overall functionality (Sadeh et al., 2001).

The distributed problem-solving paradigm in global supply chain networks is consistent with the principle of MAS. The MAS concentrates on the development of organizational structures, problem solution strategies, and cooperation and coordination mechanisms for a range of distributed knowledge-based problem-solving modules (Brenner et al., 1998). Tian et al. (2003) have observed that most decision-making entities in the manufacturing domain have their unique perspectives and economic incentives, which resemble a distributed decision-making paradigm for operations coordination among manufacturing facilities. Ertogral and Wu (2000) have demonstrated how a centralized information management can be decoupled into a distributed system by employing autonomous agents, in which each agent represents a decision entity.

The agent technology facilitates the integration of the entire supply chain as a networked system of independent echelons, each of which utilizes its own decision-making procedure (Gjerdrum et al., 2001). Through this paradigm, a global goal of the whole system is achieved as the aggregation of its local objectives by negotiation of multiple planning cycles (Kaihara, 2001). In an agent-based system, a number of heterogeneous agents work independently or in a cooperative and interactive manner to solve problems in a decentralized environment (Brenner et al., 1998). The procedure starts with task planning. The problems of the system, referred to as tasks, are decomposed into subproblems, or subtasks, in order for associated agents to make a bid to complete the tasks or subtasks. Whenever a task is announced, the agents start to bid for a contract, based on their own constraints at that moment through a communication channel. Subsequently, resources are allocated according to certain rules in relation to the bids so as to complete the task of problem solving.

Fox, et al. (1993) have proposed to organize the supply chain as a network of cooperating, intelligent agents, where each agent performs one or more supply chain functions and coordinates its actions with other agents. While applying a multi-agent framework to model supply chain dynamics, Swaminathan et al. (1996) have distinguished two categories of elements. One is structural elements that are modeled as agents, including production elements (retailers, distribution centers, plants, and suppliers) and transportation elements. The other is control elements, such as inventory, demand, supply, flow, and information controls, which are used to assist in coordinating the flow of products in an efficient manner with the use of messages. Maturana et al. (1999) have developed a hybrid agent-based mediator-centric architecture, called MetaMorph, to integrate partners, suppliers, and customers dynamically with the main enterprise through their respective mediators within a supply chain network via the Internet and intranets. In MetaMorph, agents can be used to represent manufacturing resources (machines, tools, etc.) and parts in order to encapsulate existing software systems and to function as system or subsystem coordinators/mediators. Swaminathan et al. (1998) have proposed a multi-agent approach to model supply chain dynamics. In their approach, a supply chain library of software components, such as retailers, manufacturers, inventory policy, and so forth, has been developed to build customized supply chain models from the library. Sadeh et al. (2001) have developed an agent-based architecture for a dynamic supply chain called MASCOT. The MASCOT is a reconfigurable, multilevel, agent-based architecture for a coordinated supply chain. Agents in MASCOT serve as wrappers for planning and scheduling modules. Petersen et al. (2001) have proposed a multi-agent architecture, called AGORA, for modeling and supporting cooperative work among distributed entities in virtual enterprises.

Most existing MAS approaches to supply chain coordination imply a closed environment consisting of a fixed number of entities that share a common target (Sadeh et al., 2001). Such a scenario, however, does not conform to the complex operations of a real-case global manufacturing supply chain (Chen et al., 1999). Besides different interests among supply chain entities, there is no obligation for any company to remain within a supply chain for a certain time period. Companies may join or leave the chain anytime for their own reasons. This means that functional agents must deal explicitly with the negotiation, along with the collaboration, among different supply chain entities in a dynamic environment. It is imperative to introduce a high-level negotiation mechanism to agent-based supply chain coordination systems. Moreover, all agents should be loosely coupled and not be coordinated by any central controller (Strader et al., 1998). To avoid chaotic behaviors of agents, a well-designed negotiation mechanism is conducive to making MAS operate smoothly.

Product Fulfillment in a Global Manufacturing Supply Chain

Traditional supply chain management strategies are process-driven, based on demand forecasts. This means that some specific business processes have to be benchmarked and defined as the standard, such that the execution of business activities would not deviate from the standard. This usually takes the form of business rules and/or automated workflows that execute mechanically as part of the defined process, without consideration of certain unique circumstances inherent in each application scenario. Such strategies have difficulties in supporting mass customization, where the enterprise becomes customer-driven and requires the integration of all supply chain entities dynamically (Ghiassi & Spera, 2003).

Figure 1 shows the typical configuration of a global manufacturing supply chain. There are three issues associated with the management of such a complex supply chain network: configuration, coordination, and negotiation. Configuration deals with issues related to the network structure of a supply chain, based on such factors as product architectures, lead time, transportation costs, and currency fluctuations. An important issue to be addressed is the synchronization of product, process, and supply platforms and, accordingly, the configure-to-order fulfillment of product families. Coordination tackles routine activities in a supply chain, such as material flows, distribution, inventory control, and information exchange. Negotiation involves supply contracting that controls material flows over a longer horizon, based on such factors as supplier reliability, number of suppliers, quantity discounts, demand forecast mechanisms, and flexibility to change commitments.

Multi-agent computational environments are suitable for studying classes of coordination issues involving multiple autonomous or semiautonomous optimizing agents, where knowledge is distributed and agents communicate through messages (Fox et al., 2000). Because supply chain management is concerned fundamentally with coherence among

Figure 1. Overview of a global manufacturing supply chain network

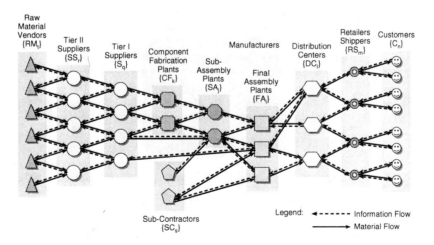

multiple decision makers, a multi-agent modeling framework, based on explicit communication between constituent agents, such as manufacturers, suppliers, and distributors, suggests itself as a distributed environment for collaborative negotiation (Chen et al., 1999).

As shown in Figure 1, product fulfillment in a global manufacturing supply chain network involves a number of parties or players and functions, including plants and production, markets and distributions, suppliers and customers, and subcontractors.

The manufacturer is a vertically integrated company comprising a few globally distributed plants. The assembly of final products is carried out in a few final assembly plants, each of which serves one or more specific distribution centers. To support final assemblies, the company usually sets up a few subassembly plants that may be located in different places from that of the final assembly plants. Every plant is associated with a planning agent, a materials agent, a production agent, and a dispatching agent. The planning agent is responsible for production planning. The materials agent handles raw product inventory, the on-order database for raw products, and reception of raw products. The production agent manages production and the work-in-progress inventory, as well as knowledge about the process architecture. The dispatching agent handles the finished goods inventory and all outbound shipments from the plant. Each plant consists of a set of workstations, bins, and stocks, each of which is modeled as an agent. To further fulfill the product orders, the company may outsource certain assembly jobs to a few subcontractor agents.

Distribution centers can be run either by the company or by third-party logistics providers. Usually, the location of a distribution center is close to the particular market to be served. From each distribution center, products are distributed to local retailers. Therefore, respective distribution center agents and retailer agents are used to model the distribution process. By modeling each customer type as an agent, retailer agents are responsible for communication with customers.

Each plant has a purchasing agent that is in charge of communication with its suppliers. Every supplier is modeled as an agent, as well. The purchasing agent possesses information regarding which parts to order from which suppliers. To support supplier agents, raw material vendors can be modeled as separate agents, as well.

Multi-Contract Negotiation

To coordinate different supply chain entities, negotiation decisions have been identified as crucial for successful global manufacturing. There are a number of negotiation systems working for e-market applications or distributed manufacturing enterprises (Lu, 2004). Most of them imply a bilateral negotiation process that corresponds to a single supply contract and focuses on the design of negotiation strategies, protocols, and mechanisms that make negotiation more efficient (Shin & Jung, 2004).

Within the global manufacturing context, negotiation among supply chain entities must coincide with the product fulfillment process. This constitutes a batch of contracts for negotiating with different supply chain echelons. Different supply chain entities deal with different types of materials associated with a product (e.g., in terms of raw materials, component parts, or subassemblies), even if they contribute to fulfilling the same customer order. When a manufacturer plans its material requirements for a customer order, it needs to execute several concurrent negotiation processes in order to arrive at a set of contracts with different materials suppliers. Because all the contracts are related to the same order, they are interdependent in terms of quantity and lead time. The goal of negotiation is to maximize not only the payoff of the end contract but also the overall payoff of all related contracts. As a result, each single negotiation must be synchronized with other negotiations throughout the supply chain. This gives rise to a multi-contract negotiation problem.

Contract Net Protocol and Negotiation Policy

In general, the negotiation process in the multi-agent paradigm is divided into three consecutive phases: inviting, bidding, and awarding. A contract net protocol defines the basic messages in accordance with these phases and how each message is to be processed. Whenever a task comes to a manager agent, it is decomposed into subtasks. Subsequently, the manager invites potential subcontractors or suppliers who possess the capability to solve the problem to bid for individual subtasks. Meanwhile, a contractor agent analyzes the tasks and prepares bids accordingly. Then the manager agent collects and evaluates all the bids for each task and selects the one with the maximal utility as the winner; thus, the winner supplier is awarded the contract.

A negotiation protocol often is used to organize the sequence of message executions among agents according to certain logics. For a specific negotiation protocol, the possible responses of agents are described by defining negotiation performative services. Table 1 shows examples of performative services defined for negotiation. An agent initiates a negotiation by sending a call-for-proposal or call-for-bidding message to other agents. A few rounds of conversation may take place, where several proposals and counterproposals are exchanged. The negotiation between agents ends when one party accepts or rejects the other party's proposal, or when any party terminates the negotiation process on its own.

Since agents may exist in various business environments with varying objectives and constraints, the same message would convey different meanings to different agents. The conversation policy is a declarative specification of the possible sequence and contracts of serial messages. It guides and restricts the way of communication by forcing the agent to follow a predefined sequence of message exchanges. The individual agent in each communication step might experience difficulties in determining how to communicate

Table 1. Performative service of negotiation

Accept	The action of accepting a previously submitted proposal.
Terminate	The action to end a negotiation process.
Call for proposal	The action of calling for proposal for a given task.
Call for bidding	The same as "call for proposal"; yet sent to multiple agents.
Send proposal	The action of submitting a proposal for a given task.
Send counter-proposal	The action of submitting a proposal based on the previous submitted proposal.

with others while choosing the right message type from many possible messages. A conversation policy consists of a conversation stage, action, and control mechanism. For example, a specific conversation policy defines that an *inform* message will be followed by a *reply* message. After agent *A* receives an inform message from agent *B*, it should understand that agent *B* intends to let *A* have a particular belief, and that *B* only expects a reply message from *A*. Because the explicit policy can guide the conversation, agent *A* does not have to perform a long reasoning process in order to evaluate all the possible goals that agent *B* might have.

Constraint-Based Material Requirement Specification

The driving force behind global manufacturing and logistics is that manufacturers are shifting from traditional make-to-stock to make-to-order or configure-to-order production. To deal with uncertainty in demands and large inventory, manufacturers can dynamically configure their supply chain networks to fulfill the customer order by outsourcing. The configuration of supply chain entities starts with material requirement planning, where the material requirements for an end product are propagated along the bill of materials (BOM).

As shown in Figure 2, the configure-to-order process starts when a customer order, $X_s(P)$, is received from a retailer agent or an order acquisition agent. Here, $X_s(P)$ denotes that customer S places an order of product P. Consequently, the configuration agent calls the MRPII/ERP system to analyze and map the order to material requirement specifications (MRSs) based on information about capabilities and resources such as inventories, production scheduling, equipment running conditions, and so forth. Make-or-buy decision making may incur for certain material types that either can be outsourced to external suppliers or made in-house. Throughout the material requirement specification process, the manufacturer and the suppliers must negotiate a number of issues, subject to different preferences and constraints.

Figure 2. Material requirement specification based on order decomposition

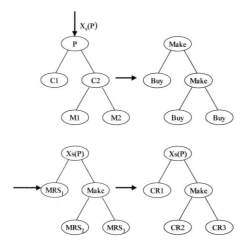

A material requirement specification (MRS) is denoted as:

$$MRS(X_s(P)) = \{MRS_i\}_N,$$

$$MRS_i = (I_i, A_i, U_i, C_i, R_i),$$

where $MRS(X_s(P))$ indicates the set of material requirement specifications for a specific order of $X_s(P)$, I_i is the required item associated with MRS_i, $A_i = \{Price, Volume, Due Date, Quality, ...\}$ denotes the attributes of MRS_i, U_i describes the utility of MRS_i, C_i is the set of constraints related to MRS_i, and R_i means the priority level of MRS_i.

Each MRS consists of five elements: item, attribute, utility, constraint, and priority. An item represents the component material in a particular product structure corresponding to the customer order. For a specific product, a variety of item sets may exist due to the changing order size or lead time requirement. Varying inventories or operational conditions also may cause different item sets for fulfilling the product. For example, for an urgent order, the manufacturer might decide to purchase the items from external suppliers for quick delivery, whereas for a regular order, the manufacturer might prefer to make the items in house for easy cost control.

An attribute represents an array of issues for describing an item requirement. It includes price, volume, delivery time, due date, quality, and so forth. According to a specific business environment, a company may employ individual attributes to reflect its unique demand. The attribute set contains fixed and variable attributes. For a fixed attribute, the attribute values are predefined and will not change during negotiation. For a variable attribute, the MRS may exhibit a range of attribute values. The specific value of a variable attribute is determined through negotiation and subsequently becomes the supply contract. For example, attribute *Due Date* might be fixed to one week, regardless of the urgency of customer orders. Attribute *Quantity* might be specified with a range between 2,000 and 2,500 to reflect negotiation with the suppliers regarding price discounts.

The utility is introduced as a benchmark of the goodness of a proposal with respect to a specific MRS. It may be defined as a function, such as a weighted sum of individual attribute evaluation. For example, a proposal with utility equal to 0.8 is better than 0.6, as higher utility means more benefit to the manufacturer. An MRS might assign attribute *Due Date* with a weight equal to 0.4 and *Price* equal to 0.2, indicating that this MRS pays more attention to the lead time performance.

Describing the interdependency among different MRSs, constraints are specified to define the relationships among MRS attributes either quantitatively or qualitatively by limiting the possible value range of a proposal.

For an outsourced material type, the manufacturer has to determine a proper MRS by negotiating with its suppliers before converting it to supply contracts. The MRSs can be used to describe the customer order and to construct messages to be transferred among agents. Based on the object-oriented concept, each element of an MRS is regarded as a class. A customer order is thus defined as:

Order = (Order_ID; Product_ID; Cust; DD; Loc; Price).

It means to deliver product *Product_ID* to customer *Cust* at location *Loc* with due date *DD* at a *Price*.

An MRS is depicted as:

MRS = (MRS_ID; Order_ID; Item; Attribute type|Value; Constraints; Priority).

An MRS instance $MRS^* = (08; 02;$ *Engine; Price|2000, DD|8; Null; Normal*) means that the #08 MRS serves for the #02 order; it needs material *Engine* at price 2,000 with due date 8; no constraint involved; and its priority level is *Normal*.

Additional constraints can be further introduced for the items of an MRS. For example, such a constraint as $MRS_2.Item_1.Attribute_2 = 1000$ means that, for the #2 MRS, the price of the #1 item is 1,000.

MRS Constraints

The configuration agent calls the MRPII/ERP system to decompose the order into a set of MRSs, which are subsequently converted to proper supply contracts. For each MRS, decisions on attribute values such as price, volume, and due date are the key issues of negotiation. Similar to production planning, the BOM is the core logic for MRS negotiation. For example, the interdependency between two MRSs is specified as the following constraints:

$C1: MRS_1.Item_1.Volume = MRS_2.Item_2.Volume*2,$

$C2: MRS_1.Item_1.DueDate = MRS_2.Item_2.DueDate+8,$ and

$C3: MRS_1.Item_1.Quality = MRS_2.Item_2.Quality.$

Constraint C1 prescribes that the purchasing volume of $Item_1$ of MRS_1 should be twice of MRS_2. Constraint C2 requires that the delivery of $Item_1$ of MRS_1 should be eight days earlier than that of MRS_2. Constraint C3 specifies that the quality of $Item_1$ of MRS_1 should be as good as that of MRS_2.

MRS Priority

There exist unexpected changes in both production and supply. Rather than fixing all the negotiation parameters for every MRS, these parameters should be kept adaptive to each specific operational environment. For example, some component parts may serve a buyer market, where the manufacturer easily could sign a contract to conform to the required price and due date. On the other hand, in a seller market, the manufacturer has to make certain concessions in either price or due date in order to attract a supplier. Such concession makes the contract for an MRS deviate from its original intention.

To avoid possible contract mismatching problems, a priority index is introduced to help an MRS adjust to different negotiation situations. This is consistent with the fact that different MRSs demonstrate different importance to serve the order. Some important MRSs need to be prioritized and handled first, while the rest could be compromised.

The MRS priority is set to three levels: critical, normal, and standard. Higher priority MRSs own high autonomous rights in order for the contract manager to adjust the contract items for more benefit. Low priority MRSs must satisfy their constraints with others and adjust negotiation conditions in accordance with the change of higher priority MRSs.

To determine the priority of an MRS, three aspects are taken into account: function, process, and market. An MRS is functionally critical, in that the required material is important in order to implement certain functions of the end product. The design department determines this type of MRS. A process critical MRS refers to the materials that serve the key operations of the end product assembly. A key operation is the one with the longest processing time and, thus, could be the key factor causing a delay. The production department justifies this type of MRS. Market critical MRSs represent those materials serving a seller market. It indicates that this type of material is difficult to obtain from the market, and, thus, the manufacturer may have to make concessions in signing a contract. This type of MRS is planned mostly by the marketing department.

Agent-Based Multi-Contract Negotiation System

The traditional contract net is employed to handle negotiations, which includes the inviting, bidding, and awarding stages. Figure 3 shows an agent-based collaborative negotiation model, based on negotiation and bidding. Compared to the traditional systems that focus on the bilateral and single-contract negotiation processes, this model enables multi-contract negotiation and coordination of multiple negotiation processes to improve the overall performance, resulting in a batch of contracts that are consistent and coherent to the ultimate goal—fulfilling customer orders.

As shown in Figure 3, a customer order first is mapped to MRSs. Then, the system starts to find proper trading partners for individual MRSs. Each contract agent bids for the relevant task, based on its production capability and resource availability. A separate configuration agent is used to solve the possible conflicts among individual tasks.

The system employs four types of functional agents: configuration agent, contract manager, information server, and negotiation agent. The configuration agent is responsible for coordination throughout the product fulfillment process. The contract manager is in charge of a specific MRS and manages the negotiation process to reach a contract for this MRS. The information server assists the contract manager in inviting the candidate suppliers and provides a message routing service. The negotiation agent executes a certain negotiation process with a supplier.

Figure 3. Agent-based multi-contract negotiation model

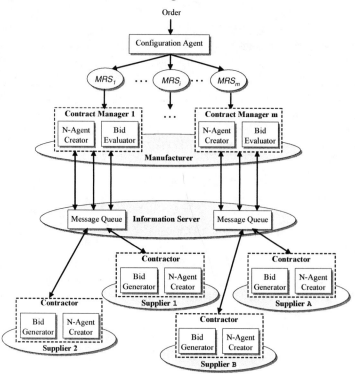

Agent-Based System Architecture

The overall system is built upon Java Agent DEvelopment (JADE) Platform (http://jade.tilab.com/). The JADE architecture enables agent communication through message exchange, based on the agent communication language (ACL). These agents work collectively to achieve the common goal by communicating and cooperating toward a better process.

To support the learning and problem-solving capabilities, blackboard architectures are used as an effective vehicle for integrating multiple sources of knowledge in order to solve complex problems. They emphasize the modular encapsulation of problem-solving knowledge within independent knowledge sources. These knowledge source modules work collectively to develop solutions to problems by communicating through a shared data structure (i.e., the blackboard).

Figure 4 presents the overall multi-agent architecture of collaborative negotiation. Each independent JADE platform typically includes (1) the main container (provides the full Java runtime environment for other agents executed inside the platform); (2) containers (may be hosted by the same computer or in remote locations); (3) agents (contained in the main container or containers for communicating via the network protocol); and (4) the system blackboard (serves as the container and domain of learning).

Figure 4. Distributed architecture of multi-agent platform

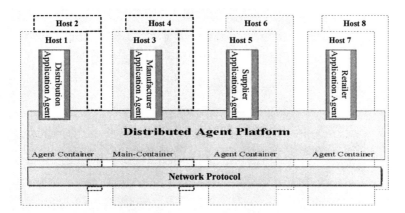

It is expected that every company or organization has its own platform consisting of a main container and a few agent containers. The platform used by different parties can be a FIPA-based or different platform that requires a specific protocol to communicate. The JADE platform supports communication between JADE–JADE, JADE–other FIPA-compliant platforms, and JADE–non-FIPA platforms, as well. The protocol used in each type relies on the capability of JADE in handling those types of communication.

System Problem-Solving Process

The blackboard provides a shared data structure for knowledge sources to post solution components (e.g., new production schedules, new capacity allocations, new parties' names, etc.), analysis results (e.g., resource/capacity utilization, failure records, etc.), and coordination/communication status information. It is partitioned into an arbitrary number of contexts that corresponds to different sets of working assumptions (e.g., sets of orders need to be scheduled, available resource capacities, etc.) and different solutions. Within each context, a summary of the current state of the solution is maintained in the form of a set of unresolved issues. An unresolved issue is an indication that a particular aspect of the current context solution is incomplete, inconsistent, or unsatisfactory. For example, a request for bid still needs to be evaluated, or a promised delivery date is violated.

Problem solving within the system, directed either by the end-user, the agent, or a combination of both, progresses in a mixed-initiative fashion so that (1) one or more unresolved issue instances are selected to be resolved; (2) a particular method of solution is selected from the set of methods applicable to the unresolved issue instance(s); and (3) the selected method is executed by invoking appropriate knowledge sources. Instances of unresolved issues are created and deleted as a result of knowledge source invocation, the incorporation of external events into a context, and/or the modification of assumptions within a context.

Figure 5. Flow of problem solving

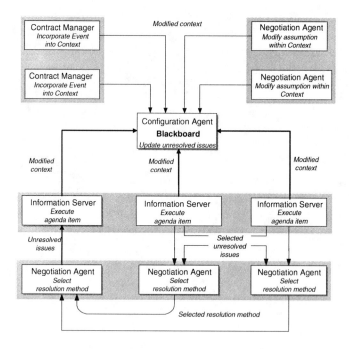

All problem-solving activities within the system architecture are triggered either by the incorporation of a new event (e.g., incoming order or status update) or modification of an assumption, both of which can be performed either by the end user or the agent. The flow of problem solving is summarized in Figure 5. It proceeds from the modification of the current working context in a clockwise direction through the following steps:

1.   Updating the set of unresolved issues within the current working context to reflect the initial problem-solving action.

2.   Selecting an unresolved issue to resolve.

3.   Selecting a solution method for the selected unresolved issue.

4.   Activating the selected solution method.

5.   Executing the problem-solving service that corresponds to the activated resolution method.

The module-activation service is invoked whenever there are problem-solving tasks on the agenda remaining to be executed or initiated by agents within the system. Knowledge sources serve as the primary problem solvers in the system. They communicate the real-time results by posting new information to the blackboard (e.g., new BOMs, new supplier selections) and by modifying existing information (e.g., re-optimized production schedules). Each domain-level knowledge source acts primarily as a server that supports a variety of problem-solving services.

Configuration Agent

The key role of the configuration agent is task generation and coordination. The production goals are broken down into more specific subgoals; based on these subgoals, the configuration agent generates executable tasks and allocates tasks to other agents. In a dynamic and open business environment, all the goals involve either bilateral or multilateral negotiations in order to reach an agreement. When a customer order arrives, the configuration agent transforms the order into a set of MRSs by calling the MRPII/ERP system. For each MRS, the configuration agent creates a contractor manager agent and assigns the MRS to the agent as its task.

Contracts reported from all contract manager agents are evaluated by the configuration agent from the overall system's perspective. The evaluation of a contract's feasibility involves four facets: (1) fulfillment of subtask objectives, (2) minimization of the total cost to complete the customer order, (3) all the contracts are consistent in terms of assembly cycle time and quantity, and (4) prevention of uncertainty in the supply chain to a certain degree.

At the negotiation preparation stage, the contract manager agent receives an MRS task from the configuration agent regarding negotiation object, value range, utility assessment, and negotiation strategy. When allocating an MRS task to a contract manager agent, the configuration agent will take into account the priority of the MRS. For example, assume two MRSs with purchasing amount constraints, as the following:

$MRS_1.Item_1.Volume = MRS_2.Item_2.Volume*2;$

$MRS_2.Priority = Critical;$

$MRS_1.Priority = Normal.$

The MRS_2 first determines its purchasing amount according to the actual demand. Then, the MRS_1 sets its purchasing amount subject to its constraint with MRS_2.

At the negotiation stage, the configuration agent needs to adjust the negotiation parameters according to the opponents' interests. Upon receiving an MRS change event, the configuration agent starts to retrieve its relevant constraints from its constraint base. If the constraints' conditions are satisfied, the configuration agent notifies the related contract manager agent regarding the negotiation parameters. For example, for a given constraint, $MRS_1.Item_1.Volume = MRS_2.Item_2.Volume*2$, two contract manager agents are involved, who are responsible for MRS_1 and MRS_2, respectively. If the volume of MRS_2 is changed due to its negotiation opponent's negative attitude toward concession, MRS_2 contract manager needs to report this change event to the configuration agent. Then, the configuration agent retrieves its constraint base and finds out any constraint associated with this change. So, the configuration agent sends a message to MRS_1 requesting that the contract manager double purchasing volume from the original setting.

Figure 6. Architecture of configuration agent

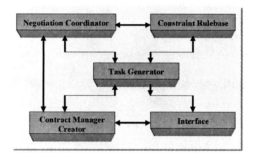

Such an event-triggered constraint-handling mechanism helps the configuration agent synchronize multiple negotiation processes while keeping the consistency among numerous contracts.

Finally, all the contract managers report their negotiation results—the best bid for each individual MRS. The configuration agent thus can evaluate all these bids and, accordingly, make the final decision from a holistic view. If certain bids conflict with the system goal, the configuration agent might require the related contract managers to renegotiate with revised settings of negotiation parameters.

As shown in Figure 6, a configuration agent contains several types of functional modules, including task generator, contract manager creator, negotiation coordinator, constraint rulebase, and interface. The task generator is the core function for decomposing a complex problem into a set of tasks. It analyzes the incoming event and maps it to subtasks that are to be processed by other functional agents. As far as product fulfillment is concerned, the task generator calls legacy systems, such as MRPII or ERP systems, to assist the decomposition. The result of decomposition is a set of MRSs. Each MRS requires a supply contract for its fulfillment. To determine an MRS contract, the task generator calls the contract manager creator to initiate the negotiation process.

The function of the contract manager creator is to generate a contract manager agent for each MRS task. While the task generator gives initial parameters, all task information is encapsulated into the contract manager agent.

Since a number of contract manager agents work independently for different MRSs, the results of negotiation may not conform to the system goal. A separate negotiation coordinator is introduced to manage the multiple negotiation processes and to synchronize different negotiation results. This is achieved by monitoring the behavior of every contract manager. Once an MRS change event occurs, the negotiation coordinator starts to retrieve the constraint base to figure out any contract manager agent to be informed of changing its MRS parameters.

The interface module manages information exchange between the configuration agent and other agents. Through the interface, the configuration agent receives order information, calls the MRPII/ERP systems, and communicates with contract manager agents throughout the negotiation process.

Figure 7. Architecture of contract manager agent

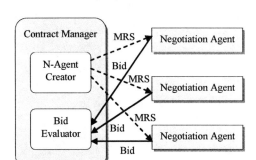

Contract Manager Agent

A contract manager agent is responsible for converting an MRS to a supply contract through the bidding and negotiation processes. The bidding mechanism is used to find the proper trading partners who are capable and available to fulfill a specific MRS. At the beginning, tasks are announced to multiple contractors through the information server. A few parallel negotiation processes may exist for the same task. A contract manager agent creates several negotiation agents to bargain with different suppliers. Each negotiation agent finds an agreement regarding negotiation parameters and submits it as a bid. Then, the contract manager evaluates all these bids and chooses the best one. As a result, the supplier offering the best bid wins the contract.

As shown in Figure 7, a contract manager includes two functional modules: negotiation agent creator and bid evaluator. The negotiation agent creator aims to generate several negotiation agents in order to solve an MRS. Each negotiation agent deals with one supplier agent. The bid evaluator analyzes all collected bids from negotiation agents and selects the best one according to the defined evaluation rules. After the bid is selected, it makes the offer and sends the awarding message to the corresponding supplier agent.

Negotiation Agent

Negotiation is an interactive process involving (1) a two-way transfer of information (the manufacturer announces tasks to suppliers, and the suppliers, in turn, send proposals to the manufacturer); (2) local evaluation (each party involved in the negotiation has its own local metrics of evaluation); and (3) mutual selection (the supplier and the manufacturer try to maximize their individual benefits while considering the opponents' interests).

Starting with the initial parameters given by the contract managers, the negotiation agent bargains with the opponent agents according to the utility assessment. Each negotiation agent interacts with one supplier agent and reaches an agreement of bid for a specific MRS. The conversation policy is applied in order to communicate with other negotiation

Figure 8. Architecture of negotiation agent

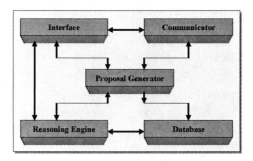

agents regarding messages of offers and counteroffers. The information server provides the message exchange service among negotiation agents via a TCP/IP protocol. A bilateral negotiation method is used to get a bid for an MRS rather than directly requesting the contractor to provide the bid.

As shown in Figure 8, the negotiation agent comprises five functional modules: interface, communicator, proposal generator, reasoning engine, and database. The interface module provides a user-friendly interface in order for a user to be involved with the negotiation. Users can check such progress of negotiation as processing time, negotiation round, and current offer, or modify the strength of negotiation, as appropriate.

The communicator deals with message exchanges among agents. All agents send their offers or receive counteroffers through the communicator. With a conversation policy, message exchange takes place in a predefined sequence.

The proposal generator constructs a proposal for a given task according to the initial parameters and the user's preference and interest. A proposal specifies a definite value for each negotiation attribute. The proposal generator gradually decreases the utility of the proposal in order to reach an agreement with the opponent.

The reasoning engine applies the utility assessment to evaluate proposals. It considers all related attributes of the given task and gives a utility assessment to represent the satisfaction level of a proposal. It also can learn from the opponent's behavior and adjusts the negotiation strategy accordingly to reach a mutually beneficial agreement.

The database contains basic information of the tasks, such as objectives, constraints, and negotiation strategies. It also stores historical negotiation data to support the reasoning process.

Collaborative Negotiation Process

To satisfy the MRSs of a customer order, multiple negotiation processes must be coordinated in accordance with task decomposition. As shown in Figure 9, the collaborative negotiation process entails four phases: decomposing, inviting, bidding, and awarding.

During the decomposing phase, the configuration agent decomposes an order into a set of MRSs. The configuration agent calls an MRPII/ERP system to analyze the order and generate production plans. According to the plan, each MRS is treated as a task and requires a contract to fulfill this task. The configuration agent then creates several contract manager agents for the task set. Each contract manager agent takes on one task with the initial parameters defined by the configuration agent.

In the inviting phase, a contract manger agent sends a request to the information server in order to search for potential suppliers. After the information server retrieves the database and communicates with other information servers, it returns a list of candidate suppliers. The contract manager agent creates several negotiation agents, each of which negotiates with a candidate supplier agent.

A negotiation agent is activated according to the task objective, the constraints, and the negotiation strategy instructed by the contract manager. The task announcement may use the following format:

Announce :=
{

        Head{Announcement_ID, Announcer_ID, Address};

        Time_Data{Announce_Expiration_Time, Bid_Validity_Time};

        Commercial_Data{Price, Volume, Penalty};

        Task_Spec{Material_Specification, Quality, Warranty, Delivery_Time};

}

In the bidding phase, each negotiation agent bargains with the supplier to maximize its benefit, often in an offer exchange mode. The agents evaluate a proposal, based on the multi-attribute utility assessment. Some heuristics, such as learning and reasoning, could be used to model an opponent's preference and interest. The result of negotiation is an agreement of the bid. The format of a bid is as follows:

Bid :=
{

        Head{Bid_ID, Announcer_ID, Bidder_ID, Address};

        Bid_Specification{Bid_Validity_Ttime};

        Commercial_Data{Price, Penalty};

        Task_Spec{Material_Specification, Quality, Warranty, Delivery_Time};

}

In the awarding phase, a contract manager collects all of the bids from negotiation agents. The bid selection decision is not made by the contract manager only. The configuration agent coordinates all the contract managers in order to synchronize the evaluation of

Figure 9. Flowchart of collaborative negotiation

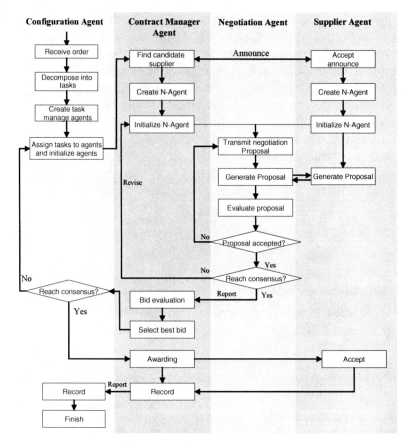

individual bids from all the contract managers. Only a global-optimized bid is selected and offered to the corresponding supplier agent. The awarding message adopts the following format:

Offer :=
{
Head{Offer_ID, Awarder_ID, Supplier_ID, Address};
Offer_Spec{Offer_Validity_Time};
Commercial_Data{Price, Penalty};
Task_Spec{Material_Specification, Quality, Warranty, Delivery_Time};
}

Case Study

A case study of the proposed agent-based collaborative negotiation framework is conducted at a leading mobile phone manufacturing company, Moxober, for the coordination of its global supply chain network. Moxober mainly serves two markets: Europe and Asia. For illustrative simplicity, this study simplified Moxober's product structure into three levels: component parts, subassemblies, and the final product, as shown in Figure 10.

Moxober used to be a vertically integrated company and produced nearly all the component parts by itself. With the development of global economy and booming telecommunication market, it has changed to a global manufacturing strategy with a focus on the key technologies and its core competency, while outsourcing major component manufacturing activities, such as the manufacturing of peripherals like batteries and chargers, memory chips, and LCD panels.

The first issue to coordinate Moxober manufacturing supply chain is the make-or-buy decisions. With respect to its BOM structures, the company decides which parts should be made in-house and which components should be outsourced to suppliers. Such decisions involve a comprehensive analysis of its market competition, core competency,

Figure 10. BOM structures of Moxober mobile phones

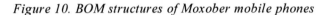
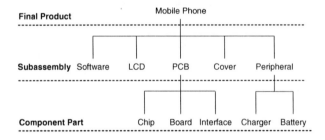

Table 2. Manufacturing BOM with make-or-buy decisions

Component Part	Importance	Competency	Impact on Measure	Impact on Production	Impact on Strategic Issue	Make or Buy Decision
LCD	Hi	Low	Med	Hi	Med	Buy
Software	Hi	Hi	Med	Med	Hi	Make
PCB	Hi	Hi	Med	Hi	Hi	Make
Charger	Low	Med	Low	Low	Low	Buy
Battery	Hi	Hi	Low	Low	Low	Buy
Chip	Hi	Low	Hi	Low	Low	Buy
Board	Med	Med	Med	Hi	Med	Buy
Interface	Med	Med	Low	Med	Hi	Buy
Cover	Hi	Med	Hi	Hi	Med	Make

and capacity planning. Based on the outsourcing decisions, the product BOM is transformed to a manufacturing BOM representing the fulfillment of individual component parts. Table 2 shows an example of make-or-buy decision making and the resulting manufacturing BOM.

For those outsourced component parts, Moxober clusters the respective suppliers to build its supply base. A multi-national company commonly involves hundreds or thousands of tier I or tier II suppliers. It would be very difficult, if not impossible, to evaluate individual suppliers on their capabilities on a case-by-case basis. Therefore, Moxober developed a taxonomy of selection criteria for systematic evaluation of its suppliers, as shown in Figure 11.

To fulfill the manufacturing BOM, Moxober starts to justify its capabilities and sourcing possibilities worldwide. Then, its global manufacturing supply chain network can be set up with right capacities and resources allocated to the right manufacturing activities. Essentially, this task is a resource allocation problem considering a number of perspectives, such as the factory loading issue of different production volumes at different manufacturing plants.

The next issue is to determine a specific configuration of the global manufacturing supply chain network for each individual customer order of a particular product model. Since each supplier possesses its unique competency and can adapt to different business situations, the actual employment of a supplier should be consistent with the product fulfillment process of a specific customer order. For example, Moxober owns final assembly plants in both Finland and China. The supply of some component parts can be assigned to either suppliers in Europe or Asia. For an order coming from China, it may be more economical to conduct the final assembly in the China plant, while still maintaining design and software programming activities in Europe.

To coordinate the fulfillment of a specific customer order across a Moxober global manufacturing supply chain, the agent-based negotiation framework comes into play. Assume that a customer order comes in from Wenzhou, China, asking for 1,000 units of model A mobile phones. Moxober needs to find suitable suppliers and synchronize the related supply contracts with material planning of its production.

At the beginning, the customer places its order through an order acquisition agent located either at a retailer side or at Moxober's online sales system. Through interaction with product catalogs, the customer can configure various ordering parameters, such as product features and quotation of price and delivery date. Order information is encapsulated as a message to be transmitted in the following format:

Order = *(0078; 013; China; 1000, 30, $500, Wenzhou)*

This order message is sent to a Moxober configuration agent. Then, the configuration agent initiates the production planning of this order. To determine material requirements, the configuration agent activates the negotiation process. Order information first is decomposed into a set of related MRSs along with the constraints among them.

The system decides to allocate the final assembly of this order to its Xiamen plant in China

Figure 11. Taxonomy of supplier selection criteria

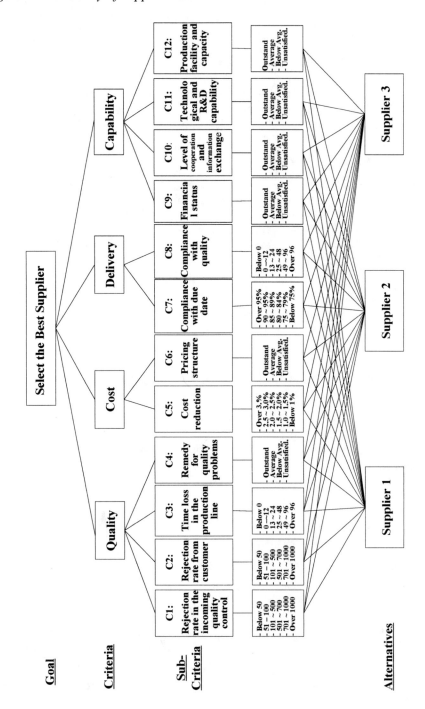

Figure 12. Moxober global manufacturing supply chain network

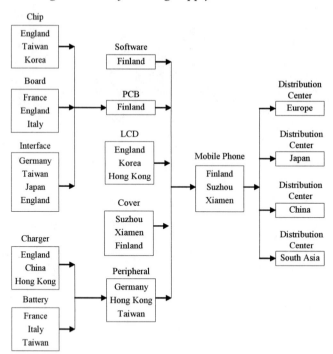

in order to expedite the delivery. The design and PCB assembly operations are still held in the subassembly plants in Finland. The Xiamen plant involves the requirement specification of three material types: LCD, charger, and battery. To take advantage of local sourcing, the configuration agent generates a set of MRSs for this customer order (ID = #13) as follows:

$MRS(013) = (MRS_1, MRS_2, MRS_3)$;

$MRS_1 = (01; 013; Charger; Volume| 600\text{-}800, Price|20\text{-}30, DD|20; Con1; Normal)$;

$MRS_2 = (02; 013; Battery; Volume| 1200\text{-}1600, Price|50\text{-}80, DD|15; Con2; Normal)$;

$MRS_3 = (03; 013; LCD; Volume| 1000, Price|100\text{-}120, DD|12; Null; Critical)$;

$C_1: MRS_1.Charger.Volume = MRS_2.Battery.Volume/2$;

$C_2: MRS_2.Battery.DD <= MRS_3.LCD.DD+5$.

Then, the configuration agent creates three contract manager agents, CM_1, CM_2 and CM_3, to deal independently with three MRSs. Each contract manager further creates three negotiation agents to tap into related supplier agents. An information server is installed to facilitate message exchange among agents. Figure 13 illustrates collaborative negotiation architecture tailored to this customer order.

Figure 13. Collaborative negotiation architecture for a specific customer order

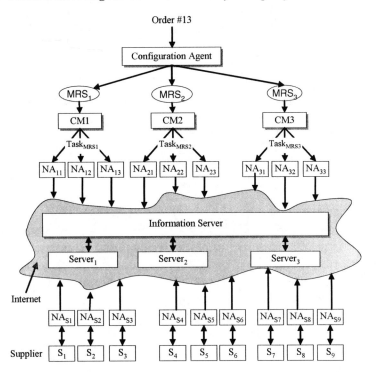

After each negotiation agent reaches an agreement with the respective supplier, a contract manager composes a bid for every MRS and returns it to the configuration agent. Then, the configuration agent checks the feasibility and consistency of all the bids from a holistic view. It ensures that no bid violates the constraints and maintains consistency of the entire production plan. Table 3 lists all the bids collected from the three negotiation agents. Each bid includes the supplier ID, material type, transaction attributes, and their values. A utility figure is used to quantify the goodness of each bid.

Table 3. Multiple bids reported from negotiation agents

Contract Manager	MRS	Bid	Utility
		Bid_{11}: (Supplier01; Charger; Volume|1000, price|25, DD|20)	0.68
CM_1	MRS_1	Bid_{12}: (Supplier02; Charger; Volume|800, price|20, DD|18)	0.73
		Bid_{13}: (Supplier03; Charger; Volume|1000, price|15, DD|22)	0.75
		Bid_{21}: (Supplier04; Battery; Volume|1400, price|70, DD|10)	0.65
CM_2	MRS_2	Bid_{22}: (Supplier05; Battery; Volume|1600, price|60, DD|16)	0.72
		Bid_{23}: (Supplier06; Battery; Volume|2000, price|45, DD|18)	0.69
		Bid_{31}: (Supplier07; LCD; Volume|1000, price|120, DD|11)	0.77
CM_3	MRS_3	Bid_{32}: (Supplier08; LCD; Volume|1200, price|100, DD|10)	0.71
		Bid_{33}: (Supplier09; LCD; Volume|900, price|90, DD|15)	0.69

Table 4. The winner of bids for each MRS

Contract Manager	MRS	Contract	Supplier
CM_1	MRS_1	(Charger; Volume|800, price|20, DD|18)	Suppier02
CM_2	MRS_2	(Battery; Volume|1600, price|60, DD|16)	Suppier05
CM_3	MRS_3	(LCD; Volume|1000, price|120, DD|11)	Suppier07

Figure 14. Supply chain network configuration specific for the customer order

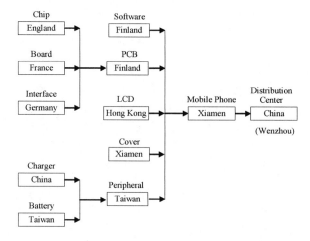

Figure 15. Multi-agent system for Moxober supply chain coordination

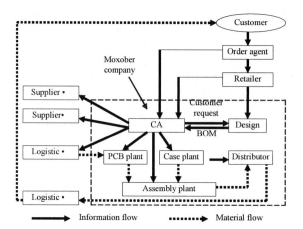

The awarding decision is made, based on the utility assessments and subject to the satisfaction of MRS constraints. For instance, the bid with the highest utility for MRS_1 is selected by CM_1 and is recommended to the configuration agent. The configuration agent has to check whether this bid is consistent with other bids. If the bid violates certain constraints, the configuration agent notifies CM_1 that the bid is unqualified and asks CM_1 to submit another bid for MRS_1. Such a negotiation process may be enacted between the configuration agent and contract managers iteratively until the winner is finally selected. Table 4 lists the winner of the bids for each MRS. Comparing Tables 3 and 4, it suggests that Bid_{13} for MRS_1 possesses the highest utility (0.75) but is not selected, because it violates constraint C_1. As a result, a configuration of the manufacturing supply chain network specific for customer order (#13) can be determined, as shown in Figure 14. Figure 15 shows the corresponding agent-based collaborative negotiation system for Moxober's supply chain coordination.

Conclusion

Highly customized customer demands and volatile markets shift manufacturing supply chain coordination from static strategic decisions to dynamic operational decisions. Global supply chain coordination must coincide with the product fulfillment process. A customer order is mapped to a set of material requirement specifications. The material requirement specifications play an important role in synchronizing interdependency among operational processes across the supply chain. Negotiation is an efficient means to quickly select the capable supplier and sign the contract to meet the material requirements. Traditional single-contract negotiation is extended to a group negotiation decision making, where multiple contracts are negotiated simultaneously to solve a batch of material requirement specifications. Several control agents, including the configuration agent and contract manager agents, are created to coordinate the multi-contract negotiation process. A constraint-triggered mechanism is conducive in order to maintain the consistency of supply contracts.

References

Anderson, C., & Bunce, P. (2000). Next generation manufacturing systems [white paper]. CAM-I Next Generation Manufacturing Systems Program. Retrieved from *http://www.cam-i.org/ngms.html*

Arntzen, B.C., Brown, G.G., Harrison, T.P., & Trafton, L.L. (1995). Global supply chain management at Digital Equipment Corporation. *Interfaces, 25*(1), 69-93.

Barbuceanu, M., & Fox, M.S. (1996). Capturing and modeling coordination knowledge for multi-agent systems. *International Journal of Cooperative Information Systems, 5*(2-3), 275-314.

Blecker, T., & Graf, G. (2003). Multi agent systems in Internet based production environments—An enabling infrastructure for mass customization. *Proceedings of the 2ⁿᵈ Interdisciplinary World Congress on Mass Customization and Personalization*, Munich.

Brenner, W., Zarnekow, R., & Wittig, H. (1998). *Intelligent software agents: Foundations and applications*. New York: Springer.

Bullinger, H.J., Lentes, H.P., & Scholtz, O.H. (2000). Challenges and chances for innovative companies in a global information society. *International Journal of Production Research, 38*(7), 1469-1500.

Chen, Y., Peng, Y., Finin, T., Labrou, Y., & Cost, R.S. (1999). Negotiating agents for supply chain management. *Proceedings of the AAAI Workshop of Electronic Commerce*, Orlando, Florida.

Cohen, M.A., & Lee, H.L. (1988). Strategic analysis of integrated production-distributed systems: Models and methods. *Operations Research, 36*(2), 216-228.

Ertogral, K., & Wu, S.D. (2000). Auction-theoretic coordination of production planning in the supply chain. *IIE Transactions, 32*(10), 931-940.

Fawcett, S.E. (1992). Strategic logistics in coordinated global manufacturing success. *International Journal of Production Research, 30*(4), 1081-1099.

Fox, M.S., Barbuceanu, M., & Teigen, R. (2000). Agent-oriented supply-chain management. *International Journal of Flexible Manufacturing Systems, 12*(2/3), 165-188.

Fox, M.S., Chionglo, J.F., & Barbuceanu, M. (1993). The integrated supply chain management system. Internal Report of the Department of Industrial Engineering, University of Toronto. Retrieved from *http://www.ie.utoronto.ca/EIL/iscm-descr.html*

Gaonkar, R., & Viswanadham, N. (2001). Collaboration and information sharing in global contract manufacturing networks. *IEEE-ASME Transactions on Mechatronics, 6*(4), 366-376.

Ghiassi, M., & Spera, C. (2003). Defining the Internet-based supply chain system for mass customized markets. *Computers and Industrial Engineering, 45*(1), 17-41.

Gjerdrum, J., Shah, N., & Papageorgiou, L.G. (2001). A combined optimization and agent-based approach to supply chain modeling and performance assessment. *Production Planning and Control, 12*(1), 81-88.

Ho, J.K.L., Fung, R., Chu, L., & Tam, W.M. (2000). A multimedia communication framework for the selection of collaborative partners in global manufacturing. *International Journal of Computer Integrated Manufacturing, 13*(3), 273-285.

Jennings, N.R., & Wooldidge, M.J. (1998). *Agent technology: Foundations, applications, and markets*. Berlin: Springer.

Kaihara, T. (2001). Supply chain management with market economics. *International Journal of Production Economics, 73*(1), 5-14.

Li, D., McKay, A., De Pennington, A., & Barnes, C.J. (2001). A Web-based tool and a heuristic method for co-operation of manufacturing supply chain decisions. *Journal of Intelligent Manufacturing, 12*(5-6), 433-453.

Lu, S.C.-Y. (2004). Engineering as collaborative negotiation: A new paradigm for collaborative engineering. CIRP Working Group on Engineering as Collaborative Negotiation. Retrieved from *http://mspde.usc.edu/ecn*

Maturana, F., Shen, W., & Norrie, D.H. (1999). MetaMorph: An adaptive agent-based architecture for intelligent manufacturing. *International Journal of Production Research, 37*(10), 2159-2174.

Petersen, S.A., Divitini, M., & Matsken, M. (2001). An agent-based approach to modeling virtual enterprises. *Production Planning and Control, 12*(3), 224-233.

Pontrandolfo, P., Gosavi, A., Okogbaa, O.G., & Das, T.K. (2002). Global supply chain management: A reinforcement learning approach. *International Journal of Production Research, 40*(1), 1299-1317.

Pontrandolfo, P., & Okogbaa, O.G. (1999). Global manufacturing: A review and a framework for planning in a global corporation. *International Journal of Production Research, 37*(1), 1-19.

Sadeh, N.M., Hildum, D.W., Kjenstad, D., & Tseng, A. (2001). MASCOT: An agent-based architecture for dynamic supply chain creation and coordination in the Internet economy. *Production Planning and Control, 12*(3), 212-223.

Shin, M., & Jung, M. (2004). MANPro: Mobile agent-based negotiation process for distributed intelligent manufacturing. *International Journal of Production Research, 42*(2), 303-320.

Strader, T.J., Lin, F., & Shaw, M.J. (1998). Information infrastructure for electronic virtual organization management. *Decision Support Systems, 23*(1), 75-94.

Swaminathan, J.M. (1996). *Quantitative analysis of emerging practices in supply chains* [doctoral dissertation]. Pittsburgh, PA: Carnegie Mellon University.

Swaminathan, J.M., Smith, S.F., & Sadeh, N.M. (1996). A multi-agent framework for modeling supply chain dynamics. *Proceedings of NSF Research Planning Workshop on Artificial Intelligence and Manufacturing*, Albequerque, New Mexico.

Swaminathan, J.M., Smith, S.F., & Sadeh, N.M. (1998). Modeling supply chain dynamics: A multiagent approach. *Decision Sciences, 29*(3), 607-632.

Tian, G.Y., Yin, G., & Taylor, D. (2002). Internet-based manufacturing: A review and a new infrastructure for distributed intelligent manufacturing. *Journal of Intelligent Manufacturing, 13*(5), 323-338.

Tso, S.K., Lau, H., & Ho, K.L. (2000). Coordination and monitoring in an intelligent global manufacturing service system. *Computers in Industry, 43*(1), 83-95.

Chapter XVI

The Critical Success Factors in Supply Chain Implementation

Panyaluck Udomleartprasert
Assumption University, Thailand

Chamnong Jungthirapanich
Assumption University, Thailand

Abstract

This chapter introduces critical success in supply chain implementation by empirical research. The widespread implementation of supply chain management induced companies to move beyond national borders and be enticed by the global competition in business. Applying supply chain management overall in organizations, companies generally considered it successful in managing their supply chains. However, some of them have not reached the magnitude of improvements or the desired results ascribed to supply chain management. With supply chain concerns and problems related to some basic companies' infrastructures, the supply chain knowledge and operational skill affected the effectiveness of supply chain practices and performances. In this research, we studied the infrastructures enhancing the success of supply chain implementation that influence supply chain performance. The author adopts three categories of infrastructure as the critical success factors of supply chain implementation: man, machines, and management. The EQS is used to analyze the data collection. A total of 114 pieces of data were completed, and the result shows the significant relationship of operational infrastructures and the success of supply chain management.

Introduction

In this chapter, we will discuss the global supply chain system in terms of operation and management. Higher competition is one of several reasons for implementing supply chain in organization. Maintaining the purchasing volume for higher purchasing power and negotiation, cost reduction in operation process, and customer satisfaction are the benefits of supply chain management. Companies that applied supply chain management considered it successful in managing their supply chain. However, while they have achieved improvement in organizational performance, they have not reached the magnitude of improvements as expectation. Supply chain concerns and problems were studied first in the year 2002. The results showed that the items of most concern were Supply Chain Coherence, such as lack of cooperation among supply chain members; Information Capability, such as lack of sophisticated information systems; and Geographical Proximity, such as customer and supplier geographical distances. All of these concerns related to some basic infrastructures of the company, the supply chain knowledge operational skill, which affected the effectiveness of supply chain practices and performances. In order to achieve the supply chain, the company needs to clearly identify the basic infrastructures and supply chain practices that will impact to the level of supply chain performance..

Supply Chain Revolutions

A supply chain company comprises geographically dispersed facilities in which raw materials, intermediate products, or finished products are acquired, transformed, stored, sold, and transported to the customers. These activities are the connected facilities along the products flow. The facilities may be operated by the company, vendors, customers, third-party providers, or other firms with which the company has business arrangements. The company's goal is to add value to the products through the supply chain and to transport them to geographically dispersed markets in the correct quantities.

In the 1950s and 1960s, most manufacturers emphasized mass production to minimize unit cost with low product flexibility. The information sharing with supplier or partnership was considered risky. In the period, there was little to find the cooperation and strategic buyer-supplier partnership, and it was rare to find the supply chain organization (Tan, 2002).

In the early 1970s, the emphasis on competitive strategy shifted from productivity and mass production to quality emphasis and cycle time reduction (Horvath, 2001). The material requirement planning (MRP) was developed, and managers realized the impact of huge WIP inventories on manufacturing cost as well as product quality, product development, and delivery lead time (Tan, 2002). All of these inconsist performances of the supplier or partnership directly and indirectly affected the company in terms of cost, customer satisfaction, and management. In this period, manufacturers resorted to new material management concepts to improve company performance.

In the 1980s, global competition forced world-class organizations to offer low-cost, high-quality, and reliable products with greater design flexibility. The JIT was developed to support and improve manufacturing efficiency and cycle time (Tan, 2002) as well as to minimize and manage inventory. In this period, the buyer-supplier relationship was accountability. The supply chain concept emerged as the experiment in manufacturing. Additionally, procurement professionals and logistics experts carried it a step further in order to incorporate physical distribution, transportation, and warehousing functions (Tan, 2001).

The evolution of supply chain management continued into the 1990s, due to the intensity of global competition. The higher demand from customers to get the product and service at the right time and at the lowest cost caused the organization or manufacturer to realize that they had to improve the overall organizational efficiency as well as the efficiency of their partnerships with both customer and supplier. Long-term and close working relationships are developed to keep the competitiveness within the chain (Li, 2002). In this period, the supply chain management was continued from the 1980s and further extended best practices in managing corporate resources to include strategic suppliers and logistics function.

At the end of the 1990s until 2000s, several developments in material management emerged. MRPII and ERP were developed as a tool in managing the material. The advanced supply chain management and logistics were studied to improve the efficiency of process, such as lean logistics, agile supply chain, and so forth. Currently, supply chain is the new business process management in almost every organization regardless of the business types or products.

As competition in the 1990s intensified and markets became global, so were the challenges associated with getting a product and service to the right place at the right time at the lowest cost. Organizations are realizing that it is not enough to improve efficiencies within an organization, but the whole supply chain has to be competitive. Developing close, long-term relationships with both customers and suppliers can take significant waste out of the supply chain and is a potentially valuable way of securing competitive advantage (Spekman et al., 1998). Understanding and practicing supply chain management have become an essential prerequisite to stay in the competitive global race and to grow profitably.

Coordination of complex global networks of organizational activities is becoming a prime source of competitive advantage in which suppliers and customers linked throughout the entire sequences of events that bring raw material from its source of supply to different value added to the ultimate customers.

In order to further understand the intricacies of supply chain management, different theories have offered insight into how and why different supply chain management practices emerge and for understanding the consequences of these practices for the efficiency and competitiveness of an organization. This chapter first will explain the theories addressing the rationale of supply chain issues, followed by the identification and discussion of various constructs of supply chain management.

Table 1. Summary of supply chain revolution

Period	Cooperative Characteristics	Authors
1950s–1960s	• Low cooperative strategy between buyer and supplier • Emphasis on mass production to minimize cost with low product flexibility • No supply chain developed	Tan, 2002
1970s	• Emphasis on high quality product • MRP is developed supporting WIP managing • Initiate the cycle time reduction, accurate lead-time delivery, and product development concept	Carter et al., 1996; Tan, 2002
1980s	• High global competition forced • Market need low cost – high quality – reliable – higher flexibility • JIT developed to minimize and manage the inventory • Realized the buyer and supplier relationship in corporate management	Tan, 2001; Tan, 2002
1990s	• Higher demand of quality product, service in the right time at the lowest cost • Partnership management emerged, the long term, partnership relationships, closely working with the supplier was developed • Supply chain management was continued from the period of the 1980s	Inman & Hubler, 1992; Morgan & Monczka, 1995; Onge, 1996
2000s	• MRPII, ERP were developed to support material management • Supply chain management is the new business process management • New supply chain knowledge was developed, such as lean supply chain management, agile management, and so forth.	Tan, 2002; Elmuti, 2002; Li, 2002

Review of Supply Chain Publications

Several supply chain publications were studied regarding supply chain topics conducted in this area, as the following summaries.

(a)   The Journal of Supply Chain Management: Year 1997-2003

(b)   The Journal of Business Logistics: Year 1970-1998

Table 2. Review of The Journal of Supply Chain Management*: Years 1997-2003*

Subject Area	1997	1998	1999	2000	2001	2002	2003	Total
Purchasing and Inventory	10	12	8	10	6	6	1	53
Supplier Management	6	5	6	4	6	6	0	33
Supply Chain Concepts	1	1	4	0	2	2	2	12
Organization and Performance	0	1	1	3	3	2	0	10
IT Application	2	1	1	2	3	0	0	9
Financial Area	2	0	0	2	1	2	0	7
Quality	0	0	2	1	1	0	0	4
Customer Management	2	0	0	0	0	0	0	2
Logistics	0	2	0	0	0	0	0	2
Outsourcing	0	0	2	0	0	0	0	2
Total by Year	**23**	**22**	**24**	**22**	**22**	**18**	**3**	**134**

Figure 1. Classification of dissertation topics in The Journal of Supply Chain Management*, Years 1997-2003*

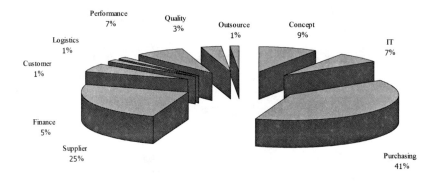

The Journal of Supply Chain Management   1997 - 2003

Table 3. Review of The Journal of Business Logistics: *Years 1970-1998 (Source: Stock, et al. The Journal of Business Logistics, 2001)*

Subject Area	1970-1986	1987-1991	1992-1998	Total
Transportation (Motor, Rail, Water, Air, Pipeline, Others)	34.8% (n = 235)	15.6% (n = 108)	22.8% (n = 63)	406
Purchasing and Inventory	20.7% (n = 142)	22.8% (n = 96)	12.6% (n = 40)	278
Information System and Decision Support System	12.5 % (n = 85)	7.6% (n = 32)	11.4% (n = 36)	153
Channel of Distribution	9.9% (n = 68)	9.0% (n = 38)	8.2% (n = 26)	132
Logistics	5.8 % (n = 40)	13.3% (n = 36)	12.9% (n = 41)	117
General Logistics	1.9% (n = 13)	4.3% (n =18)	9.8% (n = 31)	62
Location Analysis	5.6% (n = 35)	4.7% (n = 20)	1.3% (n = 4)	59
Customer Service/ Satisfaction	2.1% (n = 18)	2.6% (n = 11)	3.5% (n = 11)	40
Human Resource and Organization	0.3 % (n = 2)	0.7 % (n = 3)	5.0 % (n = 16)	21
Miscellaneous Topics	1.5% (n = 10)	0.2% (n = 1)	2.5% (n = 8)	19
Supply Chain Management	0	0	4.4% (n = 14)	14
Packaging	0.7% (n =5)	0.5% (n = 2)	0.3% (n = 1)	8
Total Quality Management	0	1.2% (n = 5)	0.6% (n = 2)	7
Total Paper Published		<u>**1316**</u>		

Figure 2. Classification of dissertation topics in The Journal of Business Logistics, *Years 1970-1998*

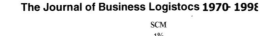

The Journal of Business Logistocs 1970- 1998

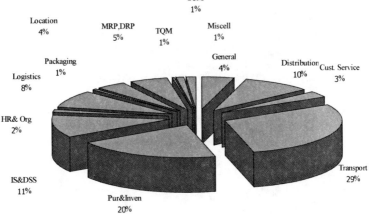

From the literature review about the published researches, the most frequent published topics are transportation, purchasing and inventory, logistics, information system, channel of distribution, MRP, DRP, JIT and Kanban, location analysis, supplier management, customer service, human resources and organization, supply chain concept, and others. The number of citations vs. the subject area is shown in the following table. From the literature review, there were rarely supply chain infrastructure topics. Therefore, this research focused on the infrastructure factors that impact successful supply chain implementation.

Research Model

From the previous section on the supply chain revolution and past researches, the supply chain benefits and its practices were studied the most. However, as a research problem, some organizations that implemented the supply chain cannot achieve the outcomes of their expectations. In this research, we are interested in the supportive infrastructures, whether they are related to and positively affect the supply chain practice and supply chain performance. The research model is proposed in Figure 3.

Supply Chain Performance

Managing a supply chain is becoming an important issue for organizations. Several researches mentioned that the competition is no longer between organizations but among supply chains (Elmuti, 2002). Wisner and Choon suggested that the intense global competition of the past decade has allowed organizations to create cooperative, mutually beneficial partnerships with suppliers, distributors, retailers, and other firms within the supply chain. The objectives of those partnerships are to offer lower-cost, higher-quality products and services with greater design flexibility (Beamon, 1999; Croteau et al., 2001; Davis, 1993), cycle time improvement, higher productivity, waste reduction, efficiency of work, and product quality (Elmuti, 2002; Inman, 1992; Jorsekog, 1998). An objective of supply chain implementation also is to achieve the financial level of firm revenue in order to maximize over time the ratio of annual revenue less operation costs (Beamon, 1999; Boudreau, 2002; Stock, 1997), sales, sales per staff, gross sales, operating income

Figure 3. The proposed research model

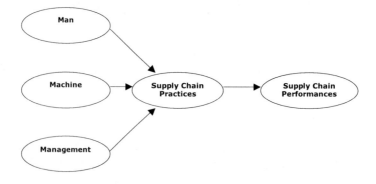

before depreciation, return on assets, net income, saving, ROE, ROI, and margin (Ahuja Saraj, 1998; Beamon, 1999; Lee, 2002; Morgan, 1995).

Several researchers focused on supply chain performance measurement and firm performance improvement objectives (Auskain, 1999; Carter, 2002; Choi, 1999; Ellram, 1990; Lambert, 2001; Lee, 2002). In 1995, McMullan (1996) studied about supply chain management practices in Asia Pacific. The researcher investigated four key areas: the management issue, role and responsibilities, competitive strategies, and performance management. McMullan (1996) (Lee, 2002) also suggested that in order to achieve a competitive advantage, the firm is required to change its organizational structures, its relationships with supply chain members, and its performance measurement systems, as well as new information technology in order to enhance communication throughout the supply chain, which will increase service levels and reduce operating costs. Lambert, et al. (2001) stated that the supply chain is to maximize the profitability at each line, supply chain performance migrations toward management's objectives, and maximize performance (Tan, 1998).

The customer management and satisfaction is the objectives of supply chain implementation (Beamon, 1999; Daugherty, 1995; Lee, 2002) in order to deliver on-time delivery product, reduce customer complaints, provide inventory accuracy, and reduce the total cycle time (Lee, 2002; Strub, 2002). The supply chain implementation in manufacturing also can reflect on customer satisfaction by increased sales volume, cost reduction in order to sell higher margin products, reducing safety stock, improving asset utilization, product development, investment plan, and resource effectiveness (Ellram, 1990; Lambert, 2001; McMullan, 1996).

For supplier management, many researchers identified it as the critical success factor in supply chain management (Ahuja Saraj, 1998; Carter, 1996; Chopra, 2001; Ellram, 2002; Handfield, 1998; Horvath, 2001). The objectives expected from the supply chain management program are to acquire the right quality products in the right supplier, time, price, and services (Christopher, 2001; Christopher, M., 2001; Fawcett, 2002; Strub, 2002). The impact of supplier selection criteria and supplier involvement can impacted firm performance by reducing the production rework cost, reducing the production costs per unit, decreasing the work-in-progress inventories, material handling, and increasing the quality of outgoing product and delivery performance from the accuracy in delivery from the supplier (Beamon, 1999; Ferrin, 2002; Strub, 1998; Tan, 2001).

The warehouse and transportation is the one component in supply chain integration; the most common measured in warehouse performance are inventory accuracy, on-time delivery, shipping error, warehouse cycle time, and so forth (Ellran, 1990; Hewitt, 2000; Lambert, 2001; Miller, 2001). Some researchers identified the benefits of supply chain in warehouse and transportation as lower inventory cost and risk, warehouse cost reduction, cost saving from overtime through increased productivity, and streamlined business processes in procurement and purchasing. The logistics system can be saved for the operation cost (Elmuti, 2002; Onge, 1996) by implementing the freight and transportation management. Some researchers studied about third-party service provided in helping cost and efficiency improvement.

The warehouse management seems to be related to information technology. Some companies have implemented software in managing warehouse and inventory processing. The software in inventory management is the most applicable to supply chain organization (Lee, 2002). So, information technology is one of the key success factors to supply chain management. It is the medium for coordination among and within organizations, but the larger of IT investment seems not to lead to higher financial performance (Ferrin, 2002; Stock, 1997). So, the firm should consider the investment level of information technology in achieving the highest benefit return. Some usage of information technology in supply chain, such as the Internet, provides the opportunity for demand data and supply capacity data to be visible to all companies within the chain (Power, 2001; Fawcett, 2002). Other applications of information technology in supply chain management concerns usage of warehousing management, fleet management, facility network planning, MRPII, bar coding, radio frequency, and EDI (Bommer, 2001; Lambert, 2001; Lee, 2002).

From these benefits, the advent of information technology and intense global competition has enticed many world-class manufacturers, service providers (Tan 2001, Tan 2002) adopt an integrated strategic approach to supply chain management. To achieve these benefits, the supply chain strategies were implemented and studied by several researchers in how the practices related to firm performance or individual studied the supply chain practices for implementation.

Supply Chain Practices

Facing the competitive global market, the revolution in manufacturers, downsizing and lean organizations in order to achieve the competitive advantage, an organization needs to adapt and implement some value-adding activities. In order to achieve financial performance, a firm should focus on profit maximization, cost reduction in manufacturing, operating costs, cost of quality, and so forth (Ellram, 2002; Ferrin, 2002). Some manufacturers are practicing the process cutting by adding some processes to supplier capacity (Morgan, 1995), such as part preparation before production.

Most practices in customer management are to identify the customers' needs, reduce customer complaints, and a score of delivery performances (Bommer, 2001; Talluri, 2002). The firm expected repeat long-term orders for these activities. On the other hand, the firm also needs the strong support of its suppliers. The supplier was monitored by the firm since the start of business; many firms implemented the supplier selection program and set up the team to control the supplier performance as well as reducing incoming inspection at the firm's receiving, provide supplier certification for the excellent supplier performance (Miller, 2001; Talluri, 2002; Tan, 2001, 2002). Currently, suppliers are treated as partners in business. Some purchasing roles in organizations have been changed, such as purchasing from individual plant sources in low-cost items, decentralizing the purchasing, and annual price negotiation activities (Tan, 2002; Talluri, 2002).

Outsourcing is another premise of supply chain management for cost reduction; outsourcing can be applied to transportation function, warehousing function, human resource management (Elmuti, 2002), and information technology. Some researchers (Ellram, 1990, 2002) identified the information technology that purchasing and supply management use in six items. The cost reduction was initiated in the JIT program to keep fewer inventories and lower risk as well as transportation, which the consolidated and postponement strategy were selected to perform the cost reduction. Generally, supply chain practices and activities were emphasized on internal competencies, which requires greater reliance. In an empirical survey, Tan, et al. (1998) identified 10 SCM practices and showed that some of the practices affected firms' performances. Later in 2002, Tan studied the 25 supply chain practices related to firm performances; the result showed that determining customers' future needs were the most practice items of the survey respondents and it leaned strongly toward customer service and competitive position performance of the firm. The use of third-party SCM specialist was the lowest activity rating from survey respondents and had no relation to any firm performances (Tan, 2001, 2002).

In this research, we are interested in three aspects of supply chain practices that contributed to the supply chain performances: partnership management, outsourcing and procurement, and flexibility.

Supply Chain Infrastructures

From past researches, there were no supply chain infrastructures found in the literature review. In this chapter, researchers divide supply chain infrastructures into three parts as follows:

Man Infrastructures

Man infrastructure is defined as the capability of people in a supply chain organization. In this research, we focus on the following:

(a)   Skill
(b)   Training

Machine Infrastructures

Machine infrastructure is defined as the equipment, tools, or necessary things to support the supply chain activities. In this research, we focus on the following:

(a)   Hardware
(b)   Software, computer program, MRP, ERP, etc.

Management Infrastructures

Management infrastructure is defined as the management vision to supply chain management and implementation. As the supply chain management being looked upon as an investment, so the budget for the implementation is affected significantly to the overall success. In this research, we focus on the following:

(a)   Management commitment
(b)   Management strategy

In this research, we study the infrastructures that directly impact supply chain practices and supply chain management. The research model is categorized into a multi-level supply chain. The basic level is the supply chain infrastructure. The intermediate level is supply chain practices, and supply chain performance is the last level.

Research Methodology

The study tools in this research are Q Methodology in clustering the basic infrastructure as the classified category. Structural equation modeling is used to validate the research result.

Inter-Rater Reliability

In this research, we apply Q methodology for inter-rater reliability analysis. It was invented in 1935 by British physicist-psychologist William Stephenson (1953). It is the most often associated with quantitative analysis, due to its involvement with factor analysis. Statistical procedures aside, however, what Stephenson was interested in providing was a way to reveal the subjectivity involved in any situation, such as in aesthetic judgment, poetic interpretation, perceptions of organizational roles, political attitudes, appraisals of health care, experiences of bereavement, perspectives on life and the cosmos, and so forth. It is life as lived from the standpoint of the person living it that is typically passed over by quantitative procedures, and it is subjectivity in this sense that Q methodology is designed to examine and that frequently engages the attention of the qualitative researcher interested in more than just life measured by the pound. Q methodology combines the strengths of both qualitative and quantitative research traditions and, in other respects, provides a bridge between the two. Some of the quantitative obstacles to the wider use of Q methodology recently have been rendered less daunting by virtue of software packages that have converted to button presses what before were tedious calculations. One such package, Q Method, is available as freeware from Kent State University's list server, as well as the way in which Q Method facilitates Q-methodological inquiries and in which such inquiries proceed. The following example describes the theoretical basis for the Q-sort method and two evaluation indices to measure inter-judge agreement level: Cohen's Kappa, Moore, and Benbasat's hit ratio. Assume that two judges independently classified a set of N components as either acceptable or rejected. After work was finished, the following table was constructed.

Table 4. Q Table shows the number of components in i row to j column

		Judge 1		
		Acceptable	Rejected	Totals
Judge2	Acceptable	X11	X12	X1+
	Rejected	X21	X22	X2+
	Totals	X+1	X+2	N

Table 5. Guidelines for kappa value

Value of Kappa	Degree of Agreement Beyond Chance
0.76 – 1.00	Excellent
0.40 – 0.75	Fair to Good (Moderate)
0.39 or less	Poor

The table of percentages will be used to describe the Cohen's Kappa coefficient of agreement. The simplest measure of agreement is the proportion of components that were classified the same by both judges (i.e., Sigma $P_{ii} = P_{11} + P_{22}$). However, Cohen suggested comparing the actual agreement with the chance of agreement that would occur if the row and columns were independent. When sampling from population where the total N is fixed, the maximum likelihood estimate of k is achieved by substituting the sample proportions for those of the population. The formula for calculating the sample kappa (k) is

$$k = \frac{N_i X_{ii} - \text{Sigma}(X_i + X_{+i})}{N_2 - \text{Sigma}(X_i + X_{+i})} \qquad (1)$$

For kappa, no general agreement exists with respect to required scores. Landis and Koch (1977) have provided a more detailed guideline to interpret kappa by associating different values of this index to a degree of agreement beyond chance. The following guideline is suggested.

Structural Equation Modeling

Statistics in SEM

The covariance-based SEM packages generate statistics at three levels: at individual path and construct level, at the overall model fit level, and finally, the individual path modification indexes.

The first set of statistics is at the individual path level; SEM estimates item loadings and measurement error along with the respective t-values. Construct reliability, the analog of a Cronbach's alpha, can be derived from these statistics; the Cronbach's statistics, in order to construct reliability, should be above 0.70. SEM also estimates the coefficients and t-values representing the relationships among the latent constructs (Betas, Gammas, Alpha, etc.). The t-values of Gammas and Betas need to be significant in order to support the hypothesized paths (1.96 for alpha protection level 0.05 and 2.56 for alpha protection level 0.01). The next important statistic in this level is the Square Multiple Correlation (SMC) of each exogenous latent constructs. Equivalent to an R^2 in linear regression, the SMC is the explained variance of each latent construct.

The second set of statistics deals with the entire model fit. The most important of these statistics is the likelihood ratio chi-square (X^2). Technically, the X^2 statistics should be insignificant with a p value above 0.05; the value above 0.05 shows the good model fit. The most widely used overall model fit indices are the Goodness of Fit Index (GFI), the Adjusted Goodness of Fit Index (AGFI), and Root Mean Residual (RMR). GFI measures the absolute fit (unadjusted for degrees of freedom) of the combined measurement and structural model to the data. AGFI adjusts this value to the degrees of freedom in the model. The standardized RMR (Root Mean Residuals), on the other hand, assesses the residual variance of the observed variables and how the residual variance of one variable correlates with the residual variance of the other items. It is important to note that the large standardized RMR values mean high residual variance, and such values reflected a poor fitting model. Generally, in the research, the GFI is above 0.90. AGFI is above 0.80, and RM is below 0.05. Another important fit index is the Normed Fit Index (NFI), which measures the normed difference in X^2 between a zero factor null model and a proposed multi-factor model (Bentler, 1990). Typically, NFI should be above 0.90.

The third set of statistics is the modification indexes. Some SEM, notably LISREL, provide modification indices that estimate the difference in model fit X^2 for each possible individual additional path. It is also called modification matrices. It is shown that the adding path may significantly improve model fit. This criterion is analogous to the way step-wise linear regression chooses to add independent variables to the regression model, except the step-wise linear regression analyzes the change in the F statistic.

Whereas reporting of RMR is roughly as deficient as reporting of AGFI and SMC, the disclosure of X^2/ df ratio, t-values, and construct reliability is generally acceptable.

Research Findings

In this chapter, the multi-level supply chain is integrated. The proposed research model is illustrated in Figure 1. From the statement of the problem—do the Man, Machine, and Management infrastructure influence the effectiveness of supply chain management?—the model is designed to study the supporting of operational infrastructures in terms of man, machine, and management in supply chain implementation.

The model is analyzed by the basic infrastructures needed for supply chain activities enhancing the effectiveness of supply chain practices and their performances. The man, machine, and management infrastructures are studied from the co-variation to the supply chain management. From the research model, an hypothesis is established:

Hypothesis: The higher supply chain infrastructures preparation, the higher the effectiveness of supply chain management.

The correlation between infrastructures, supply chain practices, and supply chain performances also were studied.

Survey Instrument and Methodology

A survey instrument in the form of a questionnaire was designed, based on the integrated model described. The respondents were asked to indicate the level of company practices and performance achievement after supply chain implementation using a five-point Likert scale (1 = strongly disagree, 5 = strongly agree). The six infrastructure variables were constructed. The questions about man, machine, and management infrastructures were asked to indicate the five-point Likert scale as well as the four group questions of the supply chain practices and performance. This survey data were collected from a single respondent from each target firm; the target respondents are in the purchasing and sale departments, because they were assumed to fully involve the company's supply chain activities. The objective in collecting the single respondent from one firm is to minimize the variation in data bias (Udomleartprasert, 2003).

The variables were checked for validity by four practitioners and academicians; the Q-sort methodology was used to ensure the variables by improving the k values from the first to second rounds. The questionnaire was pretested to check the content validity and revised where necessary to ensure the content validity. The surveys that were sent refer to the industrial estates list, a total of 114 from 986 surveys were collected (11.56%). The last wave of surveys received was considered as representative of non-respondents (Chopra, 2001; Croteau, 2001). The 30 survey items were selected for analysis randomly. Each sample was split into two groups on the basis of early and late survey return time; then, the t-test was used to analyze. The t-test yielded no statistically significant differences between early and late response groups. The non-affect of non-response bias was recommended.

Research Outcomes

The profiles of company and respondents were asked. The firms were mainly from manufacturing and trading industries. The respondent's profile is shown from firm's country of origin; they are from Taiwan, Singapore, Japan, China, and Thailand, respectively. The highest driving force of supply chain implementation is from customer requirement, cost reduction, delivery management, and inventory management, accordingly. The major business function of supply chain implementation is in electronic industry, plastic industry, trading industry, and packaging industry, respectively.

Figure 4. The research outcomes

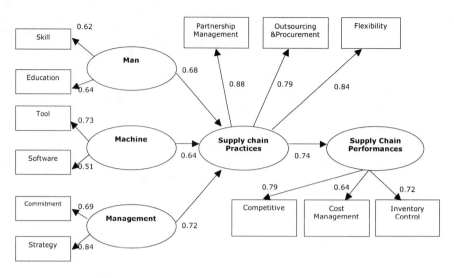

Analysis of the Research Model

The simultaneous estimation methodology is applied to test the measurement and theory. All data from 114 firms were sampled to obtain the maximum likelihood estimates of the path coefficients (γ), loading (λ), correlations, error variances, and $\chi 2$ goodness of fit test (Croteau, 2001). All of these parameters were derived from the EQS, which is a program of structural equation modeling. The advantages of EQS, other than other structural equation modeling, are the simpler represented system on two or three sets of parameter metrics. Also, the less limitation in the type of structural coefficients makes the EQS easily interpret the statistic result in the small number of variables (Croteau, 2001; Strub, 2002).

The reliability, convergent validity, and uni-dimensionalilty of infrastructure alignment and supply chain practices were analyzed by examining the level of submodel fit and estimated loading (Croteau, 2001). The uni-dimensional reliability is a model comparison with significant smaller $\chi 2$ in the proposed measurement model with the alternative measurement models. For the model, fit is assessed using chi-square statistic estimated for the hypothesized model. However, the $\chi 2$ is sensitive to the sample size, so it is a caution to only rely on the $\chi 2$. The value of $\chi 2/df$ can be used to improve this limitation, if the ratio is inferior to 5 (Croteau 2001). In EQS, the Bentler's comparative fit index (CFI) is approached to reflect the fit at all sample sizes. The CFI formula is:

$$CFI \;=\; |(\chi_0 2 - df_0) - (\chi_\circ 2 - df_k)/ (\chi_0 2 - df_0)| \qquad (2)$$

where $\chi_0 2$ is the null model and $\chi_0 2$ is the hypothesized model. Model fit is acceptable if CFI is higher than 0.90 level. The structural equation modeling assessment is shown in Figure 4. A significant value of 112.4 at df = 53, p,0.01) is the chi-square result, and confirmed fit is the $\chi 2$/df ratio at 2.18; this CFI = 0.91 is adequately supported by the uni-dimensionality of infrastructures and practices.

For the convergent validity, the underlying construct or trait is described in percentage of variance in terms of loading squared. In this model, the loading range is from 0.51 to 0.84. The loading of operational infrastructures Man, Machine, and Management are significant in enhancing the supply chain practice. A result higher than 0.5 shows the measurement is captured by the constructed variance. In this model, the ρ ranged from 0.51 - 0.74, which confirmed the reliability of this model. As shown in Table 5, the correlation ranged from 0.42 to 0.74 at 99% confidence interval. The largest correlation is between the supply chain practice and supply chain performance; the values show the acceptable discriminant validity.

For the theoretical model, the link between operational infrastructure to the supply chain practices reflect the terms of competitiveness performance, cost management, and inventory control performance. The hypothesis was confirmed by the significant path coefficient of 0.74 at 99% confidence level that enhancing of operational infrastructures of man, machine and management to the supply chain practices support the supply chain performance of the organization (Croteau, 2001; Jorsekog, 1998; Strub, 2002).

Conclusion and Recommendation

The supply chain is very important for every industrial sector. Several firms are interested in applying it to their companies. A lot of budget was spent for the expected return, but no one can guarantee the success. However, the budget is not the only critical success factor of implementation, but also human resources, technology, management, and so forth. This chapter proposes the integrated supply chain system for firms to improve their supply chain performance and to further increase their customer satisfaction, maintain supplier relationship, and compete with the competitors.

The research model herein shows the significant man, machine, and management infrastructures enhancing supply chain management. The research results indicated that the operational infrastructures highly impact the supply chain practices that reflect the success in supply chain performance.

For further research, this model can be analyzed in terms of mathematical equation in order to be the indicator of infrastructure preparation before entering the supply chain program as the following:

$$F(x) = \{Man, Machine, Management\}$$

where F(x) is the readiness indicator of infrastructure preparation.

Moreover, supply chain management in a particular type of the organization, such as SMEs and large enterprises, also are recommended to study, whether the supportive infrastructures have similar or different requirements in each type of organization as well as the business type of organization as the type of business, such as production/ manufacture; services are required at the different level of supply chain practices.

References

Ahuja, S., Lars, L., & Jaideep, M. (1998). Managing a global supply chain partnership. *Logistics Information Management, 11*(6), 349-354.

Auskain, R.J., Carter, C.R., & Ketchum, C.L. (1999). Purchasing from minority business enterprises: Key success factors. *The Journal of Supply Chain Management*, 28-32.

Beamon, B.M., Measuring supply chain performance. *International Journal of Operations and Production Management, 19*(1), 275-292.

Bommer, M., O'Neil, B., & Treat, S. (2001). Strategic assessment of the supply chain interface: Beverage industry case study. *International Journal of Physical Distribution and Logistics Management, 13*(1), 11-25.

Boudreau, M.-C., Gafen, D., Straub, D.W. (2000). Structural equation modeling and regression: Guidelines for research practice. *Communication of the Association for Information Systems, 4*(7), 1-79.

Carter, C.R., & Kaufmann, L. (2002). International supply management systems—The impact of price vs. non price driven motives in the United States and Germany. *The Journal of Supply Chain Management*, 4-17.

Carter, C.R., Hendrick, T.E., & Siferd, S.P. (1996) Purchasing's involvement in time-based strategies. *International Journal of Purchasing and Materials Management*, 2-10.

Choi, T.Y., & Rungtusanatham, M. (1999). Comparison of quality management practices: Across the supply chain and industries. *The Journal of Supply Chain Management*, 20-27.

Chopra, S., & Meindl, P. (2001). *Supply chain management: Strategic planning and operations*. Prentice-Hall.

Christopher, M., & Jutter, U. Developing strategic partnership in supply chain: A practitioner perspective. *European Journal of Purchasing and Supply Chain Management, 6*(2), 117-127.

Christopher, M., & Lee, H.L. (2001). *Supply chain confidence—The key to effective supply chains through improved visibility and reliability, global trade management*. Cranfield University and Stanford University.

Croteau, A.-M., Simons, S., Louis, R., & Francois, B. (n.d.). Organizational and technological infrastructures alignment. *Proceedings of the 34th Hawaii International Conference on System Science.*

Cutler, B.D., Christopher, R., Moberg, A.G., & Speh, T.W. Identifying antecedents of information exchange within supply chains. *International Journal of Physical Distribution & Logistics Management, 32*(9), 755-770.

Daugherty, P.J., Rogers, D.S., & Stank, T.P. (1995). Opportunities for enhancing performance. *Journal of Business Logistics, 16*(2), 43-52.

Davis, T. (1993). Effective supply chain management. *SLOAN Management Review*, 35-46.

Ellram, L.M. (1998). Supply chain management: The industrial organization perspective. *International Journal of Physical Distribution and Logistics Management, 21*(1), 13-22.

Ellram, L.M. (1990). The supplier selection decision in strategic partnership. *Journal of Purchasing and Materials Magament*, 8-14.

Ellram, L.M., & Zsidisin, G.A. (2002). Factors that drive purchasing and supply management's use of information technology. *IEEE Transactions on Engineering Management, 49*(3), 269-281.

Elmuti, D. (2002). The perceived impact of supply chain management on organizational effectiveness. *The Journal of Supply Chain Management*, 49-57.

Farris, T.M., & Hutchison, P.D. (2002). Cash to cash: The new supply chain metric. *International Journal of Physical Distribution and Logistics Management, 32*(4), 288-298.

Fawcett, S.E., & Magnan, G.M. (2002). The rhetoric and reality of supply chain integration. *International Journal of Physical Distribution and Logistics Management, 3*(5), 339-361.

Ferrin, B.G., & Plank, R.E. (2002). Total cost of ownership models: An exploratory study. *The Journal of Supply Chain Management*, 18-29.

Handfield, R.B., Kannan, V.R., & Tan, K.C. (1998). Supply chain management: Supplier performance and firm performance. *International Journal of Purchasing and Materials Management*, 2-9.

Hewitt, F. Information technology mediated bBusiness process management—Lessons from the supply chain. *International Journal of Technology Management, 17*, 37-53.

Horvath, L. (2001). Insight from industry, collaboration: The key to value creation in supply chain management. *An International Journal of Supply Chain Management, 6*(5) 205-207.

Inman, R.A., & Hubler, J.H. (1992). Certify the process—Not just the product. *Production and Inventory Management Journal, 33*(4), 11-14.

Joreskog, K.G., & Sorbom, D. PRELIS. *A program for multivariate data screening and data summarization*. Mooresville, IN: Scienctific Software.

Lambert, D.M., & Pohlen, T.L. (2001). Supply chain metrics. *The International Journal of Logistics Management, 12*(1), 1-19.

Lee, C.B. (2001). *Demand chain optimization—Pitfalls and key principles*. Nonstop Solution.

McMullan, A. (1996). Supply chain management practices in Asia Pacific today. *International Journal of Physical Distribution and Logistics Management, 26*(10), 79-95.

Mehta, S.G., & Sundaram, M,R. (2002). A comparative study of three different SCM approaches. *International Journal of Physical Distribution and Logistics Management,* 32(7), 532-555.

Miller, C.A. (2001). *The nature and design of supply chain performance measurement system—An empirical study.* Pennsylvania State University.

Morgan, J., & Monczka, R.M. (1995). Alliances for new products. *Purchasing Journal, 118*(1), 103-109.

Power, D.J., Sohal, A.S., & Rahman, S.-U. (2001). Critical success in agile supply chain management. *International Journal of Physical Distributors and Logistics Management, 131*(4), 247-265.

St. Onge, A. (1996). New concepts in supply chain management. *Modern Materials Handling, 51*(3), 33.

Stock, et al. (1997). Review of logistics research 1993-1997. *The Journal of Business Logistics.*

Strub, D.W., Gefen, D., & Boudreau, M.-C. (2002). SEM and regression. *AIS, 4*(7).

Talluri, S. (2002). Enhancing supply decisions through the use of efficient marginal cost models. *The Journal of Supply Chain Management,* 4-10.

Tan, K.C. (2001). A framework of supply chain management—Literature. *European Journal of Purchasing and Materials Management, 34*(3), 39-48.

Tan, K.C. (2002). Supply chain management: Practices, concerns, and performance issues. *The Journal of Supply Chain Management,* 42-53.

Udomleartprasert, P., & Jungthirapanich, C. (2003). Aligning the infrastructure to the supply chain management. *IEEE International Engineering Management Transaction,* 335-339.

Chapter XVII

Enabling the Glass Pipeline:
The Infusion of Mobile Technology Applications in Supply Chain Management

Umar Ruhi
Wilfrid Laurier University, Canada

Ofir Turel
McMaster University, Canada

Abstract

In recent years, the prospect of information exchange independent of time and place has been a compelling driver for organizations worldwide to adopt mobile technology applications in their various business practices. In particular, the application of mobile technology in Supply Chain Management has drawn widespread attention from researchers and practitioners who endorse adaptive and agile supply chain processes. This chapter discusses the applications of mobile technologies in various areas of supply chain management and the potential benefits of those technologies along the dimensions of reduced replenishment time and transactions and billing cycles. Among other discussions, the role of mobile procurement, inventory management, product identification, package tracking, sales force, and field service automation technologies is highlighted. To substantiate the basis for adopting mobile technologies for supply

*chain management, different market drivers for mobile applications are exemplified
and applied to the three macro-level processes of supplier relationship management,
internal supply chain management, and customer relationship management; a resulting
typology of mobile supply chain management applications is presented.*

Introduction

*The nature of competition is shifting away from the classic struggle between companies.
The new competition is supply chain vs. supply chain.* (Taylor, 2003, p. 3)

In recent years, we have seen various organizations from different industries focus their
competitive strategies on improving their supply networks rather than concentrating on
directly contending with specific companies. Companies such as Wal-Mart, Dell, and
Proctor & Gamble not only have made significant headway in optimizing their own supply
chains, they also essentially have redefined the way business is done in their particular
industries. Their competitors have had to follow suit in order to maintain their own
competitive position in the marketplace.

A major factor that has contributed to more efficient supply networks is the increasingly
unhindered and efficient flow of information within and among supply chain partners.
Several researchers and practitioners have commented on the importance of information
flow in effective supply chains (Chopra & Meindl, 2003; Handfield & Nichols, 2002;
Kalakota, Robinson & Gundepudi, 2003). Consequently, much has been said about the
role of technology in enabling effective supply chains (Holten, Dreiling, Muehlen &
Becker, 2002; Knolmayer, Mertens & Zeier, 2002; Poirier & Bauer, 2000).

Mobile technologies and applications offer an advanced level of efficient and effective
communications among business partners in supply chains. These applications augment
the static nature of their predecessor, e-commerce, phone, and fax-based technologies,
by adding flexibility and spontaneity to extant business processes. Technologies in
mobile procurement, inventory management, product identification, package tracking,
sales force, and field service automation are expected to change the current landscape
of Supply Chain Management (SCM). It is expected that mobile technologies will bridge
the functionality gap in traditional Electronic Data Interchange (EDI), Enterprise Resource Planning (ERP) and Web-based SCM technologies by providing the end-to-end
transparency that can help businesses perform better through improved supply chain
planning and execution (Kalakota et al., 2003).

In this chapter, we provide a value proposition for mobile SCM technologies and
applications. By highlighting the benefits of the latest mobile applications, this chapter
aims to explicate the role of these technologies in transforming integrated and collaborative supply chains into adaptive supply networks. We start this discussion with our
working definition of SCM, which will be the gate to our analysis of various technology
applications. Following that, we discuss the current state of information technologies
in SCM and subsequently rationalize the business drivers for implementing mobile SCM

technologies. This is followed by an elaboration of a typology of mobile SCM technology applications. Our conclusion and ensuing inferences follow after a discussion on the future outlook for mobile SCM technologies vis-à-vis other SCM information systems.

Supply Chain Management: A Working Definition

There are as many definitions of SCM as there are publications, which is quite enormous within the supply management literature. Furthermore, the terminology used to describe the concept or idea behind SCM is interchangeably used in various contexts to refer to the same thing. For example, supply chains, supply networks, and supply webs often are used to describe the same idea—coordination and collaboration across business partners. Recently, however, there is an increasing tendency to use the terms *supply networks* and *supply webs* as opposed to the notion of *supply chains*. The advantage of using the former terms over the latter, is to emphasize that the links among business partners are not linear and sequential but are, instead, dynamic, interdependent, and flexible (Bovet & Martha, 2000; Murphy, 2000; Rayner, 2004).

In this chapter, we use the terms *supply chains* and *supply networks* interchangeably, with the proviso that the nature of relationships among business partners is, indeed, more than just linear and sequential. As highlighted in the introduction and for the purpose of this discussion, we adopt a definition of SCM that incorporates the management of information flow as the primary functional component—material flow and financial flow both upstream and downstream the supply chain. For a descriptive and formal characterization, we adopt Handfield and Nichols' (2002) definition of SCM. The authors define SCM as:

The integration and management of supply chain organizations and activities through cooperative organizational relationships, effective business processes, and high levels of information sharing to create high-performing value systems that provide member organizations a sustainable competitive advantage. (Handfield & Nichols, 2002, p. 8)

In addition to affirming the importance of high levels of information sharing, the definition prominently highlights the concept of a value system for sustainable competitive advantage.

The notion of a value system (also known as a value chain) is intertwined with that of a supply chain and needs some elaboration. Introduced by Michael Porter in his widely acclaimed book, *Competitive Advantage* (Porter, 1985), the idea of a value chain has been used to model a firm on the basis of its value-creating activities. The primary activities in the value chain include inbound logistics, operations, outbound logistics, marketing and sales, and service. Noticeably, it is several different business processes within the value-creating functions of a firm that constitute the various components in an organization's supply chain, as well. In fact, Chopra and Meindl (2003) classify all supply

Figure 1. Supply chain management functions and processes

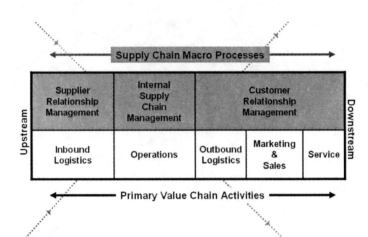

chain processes into three main macro processes; namely, Supplier relationship management (SRM), internal supply chain management (ISCM), and customer Relationship
Management (CRM). Juxtaposing the value creating functions described by Porter (1985)
with the three macro processes in a supply chain, it can be seen that inbound logistics
and operations functions map diametrically to supplier relationship management and
internal SCM, respectively, while the marketing, sales, and service functions map to the
processes in customer relationship management. It is this inclusive framework of value-
creating activities and supply chain macro processes that forms the basis of our
discussion throughout the rest of this chapter. Figure 1 summarizes these processes and
functions in an inclusive conceptual model for SCM.

Current State of Mobile SCM
Technologies and Applications

As an affirmation of the prevalent adoption of wireless technologies, the Yankee Group
predicts that close to 50% of large US enterprises will employ wide area wireless
solutions, and that 3,000,000 mobile users will use these services (Yankee Group, 2004).
In terms of technological maturity, third-generation (3G) technologies are emerging
quickly, while more established technologies, such as Short Messaging Services (SMS)
and the wireless Internet (e.g., Wireless Application Protocol [WAP]) are serving
organizations to help fulfill their current business requirements. It is these existing and
emerging technologies that act as the bearers of a large and ever increasing number of
mobile SCM solutions. Furthermore, the diffusion of more advanced packet-switched
data networks (e.g., GPRS, 1XRTT, etc.) is giving rise to innovative communication
solutions. For example, Push-to-Talk services (P2T) that previously were available only
to niche markets are now being deployed effortlessly over packet switched data networks

and are being used to facilitate inexpensive interorganizational voice communications (Guy, 2003). At the same time, short-range wireless technologies, such as Radio Frequency Identification (RFID), Wireless Personal Networks (WPANs) such as Bluetooth, and Wireless Local Area Networks (WLANs) such as the 802.11, are becoming commonplace, forming the basis of wireless networking standards.

As anticipated, the previously mentioned technologies are finding their applications in various business processes in the organization's SCM, as well. A case in point is the recent adoption of RFID solutions by Wal-Mart, exemplifying the wireless services market trends and opening doors for next-generation logistics management (Emily, 2004). Additionally, WLAN technologies already are being used widely in many industries, such as the energy sector (Yankee Group, 2001). Decreasing deployment costs as well as communication and network costs are being proclaimed as the primary drivers for the growth of this market (Rao & Parikh, 2003).

To capitalize upon the opportunities presented by mobile technologies, vendors of traditional SCM systems, such as SAP and Oracle, and new ones, such as HighJump and @Par, are vying for a piece of the pie. Most of the mobile SCM technology vendors currently offer their solutions in bundled packages as part of their m-business or m-commerce technology suites. Such an offering (under a broader umbrella of m-commerce) is in line with the treatise of mobile SCM solutions by researchers (Burchett, 2000; Cousins & Varshney, 2001). M-commerce can be succinctly defined as "a layer of applications atop the mobile Internet" (Rulke & Iyer, 2003) or explicitly as "an extension of e-commerce in a mobile environment" (Dholakia, 2002). Consequently, Mobile Supply Chain Management (MSCM) can be regarded as a specific branch of m-commerce, and it can be characterized as a layer of mobile applications that enhances existing supply chain mechanisms while enabling efficient business processes. Just like their e-commerce counterparts, the incumbent technologies in MSCM are being used increasingly to support an evolving complex transactions landscape. Researchers classify the types of transactions supported through mobile technologies under the business-to-consumer (B2C), business-to-business (B2B), employee-to-employee (E2E), business-to-employee (B2E), and machine-to-machine (M2M) domains (Alanen & Autio, 2003). With this transactions landscape in mind, let us now examine the driving factors behind the adoption of mobile technologies in SCM.

Drivers for Mobile Technologies in Supply Chain Management

The use of information systems in any business context always has been driven on the basis of available technological capabilities as well as on managerial vision toward fulfilling certain business requirements via those technologies. This is why we see the proliferation of different types of information systems, depending on different eras in which they are adopted. For example, whereas data and transaction processing systems were the order of the day in the 1950s, decision support systems started emerging in the

Table 1. Drivers for information systems in SCM

Driver:	Applications:				
	Enterprise Resource Planning	Data Warehouses	Customer Relationship Management	Decision Support Systems	Mobile Technology Applications
Internal Integration	•	•	•	•	•
External Integration			•	•	•
Globalization	•	•	•	•	•
Data Information Management		•	•		•
New Business Processes	•		•		•
Replace Obsolete Systems	•		•		•
Strategic Cost Management	•	•	•	•	•

(Adapted from Handfield & Nichols, 2002)

1970s, followed by e-business systems in the 1990s. The current trend is on the collaborative aspect of information systems.

Within specific business contexts of the current era, SCM has attracted myriad information systems (e.g., Materials Requirements Planning [MRP I] systems, Manufacturing Resource Planning [MRP II] systems, Enterprise Resource Planning [ERP] systems and Advanced Planning and Scheduling [APS] systems), which all have seen their peaks during the evolution of SCM as a discipline. Whereas, these systems all have a distinct logistics-oriented flare to them, SCM also utilizes cross-functional information systems, such as decision support systems and customer relationship management systems in day-to-day activities.

There have been several drivers that have led to the adoption of different types of information systems in SCM. Perhaps the most significant driver in the adoption of such systems has been the realization of an increasing need to internally integrate within and among different business functions as well as to integrate externally with supply chain business partners (Holten et al., 2002; Poirier & Bauer, 2000). Handfield and Nichols (2002) highlight additional drivers that have led to the adoption of various types of information systems in SCM. These additional drivers include trends emerging from globalization, information management requirements, the need for new business processes, the desire to replace obsolete systems, and ensuring strategic cost management. Table 1 summarizes a mapping of these drivers to different types of information systems in SCM and presents our extension of this framework to assimilate the drivers for mobile technologies. An elaboration of the specific drivers for mobile technologies follows.

Internal and External Integration (Toward Pervasive Computing)

As highlighted earlier in this chapter, internal and external integrations are extremely important drivers in the adoption of information systems in today's business environment. Whereas, systems such as MRP I and MRP II lacked the functionalities that allowed effective internal integration among various supply chain functions, external integration with supply chain partners is a challenging problem for even modern-day ERP systems. It was only with the advent of the Internet and the connectivity accorded by it that the newer Web-based applications, including the likes of CRM systems, were made possible; these applications enabled more cross functional operations inside the firm and outside, to a certain extent.

The adoption of mobile technologies in SCM promises to take the integration phenomenon to the next level (i.e., pervasiveness). Gupta and Moitra (2004) characterize pervasive computing as saturating an environment with computing and communication capability, yet having those devices integrated into the environment such that they disappear. The same authors also consider mobility and wireless connectivity as an essential component in pervasive computing. Accordingly, the adoption of mobile applications in supply chains is driven partially by their capabilities to enhance internal and external integration. Internal integration at the systems level is enhanced through seamless network connectivity between the front end and back end systems through wireless local and personal area networks (WLAN and WPAN). Basic voice communication capabilities, like cellular technologies and push-to-talk (P2T), further allow employees to connect effortlessly to one another. Moreover, remote data access by employees increases the internal integration by allowing internal users to access organizational data from anywhere at anytime. Similarly, external integration is enhanced, as mobile applications enable remote access to relevant information for customers, retailers, and distributors through wireless wide area networks. This is particularly important with the increasing trend in large-scale organizations to establish supplier parks in geographic vicinities around their main manufacturing and fabrication plants (Moline, 2002). Furthermore, mobile applications also enable the organization to access external mobile data resources. For example, using a global positioning system (GPS) and wireless data services, an organization can view the location and status of a shipment arriving from one of its upstream suppliers and prepare for it accordingly. Late delivery of shipment (as well as occasional early delivery) requires careful planning, especially in case of time-sensitive goods, and mobile technologies and applications provide hitherto unknown possibilities in improving the efficiency of managing this supply chain.

Globalization

Globalization is another factor that is driving the infusion of mobile technology applications in supply chains. In remote locations, specifically where fixed landlines and other forms of communications are not available, mobile communications can provide a valuable means for voice and data transmission. Many researchers and visionaries have suggested that a wireless infrastructure can reduce the great divide between the developed and the underdeveloped countries, and it has the potential to facilitate and promote business prosperity (Parker, 2000; Rice & Katz, 2003; Wareham, Levy & Shi, 2004). For example, the wireless infrastructure in China now has surpassed the fixed-line infrastructure in terms of penetration and coverage (GSM Association, 2004). This implies that businesses and people from other countries are more likely to engage in commercial transactions with firms located in China through mobile communication networks. The ascent of this mobile penetration, especially in developing countries, also can be attributed to the fact that once a mobile infrastructure (e.g., a mobile transmission tower) is set up, it does not require any additional work, such as installation and maintenance of landlines for communication. Furthermore, mobility is now regarded as a predominant characteristic of knowledge workers, and with the widespread availability and standardization of roaming capabilities, these knowledge workers are more likely to collaborate with other businesses through mobile technologies. Whereas, 15 years ago it was unthinkable to even call someone in a different part of the world, not to mention wireless connectivity with them while on the move, today, roaming agreements have made wireless connectivity around the globe a reality by connecting over 500 GSM/GPRS (Global System for Mobile/General Packet Radio Service) networks in almost 200 countries (GSM Association, 2004).

Also, with particular reference to SCM, there is an increasing tendency to outsource non-core functions to external service providers, such as third party logistics (3PL) companies. With contemporary provisions for boundary-less commercial exchanges under global economic forums, such as the North American Free Trade Agreement (NAFTA) and the European Union (EU), there is greater potential to offshore business functions to supply chain service providers in different countries. In fact, offshoring as a global phenomenon has been fueled by organizational attempts to gain competitive advantage through concentration on their core competencies while minimizing the costs of outsourcing at the same time (Bardhan & Kroll, 2003; Nair & Prasad, 2004).

Data Information Management

Mobile applications can improve the frequency and speed of communication (Gebauer, Shaw & Zhao, 2002). With data collection at the point of activity and the elimination of paper-based desktop-centric workflows, the velocity of transactions can be increased greatly. Proof of delivery and electronic signature capture technologies are being used in various businesses to enable more efficient and more streamlined information processes within the supply chain. Moreover, these processes, enabled through mobile technologies, allow real-time data access from the source, as opposed to batches of information being transmitted through various information systems at different times. Consequently, information synchronization errors that are attributed to batch processing can be reduced greatly.

While, on the one hand, real-time data transmission helps to increase the fulfillment velocity by making information instantaneously available throughout the supply chain, on the other hand, it facilitates enhanced visibility of supply chain processes by interacting directly with concerned parties through notification and alert mechanisms. The end result is reduced order-to-delivery time and more responsive service management.

New Business Processes

Mobile applications also are driven by the need to innovate operational business processes. Companies like Wal-Mart and McDonald's are well known for acquiring favorable market positions and competitive advantage through novel business processes. In fact, it has been conferred by many authors that it is the processes and not merely the underlying IT infrastructure that enables strategic advantage (Hurst, 2003). Hence, the need to gain and sustain competitive advantage can drive companies to innovate and re-engineer their business processes using new technologies (Barney, 1995; Porter, 1980).

The well-known market leaders in SCM are just beginning to avail the opportunities afforded by mobile technologies, as well. For example, Wal-Mart's adoption of Radio Frequency Identification (RFID) and subsequent coercion of its suppliers to do the same will be indubitably accompanied by the establishment of new business processes. The workflows associated with tracking pallets and items from receiving to sales and the management of inventory status all will be affected. Among other benefits, RFID technology is being touted as an enabler for improved inventory accuracy, reduced receiving costs, lower safety stock levels, and reduced cycle count efforts. With mandates from companies such as Wal-Mart, other businesses in various industries also will be driven to explore such technologies in order to revamp their own business processes.

Replace Obsolete Systems

The adoption of mobile technology applications also is being driven by the need to replace obsolete systems and associated business processes. For example, mobile telemetry services (i.e., the use of telecommunication devices to automatically record measurements from a distance) can replace manual on-site data entry and other forms of continuous monitoring (Salz, 2003). With the proliferation of cellular networks, it makes sense to monitor remote resources and assets using wireless technologies.

The previous example is not a completely new technology phenomenon. Often, information systems from one industry find their way into other industries with a certain level of customization. Telemetry solutions have prevailed in the agricultural and military sectors for years. Feeding livestock and examining contamination levels in water are among the applications that use telemetry in an agricultural context. Similarly, remote surveillance using airborne and satellite-based cameras is an example of a telemetry application used by the military (Forrester Research, 1998).

Changing business contexts necessitate newer technology infrastructures. As illustrated in the example, wireless services and applications have the potential to steer more versatility in today's supply chains by offering features and functionalities that may have been tested in other business functions or in totally different industries. It is only a matter of time before more mobile technology applications emerge and change the current supply chain landscape.

Strategic Cost Management

As elaborated throughout this chapter, cost reduction is a major driver in adopting any new technology in SCM. Under compelling demands from various stakeholders, supply chain managers constantly are looking for ways to optimize operations with the objective of reducing operating costs. A feature that makes mobile technologies a viable contender for the supply chain applications market is their ability to account for financial information in real time. Technologies such as GPS (Global Positioning Systems), telemetry, and RFID can feed real-time data to static tethered information systems. Furthermore, by streamlining the order-to-cash process, mobile technologies can reduce the complexity in the overall supply chain execution (Kalakota et al., 2003).

Overall, it can be said that mobile technology applications are driven by a multitude of market forces, and the adoption of such applications is likely to have an impact on business functions across different industries. Mobile SCM technologies can provide processing efficiency in the form of time, cost, and quality of operations. Based on these various benefits that can be availed through the adoption of mobile SCM technology applications, organizations need a road map to implement these technologies in their various business functions and subsequently integrate these into a seamless mobile infrastructure. The next section provides a typology of mobile SCM technology applications that can facilitate an organization's efforts in this area.

A Typology of Mobile Technology Applications in Supply Chain Management

In presenting our system of classification for mobile technology applications in SCM, we will discuss various mobile applications vis-à-vis their associated bearer technologies. Furthermore, to help us with our analysis, we will utilize the functions and processes from the inclusive SCM framework elaborated earlier in this chapter (see Figure 1). Table 2 at the end of this section illustrates the dimensions of our typology and the incumbent technology applications that are described herein.

Mobile Technology Applications in Supplier Relationship Management (Upstream Processes)

Three things in the life of a supply chain planner are for certain: death, taxes and reconciliation. (Hammer, 1997, p. 18)

This statement by Michael Hammer (1997) epitomizes a classic problem in SCM. Traditional information systems fall short in their functionality in order to reconcile cash and inventory at various points in the supply chain. It is not surprising, then, that manifest reconciliation emerges as the most popular application in mobile SCM (see Table 2). An example in upstream supply chain processes is the enduring difficulty in reconciling purchase orders to truck manifests at check-in times and freight pickups. The solution to such problems lies in the integrated use of bearer technologies, such as RFIDs, WWANs, and WLANs. Using emerging technologies in smart bar coding, the receiver can seamlessly scan incoming shipments, note discrepancies between purchase orders and truck manifests, make relevant changes to purchase orders, and update back-office systems as well as supplier databases at the same time. Furthermore, the ability for the driver to connect instantaneously with the materials planner for the upstream supplier helps to resolve exceptions and system errors at the point of delivery. Together, these technologies allow increased transaction velocity in the supply chain and higher levels of supplier coordination versatility (Kalakota et al., 2003).

Also, mobile technologies based on GPS allow for greater inventory visibility throughout the supply chain. By pinpointing the location of delivery trucks and the status of delivery packages, upstream suppliers can coordinate shipment schedules with downstream customers, who, in turn, can communicate expectations to their own downstream business partners. Telematics, which is defined as the integration of wireless communications, vehicle monitoring systems, and location devices (GSM Association, 2004), is one such suite of applications that is known to enhance confidence in business functions, including SCM, through facilitating greater visibility and enabling greater control in the supply chain (Hanebeck & Tracey, 2003).

Mobile Technology Applications in Internal Supply Chain Management (Internal Processes)

Mobile technologies also offer significant advantages to internal business operations by facilitating express and streamlined workflows. Among others, workflow applications in business operations include document approval, expense reporting, payment, and purchase orders (Kalakota et al., 2003). According to a recent pilot study by Gebauer, Shaw, and Zhao (2002), the most significant benefits in wireless procurement services result from speeding the overall processing time of an approval request. It is estimated that close to half of the processing time of a purchasing request is due to managers being out of the office, and, from their study, the researchers conclude that wireless technologies can appreciably help manager approvers as well as finance and accounting approvers by providing support for delegation, communication, notification, and information access (Gebauer et al., 2002).

Another major category of mobile technologies that is redefining internal supply chain processes is wireless product identification. This suite of technologies is regarded as an enabler for handling efficiency, customisation, and information sharing (Karkkainen & Holmstrom, 2002). An example of wireless product identification technology is an RFID system that comprises electronic product codes stored on RFID tags. These tags can be read seamlessly through tactically placed RFID scanners, which, in turn, transmit inventory information to back-office systems through specific middleware. The advantage of such systems is that they can be used without requiring line of sight. The tag readers, hence, can be attached to forklifts, mounted in freight and shipment pathways, or built into stacking shelves. The idea in using such a technology is to eliminate the extra step in scanning pallets or items and to automate the process.

Other internal mobile applications that drive process efficiencies include direct machine-to-machine data exchanges through telemetry. As defined in the previous section, telemetry is the use of telecommunication devices (including wireless) to automatically record measurements from a distance. The automatic notification of inventory management system by an RFID reader when inventory gets depleted below a certain level would be an example of a telemetric application. Again, this type of application can facilitate efficient and streamlined process flows in warehouse and inventory management systems.

Finally, as mentioned earlier, wireless technologies usually are always strongly integrated with other SCM enterprise systems. Back-office updates resulting from real-time data capture at the source are almost never stored or used independently of these systems. The medium of transmission for updates between wireless devices and enterprise systems can be in the form of a WLAN, based on short-range Wi-Fi technology or the proximity-based Bluetooth technology.

Mobile Technology Applications in Customer Relationship Management (Downstream Processes)

Many technology applications in the outbound logistics function coincide with those in the inbound logistics function. This is because of the sophisticated omni-directional nature of supply networks of today, where the position of an organization might be that of an upstream supplier as well as a downstream customer at the same. Similar technologies can be utilized in both cases, albeit in different business contexts. For example, in the instance of delivering a package to a customer, the manifest reconciliation is still a useful application, except this time, the customer invoice will be reconciled with the bill of loading. Similarly, GPS bearer technologies can be used in conjunction with transportation management systems to determine dispatching routes and daily delivery schedules for outbound freight drivers and delivery personnel.

The marketing and sales function in customer relationship management can benefit greatly from information access provided through wireless handheld and pocket-pc-type devices. Using their handhelds, field sales employees can connect directly to back-office

Table 2. A typology of mobile technology applications for SCM

Bearer Technologies	Supplier Relationship Management — Inbound Logistics	Internal Supply Chain Management — Operations	Customer Relationship Management — Outbound Logistics	Customer Relationship Management — Marketing & Sales	Customer Relationship Management — Service
GPS	Load Verification; Vehicle Dispatching; Package Tracking; Asset Tracking; Telematics		Route Management; Vehicle Dispatching; Package Tracking; Asset Tracking; Telematics	Location-based Information Access	Telemetry
WWAN	Advance Shipping Notifications; Manifest Reconciliation		Advance Shipping Notifications; Manifest Reconciliation		
Cellular	Delivery Confirmation; Manifest Reconciliation; Electronic Signature Capture; Exception Notification; Driver Contact	Approval Workflows; Managerial Contact; Employee Contact	Delivery Confirmation; Manifest Reconciliation; Electronic Signature Capture; Exception Notification; Driver Contact	Sales Promotion; ATP/CTP Channel; Reverse Logistics; Location-based Push Services; Sales Contact	Service Contact; Telemetry
P2T	Delivery Confirmation; Exception Notification	Employee Contact	Delivery Confirmation; Exception Notification		Employee Contact
RFID	Asset Tracking; Barcode Scanning	Barcode Scanning; Telemetry	Asset Tracking; Barcode Scanning		
WLAN (Wi-Fi / Bluetooth)	Back-office Updates	Telemetry; Manifest Reconciliation; Receiving & Payment Workflows	Back-office Updates		

Supply Chain Macro Processes & Value Chain Activities

Mobile SCM Applications

Acronyms Glossary: ATP/CTP—Available-to-Promise/Capable-to-Promise; GPS— Global Positioning System; P2T—Push-to-Talk; RFID—Radio Frequency Identification; WLAN—Wireless Local Area Network; WWAN—Wireless Wide Area Network inventory management systems or enterprise resource planning systems in order to perform available-to-promise (ATP) checks or capable-to-promise (CTP) checks, respectively (May, 2001). They then can provide up-to-the-minute information to their customers. Not only do these types of applications result in lower costs, due to increased employee productivity and more streamlined workflows and faster decision-making, they also result in higher levels of customer satisfaction. Returns processing and reverse logistics presents yet another area where mobile technologies can help alleviate business pain spots. By allowing drivers and field service representatives to accept returns (due to product defects or a change of mind from the customer) and with the ability to dispatch pickup trucks in near vicinity, if need be, businesses can drastically increase customer satisfaction levels and operational productivity.

Lastly, with respect to mobile technology applications in the service function, telemetry applications have the potential to provide yet again an effective means of monitoring and controlling remote resources. Service levels can be monitored, and personnel can be assigned, based on the type of problem incurred. These applications can help to reduce employee time and costs associated with routine administration of assets in remote locations.

From the discussion in this section, it should be evident that the mobile supply chain applications described herein, along with their respective bearer technologies are indeed in harmony with the various drivers for mobile technologies described earlier. Table 2 presents our typology of mobile technology applications as a juxtaposition of bearer technologies and their functional scope in different supply chain activities. In the next sections, we discuss our future outlook for these mobile technology applications followed by our conclusions.

Future Outlook

Recent developments in new wireless technologies, more sophisticated end-user devices, and improved network coverage all have resulted in greater adoption rates for mobile applications (Alanen & Autio, 2003). However, in order to predict the future pathway of different types of mobile technology applications described in this chapter, we need to consider them vis-à-vis other technologies that have been used in SCM for some time, such as MRP I, MRP II, APS, ERP, EDI, and e-commerce systems. It is the combination of these functional and enabling technologies that constitutes the essential technology base for different supply chain environments. As elaborated throughout this chapter, mobile technology applications have the potential to assimilate in this current portfolio of technologies by improving process efficiencies and allowing streamlined access to these traditional back-end systems.

First, let us consider the technical interaction between current systems and how mobile technology applications are changing the current landscape. To reiterate our point from the previous section, mobile technologies currently are being used in conjunction with other systems, such as enterprise resource planning (ERP) systems, and it is our belief that this joint utilization will prevail at least in the short-term future. In order to explicate

Figure 2. Positioning of various SCM systems in the range/reach framework (adapted from Broadbent et al., 1999)

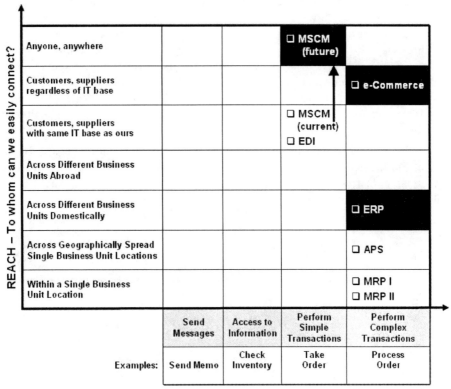

our position further and discuss our viewpoint for the future of mobile SCM technologies, we utilize the range/reach framework developed by Broadbent, Weill, and Clair (1999). The framework was used originally to explain the findings of an academic study that explored the functionalities of different types of information systems, and it lends well to our discussion of SCM systems. Figure 2 depicts our conceptual positioning of various SCM systems along the two dimensions.

As depicted in Figure 2, it can be seen that the current positioning of MSCM applications is such that these applications are bound to augment the reach and range of other enterprise systems (including ERP, MRP, and APS systems) that support various supply chain processes. The two types of technologies are complementary, in that although contemporary enterprise systems such as ERP are capable of performing complex transactions, they are limited to operations cross-functionally across the same organization. Wireless applications can help overcome these spatial boundaries in order to allow communication, collaboration, and coordination across different businesses. Furthermore, with the ongoing standardization of communication protocols, the introduction of new transmission mechanisms (e.g., GSM/GPRS), and improved network coverage worldwide, wireless connectivity very soon can enable the anytime/anywhere business paradigm across global supply chain partners. Figure 2 illustrates the direction of this shift upwards from the current position of MSCM applications along the dimensions of range. However, it should be noted that, although this advancement in mobile technologies may enable more complex transactions to be executed than is possible today, the level of complexity cannot catch up to that of e-commerce and ERP systems. This is because of the nature of computing resource requirements for these complex systems. Hence, in the near to medium future, mobile technology applications in SCM will complement other more complex technologies, such as ERP systems and e-commerce systems. The shaded cells in Figure 2 illustrate this unison among the three systems.

Lastly, theorists and practitioners also envisage that mobile technologies will find their way into horizontal, function-specific services, only after they have been tried and tested in vertical, industry-specific applications (Alanen & Autio, 2003; Forrester Research, 2001).

Conclusion

The adoption of mobile technology applications for SCM is being driven by various business and technical factors. At the end of the day, managers at the helm of decision making are interested in increasing productivity by reducing process costs and time, increasing process responsiveness, and improving product and service delivery quality. Researchers and futurists contend that MSCM technology applications can turn that vision mentioned previously into a reality by enabling new processes in order to seamlessly connect into existing supply chain planning and execution systems. Through omni-directional, real-time transmission of information, instantaneous reconciliations, and elimination of non-value-added activities from the supply chain, these new mobile applications are enabling increased fulfillment velocity, improved inventory visibility, and higher levels of supplier coordination versatility in the supply network.

In this chapter, we have discussed various categories of mobile technology applications for SCM. A typology based on these applications and associated bearer technologies was presented to highlight various applications within the three supply chain macro processes of supplier relationship management, internal SCM, and customer relationship management. The current and predicted positioning of these technologies in the near to medium time frame shows that the business process changes that will be instigated by the introduction of mobile technologies will lead to gradual, albeit fundamental, trans-formations in the organization's operations.

It is hoped that the discussion of technology drivers and the typology of mobile applications will prove to be a useful conceptual vehicle for understanding mobile SCM technologies and aid practitioners in making a business case for adopting these technologies. Finally, organizations that recently have undertaken MSCM initiatives can provide useful test beds for the validation of these conceptual models. Case studies investigating the undertakings of these organizations and their experiences with different technologies can provide valuable insights for revising and improving the ideas presented in this chapter.

References

Alanen, J., & Autio, E. (2003). Mobile business services: A strategic perspective. In M.B.E. Strader & T.J. Strader (Eds.), *Mobile commerce: Technology, theory, and applications* (pp. 162-184). Hershey, PA: Idea Group Publishing.

Bardhan, A.D., & Kroll, C.A. (2003). *The new wave of outsourcing*. Berkeley: University of California.

Barney, J. (1995). Firm resources and sustained competitive advantage. *Journal of Management, 17*, 99-120.

Bovet, D., & Martha, J. (2000). *Value nets: Breaking the supply chain to unlock hidden profits*. New York: John Wiley & Sons.

Broadbent, M., Weill, P., & Clair, D.S. (1999). The implication of information technology infrastructure for business process redesign. *MIS Quarterly, 23*, 159-182.

Burchett, C. (2000). Mobile virtual enterprises: The future of electronic business and consumer services. Paper presented at the *Acadmia/Industry Working Conference on Research Challenges (AIWoRC)*, Buffalo, NY.

Chopra, S., & Meindl, P. (2003). *Supply chain management: Strategy, planning, and operation*. Upper Saddle River, NJ: Pearson Education Inc.

Cousins, K., & Varshney, U. (2001). *A product location framework for mobile commerce environment. Proceedings of the International Conference on Mobile Computing and Networking*, Rome, Italy.

Dholakia, R.R., & Dholakia, N.D. (2002). Mobility and markets: Emerging outlines of m-commerce. *Journal of Business Research, Article in Press*.

Emily, K. (2004). Wal-Mart starts RFID test, promises privacy. *Forbes.com*. Retrieved April 4, 2004, from *http://www.forbes.com/reuters/newswire/2004/04/30/rtr1355059.html*

Forrester Research. (1998). *Telemetry's time is coming*. Cambridge, MA: Forrester Research.

Forrester Research. (2001). *Mobile data finds niche in risk-tolerant firms*. Cambridge, MA: Forrester Research.

Gebauer, J., Shaw, M., & Zhao, K. (2002). *The efficacy of mobile e-procurement: A pilot study. Proceedings of the Hawaii Conference on Systems Sciences*, Los Alamitos, California.

GSM Association. (2004a). *Mobile terms & acronyms*. Retrieved August 03, 2004, from *http://www.gsmworld.com/technology/glossary.shtml*

GSM Association. (2004b). *GSMA statistics Q1 04*. Dublin, Ireland: GSM Association.

Gupta, P., & Moitra, D. (2004). Evolving a pervasive IT infrastructure: A technology integration approach. *Personal and Ubiquitous Computing, 8*(1), 31-41.

Guy, A. (2003). *The evolution of push-to-talk represents a powerful carrier weapon*. Boston: The Yankee Group.

Hammer, M. (1997). *Beyond reengineering: How the processed-centered organization is changing our work and our lives*. New York: Harper Business.

Handfield, R.B., & Nichols, E.L. (2002). *Supply chain redesign: Transforming supply chains into integrated value systems*. Upper Saddle River, NJ: Financial Times Prentice Hall.

Hanebeck, H.-C.L., & Tracey, B. (2003). The role of location in supply chain management: How mobile communication enables supply chain best practice and allows companies to move to the next level. *International Journal of Mobile Communications, 1*(1/2), 148-166.

Holten, R., Dreiling, A., Muehlen, M.Z., & Becker, J. (2002). Enabling technologies for supply chain process management. *Proceedings of the Information Resources Management Association International Conference*, Seattle, Washington.

Hurst, S. (2003). IT doesn't matter—Business processes do: A critical analysis of Nicholas Carr's IT article in the *Harvard Business Review Library Journal, 128*(19), 78.

Kalakota, R., Robinson, M., & Gundepudi, P. (2003). Mobile applications for adaptive supply chains: A landscape analysis. In K. Siau, & E.-P. Lim (Eds.), *Advances in mobile commerce technologies*. Hershey, PA: Idea Group Inc.

Karkkainen, M., & Holmstrom, J. (2002). Wireless product identification: Enabler for handling efficiency, customisation and information sharing. *Supply Chain Management: An International Journal, 7*(4), 242-252.

Knolmayer, G., Mertens, P., & Zeier, A. (2002). *Supply chain management based on SAP systems*. Berlin, Germany: Springer-Verlag.

May, P. (2001). *Mobile commerce: Opportunities, applications, and technologies of wireless business*. Cambridge, UK: Cambridge University Press.

Moline, A. (2002). Supplier parks—The wave of the future? *Plants Sites & Parks, 29*(1), 18-19.

Murphy, J. (2000). Internet technology both forces and enables transformation of supply chains. *Global Logistics & Supply Chain Strategies*, March. Retrieved June 8, 2004, from *http://www.glscs.com/archives/3.00.intro.htm?adcode=10*

Nair, K.G.K., & Prasad, P.N. (2004). Offshore outsourcing: A SWOT analysis of a state in India. *Information Systems Management, 21*(3), 34-40.

Parker, E.B. (2000). Closing the digital divide in rural America. *Telecommunications Policy, 24*(4), 281-290.

Poirier, C.C., & Bauer, M.J. (2000). *E-supply chain: Using the Internet to revolutionize your business*. San Francisco: Berrett-Koehler Publishers Inc.

Porter, M. (1980). *Competitive strategy: Techniques for analysing industries and competitors*. New York: Free Press.

Porter, M.E. (1985). *Competitive advantage*. New York: The Free Press.

Rao, B., & Parikh, M.A. (2003). Wireless broadband drivers and their social implications. *Technology in Society, 25*, 477-489.

Rayner, B. (2004). More than a supply chain. *Electronics Supply & Manufacturing*. Retrieved June 8, 2004, from *http://www.my-esm.com/oped/showArticle.jhtml? articleID=21400478*

Rice, R.E., & Katz, J.E. (2003). Comparing Internet and mobile phone usage: Digital divides of usage, adoption, and dropouts. *Telecommunications Policy, 27*(8-9), 597-623.

Rulke A., Iyer, A., & Chiasson, G. (2003). The ecology of mobile commerce: Charting a course for success using value chain analysis. In B.E. Mennecke & T.J. Strader (Eds.), *Mobile commerce: Technology, theory and applications* (pp. 114-130). Hershey, PA: IRM Press.

Salz, P.A. (2003). New high-tech strategies aim to make supply-chain management smoother. *Wall Street Journal Europe*, November 2. Retrieved June 8, 2004, from *http://www.sensile.com/sentech/download/wsje_article.pdf*

Taylor, D.A. (2003). *Supply chains: A manager's guide*. Boston: Pearson Education Inc.

Wareham, J., Levy, A., & Shi, W. (2004). Wireless diffusion and mobile computing: Implications for the digital divide. *Telecommunications Policy, 28*(5-6), 439-457.

Yankee Group. (2001). Wireless technology in the energy industry. Boston: The Yankee Group.

Yankee Group. (2004). *The Yankee Group predictions for 2004*. Boston: The Yankee Group.

Chapter XVIII

Determinant of E-Based Success Attributes for Integrated Supply Chain System

Wing S. Chow
Hong Kong Baptist University, Hong Kong

Abstract

An e-integrated supply chain system is an enabler that enriches the effectiveness of global supply chains. This chapter adopts factor analysis to determine four success factors: work performance quality, system quality, information quality, and service quality. A critical analysis of areas that require improvement is also conducted

Introduction

Supply chain is a management philosophy that links all logistics activities of parties involved into a single entity so that production orders can be delivered in a short life span. An effective way for linking all logistics activities together is to implement an integrated supply chain information system. Laudon and Laudon (2004) discuss the basic structure and system components of an integrated supply chain information system. Vakharia (2002) points out that the adoption of e-business technologies has been the main focus of the development of supply chain information systems. Frohlich (2002) verifies that an e-based integrated information system has a positive effect on supply chain performance.

The applications of e-based supply chain systems have played a significant role in the fast changing business environment in the Asia Pacific region. In Hong Kong, the state of economy has gradually merged with mainland China; the local government has propelled the idea of setting an e-based logistics center, which includes the development of a super-computer platform that aids for fast e-business exchanges among trading partners in the region. This logistics center serves the role of third-party logistics, and the e-based integrated supply chain system (e-ISCS) is the basic platform for its e-based information system. In practice, e-ISCS operates differently than a conventional e-based supply chain information system; the third party logistics firms are fully responsible for the design, development, implementation, and service supports of the system. Thus, the study of e-ISCS quality has played an important role in supply chain performance.

The modeling and study of system quality of supply chain practices are well documented in the literature. Kuei and Madu (2001) identify the critical success factors for the implementing supply chain quality management concept. Narashimhan and Kim (2001) confirm a set of quality factors that contributes to the success of a conventional supply chain information system. However, literature directly linked to the e-ISCS quality is not noticeable. The e-ISCS quality has online features like Internet attributes, which were reviewed by Madu (1998), and intranet benefits, revealed by Lai (2001). This chapter determines the critical success factors for the e-ISCS and examines its performance in the supply chain. The following section will review relevant system features and practices of e-ISCS, discuss the model development, present research methodology, and discuss the findings before concluding the chapter.

E-Supply Chain System Features and Practices

This section reviews system features and practices of e-ISCS. However, the existing literature on e-ISCS features and practices are relatively sparse. This chapter borrowed system features and practices from the intra-organizational system literature. The reason is that both systems share similar features, except that e-ISCS is a totally open system and third-party logistics firms are managing their design and operations. Twenty-four common system features and practices were identified initially from literature, but these were reduced to 18 after verifying their applicability in personal interviews with five local supply chain firms and five third-party logistics firms. The following will discuss the contents of these 18 system features and practices with supporting references.

1.   The system regularly enhances maintenance. Maintenance is a critical process to the success of an information system (Laudon & Laudon, 2004). Cupito (1997) states that an effective e-based system is not something we put up but something

we keep up. Thus, scheduling regular maintenance must be enhanced.

2. The system provides user manual/instructions. User manual explains all systems features and operations to users. Without a proper non-technical user manual, users may abandon the system, because they failed to see the full benefits (Misic & Hill, 1994).

3. The system enhances collaboration among users. An effective system allows users to exchange information directly and, thus, enhances the collaboration among users (Lynch, 1997). In addition, the supporting feature of many-to-many interactions in the e-based environment also helps to elevate the collaboration between all decision makers (Campbell, 1997).

4. The system produces accurate search results/information. The ability to provide accurate information is a key success feature of an e-based system (Baines, 1996). In addition, the system must ensure that changes must be updated and integrated before any search commands are executed (Foo & Lim, 1997).

5. The system provides a standardized display format (i.e., screen layout). Authorized personnel from different locations easily can place and upload relevant information onto the system. Thus, a standardized display format should be enhanced, so that all users easily can read and understand information (Foo & Lim, 1997).

6. The system adopts data security/privacy. The system feature of openness in the e-environment brings many benefits but also imposes many internal securities, like data privacy (Liddy, 1996). The design of tight control that delimits authorized access to all sensitive information is needed (Adhikari, 1997; Fuller & Pagan, 1997; Pagan, 1997).

7. The system improves personal productivity. An e-based system enhances personal productivity, because critical information easily can be accessed for decision making (Koprowski, 1997; Sridhar, 1998). Additional system features like communications and collaboration also can help to elevate the performance of individuals.

8. The organization provides technical support competently. The competency of technical support staff plays an influential role in the success of a system (Huff & Munro, 1985). Users would be highly motivated to use the system, if technical assistance and problem resolution were available online (Madu, 1998).

9. The system improves business communications. An e-based system easily could be installed across many different platforms and would permit users to be connected worldwide (Lynch, 1997). With this online connection, communications between users can be enhanced (Tabor, 1997).

10. The system enhances fast response time. Time is money. For the success of any e-based system, the response time should be a critical system feature (Lai, 2001). It reveals that fast response time gains a higher rating and that it becomes an ever more key system feature.

11. The system provides standardized retrieval procedures. An e-based system facilitates the ease of data and program uploading but also imposes difficulty in retrieving the desired information. Foo and Lom (1997) point out that all information to be posted should be indexed hierarchically, so that standardized retrieval procedures can be implemented.

12. The organization provides minimal system training. Technology helps organizations to achieve a higher level of productivity, only if users are conversant with them. Therefore, it is suggested that a minimal level of training should be provided to all users when a system is implemented (Misic & Hill, 1994).

13. The system provides up-to-date information. The ability to guarantee the most up-to-date information is a key criterion for an effective e-based system (Baines, 1996). Ba, et al. (1997) point out that such an effective system also helps to eliminate the bulky paper-based information system.

14. The system provides a standardized search procedure. Similar to the retrieving procedure, a standardized search procedure is an important system feature. Foo and Lim (1997) suggest that data and information should be indexed clearly and arranged in a hierarchical fashion, so that users can locate them easily.

15. The system is easy to use. Ease of use is an important feature, because it reduces the need for user training (Campbell, 1997; Lynch, 1997). Furthermore, this system feature also helps to diminish the user's resistance to the system (Johnson, 1995).

16. The system improves the quality of decision making. An effective e-based system transforms scattered data into meaningful business information (Sridhar, 1998). With the ability to access rich information from the e-based system, the quality of the decision made is improved.

17. The system helps to make decisions more quickly. With e-based technology, integrated information is readily available to all users for decision making. Therefore, the time spent making quality decisions is shorter when compared to a conventional system (Sridhar, 1998).

18. The system allows fast information exchange. In today's competitive business world, fast exchange of business information is key to survival. With the help of Internet technology, an e-based system ensures that critical business information could be disseminated efficiently throughout business partners (Baines, 1996).

Study Design and Measures

Study Subject

The respondents were the supply chain firms hiring third-party logistics services. Supply chain firms were selected here because they were the users of the e-ICSC. They were asked first to evaluate the 18 system features and practices and then to rate their e-ISCS performances: actual performance and overall satisfaction.

Measures

Eighteen system features and practices were used as the first part of our questionnaire. Supply chain firms were asked to evaluate the importance of these system features and practices in a scale of 1 to 5; where a value of 5 represents the most important one and a value of 1 is the least important one. These measurement scores are known as expected scores and were used to determine the success factors of e-ISCS. Three questions were adopted to measure the performance of e-ISCS; they were based on questions developed by Chow and Lui (2001) with modifications. The mean score of the three questions was treated as the e-ISCS overall user satisfaction. In this study, we also collected the views of actual performance for those 18 system features in a measurement scale of 1 to 5, with a value of 5 representing excellent performance and a value of 1 representing poor performance. These measurements will be used to compute perceptual scores, which also will be elaborated later.

Data Collection Procedure

A structured questionnaire with a cover letter was used for the data collection. A telephone interview was adopted to follow up with those respondents who did not reply within four weeks after the questionnaires were posted. A total of 380 respondents were selected randomly from the http://www.tdctrade.com. This database was selected mainly because it provides a comprehensive database that consists of supply chain companies practicing third party logistics management. Telephone calls were made to confirm their adoption.

A complete set of questionnaires was sent to each selected candidate with a return envelope, and 105 replies were returned. Two incomplete questionnaires were discarded. Therefore, 103 questionnaires were used for the data analysis, which constituted the response rate of 27.6%. The average experience of e-ISCS was reported as 2.95 years with a standard deviation of 0.51 year. Participants have been with the present company for an average of 5.46 years, which indicated that they were conversant about their system. Our participants all held a managerial position and were from the industries of delivery services (including air cargo services), freight, transportation, wholesalers, trading, and logistics. The mean score of e-ISCS overall user satisfaction was reported as 3.18.

Data Analysis

Factor analysis with varimax rotation was used to determine the e-ISCS success factors. Factor loadings of ≥ 0.5 was considered as a significant contribution to a factor cluster. The internal consistency method was adopted to check for homogenous data, with $\alpha \geq 0.6$ as a sufficient condition for an exploratory study. KMO (Kaiser-Meyer-Olkin) values were used to measure the adequacy of the samples, with KMO ≥ 0.5 as an acceptable condition. A regression model was used to study the effect of perceptual scores of e-ISCS success factors to the overall user satisfaction. The perceptual scores are computed by subtracting the expected scores of performance from the actual scores (Kettinger & Choong, 1997).

Result Findings

Factor Analysis

Table 1 shows the results of e-ISCS success factors. The first e-ISCS success factor is labeled as *work performance quality*, and it has six system features and practices: (3) = The system enhances the collaboration among group members, (7) = The system improves personal productivity, (9) = The system improves business communication, (16) = The system improves the quality of decision making, (17) = The system helps to make decisions faster, and (18) = The system allows fast information exchange. Their factor loadings ranged from 0.696 to 0.813. Their values of α and KMO are 0.850 and 0.76. The second e-ISCS success factor is labeled as *system quality*, and it has six system features and practices: (2) = The system provides user menu, (6) = The systems adopts data security/privacy, (10) = The system enhances fast response time, (11) = The system provides standardized retrieval procedure, (14) = The system provides standardized search procedure, and (16) = The system is easy to use. Their factor loadings range from 0.590 to 0.771. Their values of α and KMO are 0.761 and 0.76.

The third e-ISCS success factor is called *information quality*, which comprises three e-ISCS system features and practices: (4) = The system produces accurate search results/ information, (5) = The system gives a standardized display format (screen layout), and (13) = The system provides the most up-to-date information. Their factor loadings range from 0.707 to 0.904. Their α and KMO values are 0.71 and 0.72. The fourth e-ISCS success factor is the *service quality*, which has three system features and practices: (1) = The system enhances maintenance regularly, (8) = The organization provides technical support competently, and (12) = The organization provides minimal training. Their factor loadings range from 0.729 to 0.835. Their values of α and KMO are 0.662 and 0.63. The previous four e-ISCS success factors are considered critical, and third-party logistics firms should treat them seriously in their e-ISCS systems. In the next section, using these four e-ISCS success factors to analyze e-ISCS performance is presented.

Regression Model

Table 2 shows the perceptual scores for the four e-ISCS success factors. All perceptual scores have a negative value, which implies that users considered that the expected performances of those factor features are undermined when compared to their actual perceptual scores. It reveals that only two perceptual scores of e-ISCS are significant. The perceptual score of e-ISCS success factors of system quality has a positive effect on overall user satisfaction, $\rho < 0.0001$. The perceptual score of the e-ISCS success factor of service quality has a negative effect on overall user satisfaction, $\rho < 0.01$. The other two insignificant perceptual scores have coefficients of 0.191 and 0.043. The proposal explained 28.8% of the observed variation. The implication of these results will be discussed.

Table 1. Rotated factor matrices of success factors

Proposed Features/ Practices	Extracted Factors			
	1	2	3	4
(9)	0.813			
(17)	0.791			
(16)	0.776			
(3)	0.758			
(7)	0.708			
(18)	0.696			
(6)		0.771		
(11)		0.754		
(14)		0.716		
(10)		0.642		
(15)		0.642		
(2)		0.590		
(13)			0.904	
(4)			0.880	
(5)			0.607	
(1)				0.835
(8)				0.771
(12)				0.729

Table 2. Regression model for the perceptual scores of e-ISCS success factors

e-ISCS Success Factors	Perceptual Scores		Regression Model $R^2 = 0.228$		
	μ	σ	β	t values	significant
Work performance	-0.8366	0.9086	0.191	1.477	0.143
System	-0.8123	0.7707	0.580	4.210	0.000
Information	-0.7346	0.8263	0.043	0.372	0.710
Service	-1.0421	1.005	-0.397	-2.677	0.009

Where (1) the system enhances maintenance regularly, (2) the system provides user-menu/instructions, (3) the system enhances collaboration among trading partners, (4) the system produces accurate search results/information, (5) the system provides a standardized display format (i.e., screen layout), (6) the system adopts data security/privacy, (7) the system improves personal productivity, (8) the organization provides technical support competently, (9) the system improves business communications, (10) the system enhances fast response time, (11) the system provides standardized retrieval procedure, (12) the organization provides minimal system training, (13) the system provides up-to-date information, (14) the system provides a standardized search procedure, (15) the system is easy to use, (16) the system improves the quality of decision making, (17) the system helps to make decisions more quickly, and (18) the system allows fast information exchange.

Discussion

Many supply chain practitioners advocate the esteem of e-based integrated information systems (e-ISCS), but the success factors of e-ISCS remain opaque. Based on a survey from supply chain firms, this study identifies four e-ISCS success factors: information quality, service quality, system quality, and work performance quality. Third-party logistics firms now can identify these system features and practice closely, so that the identification and implementation of a successful e-ISCS can be established. The success factors identified herein also can serve as a basis for developing a strategy of supply chain quality management (SCQM), as proposed by Kuei and Madu (2001).

This study also contributes to the understanding of e-ISCS performance. Two e-ISCS perceptual scores are singled out as having a significant effect on overall user satisfaction: system quality and service quality. To further allow practitioners to appreciate what system features contribute to these two significant e-ISCSs, we conducted regression tests to examine the effects of each perceptual score of system features on overall user satisfaction. Findings are elaborated in the following.

In the e-ISCS perceptual score of system quality, the regression analysis singles out four system features as critical sources to improve user satisfaction. They are (10) = the system enhances fast response time, (11) = the system provides standardized retrieval procedure, (14) = the system provides standardized search procedure, and (15) = the system is easy to use. These four system features and practices are associated with end-user orientation of a system. An effective information system should cater to the needs of the users, and thus, the capture of user's requirements is absolutely essential. One way to achieve this goal is for practitioners first to gain first-hand experience on how these features are implemented in their clients' information systems, and then to use them as a guideline to develop the standardized features for e-ISCS.

In the e-ISCS perceptual score of service quality, the regression analysis reveals that only one system feature has a negative effect on user satisfaction; namely, (8) = the organization provides technical support competently. This result of negative effect suggests that e-ISCS should be designed in a user-oriented fashion, so that real-time information could be accessed readily without waiting for technical support from third-party logistics firms. Supply chain firms are highly dependent on the e-ISCS provided by the third-party logistics firms, and they would be totally paralyzed, if the system does not support their requests promptly. Thus, third-party logistics firms are advised to identify what features they should focus on, so that their users are virtually free from the minimal need of their technical support. It should be noted that this feature is a critical one, and thus, it always should be made available to users.

Conclusion

The globalization of business ventures has elevated the emphasis of an integrated supply chain system. In an e-integrated supply chain system, the success story depends on collaboration and information exchange among trading partners. This chapter first determines four critical success factors of e-integrated supply chain systems and areas in which to improve their effectiveness of adoption.

References

Adhikari, R. (1997). Security of an intranet. *Information Week, 5*, 151-156.

Ba, S., Lang, K.R., & Whinston, A.B. (1997). Using client-broker-server architecture for intranet decision support. *Decision Support Systems, 19*, 171-192.

Baines, A. (1996). Intranets. *Work Study, 45*(5), 5-7.

Campbell, I. (1997). The intranets: Slashing the cost of business. Retrieved from *http://www.home.netscape.com/comprod/annunce/idc/summary.html*

Chow, W.S, & Lui, K.H. (2001). Discriminating factors of information systems function performance in Hong Kong firms practicing TQM. *International Journal of Operations and Production Management, 21*(5/6), 749-771.

Cupito, M.C. (1997). Intranets: Communication for the internal universe. *Health Management Technology, 6*, 20-58.

Foo, S., & Lim, E.P. (1997). Managing World Wide Web publications. *Information Management & Computer Security, 5*(1), 11-17.

Frohlich, M.T. (2002). E-integration in the supply chain: Barriers and performance. *Decision Sciences, 33*(4), 537-556.

Fuller, S., & Pagan, K. (1997). *Intranets firewalls*. New York: Ventana.

Hills, M. (1997). *Intranet business strategies*. Canada: Wiley Computer Publishing.

Huff, S.L., & Munro, M.C. (1985). Information technology assessment and adoption: A field study. *MIS Quarterly, 9*(4), 327-340.

Johnson, J.T. (1995). Web servers get ready for some real work. *Data Communications, 11*, 57-68.

Kettinger, W.J., & Choong, C.C. (1997). Pragmatic perspectives on the measurement of information systems service quality. *MIS Quarterly, 21*(2), 223-240.

Koprowski, G. (1997). Intranets unleashed. *Computing, 8*, 76-83.

Kuei, C., & Madu, C.N. (2001). Identifying critical success factors for supply chain quality management. *Asia Pacific Management Review, 6*(4), 409-423.

Lai, V.S. (2001). Intraorganizational communication with intranets. *Communications of the ACM, 44*(7), 95-100.

Laudon, K.C., & Laudon, J.P. (2004). *Management information systems: Organization and technology*. New York: Prentice Hall.

Liddy, C. (1996). Commercial security on the internet. *Information Management & Computer Security, 4*(1), 47-49.

Lynch, G. (1997). Intranets—Just another bandwagon? *Industrial Management & Data Systems, 97*(4), 150-152.

Madu, C. (1998). Development attributes of quality for Internet applications. In C.N. Madu (Ed.), *Handbook of total quality management* (pp. 154-164). London: Kluwer Academic Publisher.

Misic, M.M., & Hill, J.A. (1994). Keys to success with the Internet. *Journal of Systems Management, 11*, 6-10.

Narashimhan, R., & Kim, S.W. (2001). Information system utilization strategy for supply chain integration. *Journal of Business Logistics, 22*(2), 51-75.

Sridhar, S. (1998). Decision support using the intranet. *Decision Support Systems, 23*, 19-28.

Tabor, S.W., Pryor, A.N., & Gutierrez, C.F. (1997). Improving corporate communications with intranets. *Information Strategy: The Executive's Journal*, Fall, 7-12.

Vakharia, A.J. (2001). E-business and supply chain management. *Decision Sciences, 33*(4), 495-504.

Chapter XIX

Business Continuity Challenges in Global Supply Chains

Steve Cartland
HP, Australia

Abstract

This chapter examines the relevance of business continuity to supply chain management. Business continuity has focused on the business processes of individual organizations. A business process in a supply chain can involve multiple discrete organizations. This chapter draws on the approaches used by individual organizations to implement continuity and apply them to a supply chain. Typically, supply chains are dependent on IT and workplace for staff. Both can be impacted in a disaster. If one member of a supply chain is affected, this will affect other organizations in the supply chain, magnifying the impact of the initial disaster. The chapter also examines the issues of service supply chains as well as physical goods. A practical outline plan for the development, auditing, and testing of a continuity plan for a supply chain and its management within an overall supply chain governance is proposed as a starting point for supply chain managers.

Introduction

Business continuity is a crucial ingredient of supply chain management. This chapter discusses this significance and the impact of business continuity on supply chain systems. The discussion is based on the author's experience of working in an environment that is dependent on supply chains, as well as helping many of his clients in achieving uninterrupted business continuity.

Business Continuity Today: A Background

Business continuity is essentially a simple concept. Strategically, it should be simple for an organization to implement and manage business continuity. This is not to argue that the detail of a successful business continuity plan is straightforward. In fact, the detailed planning and execution of a business continuity initiative is not always simple, as there is a staggering amount of details resulting from bringing numerous business processes together with many knowledgeable people to develop a successful outcome for an organization. However, at the strategic level, it can be made simple. In fact, at the strategic level, business continuity is the process of ensuring that all critical business processes are available to meet the business needs under all agreed scenarios in case of an emergency or a disaster.

There are three key points in this definition.

1. An organization must be able to identify and to agree on what its critical business processes are. The best approach to understand this is determined through business impact analysis. A business impact analysis is a process to identify the impact on an organization of a significant incident, such as a fire that will affect the running of the business. The outcomes of a business impact analysis are the identification of critical business processes on which the organization depends, their interrelationships, the components that the process requires, the cost of down time, and the maximum time that the organization can operate without the process. The key point is that the definition of critical business processes will differ from one organization to another, and it is reached through consensus of senior management.

2. Critical business processes do not have to be available all the time. Therefore, senior management needs to agree on how long the organization can cope without them (this is called the maximum tolerable outage) and the hourly cost of down time. Typically, the hourly cost of down time will increase exponentially (i.e., the cost of down time for the first hour will be much lower than that of the 10th hour). Eventually, the cost of down time will exceed the revenue from continuing business, so the private sector organization will fail. In the public sector, there will be major political intervention and significant reorganization.

3.   The scenarios that an organization needs to safeguard against need to be agreed on. This can be simplified by considering a denial of access strategy, regardless of the various causes of a disaster. Therefore, senior management should think about its various locations in order to consider denial of access to a floor of a building, the whole building, the city block, a half of a kilometer radius from the building, the whole metropolitan area, and beyond, as a denial zone. The likelihood of each scenario needs to be considered separately. To add to the reality, possible causes also ought to be considered. For instance, loss of power supply is one that senior managers can readily understand. What would be the impact if the organization lost power to its building due to a malfunction in its power distribution boards? What if there were a regional power failure that affected a significant portion of a central business district or a total blackout?

This leads to risk analysis and mitigation.

For example, if we consider the power outage, an organization may protect certain parts of it premises (e.g., call center and computer room) with a UPS (uninterruptible power supply) and generator. But how often are the UPS and generator tested? Is the switch across and switch back seamless? Is the fuel for the generator checked for quality regularly, and is fuel supply service in place that can be relied on during a major prolonged power outage?

We have been considering the approach a discrete organization needs to take. A supply chain could be considered to be a super-organization; therefore, the same basic issues will apply.

A simple seven-step model to develop and maintain a plan at the strategic level is shown in Figure 1.

•   **Current Situation:** Most organizations have some level of business continuity capability. After all, their management and staff are dealing with the daily issues of keeping the business going. However, this capability is not readily recognized

Figure 1. The 7 steps model

© *Hewlett-Packard*

and coordinated, which means its effectiveness will not be maximized in a crisis situation. Identifying and documenting this capability is the first step.

- **Business Impact Analysis:** This is a standard consulting engagement or internal process that helps to identify the critical business processes, their interconnections, the cost of down time, and maximum tolerable outage for each critical business process.

- **Risk Assessment:** This identifies the risks that may impact the organization, their severity, likelihood, and ways they can be ameliorated.

For an organization developing a continuity capability, there are advantages to using an external organization to provide guidance during these first three steps, as the experience may not be available in the organization to ensure all assumptions are appropriately challenged.

- **Define Strategy:** Using the data collected during the first three steps, senior management then can determine the level of protection desired, the probable causes of an impact, and the resources they are willing to commit. This will depend on the organization's appetite for risk, formal supply service levels, and the cost of various plans vs. the cost of down time. At this stage, the individual(s) and the sponsor(s) (including the CEO) that are responsible for managing the continuity plans should be identified.

- **Define Solution:** Senior management can pass on its strategic requirements, together with the implementation and operational budget plans, to departments such as facilities, IT (including voice), and human resources (HR) to work with various line managers.

- **Select or Build Solution:** An organization can choose to build its own solutions, outsource, or use a mixture of both.

- **Document, Plan and Test:** A range of documentation needs to be prepared as part of the overall solution. First, the description of the objectives, together with how these objectives will be achieved. Second, documentation for users needs to be made available. Great care needs to be taken to ensure that it is appropriately used in a crisis situation. This means that it must be brief and straightforward. Finally, the plan must be tested on a regular basis, at least annually and more regularly, if the organization is undergoing change. This is vital. Without regular complete testing, organizations have no proof that the plan will work.

Most senior managers will acknowledge readily that their organizations need a business continuity plan to ensure they can continue to operate, if they are affected by a disaster. The need is built into corporate consciousness in that only a few would state that a plan is not required. However, according to research undertaken by Macquarie Graduate School, fewer than 12% of organizations in the public and private sectors have fully tested plans.

There are many reasons why organizations do not have business continuity plans. They include:

- Denial (it cannot happen to us)
- The generally low likelihood of a disaster (ignoring the major impact, if one does occur)
- Pressure to undertake other work
- Inability to see a return on investment
- No obvious owner for the responsibility in the organization

However, regulators around the world are addressing the issue of organizations that lack business continuity preparation plans. For instance, the Australian finance industry regulator, the Australian Prudential Regulatory Authority, released a standard for business continuity plans. In part, it stated that certain categories of organizations that it regulates must have a plan as part of their risk management and assigned this responsibility to the boards of directors.

With so few organizations having fully tested plans in place (and if it is not fully tested, it is of dubious worth), it will be more difficult to develop supply chain continuity plans. Until this is done, supply chains will be at serious risk.

The corollary, however, is that the great incidence of supply chains may be a driver to organizations developing business continuity plans, as customers demand them of their suppliers.

Some organizations delegate the task of implementing a business continuity plan to the IT function, as IT disaster recovery has been a part of IT management for larger organizations for a number of decades. However, while this approach protects IT functionality, it isolates other critical business processes by leaving them vulnerable to disasters and unprotected. This is due to the fact that most organizations consider the cost rather than the long-term benefits of implementing a business continuity plan. Organizations should consider the cost of down time in order to recognize the urgency of planning for business continuity This requires the support of senior executives. For example, in the financial services industry, in the banking sector, in particular, certain regulations are adopted by many OECD countries because of the support and the backing of a risk management executive who can influence the decisions of top management.

However, the very nature of a supply chain involves a number of organizations that are dependent on each other for daily business operations. Therefore, an increasing number of organizations are putting a greater emphasis on developing continuity plans that work. The reasons for this are:

1. **The Current Worldwide Situation:** Although relatively few organizations have been affected by terrorism or by any politically based activity, the headlines cause senior management to wake up and to act.

2. **Corporate Governance:** This has been an issue of growing importance since the mid-1980s. The importance of good corporate governance grew out of some of the corporate excesses in the 1980s. There has been a number of reports (shown in the following chart) from many countries that have been built on the importance of good corporate governance. The most recent, the Turnbull Report (London Stock

Exchange, 1999), identified risk management as a key part of corporate governance and business continuity as a key part of risk management. Companies listed on the London Stock Exchange are now required to report annually on their risk management approaches.

3. **Outsourcing:** Organizations outsource activities that are not core to their operations and that a specialized contractor will be able to undertake more efficiently and provide enhanced efficiencies through transformation of the process. Common examples are IT (infrastructure management, applications development), logistics, and manufacturing. Typically, each of these activities is critical to the operation of the organization, but they don't define the organization, and there are savings and flexibilities to be obtained.

Treadway Report	USA	1987
Cadbury Report	UK	1992
King Report	South Africa	1994
Dey Report	Canada	1994
Vienot Report	France	1995
Peters Report	Netherlands	1996
Turnbull Report	UK	1999

When activities are outsourced, they become part of a supply chain. An essential part of the outsourcing process is to review risks and benefits, which requires potential outsourcing contractors to demonstrate a business continuity plan. However, there are rarely processes in place to review that plan on a continuing basis.

There is some guidance available as to what a continuity plan should contain. For example, there are two global professional bodies, the US-based DRI International and the UK-based Business Continuity Institute. The latter states that the components of a continuity plan are:

1. Initiation and Management
2. Business Impact Analysis
3. Risk Evaluation and Control
4. Developing Business Continuity Management Strategies
5. Emergency Response and Operations
6. Developing and Implementing Business Continuity and Crisis Management Plans
7. Awareness and Training Programs

Figure 2. Relationship between critical business process and infrastructure

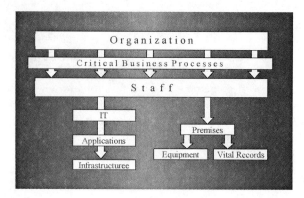

© Hewlett-Packard

8. Maintaining and Exercising Business Continuity and Crisis Management Plans
9. Crisis Communications
10. Coordination with external agencies

However, as each organization is different (even those in the same industry), effectively, each management will need to make its own decisions.

The following model (Figure 2) can be a useful guide, because it is anchored to the critical business process.

The model's focus is to keep member organizations of a supply chain operating. This requires that the critical business processes (identified by senior management) continue to operate in order to meet the business needs under all agreed scenarios (as defined in the definition of business continuity earlier).

The key force behind the operation of any critical business process is the employee (staff). It is difficult to think of any critical process that does not involve some human intervention (staff involvement). Automatic teller machines, for instance, as automated as they can be, still need some human intervention for the replenishing of cash, the removal of deposits, and the human oversight of network management systems.

Generally, staff needs two facilities to operate—IT and premises.

For most organizations, it is increasingly difficult to think of any critical business process that can operate effectively without some kind of IT support. For example, staff needs access to the applications; however, these applications will not run without the appropriate IT infrastructure.

Staff also needs access to a suitable premises in order to work and to perform its daily operational activities. A mobile workforce may be able to satisfactorily work from home, if an IT remote access capability is dysfunctional as a part of a continuity planning exercise. Other groups may need access to different work environments or to more suitable premises. Such groups would include those where interaction is important; supervision is required; or access to special tools, information, or equipment is required.

Working from home can be an effective part of a continuity solution for organizations that have successfully implemented this approach as part of their normal working arrangements. However, the implementation of such a program often takes a long time to complete; therefore, an organization must proceed with caution and not fall into a trap of a long-term commitment that would be difficult to get out of. In addition, there may be workplace safety and liability issues, if a staff member is directed rather than being given the choice of working from home.

At the new selected alternative workplace, there may be a need for specialized non-IT equipment. An example is a specialized telephone service with automatic call distribution, hunt groups, and so forth. These services are used not only by call centers but increasingly by any organization that undertakes a lot of its customer contacts via the phone.

Finally, non-IT vital records also must be available at the alternative workplace. Examples are contracts and building plans, which should prove very useful, if any of the production offices were to be damaged.

Using this model, it is possible to connect the cost of recovering the IT infrastructure to the cost of down time for a business process. Therefore, senior management can make a standard cost-benefit analysis to determine how much should be invested in a continuity capability.

So far, we have discussed business continuity planning, its various issues to consider, and its tremendous importance. We now consider the relevance and the importance of supply chain systems on the business continuity.

Supply Chain from a Business Continuity Perspective

When a single business considers its business continuity needs, it tends to look at its internal processes. A formal supply chain initially needs to take a similar approach; that is, it needs to look at the overall processes within the supply chain. The difference is that there are more potential points of failure, less control as discrete organizations are involved, and potentially less overall clarity.

The greater potential points of failure arise where a process goes across a number of organizations with no single management. No matter how closely organizations work together, they are unlikely to have the same cohesion as a single organization with a single CEO. This will be compounded, if an organization is in multiple unrelated supply chains, such as a global logistics organization may be.

This is where supply chain governance becomes important, which is discussed later in this chapter.

As individual organizations review their own internal procedures, there is a natural boundary to the development of an internal continuity plan (i.e., internal activity only). There is a similar boundary for the supply chain, where the process relates only to the members of the private exchange, industry vertical marketplace, or other structure. If members of a supply chain already are working across organizational boundaries, they should seriously consider extending the business continuity process used in the formal supply chain to the suppliers that support their critical business processes.

As organizations increase the amount of outsourcing, supply chains get more complex, which has an impact on the management of a continuity plan. For example, in a four-organization supply chain, if each organization outsources three extra-critical activities (e.g., IT, transport, plus some manufacturing activity) to different suppliers, the number of organizations in the supply chain increases to 16. Potentially, this could vastly complicate the management of a continuity plan, which is why a simple high-level approach should be adopted to manage continuity for the supply chain.

Even when operating domestically, an organization should conduct its analysis of the whole supply chain, taking into consideration potential risks from overseas suppliers that also may become a threat, which is crucially relevant, when at least one of the member organizations of the supply chain relies on overseas supply. The process of comparing a particular impact on a domestic level is far less complex than that of the whole supply chain. Although it is a challenge to an organization, it can be simplified by addressing critical suppliers only. Again, deciding how much time to spend can be based on a simple cost-benefit analysis so it remains straightforward.

As with a single vertically integrated organization, synchronization is the key to an efficient supply chain. Synchronization is more difficult to achieve than in a single organization, because there is less control, and that synchronization typically is achieved by the interconnection of IT systems.

The basic driver for business continuity within an organization is risk management, which is part of corporate governance. Corporate governance and risk management together should be the driving force in any successful supply chain. Without undertaking a risk-management-driven business continuity approach, supply chain members simply would not be able to identify where the potential risks are, let alone be able to manage them.

As previously mentioned at the beginning of this chapter, the point of a business continuity plan is to protect the critical business processes of an organization. A supply chain has two effects—it spreads the critical business process beyond the boundaries of the organization, and it diffuses the responsibility for continuity throughout the supply chain. In a single organization, there is a growing acceptance that the board of directors has the overall responsibility of implementing the business continuity initiative; however, depending on the nature and the infrastructure of a supply chain, the responsibility is spread among all the participants.

Supply chain governance can be implemented in many forms and will be dependent on the type of supply chain. Typically, there is one organization that is responsible for the management of the supply chain, and that is where the responsibility for governance lies.

The challenge is to define the beginning and the end of the supply chain. For example, a white goods manufacturer may develop a supply chain that upstream involves suppliers of electric motors, gear boxes, electronic control panels, packaging, steel, and other components. Downstream, the chain may involve transport, warehousing, and major retailers. It can be argued that downstream, the chain ends at the retailer. Upstream,

Figure 3. SCS for a white goods manufacturer

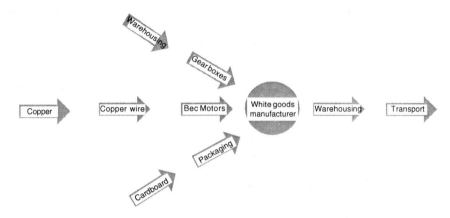

from a supply chain management perspective, it can be argued that the supply chain ends with, for instance, the electric motor manufacturer. However, this motor manufacturer has its own supply chain for its components and may have little awareness of the white goods manufacturer's transport and warehousing issues.

A simplified supply chain map for the white goods manufacturer may look like Figure 3.

However, if a supplier to the electric motor manufacturer has an incident that disrupts its ability to supply, then the white goods manufacturer, warehousing, and transport contractors all may be impacted. In addition, the other supply chain lines upstream from the white goods manufacturers (e.g., gear box, control panel, etc. suppliers) also may be impacted, because there will be a reduced demand for their products. The supply chain map then looks like Figure 4, where organizations on either side of the impacted organization are most impacted, but, with the white goods manufacturer having to use its stocks of electric motors, the gear box manufacturer and packaging supplier are likely to be affected.

Figure 4. SCS for a white goods manufacturer (disrupted)

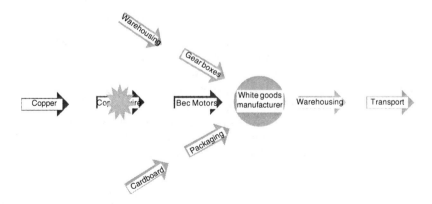

The more tightly integrated the supply chain is, the greater is the impact.

Supply chain governance needs to consider the causes of an incident. In a physical goods supply chain, these include the inability to supply physical goods or the total loss of a business process, as demonstrated in the following section.

- **Loss of Physical Goods:** This can be caused by damage to the manufacturing plant, warehousing, or (for imported goods) by the loss of a shipping vessel. This can be addressed by increasing stock or duplicating warehouses or suppliers. However, these measures are very expensive to implement and should be weighed against the cost of not being able to supply.

- **Failure of Business Process:** An organization may have the goods but are not able to supply them, because, for example, the shipping process has failed. As explained above, some critical business processes require both IT systems and people. If a supplier organization suffers an incident that affects its head office and computer center, it may not be able to control its manufacturing, quality checking, and shipping. This would reduce greatly its ability to ship goods, especially in a tightly integrated supply chain, where shipping advices, invoicing, and quality reports are provided electronically.

The supply chain, as a super-organization, is unable to undertake one of its critical business processes.

The above model needs to be considered from the ordering, fulfilment, and service supply chain perspective.

Ordering

Organizations typically require that ordering and confirmation take place as a single speedy process. In a supply chain situation (which implies that there is an ongoing relationship between the parties), any supplier that requires 24 hours to confirm the ability to supply is at a severe disadvantage and will introduce inefficiencies to the supply chain.

Ordering, for example, is a business process (i.e., no physical goods or services are provided at this point). A business process requires that people and IT be able to react rapidly to filling orders and confirming their delivery. This must be undertaken with a predictable level of service. Within a supply chain, there may be many order receiving points, and the failure of any can affect the efficiency and, therefore, the overall cost to members of the supply chain. Therefore, such processes must be protected as part of a business continuity plan; that is, the connections between processes should be identified, the critical business periods agreed on, the cost of down time calculated, the risks identified, and the continuity processes established following a cost-benefit analysis that explicitly considers the cost of down time.

Fulfillment

Predictable fulfillment increases in importance as the supply chain becomes more tightly integrated and inventory costs are reduced through just-in-time deliveries. There are two parts of fulfilment—the physical provision of the goods and the business processes that support the fulfillment process.

If the goods are being supplied from inventory, the basic key processes are the suppliers' inventory and shipping; transport contractors booking, tracking, tracing, and proof-of-delivery; and the purchasers receiving. In any supply situation of any size, it is unlikely that supply can take place if any of these processes fail. They all rely on people and IT; therefore, these critical processes must be protected by a business continuity plan.

If the goods are not being supplied from inventory, the process becomes more complex, as back-order management and manufacturing processes also are involved.

In addition, there is the issue of the protection of the physical goods.

Services Supply Chains

As a result of organizations outsourcing a greater number of services, this type of supply chain is increasing. Examples are IT, legal, and travel. The increasing flexibility of communications makes it possible to provide services from lower-cost countries encouraging providers of services to introduce further suppliers into the chain. For example, an IT outsourcer based in Europe may use a help desk company in India and an applications developer in Australia.

Similarly, an online stockbroker in Singapore may use a number of intermediaries to enable their customers to buy shares on the New York Stock Exchange.

In the IT outsourcing example, applications development has an ordering phase (i.e., we need these changes made) and a fulfillment phase (i.e., completion of the changes). With the help desk, ordering of the service ("I have a problem") and the fulfillment (problem fixed) should take place in a very short time. The same applies to the online stockbroker. The failure of a help desk service or an online stockbroker can cause potential significant loss. However, the same approach to protecting the process via a business continuity plan can be taken.

One of the key differences between physical goods supply chains and services supply chains is that the service supply chain may not be recognized as such; so, it may not have the same level of management recognition, governance, and, therefore, business continuity protection.

Implementing a Business Continuity
Plan for a Supply Chain

Essentially, there is no difference between developing a continuity plan for a single organization and a formal supply chain. Therefore, standard proven methods can be adopted. The two areas that require extra attention are the greater *complexity* due to the increase in the number of unrelated organizations working together and *governance*.

Both the complexity of the supply chain architecture and the governance issue can be addressed, provided the strategic development and the tactical management of the continuity plan are not in conflict with one another.

Essentially, each organization in the supply chain needs to make sure that upstream suppliers and downstream customers that support its critical business processes have a suitable continuity plan in place.

It is not unusual for an organization to ask for details of a critical supplier's continuity plan, but at this stage, it is uncommon to ask for details of a major customer's plan. However, this is quite logical.

A supply chain is a symbiotic relationship. Suppliers provide customers with benefits, such as lower prices, guaranteed delivery, guaranteed quality, and cooperation to improve flexibility and time to market. Customers provide suppliers with guaranteed business. This is the essence of the point and the driving force behind the architecture of a business continuity plan. The guarantee of business continuity needs to be there in the event a customer suffers an incident that disrupts the supply chain business continuity.

Therefore, a tested continuity plan not only shows a commitment from the supplier but also from the customer. In addition, no organization is just a supplier or just a customer; it is both. An organization increasingly needs a continuity plan to demonstrate its commitment as a reliable supplier to downstream customers and as a committed customer to upstream suppliers.

It follows that this approach will have significant benefits in reducing risk to a formal supply chain and can be used as a competitive advantage against the competition.

The Steps to Developing a Supply Chain Continuity Plan

The key point in developing a continuity plan, whether it is internally within the organization or externally to include member organizations of a supply chain, is simplicity; keep it simple. If it becomes complex, it may develop into a tactical plan that may need to be taken up a level.

The seven steps described earlier (Figure 1) to develop a continuity plan for a single organization are:

1. Review current continuity situation
2. Undertake a business impact analysis
3. Undertake a risk assessment
4. Define the continuity strategy
5. Design the solution
6. Select or build the solution
7. Document the plan and test

Assuming your organization has an appropriate continuity plan in place, the following steps should be followed to include a supply chain:

1. Map your supply chain
2. Review suppliers' current capabilities
3. Compare their capabilities to meet the recovery times with your maximum tolerable outage (as identified by your business impact analysis)
4. Review suppliers' risk analyses for assumptions, impacts, and likelihoods
5. Compare each supplier's ability to satisfy your continuity strategy
6. Develop improvement program
7. Implement the improvement program
8. Document and test

As can be seen, the development of a continuity plan for a supply chain is very similar to developing one for an individual organization. Indeed, if an organization has the experience and the skills from developing and managing its own continuity plans, it is in a very good position to extend its expertise across the supply chain.

Assuming that a supply chain partner appreciates the benefits of a continuity plan for its business and for its customers, then senior managers that insist on or demand a business continuity plan to be adopted by all business partners will be involved. One way to do that is by making it a prerequisite to bidding for work.

The following addresses the steps in detail.

1. **Mapping the supply chain.**

Mapping can be a simple procedure, if organizations are in a formal supply chain run by a major manufacturer that is part of an industry vertical market. However, many supply chains do not have this formal structure.

Use the process map that is the outcome of your own business impact analysis to identify all external organizations that are critical to each process. This can be done in an internal workshop.

Rank suppliers by the value they bring to your organization. Suggested categories are critical, important and transactional. These categories should be kept to a minimum to support simplicity. This categorization will enable you to prioritize the suppliers you work with.

You also should rank them by the value you bring to their business. For example, if you have a supplier that is critical to your success, but you are not as critical to theirs, then you are in no position or have no leverage to influence them to develop a business continuity plan in order to protect your business. This is critically important information, because if they do suffer a disaster, you may not be a priority customer.

In producing the supply chain map, service suppliers and utilities should be included.

Identify supply type product (e.g., raw material, simple-built product, complex-built product) and service (e.g., utility, professional, financial, logistics). Add criticality (as perceived by management) and ease of replacement (e.g., legal services, which know the organization, but a tactical view of an agreement could be obtained from another source; and logistics, wherein a simple transport easily could be arranged, but a complex warehousing and fulfillment operation could not). This will help identify their criticality and the likelihood of easy replacement.

The supply chain map can be color coded to identify criticality, supply type, and single source suppliers. In this way, the map can be used as an ongoing tool to identify weaknesses in the supply chain and threats to your organization. This is an example of using business continuity tools to improve the business process.

As discussed earlier, a simple way to consider disaster scenarios is to consider denial of access. This avoids becoming caught in the detail trap of contemplating all the issues that could cause a disaster.

The same approach can be used to test your supplier's disrupted ability to supply your organization. Just consider a denial of access to that supplier. What would be the impact on your organization? If the impact is major, and if your supplier is the sole provider of a certain category, then you need to ensure that the supplier has a strong business continuity plan.

Building an accurate map is the foundation activity in ensuring business continuity for the supply chain. The emphasis should be on thoroughness rather than speed, ensuring that many people throughout your organization are involved. As with other areas of data collection and assembly in business continuity, there are advantages in engaging an outside specialist to ensure that all questions are asked, all assumptions are challenged and structured documentation is produced.

2.   Review suppliers' current capabilities.

You are only concerned with the information that affects your critical business processes, but sometimes, other processes can have an impact, too. For example, if you are dealing with a transport company, you may be interested only in its ability to take orders, run its track, trace shipments, and provide a proof of the delivered product. However, if an organization is a unionized shop running under an agreement, there may be issues about its staff being paid on a certain day of the week. Therefore, you may need to check how the payroll system is protected, as industrial unrest could affect their ability to operate.

Having said that, the main focus needs to be on their processes that affect you.

Building and strengthening business continuity plans takes time, so it is better to base it on an audit plan that is consistent and sharable.

The best approach is to give information about your plan and needs before asking for information so the context is set. This has the advantage of outlining the type of information you require and establishing an open, sharing environment so that broader information sharing can take place.

Start off with key points from your recovery plan, such as the following:

- Key business processes
- Processes that rely on this particular supplier
- Maximum tolerable outage
- Scenarios from which you plan to protect your organization
- Outline of continuity plan to ensure that critical business process can continue.

This is best done with a standardized template.

The following are examples of questions to ask suppliers:

a. Do they have a continuity plan? If they do:
   - When was it last tested?
   - What were the results, and will they share the reports with you?
   - Have they conducted a business impact analysis? Will they provide a synopsis to you? (Few organizations will share their complete business impact analysis, because it may contain financial and other confidential information.)
   - Have they conducted a risk analysis? Will they provide a synopsis for you?
   - What are the critical business processes they aim to protect? What is the maximum tolerable outage for each of those processes?
   - What disaster scenarios was their planning based on?
   - How do they protect them?
   - What is the maximum tolerable outage for the processes that your organization relies on?
   - Who has management responsibility for the continuity plan?

b. If they don't:
   - What plans do they have? If they don't, what plans do they have to implement one?
   - What are the key processes for their whole business? What agreements do they have in place? How will they be reviewed?

- What do they see as the major risks to their ability to supply?
- Who are their key suppliers, and do those organizations have a satisfactory continuity plan?
- What workarounds do they rely on? Workarounds can be a major trap in continuity planning. They can include reverting to manual processes if a computer system is not available or assuming that a product or service is available from an alternative supplier. All workaround assumptions need to be tested rigorously. For example, in the case of reverting to the manual system that was in place before the computerized system, you should ask how often the manual system is exercised and how experienced those using the manual system are. It may be that those who used to run the manual system are no longer with the organization or are in a completely different role. In this circumstance, the future of your supply chain is in some very inexperienced hands.

  In the case of reliance on an alternative supply, the failure of the main supplier may lead to shortages in the market, so any secondary supplier may not be able to meet demand, unless there is a service level agreement in place. In addition, the alternative supplier may not be familiar with the level of service required. It may be necessary to provide the alternative supplier with some ongoing business in order to ensure the relationship and their interest.

  All assumptions supporting workarounds need to be documented and each one challenged.

3. **Compare their capability to meet the recovery times with your maximum tolerable outage (as identified by your business impact analysis).**

At this point, you need to make a judgment as to whether this plan will support your processes satisfactorily. This decision will draw on your own organization's growing knowledge of business continuity.

4. **Review suppliers' risk analysis for assumptions, impacts, and likelihoods.**

Again, as you will have carried out an analysis for your own organization, you will draw on your own growing knowledge.

5. **Compare the supplier's ability to satisfy your continuity strategy.**

This will require the involvement of your operations staff that has the day-to-day responsibility of running the critical business processes with which the supplier in question interfaces. They would know impacts and potential workarounds.

6. **Develop an improvement program.**

On the first review, it is highly likely that a critical supplier's continuity plan would not meet your requirements, as it would have been developed in isolation from your needs. If, however, it was developed in conjunction with you as a customer and your supplier's upstream suppliers (based on a spirit of cooperation within the supply chain), it stands a much better chance of satisfying your needs and will probably be a lower cost to all concerned parties. This is because unnecessary features would not have been included.

7.   Implement the improvement program.

This needs to be run as a standard project with full project management support. It is likely that your organization and the supplier organization will use different project management methodologies; this may complicate the implementation. It also is likely that the improvement program will involve people from many different parts of the supplier organization, so adequate time and resources should be allowed.

8.   Document and test.

One of the traps for an organization testing its own continuity plan is that it only may test one part of its plan at a time. This is only appropriate if full locations are tested together. For example, sometimes organizations split the recovery testing of applications that are provided from a single data center. This can be quite dangerous, because a full test will not have been carried out if that data center is not destroyed.

One of the benefits of testing a continuity plan for a supply chain is that parts of it can be tested at a time.

In a supply chain, it is likely that the various organizations will be geographically distributed. So, individual organization testing may be appropriate. However, the locations of all facilities that support the critical business processes must be identified and their distances from each other noted. If, for example, the data center of one member of the supply chain is half of a kilometer from the data center of another member of the supply chain, the risk should be noted, and the test to recover both should be scheduled for the same time that a single incident could affect both sites.

This is becoming increasingly important with the development of large technology parks. The trend toward outsourcing also impacts this, as two or more supply chain members may have outsourced their help desks to the same organization, making the outsourcer a member of the supply chain.

There is no fixed rule as to how often a continuity test should be undertaken; however, it should not be less often than once a year. Greater frequency is driven by the rate of change within the supply chain itself and the members of the supply chains. Any significant change to a critical business process or infrastructure to support those processes should trigger a test.

9.   Ongoing Review.

After the supplier's plan has been established to your satisfaction, it will be necessary to review it on a regular basis.

A key question is how far back do you follow the chain of continuity capability? Each organization in the supply chain is dependent on others further up the chain. This is where the categorization of suppliers into critical, import, and transactional can be used.

By reviewing your critical suppliers and ensuring they have reviewed their critical suppliers, you can address the most important parts of the supply chain. This also will provide an understanding of the impact of failure by an organization with which you do not have a contractual relationship, but which could have a severe impact on your business.

If this can be approached as a collaborative program jointly managed by all key members of the supply chain, experience will be shared in an open forum, which will make the whole process much more efficient and will support the development of best practice.

The more strategic and balanced the relationship (i.e., the more important you are to each other), the more it is reasonable to ask. The issues should be the same as those addressed within your own organization—key business processes, key external suppliers (and whether their continuity plans have been checked), major perceived risks, and results of last tests.

The review approach should be developed so that it helps the suppliers. There should be no use of language internal to your organization, and reports should be sharable. Openness can be encouraged by sharing the results of your organization's tests.

The review comprises two functions: ensuring it meets your changing business needs (including any changes driven by regulators, legislation, the market, etc.) and ensuring it operates as documented.

By keeping the critical process documentation and the supply chain map up to date, it is straightforward to check whether, at the strategic level, the continuity needs of your organization are being met. This should be a senior management responsibility and should be reviewed on a quarterly basis or more, if the organization is undergoing significant change.

Ensuring that suppliers' plans operate as documented will involve close and trusted working with suppliers. The best situation is if they will allow someone from your organization to attend their rehearsals. In this way, you will gain a greater understanding of their thoroughness of testing and continuity. Alternatively, you can ask for copies of reports that the testing team should be sending to their own management. This should include objectives and outcomes, scenario, and how the activities being tested fit into their overall plan.

Conclusion and Future Trends

This chapter discussed business continuity within the context of supply chain management. Continuity planning is growing slowly but principally in individual organizations. The only signs of growth in supply chain is that, as organizations outsource requirements, they are looking for strong evidence of continuity capability in potential suppliers.

As sectors become regulated (e.g., financial services), they will demand continuity from their supply partners.

As regulators make boards of directors responsible for continuity, directors will question what continuity capability their organisation and supply chains have. Certain sectors, particularly financial services, are becoming increasingly regulated globally. Often, the regulators are stating that the board has overall responsibility to ensure that an appropriate continuity plan is in place. Typically, directors of financial services company boards also sit on a number of other boards so we could see these other boards also requiring that a continuity plan is in place for these other organizations. In this way, we could see the requirement for strong continuity plans spread.

Some other issues and trends that may emerge include the following:

- As organization seek to concentrate on their key differentiators, more outsourcing will take place; therefore, supply chains will become more complex.

- As supply chains become more complex, there is an increased likelihood that organizations will be impacted by a continuity issue somewhere in their increasingly complex chains.

- In an attempt to effectively manage outsourcing, service level agreement will become more prevalent and sophisticated. There will be a lower tolerance of failure to meet service levels based on an incident (i.e., some type of preventable disaster), forcing organizations to develop continuity plans.

- We cannot foresee events that will strike; therefore BCP development can and should be seen as a training exercise. If you undertake the planning, your organizations will be far more able to adapt than if none had taken place. Organizations should keep their thinking broad concerning likely causes and think of a denial of access.

- There will be a need for a standardized auditing process or maybe even a continuity standard so organizations can show they have a plan that meets a basic requirement. Singapore has adopted this approach in order for organizations to obtain certification to the business continuity standard adopted by SPRING Singapore (the Standards, Productivity, and Innovation Board). We have a long way to go before that happens more generally, as there is still too little understanding and adoption of continuity as a standard approach to business. Therefore, organizations and their supply chains will continue to be at risk. Even if this were to happen, a standardized approach still would not be satisfactory for critical suppliers, as a higher standard may be required, so an audit based on strong symbiotic relationship still would be required.

References

This chapter is based on the author's work at Hewlett-Packard in Sydney, Australia.

About the Authors

Yi-chen Lan (BCom, Honours, PhD; MACS) is a senior lecturer at the School of Computing and IT, University of Western Sydney, Australia. The author of three books in the area of globalization, he teaches information systems and management courses at both undergraduate and graduate levels. Prior to his current academic work, Lan worked in industry for five years, wherein he held senior management responsibilities in the areas of information systems and quality assurance programs in a multi-national organization. His main areas of research are global transition process, global information systems management issues, and globalization framework development. In addition to his Honours degree, he has his PhD from the University of Western Sydney in the area of global transitions.

Bhuvan Unhelkar (BE, MDBA, MSc, PhD; FACS) has 23 years of strategic as well as hands-on professional experience in information technology, including recent academic work at the University of Western Sydney, Australia where he leads the emerging technologies research group. He is the author of eight books and has published numerous papers and presented and chaired seminars and conferences. Unhelkar is a fellow of the Australian Computer Society and a rotarian.

*   *   *   *   *

Lynn Batten is a professor at the School of Information Technology, Deakin University, Australia, and co-director with Professor Tanya Castleman of SWEEP, a supplier-wide electronic engagement project analyzing the reasons for and against the uptake of electronic commerce by Australian SMEs. Batten's principal research interests lie in the applications of mathematical methods to communication security; she has organized many conferences on this subject and has been a member of the scientific program committee for major Australian conferences on this theme. She received her PhD from the

University of Waterloo, Canada, and has held positions of head of department and associate dean of research at several universities.

Steve Cartland is the South Pacific manager for Hewlett-Packard's Business Continuity Services, Australia. His responsibilities include managing recovery centers in Auckland, Melbourne, and Sydney, consulting with customers to define their business recovery needs as well as designing and delivering solutions to satisfy these requirements. In addition, Cartland serves as part of the Asia Pacific and worldwide teams involved in the development and deployment of new services and service enhancements. He is a frequent presenter at business continuity seminars. Cartland has more than 28 years of commercial IT experience with organizations in financial services and manufacturing IT services markets. He has been with Hewlett-Packard for more than six years. In previous organizations, he has been responsible for managing multiple data centers, consulting teams, software development groups, and service businesses. Cartland is based in Sydney.

Chian-Hsueng Chao is an assistant professor at the Department of Information Management, National University of Kaohsiung (NUK), Taiwan. He earned his PhD in civil engineering – construction management from Northwestern University (2001). Chao has great interests and extensive knowledge in information technology, which eventually led him to become a professor in this field. Prior to joining NUK in 2002, Chao worked in both public and private sectors, where he also made several significant contributions in industry. Chao's research interests are in the areas of e-commerce, enterprise application integration, supply chain management, and issues of how IT gives enterprises competitive advantages and how to manage technologies better.

Huey-Kuo Chen earned an MSc in civil engineering from the National Taiwan University (1979) and from Purdue University (1989), and a PhD from the University of Illinois at Urbana-Champaign (1989). Currently, he is a professor at the Department of Civil Engineering, National Central University, Taiwan. He has co-authored more than 50 journal papers and chapters in books and has published a research monograph titled *Dynamic Travel Choice Models* (Berlin, Springer, 1999). His research interests include dynamic traffic assignment, logistics, and supply chain network models.

Huey-Wen Chou earned a BA in Chinese literature from the National Taiwan Normal University (1982), an MA from the College of Education, Purdue University (1986), and a PhD from the Educational Psychology Department, University of Illinois at Urbana-Champaign (1990). She is currently a professor at the Department of Information Management, National Central University, Taiwan. Her research interests include supply chain management, e-commerce, and IT and organizational change.

Wing S. Chow is an associate professor of MIS at the School of Business, Hong Kong Baptist University. He earned his master's and PhD degrees from the University of Manitoba. Chow has published many papers in top journals and conference proceedings.

His name has been included in *Who's Who in Science and Engineering* since 2002. His research interests are in manufacturing and business information management. For more information on his publications, please visit http://www.hkbu.edu.hk/~vwschow/.

Edward D'Souza (B Eng, MBA, CISA, PMP, CISSP, CISM) is an emerging technology projects executive with more than 22 years of experience spanning project management, application development, product management, marketing, sales, and customer support. D'Souza has worked on projects spanning Internet, smart cards, and wireless technologies. These projects involved working with world-renowned research institutions, including Bell Labs and Schlumberger's Austin Product Research Center. D'Souza's physical work locations include India, Bahrain (Middle East), U.S., and Canada. While working in these locations, his regions of responsibility included North America, Latin America, the Middle East, Africa, Asia Pacific, and Europe. His technological expertise and international business experience have contributed to successful implementation of solutions for international deployment. In 1996, he was the program manager for the Internet-based Home Banking Solution that was deployed to banks in North America, Europe, and Asia. In 2000, he managed a hybrid smart card deployment for secure network and premises access in Canada. D'Souza currently works as an independent consultant based in Toronto, Canada.

Jianxin (Roger) Jiao is an assistant professor of systems and engineering management at Nanyang Technological University, Singapore. He is convener and coordinator of the Global Manufacturing and Logistics Forum at Nanyang. He earned a PhD from the Department of Industrial Engineering and Engineering Management, Hong Kong University of Science & Technology. He has worked as a lecturer at the Department of Management, Tianjin University, China. His research interests include mass customization, design theory and methodology, reconfigurable manufacturing systems, engineering logistics, and intelligent systems.

Chamnong Jungthirapanich is currently dean of the Graduate School of Computer and Engineering Management at Assumption University, Thailand. He received bachelor's and master's degrees in electrical engineering from King Mongkut's Institute of Technology, Thailand, and the University of Missouri-Columbia, respectively. He earned a PhD in engineering management from the University of Missouri-Rolla. His expertise fields are location management, production management, quality management, and supply chain management.

Takefumi Konzo earned his BE and ME from Osaka Prefecture University, Japan (2003 and 2005, respectively). He won the Shirasagi Prize in 2004 from Osaka Prefecture University. In 2005, Konzo joined Sharp, Ltd. His research interests include a wide range of industrial engineering.

Akihiro Koretsune graduated from Osaka Prefecture University, Japan (2004) and is a graduate student at Osaka Prefecture University. He is developing an SCM simulator.

Arun Kumar is an associate professor of systems and engineering management at Nanyang Technological University, Singapore. Prior to joining Nanyang Technological University, he worked as an associate professor of decision sciences at the State University of New Jersey. He earned his PhD in operations research from Virginia Tech. His research interests are in the applications of probability to problems in reliability, logistics, and healthcare systems. He is a member of INFORMS, WDSI, and SIAM.

Yei-Chun Kuo is a lecturer of international trade at Van-Nung University, Taiwan. She is a PhD student with a major in business administration from National Central University. She has been teaching international trade and global logistics courses at Vanung University since 1992. Her research concentrates on logistics and supply chain management.

Chean Lee began his career in a NASDAQ listed e-business solution company as a marketing executive responsible for business development and advised SMEs and telecoms in e-commerce solutions. After completion of his postgraduate study, Lee worked as a contract e-business analyst for a Web development company in Malaysia. His main focus was designing information architecture for intranet/extranet and Web applications. He then worked as a business consultant for an ERP solution vendor. Lee currently resides in Australia and is a consulting staff for Methodscience.com. He holds a Bachelor of Commerce degree from Griffith University and a Master of Information Technology from University of Western Sydney.

E. Stanley Lee earned his PhD in chemical engineering from Princeton University (USA) and has been working in the area of operations research and applied mathematics for several years. His current interest is in the area of artificial intelligence and soft computing techniques, such as support vector machines, evidence theory, fuzzy set theory, probabilistic approaches, and neural networks, and on the application of these techniques to engineering and social problems.

Wei Liu has undertaken an e-commerce degree course at Nanjing University of Traditional Chinese Medicine (NUCM) in China. His research interests include application of information technology to enhance global business.

Mahesh S. Raisinghani is an associate professor at Texas Woman's University, School of Management (USA). Dr. Raisinghani was the recipient of the UD Presidential Award and the King Haggar Award for excellence in teaching, research, and service. His previous publications have appeared in *Information and Management, Information Resources Management Journal, Information Strategy: An Executive's Journal, Journal of Global IT Management, International Journal of E-Business Research, Journal of IT Cases and Applications, Journal of IT Theory and Applications, Enterprise Systems Journal, Journal of Computer Information Systems, Asian Journal of Information Technology, Annals of Cases in Information Technology*, and *Information Systems*

Managmenet among others. He serves on the editorial review board of leading information systems/e-commerce academic journals; on the board of directors of Sequoia, Inc., and is included in the millennium edition of *Who's Who in the World, Who's Who Among America's Teachers,* and *Who's Who in Information Technology.*

Umar Ruhi is a lecturer in management information systems, operations management, and e-business at the School of Business and Economics, Wilfrid Laurier University, Canada. With more than five years of experience in e-business consulting, Ruhi has managed operational technology projects from the design to the deployment stages, and consulted for multi-national organizations, such as General Electric and Cisco Systems. His professional qualifications include various industry-endorsed certifications, including those from IBM, Cisco, Novell, and Sun Microsystems. Additionally, Ruhi has lectured in various information systems and e-business courses at the college and university level throughout Canada. Ruhi's research interests include mobile services, knowledge management, and community informatics.

Ryosuke Saga earned his BE and ME degrees from Osaka Prefecture University, Japan (2003, 2005). He is currently a PhD student at Osaka Prefecture University. His research interests include agent system and intelligent systems for e-commerce. He is a student member of IEEJ.

Ron Savage earned a BSc Monash University (1971) with a major in applied mathematics. Since, he has worked on numerous projects in software development for organizations, including Telstra, BHP, HP, and Monash University. In 2002, Savage joined Deakin University, Australia, as an associate lecturer and began a master's degree program as a member of the SWEEP research project team, along with Professor Batten. As part of this team, his primary responsibilities are data management.

Margaret L. Sheng earned her PhD from the University of Minnesota - Twin Cities (USA). Currently, she is an assistant professor at Hamline University in Minnesota. Sheng also had several years of industry experience in major multi-national corporations, specializing in international business and marketing with the applications of information technology. Besides maintaining her ongoing research interests in international business and marketing, her current work also involves e-commerce and high-technology marketing.

Xinping Shi (xpshi@hkbu.edu.hk) is an associate professor of decision sciences and director of the Logistics Management Research Centre at Hong Kong Baptist University. His research interests include operational research, management information systems, and logistics and supply chain management, and he has published many academic and professional articles in *International Business Review, Management International Review, Communications of the ACM, Journal of Managerial Psychology, Journal of Multi-Criteria Decision Analysis,* and other referred international journals.

Ling-Lang Tang has been an associate professor of Yuan-Ze University (Taiwan) since 1993 and is a board member of Philips Taiwan Quality Foundation. He earned his PhD degree from the National Sun Yat-Sen University and has 10 years working experience in Philips Taiwan. His current research interest is in the areas of supply chain management, information management of e-commerce, and total quality management in service/ manufacturing industry.

Denise Taylor is an information technology staff consultant for a telecommunications company where she creates and implements business solutions across various business channels. Taylor holds a Master of Business Administration from Amberton University and is completing a Master of Management in information technology from the University of Dallas (USA). She is member of the Sigma Zeta Chapter of Sigma Iota Epsilon Honor Society.

Hiroshi Tsuji earned his BE, ME, and PhD degrees from Kyoto University (1976, 1978, and 1993, respectively). He joined Hitachi, Ltd. in 1978 and was a visiting researcher of Carnegie-Mellon University (1987-1988). He is currently a professor at Osaka Prefecture University, Japan. He has engaged in research and development of management information systems, enterprise system, and human-computer interaction. He is a member of ACE, IEEE, IEEJ, among others.

Ofir Turel is a PhD candidate at the Michael G. DeGroote School of Business, McMaster University, Canada. Turel holds an MBA in technology management and a BSc in industrial dngineering. Before joining the School of Business, Turel held senior positions in the IT and telecommunication industries. He served as a delegate of the GSM (Global System for Mobile) Communications Association's working committees and contributed to the development of standards and value added wireless services. His research interests include mobile services and online dispute resolution.

Christopher Van Eenoo has five years of commercial experience in business analysis and software engineering in global supply chain and logistics environments. He has worked as a project leader in many software projects throughout North America and Europe. He is a member of the Australian Computer Society. He earned his Bachelor of Business in computing and information systems as well as his Master of Computing in software engineering from the University of Western Sydney, Australia.

Ketan Vanjara currently works as a lead program manager with Microsoft, India. Prior to this, he held several senior positions in the software industry and led large software teams to develop enterprise application software and software products on diverse domains and technology platforms ranging from mainframes to handheld devices and COBOL to J2EE and .NET. He specializes in application software for healthcare and knowledge industries, including implementation of effective workflows and quality frameworks. Apart from books, he has interests in photography and music. He lives in India with his wife and daughter.

Chen Xiao is finishing his final year of double bachelor degrees as an international student at the University of Western Sydney, Australia. His research interests are in international economics and e-commerce. He also has working experience in enterprises such as Siemens AD and Gori in China.

Panyaluck Udomleartprasert earned a bachelor's degree in electronics engineering from Assumption University, Thailand. She earned a master's degree and PhD in computer and engineering management from the same university. Her research interests include supply chain management, quality management, operation management, and supportive infrastructures for organization performance.

Xiao You is a PhD candidate in the School of Mechanical and Production Engineering at Nanyang Technological University, Singapore. He earned his bachelor's degree in automobile engineering from Hubei Automobile Industry College, China, and a master's degree in mechanical engineering from Huazhong University of Science and Technology, China (1995 and 2003, respectively). His current research interests are supply chain management, global manufacturing, and multi-agent systems.

Chan Pui Yuk (lmrc@hkbu.edu.hk) is a PhD candidate at the Department of Finance and Decision Sciences and a research fellow at Logistics Management Research Centre, Hong Kong Baptist University. His research interests are enterprise resource planning, information technology and information systems applications, and supply chain management. He has published research papers in a number of international conference proceedings and journals.

Ed White (H BSc, CPIM, CIRM) is a supply chain specialist with Bayer Material Science, with responsibility for supply chain, cost saving, and education projects at local, regional, and global levels. He is currently splitting his time between the Regional Service Center of Bayer Canada Inc. and the Bayer Global Supply Chain Management group. White also is active in the APICS organization as both an instructor and a member of the board of directors for his local chapter in Hamilton, Ontario (the chapter that made APICS International). He is the current director of education but also has held both the administration and communications portfolios. Over the years, he has had several articles published in various publications as well as presenting at local and international conferences for APICS (Association of Operations Management) and the Institute of Business Forecasting (IBF).

Wu Dan (Lisa Wu) has undertaken an e-commerce degree at Nanjing University of Chinese Medicine (NUCM) in China. Her research interests are focused on supply chain management (SCM), especially within the context of China, where she is studying both successful and unsuccessful implementations of SCM.

Index

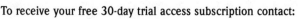